German Grammar in Context
SECOND EDITION

'*German Grammar in Context* is popular with our students and highly suitable for use both in classroom teaching and for self-study. The range of authentic source material offers something for all interests, and the user-friendly organisation of the book allows learners of different levels to progress at a comfortable pace, thereby facilitating a sense of achievement and confidence.'

Annemarie Kunzl-Snodgrass and Silke Mentchen, *University of Cambridge, UK.*

German Grammar in Context presents an accessible and engaging approach to learning grammar. Each chapter opens with a real-life extract from a German newspaper, magazine, poem, book or internet source and uses this text as the starting point for explaining a particular key area of German grammar. A range of exercises follow at the end of the chapter, helping students to reinforce and test their understanding, and an answer key is also provided at the back of the book.

This second edition features:

- Updated texts with current newspaper and magazine articles and new extracts from digital media such as chatrooms and blogs
- Inclusion of a wide-ranging selection of sources and topics to further students' engagement with issues relevant to contemporary Germany and Austria
- Clear and user-friendly coverage of grammar, aided by a list of grammatical terms
- A wide variety of inventive exercises designed to thoroughly build up grammatical understanding, vocabulary acquisition and effective comprehension and communication skills
- Helpful 'keyword boxes' translating difficult vocabulary in the texts
- A recommended reading section offering advice on additional grammar resources and website links.

German Grammar in Context is an essential resource for intermediate to advanced students of German. It is suitable for both classroom use and independent study.

Carol Fehringer is Senior Lecturer at Newcastle University, UK.

LANGUAGES IN CONTEXT

The *Languages in Context* series presents students with an engaging way of learning grammar while also acquiring cultural and topical knowledge. Each book in the series uses authentic texts, drawn from a generous variety of sources, as the starting point for the explanation of key areas of grammar. Grammar points are then consolidated with a wide range of exercises to test students' understanding.

Aimed at intermediate to advanced students, *The Languages in Context* series is suitable for both class use and independent study.

The following books are available in this series:

French Grammar in Context
Spanish Grammar in Context
German Grammar in Context

German Grammar in Context

Analysis and Practice

SECOND EDITION

CAROL FEHRINGER

Routledge
Taylor & Francis Group

LONDON AND NEW YORK

Second edition published in 2014 by Routledge
2 Park Square, Milton Park, Abingdon, Oxon OX14 4RN

Simultaneously published in the USA and Canada
by Routledge
711 Third Avenue, New York, NY 10017

Routledge is an imprint of the Taylor & Francis Group, an informa business

First published in 2002 by Arnold, a member of the Hodder Headline Group,
338 Euston Road, London, NW1 3BH

British Library Cataloguing in Publication Data
A catalogue record for this book is available from the British Library

Library of Congress Cataloging in Publication Data
Fehringer, Carol.
German grammar in context : analysis and practice / Carol Fehringer, Senior Lecturer in
German Studies, Newcastle University. – Second Edition.
pages cm. – (Languages in context)
Text in English and German.
Includes bibliographical references and index.
1. German language–Grammar. 2. German language–Textbooks for foreign speakers–
English. 3. German language–Grammar–Problems, exercises, etc. I. Title.
PF3112.F39 2013
438.2'421–dc23
2013005375

ISBN: 978-0-415-86991-1 (hbk)
ISBN: 978-1-4441-6726-9 (pbk)
ISBN: 978-0-203-78485-3 (ebk)

Typeset in Minion Pro
by Saxon Graphics Ltd, Derby

Contents

Foreword

The purpose of this book is to provide an accessible text-based reference grammar of the German language for English-speaking students of German and to help consolidate their knowledge through practical exercises on a whole range of grammatical topics. It is aimed at first- and second-year undergraduate students, although more advanced students wishing to revise particular grammatical points may also benefit from this book. As one of the main aims of the book is accessibility, grammatical terminology is kept to a minimum and only traditional terms are used. There is also a list of grammatical terms and their definitions at the beginning of the book.

The book is based on the premise that grammatical issues are more easily explained and understood within the wider context in which they appear, i.e. within whole texts, rather than in terms of isolated rules and fabricated examples. Thus, in each chapter an authentic German text is chosen which illustrates a particular grammatical feature, e.g. the past tense, the subjunctive or personal pronouns, and the necessary rules are set out in relation to the occurrence of the grammatical forms within the text. Later in the chapter supplementary rules are given which are not illustrated in the text, for the sake of completeness. Each grammatical point is explained as concisely as possible and is illustrated, if not by directly referring to the text, by the use of everyday German examples of the kind likely to be encountered and used by the student. Some of the larger chapters contain charts and tables to help the student focus on the main points in question. These usually follow the principle of 'grammar in context' in that they rarely consist of lists of isolated words but usually of words co-occurring with other forms in the language, e.g. prepositions listed with a following definite article and noun to show the case that they take. Unpredictable exceptions to rules and more complicated issues, which may be of interest to more advanced learners, are usually dealt with in footnotes.

The chosen German texts are extremely varied both in style and in subject matter, yet they have in common that they are all authentic and are examples of modern standard German. The styles range from journalistic writings to literary excerpts, from prose to poetry, from scientific writings to song lyrics, from transcripts of dialogue from TV shows to excerpts from blogs and internet forums. The subject matter ranges from discussions on study abroad and career choice to humorous texts on dating and relationships, from technical developments in web-based media to recipes for sausage and sauerkraut. In particular, many of the texts chosen reflect German or Austrian life and culture.

Each chapter ends with a set of exercises designed to practise the particular grammatical topic under discussion. Some of these exercises are organised according to complexity: e.g. 1a) deals with regular forms while 1b) deals with irregularities and more complicated issues. The exercises are varied in style: from reformulation and gap-filling exercises, many of which are based on authentic texts themselves, to translation exercises and crosswords. In addition, the exercises in each chapter are based on a particular vocabulary topic in order to build up students' vocabulary at the same time as practising their grammar. These are useful everyday topics which students should be familiar with: e.g. food, transport, holidays, school and university subjects, careers, garden and household, hobbies and entertainment etc. There is a key to the exercises towards the back of the book.

At the end of the main part of the book are four revision texts, each of which deals with a number of key grammatical issues together so that students can revise the grammatical topics which they have learned earlier in the book. Each of the revision texts is followed by two sets of exercises, the first of which deals with recognising particular forms and explaining why they are used, while the second requires the students to practise using the forms themselves. These are also followed by a key.

At the end of the book there is a comprehensive index covering both the main issues and the more specific grammatical problems and particular forms dealt with in the book. In the appendices are also included an alphabetical list of common irregular verbs and a set of article-adjective-noun paradigms for students to learn. A selection of recommended reading is also given, which covers both print and web-based material.

Acknowledgements

I would like to thank my German colleagues (and former colleagues) in the School of Modern Languages at Newcastle University for their help with both this and the earlier edition of the book, in particular Ms Franziska Schulz, Dr Simone Schroth, Mr Sascha Stollhans, Ms Aletta Rochau, Dr Beate Müller, Professor Henrike Lähnemann, Ms Andrea Wilczynski, Dr Helen Ferstenberg, Ms Anke Neibig and Professor Jens Hentschke. Thanks also go to colleagues in linguistics: Dr Richard Waltereit, Ms Nicole Böheim, Dr Tina Fry and Dr Jonathan West; and to German linguists further afield, who have given useful feedback on specific points of grammar: Professor Martin Durrell, Dr Nils Langer, Dr Nicola McLelland, Dr Alan Scott, Professor Andreas Musolff and Dr Sheila Watts. I am grateful to my husband Gerhard for his Austrian perspective, and I am also very grateful to the German teaching team at Cambridge University for their detailed feedback on the first edition, which I found extremely helpful: Ms Silke Mentchen, Mrs Annemarie Künzl-Snodgrass, Mrs Britta Förster and Dr David Wachter. My thanks also go to the anonymous reviewers of the second edition manuscript for their very valuable comments and, finally, I would also like to thank the authors and publishing agents of my chosen texts for giving me permission to use their work.

List of grammatical terms

Abstract noun A noun referring to an abstract concept or idea rather than to a concrete object: e.g. 'length', 'friendship'; *Gesundheit, Höhe.*

Accusative In German, the case used to express the direct object of the verb and also after certain prepositions: e.g. *Ich liebe **dich/den** Mann/**diesen jungen** Mann, Ein Brief für meinen Freund.*

Active A grammatical construction in which the agent of the verb is also its subject: e.g. '**He** likes me'; *Ich fragte ihn (contrast passive).*

Adjective A word used to describe a noun or pronoun: e.g. 'A **shy** boy', 'She is **tall**'; *Ein großes Zimmer.*

Adverb A word used to describe a verb or adjective: e.g. 'He got up **slowly**', 'They were **annoyingly** loud'; *Er spielt **gut**.*

Agent The person (or, less commonly, thing) that carries out the action described by the main verb: '**He** hit me', 'I was warned by **my friend**'; *Er wurde von **dem Lehrer** bestraft.*

Article A word meaning '**the**' or '**a**' used before nouns (*see* definite article *and* indefinite article).

Auxiliary verb A verb used together with other verbs to form different tenses: e.g. 'I **have** finished', 'He **will** come'; *Er **hat** gesagt, Sie **ist** gegangen.*

Bare infinitive In German, the infinitive used without *um* or *zu*: e.g. *Er will **spielen**.*

Case In German, a grammatical category shown by changing the forms of articles, pronouns, demonstratives and adjectives depending on their relationship to other words in the sentence (*see* accusative, dative, genitive *and* nominative).

Clause The part of the sentence which contains a finite verb (usually accompanied by a subject): e.g. '[I am hungry _Clause 1_] but [there is nothing in the fridge _Clause 2_]'; *[Er ist früh ins Bett gegangen _Clause 1_], weil [er müde war _Clause 2_].*

Comparative The form of the adjective used to compare two or more persons or things: e.g. 'You're **fatter** than me'; *Das Zimmer ist **größer** als die anderen.*

Compound (word) A word made up of two or more other words: e.g. 'house' + 'wife' = **housewife**; *Universität + Professor = **Universitätsprofessor**.*

Conditional A tense used to refer to hypothetical situations in the future: e.g. 'I **would buy** a new car'; *Er **würde** seinen Freund **besuchen**.*

Conditional perfect A tense used to refer to hypothetical situations in the past: e.g. 'I **would have bought** something cheaper'; *Er **hätte** es nicht **gemacht**.*

Conjunction A word that links clauses together: e.g. 'I came in **and** sat down'; *Er war müde, **weil** er schlecht geschlafen hatte; **Obwohl** er schlecht geschlafen hatte, war er nicht müde.*

Co-ordinating conjunction A conjunction, such as German **und, aber, oder**, which does not affect word order (*contrast* subordinating conjunction).

Dative In German, the case used to express the indirect object of the verb and also after certain prepositions: e.g. *Ich gebe **dir/dem** Mann/**diesem jungen** Mann einen Kuss, Ich gehe <u>mit</u> **meiner** Freundin aus.*

Definite article A word placed before a noun to make it definite or specific: e.g. 'the dog'; *der Mann, **die** Tür, **das** Haus* (*contrast* indefinite article).

Demonstrative A word used to point out a specific person or thing and differentiate it from other members of its class: e.g. '**this** wine', '**that** bread', ***dieser** Mann, **der** Wagen.*

Diminutive A word with a special ending used to express smallness (and also endearment or contempt, depending on the context): '**piglet**'; ***Kätzchen, Schwesterchen.***

Direct object A noun/pronoun which is the direct recipient of the action described by the main verb. It is usually expressed by the accusative case in German: e.g. 'He loves **me**'; *Sie küsst **ihren Freund*** (*contrast* indirect object).

Expanded attribute In German, a phrase of two words or more ending in an adjective which describes a following noun: e.g. *der **für meinen Geschmack etwas zu große** Tisch.*

Finite verb The part of the verb which may change its form (i.e. by adding an ending or changing its vowel) to show person, number and tense: e.g. 'He **works** hard'; *Ich **liebe** dich, Du **bist** gegangen, Wir **haben** ihn gesehen.*

Future perfect A tense used to express completed actions either in the future or as an assumption: e.g. 'He **will have finished** it by tomorrow'; *Er **wird** schon **losgefahren sein.***

Future tense A tense used either to refer to future time or to express an assumption: e.g. 'John **will arrive** tomorrow'; *Er **wird** jetzt zu Hause **sein.***

Gender In German nouns, the categories 'masculine', 'feminine' and 'neuter' which determine the forms of co-occurring articles, pronouns, adjectives etc.: e.g. Masc. ***der/ein** Hund*, Fem. ***die/eine** Blume*, Neut. ***das/ein** Haus.*

Genitive In German, the case used chiefly to express possession, corresponding to English *'s* or *of*, and also after certain prepositions: e.g. *Ein Freund **meines Vaters**, das Haus **der** Nachbarin, <u>Während</u> **des ersten Weltkriegs.***

Imperative The form of the verb used in commands: e.g. 'Go away!'; ***Sei brav!, Kommen Sie** herein!*

Indefinite article A word placed before a noun to indicate that it is not specific: e.g. '**a** house'; ***ein** Freund, **eine** Katze* (*contrast* definite article).

Indirect object The noun/pronoun (usually a person) which is the recipient of the direct object (usually a thing). It is usually expressed using 'to' in English and the dative case in German: e.g. 'I sent the letter **to my friend**'; *Er erzählte **den Kindern** einen Witz.*

Infinitive In German, the part of the verb always listed in dictionaries which does not change its form to express person, number etc.: e.g. ***machen, gehen, sein.***

Infinitive clause In German, a clause consisting of an infinitive preceded by *zu*: e.g. *Ich habe versucht, **dem alten Mann <u>zu helfen.</u>***

Inseparable verb In German, a verb beginning with a prefix such as *be-, ent-, er-, ge-, ver-* which is never separated from the verb and does not take *ge-* in the past participle: e.g. *Es **beginnt**, Du hast mich **erkannt**, Um besser zu **verstehen*** (*contrast* separable verb).

Intransitive verb A verb not taking a direct object: e.g. 'I **stay**'; *Er **kommt*** (*contrast* transitive verb).

Irregular Not following the usual rules: e.g. 'I **thought**' (not **'thinked'); *Er **sang*** (not **singte*).

Main clause In German, a clause that does not begin with a subordinating conjunction or relative pronoun: e.g. ***Ich habe dich angerufen***, *aber **du warst nicht zu Hause*** (contrast subordinate clause).

Manner An expression of manner refers to *how* the action of the verb is carried out: e.g. 'He left **in a hurry**'; *Ich bin **mit dem Bus** gefahren.*

Modal verbs A set of verbs expressing a range of moods such as ability, obligation and volition which are often used in combination with the bare infinitive form of other verbs: e.g. 'He **can** come'; *Ich **will** dich sehen; Du **musst** hier bleiben.*

Nominative In German, the case used to express the subject of the verb: e.g. ***Du*** *liebst mich,* ***Der*** *Chef kommt, Klaus ist **mein bester** Freund.*

Noun A word used to name a person, thing or concept which, in English and German, may appear after an article and may be singular or plural: e.g. 'My **friend**'; *der **Tisch**, die **Probleme**.*

Number A term used to refer to the grammatical categories of singular and plural (*see* singular *and* plural).

Object *See* direct object *and* indirect object.

Participle *See* past participle *and* present participle.

Passive A grammatical construction which shifts the emphasis away from the agent of the verb to the **recipient of the action** described by the verb. This recipient becomes the subject of the passive construction: e.g. '**I was asked** by him' (contrast the active 'He asked me'); *Er **wurde** vom Lehrer **bestraft*** (and without the agent: *Er wurde bestraft* 'He was punished').

Past participle The non-finite part of the verb used in the perfect tenses and the passive: e.g. 'I have **seen** him'; *Du hast es **gemacht**, Er war **geblieben**.*

Past tense A tense used to refer to past events. In German, this is mainly used in the written language: e.g. 'He **came**'; *Ich **machte** es, Er **wartete** auf mich.*

Perfect tense A tense used to refer to past events. In German, this is mainly used in the spoken language: e.g. *Er **hat** auf mich **gewartet**.* In English, the perfect is used when the actions in the past are still relevant to the present: e.g. 'He **has arrived**' (and is here now)'.

Person The grammatical category used to indicate which person or thing is being referred to: e.g. the first person refers to 'I', 'we'; the second person to 'you' (singular and plural); the third person to 'he', 'she', 'it', 'they'. Person is shown on some pronouns: e.g. *ich, du, mein* and also on verbs: e.g. *mache, machst, macht.*

Personal pronoun A pronoun referring to one or more persons or things: e.g. 'I', 'me', 'you', 'we', 'it'; *du, dich, er, sie, es, wir, uns, Sie, Ihnen.*

Pluperfect tense A tense used to refer to events in the past which precede other events in the past (i.e. a past within a past): e.g. 'He **had expected** her to ring but she didn't'; *Er **war** lange krank **gewesen**, bevor er starb.*

Plural The grammatical category used to refer to more than one person or thing: 'My **friends**', '**They are** here'; *Die **Probleme sind** noch nicht gelöst.*

Possessive A word used to denote possession: '**My** dog', '**Her** cat'; *Unser Haus, Das ist **meiner**.*

Predicative adjective An adjective used after the verb: e.g. 'He is **rich**'; *Sie sind sehr freundlich.*

Prefix A grammatical element attached to the beginning of a word: e.g. '**un**usual', '**ex**-husband'; *verstehen, **an**rufen.*

Preposition A word, such as *in, on, under* etc., usually placed before nouns or pronouns to relate them to other words in the sentence: e.g. 'He hid **behind** the tree'; *Ich warte **auf** dich, Wir fahren **mit** dem Bus.*

Prepositional prefix In German, a preposition attached to the beginning of a word: e.g. ***an**rufen, **aus**gehen, **mit**kommen.*

Present participle In English, the form of the verb ending in '-ing': e.g. 'I was **thinking**'. In German it ends in *-end* and is mainly used as an adjective or adverb: e.g. *Wir haben kein **laufend**es Wasser.*

Present tense A tense used primarily to refer to the present (or to general/habitual occurrences and states): e.g. 'It **is** two o'clock'; *Er **spricht** Deutsch, Wir **gehen** jeden Samstag ins Kino.*

Productive A grammatical rule is productive if it still operates in the language: e.g. if it can apply to new words, such as recent technological terms or loanwords from other languages: e.g. Adding '-s' to form plurals in English: 'i-pod**s**', 'app**s**', versus the unproductive endings '-en' and '-ren' in 'ox**en**, child**ren**'; Forming past participles with ***ge-** ... **-t*** in German: *Ich habe dich **ge**mail**t**, **ge**fax**t*** as opposed to unproductive ***ge-** ...-**en*** in *ge**fang**en, ge**schlaf**en.*

Progressive forms In English, verbal constructions using the forms of 'to be' plus a present participle: e.g. 'He **is working**'. In German, the progressive aspect is expressed using words such as *eben, gerade* etc.: e.g. *Er arbeitet **gerade**.*

Pronoun A word which takes the place of a noun: e.g. 'the man → **he**', 'the coffee → **it**'; *ein Bleistift → **einer**; dieser Rock → **dieser**; mein Bier → **meins**.*

Proper noun A noun which is the name or title of a person, thing or place: e.g. 'John', 'the Titanic', 'Manchester'; *Schmidt, Deutschland, Europa.*

Reflexive verb A verb whose subject and object refer to the same person or thing: e.g. '**He hurt himself**'; *Ich dusche **mich**.* These objects ('myself', 'yourself' etc.) are known as reflexive pronouns.

Relative clause A clause beginning with a relative pronoun: e.g. 'The job **that he hates**'; *Der Mann, **der im Restaurant saß**.*

Relative pronoun A pronoun that refers back to a noun or pronoun already mentioned in the sentence: e.g. 'The boy **who** was ill', 'The issue **that** was raised'; *Die Frau, **die** da sitzt, Der Lehrer, mit **dem** ich gesprochen habe.*

Sentence A group of words containing one or more clauses. In writing it begins with a capital letter and ends with a full stop: e.g. 'He speaks fluent French'. *Sie möchte Spanisch lernen, aber sie hat keine Zeit, weil sie vier Kinder hat.*

Separable verb In German, a verb beginning with a prefix such as *an, auf, aus, mit, zu* etc. which is separated from the verb in certain grammatical constructions: e.g. *Ich **rufe** dich **an**; Du hast mir nicht **zugehört**, Ich habe keine Lust **aus** zu **gehen*** (*contrast* inseparable verb).

Singular The grammatical category used to refer to one single person or thing: '**The man**', 'A **girl**'; *Mein **Freund** ist krank.*

Stem *See* verb stem.

Stress In the spoken language, emphasis placed on a particular syllable of a word: e.g. 'per**for**mance'; *ver**steh**en, **auf**stehen.*

Strong verb A verb that forms its past tense and/or past participle by changing the main vowel: e.g. 'sw**i**m – sw**a**m – sw**u**m'; *n**e**hmen – n**a**hm – gen**o**mmen.*

Subject In an ordinary active sentence, the person or thing that carries out the action described by the verb, e.g. '**She** hit him', or experiences the state described by the verb, e.g. '**My friend** is ill'. In German, the subject has nominative case: e.g. *Der Lehrer fragt den Jungen, Wo ist mein neuer Regenschirm?*

Subordinate clause In German, a clause beginning with a subordinating conjunction: e.g. *Ich gehe ins Bett,* **weil ich sehr müde bin** (*contrast* main clause).

Subordinating conjunction In German, a conjunction such as *bevor, bis, da, nachdem, obwohl, weil* etc. which sends the following finite verb to the end of its clause: e.g. *Ich wartete,* **bis** *er von der Arbeit <u>zurückkam</u>.* (*contrast* co-ordinating conjunction).

Suffix An element attached to the end of a word or a stem, otherwise known as an 'ending': e.g. 'sad**ness**', 'quick**ly**'; *freund**lich**, Mein**ung**, Lehr**er**.*

Superlative The form of the adjective used to express the most extreme degree of its meaning: e.g. 'The **hottest** day'; *Der **älteste** Mann, Die **schönsten** Bilder.*

Syllable The part of a word which usually contains a vowel. The words '**man**' and *Maus* have one syllable; '**husband**' and *Katze* have two syllables; '**Germany**', and *Elefant* have three syllables.

Tense A grammatical term used to refer to relations of time: e.g. present tense, past tense, future tense.

Transitive verb A verb taking a direct object: e.g. 'I **love** <u>him</u>'; *Er schreibt <u>einen Brief</u>* (*contrast* intransitive verb).

Verb A word denoting an action or a state. In English and German it usually occurs with a subject and can change its form depending on its tense and the person and number of its subject: e.g. 'He **loves** me'; *Wir **spielten**, Du **warst** krank.*

Verb stem The part of the verb without any endings for person and number. In German, this usually means the infinitive minus *-en*: e.g. ***mach-, les-, arbeit-.***

1 | Gender

> Kommt **eine** Maus – baut **ein** Haus.
> Kommt **eine** Mücke – baut **eine** Brücke.
> Kommt **ein** Floh – **der** macht so!   [**Das** Kinn des Kindes kitzeln].
>
> Da kommt **der** Bär – **der** tappt so schwer,
> 5 Da kommt **die** Maus – in Hänschens Haus,
> Da hinein, da hinein!   [**Die** Halsgrube des Kindes kitzeln].
>
> Da kommt **die** Maus – da kommt **die** Maus.
> Klingelingeling!
> „Ist **der** Herr zu Haus?"   [**Das** Ohr des Kindes zupfen].

Aus: *Das ist der Daumen*. Fingerspielreime für Kinder, © Pestalozzi-Verlag, 1992.

die Mücke – midge	*der Halsgrube* – pit of the throat
die Brücke – bridge	*kitzeln* – to tickle
der Floh – flea	*Klingelingeling!* – ding dong!
tappen – to lumber	*zupfen* – to pull at

Gender in the text

1.1   GENDER ON ARTICLES AND PRONOUNS

German nouns must have a gender, either **masculine**, **feminine** or **neuter**, which shows up on the articles and pronouns (and adjectives) used with the nouns in the singular. (Gender differences are not shown on the articles/pronouns in the plural.) **1.1a** and **1.1b** below give the different gender forms of the definite and indefinite articles in the nominative case.[1]

> [1]   See **Ch. 3** for other case forms and **Ch. 5** for gender on adjectives.

1.1a   Definite article 'the': *der Mann, die Frau, das Kind* (pl: *die* for all genders)

Common pronouns which follow the same pattern are the demonstratives *dieser* 'this', *diese*, *dieses* and *jener* 'that', *jene*, *jenes*; *jeder* 'each/every'; *jede*, *jedes*; *welcher?* 'which?', *welche?*, *welches?* and the **relative pronouns** which are mostly identical to the definite articles (see **Ch. 9**).

Some examples from the text are: masc. *der Bär* (line 4), *der Herr* (9); fem. *die Maus* (5, 7), *die Halsgrube* (6); neut. *das Kinn* (3), *das Ohr* (9). In line 4, the definite article[2] is used as a pronoun: *der tappt so schwer* 'i̲t̲ (masc., i.e. the bear) is lumbering heavily'. Similarly *der macht so* (3) 'i̲t̲ (masc., i.e. the flea) does this'.

> [2] Technically this is a demonstrative pronoun, which is identical to the definite article (see **8.2**).

1.1b   Indefinite article 'a': *ein Mann, eine Frau, ein Kind* **(no plural)**

Here the masculine and neuter forms are identical. Common pronouns which follow the same pattern are *kein* 'not a/no' and the possessives *mein, dein, sein, unser, euer, ihr* (see **7.3**). These also have plural forms ending in *-e*: e.g. *keine, meine*.

Some examples from the text are: masc. *ein Floh* (3); fem. *eine Maus* (1), *eine Mücke* (2), *eine Brücke* (2); neut. *ein Haus* (1). The last two examples are in the accusative case but this is identical to the nominative for all but masculine singulars (see **3.2b**)

Other points to note in the text

- Genitive case: *des Kindes* (6), *Hänschens* (5) (see **3.1a(iv)**).
- Use of *hin-* to indicate movement away from speaker: *da hinein* (6) 'in there' (see **19.2a**).
- Verb first for poetic effect: *Kommt...* (1–3).
- Missing pronoun and *und* to create rhythm: *baut ...* (1–2).
- Omission of final *-e* in *zu Haus* to create rhyme (9).

Discover more about gender

1.2 WHICH GENDER?

It is often not possible to predict which noun will take a certain gender, particularly in the case of nouns referring to inanimate objects, and therefore when students learn individual nouns they must also remember their gender (e.g. by learning the nouns together with a definite article). There are, however, a few correlations between certain characteristics of the noun and its gender that can be given to help students remember and predict which nouns tend to take a certain gender. First, gender is often determined by the **ending** of the noun (see **Table 1.1**).

Sometimes an ending will signal a *preference* for a particular gender rather than conforming to a hard and fast rule. For example, nouns ending in *-nis* and *-sal* tend to be neuter (e.g. *das Gefängnis, das Schicksal*) but this is not always the case. Nouns ending in *-iv* tend to be masculine if referring to people and to grammatical terms (e.g. *der Imperativ, der Akkusativ*), but there are exceptions (e.g. *das Adjektiv, das Substantiv*). Nouns ending in *-ekt* tend to be masculine (e.g. *der Aspekt*) but can also be neuter (e.g. *das Insekt*, and particularly for grammatical terms, e.g. *das Subjekt*).

Second, gender may also be determined by the **meaning** of the noun (see **Table 1.2**), although it should be pointed out that we are dealing with general tendencies here rather than rules. The correlation between meaning and gender is, on the whole, less reliable than that between endings and gender.

Table 1.1 The gender of nouns according to their endings

MASC.		FEM.		NEUT.	
-ant/-ent*	der Student	-anz/-enz	die Prominenz	-chen/-lein	das Mädchen
-ast	der Palast	-e†	die Limonade	-en (infinitive)	das Essen
-er*	der Arbeiter	-ei	die Polizei	-ett	das Duett
-ich	der Teppich	-ette	die Zigarette	-icht	das Licht
-ig	der Käfig	-heit/-keit	die Schönheit	-il	das Wohnmobil
-ling	der Flüchtling	-ie	die Chemie	-ma	das Thema
-ist	der Polizist	-ik	die Musik	-ment	das Testament
-or	der Traktor	-in	die Lehrerin	-o	das Auto
-us	der Sozialismus	-ion	die Situation	-tel	das Drittel
		-sis	die Dosis	-tum	das Wachstum
		-tät	die Pubertät	-um	das Studium
		-ung	die Zeitung		
		-ur	die Figur		

* When referring to people

† Except for weak masculine and masculine/neuter adjectival nouns (see **3.3a**, **3.3b**)

Table 1.2 The gender of nouns according to their meaning

MASC.		
	• Males:	der Mann, der Lehrer, der Löwe, der Kater, der Stier
	• Days, months, seasons:	der Montag, der April, der Herbst, der Winter
	• Points of compass & weather:	der Norden, der Süden, der Wind, der Hagel, der Regen
	• Many drinks:	der Tee, der Kaffee, der Saft, der Wein, der Cognac (but: das Wasser/Bier)
	• Makes of car:	der Volvo, der Audi, der BMW
FEM.		
	• Females:*	die Frau, die Mutter, die Tochter, die Katze, die Kuh
	• Trees and flowers:	die Tanne, die Birke, die Rose, die Nelke
	• Most native rivers:†	die Donau, die Elbe, die Ruhr (yet: der Rhein)
	• Nouns denoting numbers and size:	die Eins, die Zwei, die Größe, die Breite, die Länge
NEUT.		
	• Young persons/animals:	das Baby, das Kind, das Kalb, das Ferkel, das Küken
	• Towns, countries,‡ continents:	das Berlin, das Deutschland, das Europa, das Afrika
	• Units of measurement:	das Kilo, das Gramm, das Pfund (das or der Liter, Meter)
	• Metals:	das Gold, das Silber, das Blei, das Eisen
	• Colours:	das Rot, das Blau etc.
	• Languages:	das Deutsch, das Englisch etc.
	• Letters of alphabet:	das A, das B etc.

* Except diminutives in -chen, -lein, e.g. das Mädchen, das Fräulein

† Rivers outside the German-speaking area are usually masculine, unless they end in -a or -e, in which case they are feminine: e.g. die Themse.

‡ There are some exceptions to this: e.g. die Schweiz, die Türkei, der Iran.

Occasionally these two main criteria (i.e. meaning and ending of word) may conflict when determining a noun's gender. For instance, nouns in -*ei* are usually feminine, yet *der Papagei* 'parrot' is masculine because it is a male animal; nouns in -*er* are usually masculine when referring to people, yet *die Mutter* and *die Tochter* are feminine as they are females. Conversely, a girl is a female person, yet it is *das Mädchen* because of the diminutive -*chen*.

1.3 **FURTHER NOTES ON GENDER**

i) **Compound nouns**: The gender of compounds is determined by the last element: e.g. *das Haus* + *die Frau* = *die Hausfrau*.

ii) **Derived nouns without an ending:** Nouns derived from a **bare verb stem** are usually masculine: e.g. *der Schlaf*; nouns formed with the **prefix *ge-*** are usually neuter: e.g. *das Gebäude*.

iii) **Abbreviations**: The gender of these is determined by that of the **whole word**: e.g. *die Limo* (< *die Limonade*), *das Labor* (< *das Laboratorium*), despite the fact that -*o* is usually neuter and -*or* usually masculine. In the case of whole phrases, the main noun determines the gender: e.g. *die SPD* (< *die Sozialistische **Partei** Deutschlands*), *die BRD* (< *die **Bundesrepublik** Deutschland*), *die DDR* (< *die Deutsche Demokratische **Republik***).

iv) Regional variation: The gender of some words differs depending on whether the speaker is German, Austrian or Swiss: e.g. German *die Butter, das Radio* vs. Austrian *der Butter, der Radio*.

EXERCISES

Vocabulary topic: *Grammatische Terminologie*

1 Fill in the gaps with the correct form of the definite or indefinite article, as appropriate.

1 D__ Substantiv: ein__ Wort, das z.B. ein__ Ding oder ein__ Lebewesen bezeichnet.

2 D__ Satz: ein__ sprachliche Einheit, die aus Subjekt und Prädikat besteht.

3 D__ Kongruenz: d__Übereinstimmung und Gleichheit zusammengehöriger Teile eines Satzes in Kasus, Numerus und Genus (bei Nomen) oder in Person und Numerus (Subject zu Verb).

4 D__ Hilfsverb: ein__ Verb, das zusammen mit einem Vollverb ein__ bestimmte Tempus- oder Modusform bildet (z.B. Ich <u>habe</u> es getan).

5 D__ Präteritum: d__ Vergangenheitsform, die abgeschlossene Ereignisse beschreibt.

6 D__ Objekt: ein__ Ergänzung, auf die sich d__ Prädikat bezieht.

7 D__ Perfekt: ein__ grammatischer Terminus, der einen Aspekt oder ein Tempus eines Verbs bezeichnen kann. Er wird auch d__ *2. Vergangenheit* genannt.

8 D__ Wortstellung (auch d__ Wortfolge): d__ Anordnung der Wörter oder Satzglieder innerhalb eines Satzes.

9 D__ Genus: ein__ Klassifikationsmerkmal von Substantiven. Ein__ Sprache hat ein__ Genus-System, wenn es Kongruenzeffekte gibt, die sich auf verschiedene Klassen von Substantiven zurückführen lassen. Die drei Genera des Deutschen sind d__ Maskulinum, d__ Femininum und d__ Neutrum.

10 D__ Kasus: ein__ morphologische Kategorie, die durch ein__ System einander gegenüberstehender Formenreihen gekennzeichnet ist, wobei diese Formen d__ Beziehung eines Gegenstandes zu anderen Gegenständen in einer bestimmten Situation wiedergeben. Die vier Fälle im Deutschen sind d__ Nominativ, d__ Akkusativ, d__ Dativ, und d__ Genitiv.

✎ FURTHER EXERCISES

2 Out of the 30 words below, 10 are masculine, 10 are feminine and 10 are neuter. Rearrange the words into three columns according to their gender, bearing in mind the two main factors determining gender: i) ending of word; ii) meaning of word. Place *der*, *die*, *das* in front of each word as appropriate:

Bruder	Kind	Polizist
Blume	Frühling	Höhe
Schnee	Französisch	Osten
Foto	Whisky	Erde
Regierung	Viertel	Motor
Politik	Lesen	Geräusch
Liebling	Lehrer	Freundin
Gesundheit	Natur	Fräulein
Ereignis	Tourismus	Klima
Universität	Grün	Bäckerei

For further exercises on gender see Ch. 27, Exs. 4b and 5, and Revision Text 4, Exs. 1 and 5.

2 | Noun plurals

Text

> ## *Beliebte **Rezepte** für **Gäste**:* <u>Wurstgulasch mit Sauerkraut</u>.
>
> <u>Portionen</u>: 4. <u>Nährwerte</u>: pro Portion ca 656 Kcal 50g Fett.
>
> <u>Zutaten</u>: 1 Fleischwurst (400g), 100g geräucherter durchwachsener Speck, 2 **Zwiebeln**, 1 Dose Sauerkraut, 1-2 **Esslöffel** Butter, 1 Dose rote **Bohnen**,
> 5   3/4 L. Brühe, 2 **Lorbeerblätter**, Salz, Pfeffer, Zucker, gemahlene **Nelken**, 150g Crème fraîche.
>
> <u>Zubereitung</u>: Die Fleischwurst aus der Haut lösen, längs vierteln und in etwa 2cm dicke **Scheiben** schneiden. Speck würfeln. **Zwiebeln** abziehen und in feine **Spalten** schneiden. Sauerkraut fein schneiden. Die Butter erhitzen
> 10   und Speck und **Zwiebeln** darin anbraten. Die Fleischwurst dazugeben und kurz mit anbraten. Die **Bohnen** auf einem Sieb unter fließendem kaltem Wasser abspülen. Sauerkraut, Brühe, **Bohnen** und **Lorbeerblätter** dazugeben. Bei kleiner Hitze etwa 15 **Minuten** schmoren lassen. Mit Salz, Pfeffer, Zucker und **Nelken**pulver abschmecken. Auf **Teller**
> 15   verteilen und je einen Klaks Crème fraîche daraufgeben.

Aus: *Brigitte*, 28/2/01.

das Rezept – recipe	*die Bohne* – bean	*anbraten* – to brown
der Gast – guest	*das Lorbeerblatt* – bay leaf	*das Sieb* – sieve
der Nährwert – nutritional value	*gemalen* – ground	*abspülen* – to rinse
die Zutaten – ingredients	*die Nelke* – clove	*die Brühe* – stock
geräuchert – smoked	*vierteln* – to quarter	*schmoren* – to stew
durchwachsen – streaky	*die Scheibe* – slice	*der Klaks* – dollop
der Esslöffel – tablespoon	*die Spalte* – strip	*abschmecken* – season
die Dose – tin, jar	*erhitzen* – to heat up	to taste

Noun plurals in the text

2.1 PLURAL FORMATION

There are seven ways of forming noun plurals in German, five of which are illustrated in the above text:

1	Add **-e**:	*Rezept-e* (1), *Nährwert-e* (2)
2	Add *umlaut* and **-e**:	*Gäst-e* (1)
3	Add **-(e)n**:[3]	*Portion-en* (2), *Zutat-en* (3), *Zwiebel-n* (4, 8, 10), *Bohne-n* (4, 11, 12), *Nelke-n* (5, 14), *Scheibe-n* (7), *Spalte-n* (9), *Minute-n* (13)
4	Add **-er**: (and *umlaut* the preceding vowel where possible)	*Lorbeerblätt-er* (5, 12)
5	**No change**:[4]	*Esslöffel* (4), *Teller* (14)

---

[3] -*en* is reduced to -*n* after nouns ending in -*e*, -*el*, -*er*.
[4] When the noun plural is the same as the singular, the difference is marked elsewhere, e.g. by changing the definite article: *der Teller* – **die** *Teller*.

In addition, there are two markers which are less widely used and therefore do not occur in our text:

6	Add *umlaut* alone:	e.g. *Vater – Väter, Bruder – Brüder*
7	Add **-s**:	e.g. *Foto-s, Baby-s*

As it is often not predictable which plural marker a certain noun may take, this information is always given in dictionaries, along with information about the noun's gender, so that students can learn the plural form together with the singular. It is, however, of some help to note that the choice of plural marker can sometimes be predicted on the basis of gender or phonological shape of the noun. These correlations will be dealt with under **2.2** below.

Other points to note in the text

- Use of infinitive as an imperative: *lösen* (7), *vierteln* (7), *schneiden* (8, 9), *würfeln* (8), *abziehen* (8), *erhitzen* (9), *anbraten* (10, 11), *dazugeben* (10, 13), *abspülen* (12), *schmoren lassen* (13), *abschmecken* (14), *verteilen* (15), *daraufgeben* (15) (see **11.1**).
- Prepositions + case: *aus der Haut* (7), *in... dicke Scheiben*, accusative expressing 'into' (8), *in feine Spalten,* accusative 'into' (9), *auf einem Sieb* (11), *unter fließendem kaltem Wasser* (11–12), *bei kleiner Hitze* (13), *auf Teller*, accusative expressing 'onto' (14) (see **24.1a–b**).
- Prepositions with *da(r)*: *darin* (10), *dazugeben* (10, 13), *darauf*geben (15) (see **7.5**).

Discover more about noun plurals

2.2 **GENERAL TENDENCIES: CORRELATION BETWEEN PLURAL MARKER AND GENDER/PHONOLOGICAL SHAPE OF NOUN**

Although, generally speaking, noun plurals must be learned individually, alongside their corresponding singulars, some general tendencies in their distribution can be observed which may be helpful to the foreign learner. These are given in **Table 2.1**.

Table 2.1 Noun plural markers

Marker	General use	
-e	Many **masculines**	e.g. *Tage, Hunde*
	Some neuters	e.g. *Jahre*
-"e	Many **masculines**	e.g. *Bäume, Köpfe*
	Some feminines	e.g. *Hände*
-(e)n	Most **feminine** nouns (over 90%)	e.g. *Frauen, Blumen*
	All 'weak' nouns (see **3.3b**)	e.g. *Jungen, Polizisten*
	Some neuters	e.g. *Ohren*
-"er	Many **neuter** nouns	e.g. *Kinder, Länder*
	A few masculines	e.g. *Männer*
	No feminines	
-	Most nouns in **-er, -en, -el** (except feminines)	e.g. *Fenster, Wagen*
	Diminutives in **-chen, -lein**	e.g. *Händchen*
-"	Some masculines in -er, -en, -el with an umlautable vowel:	e.g. *Brüder, Väter*
	Two feminines:	e.g. *Mütter, Töchter*
-s	Most nouns ending in a **vowel** other than -e	e.g. *Autos, Omas*
	Some foreign loanwords*	e.g. *Champignons*

* People's names tend to be pluralised with *-s*, e.g. *die Müllers* 'the Müllers'.

2.3 COMMON NOUNS AND THEIR PLURAL FORMS

Below is a list of frequently occurring German nouns (many of which are very often used in the plural) together with their plural forms which you should learn. Examine to what extent the plurals correspond to the general tendencies set out in **Table 2.1**.

der Apfel – die Äpfel	*der Garten – die Gärten*	*der Student – die Studenten*
der Arm – die Arme	*der Herr – die Herren*	*der Stuhl – die Stühle*
der Baum – die Bäume	*der Hund – die Hunde*	*der Tag – die Tage*
der Brief – die Briefe	*der Junge – die Jungen*	*der Tisch – die Tische*
der Bruder – die Brüder	*der Kopf – die Köpfe*	*der Vater – die Väter*
der Bus – die Busse	*der Mann – die Männer*	*der Vogel – die Vögel*
der Chef – die Chefs	*der Mensch – die Menschen*	*der Wagen – die Wagen*
der Finger – die Finger	*der Monat – die Monate*	*der Weg – die Wege*
der Fisch – die Fische	*der Opa – die Opas*	*der Zahn – die Zähne*
der Freund – die Freunde	*der Schuh – die Schuhe*	*der Zeh – die Zehe*
der Fuß – die Füße	*der Sohn – die Söhne*	*der Zug – die Züge*
die Blume – die Blumen	*die Minute – die Minuten*	*die Stunde – die Stunden*
die Flasche – die Flaschen	*die Mutter – die Mütter*	*die Tasse – die Tassen*
die Fliege – die Fliegen	*die Nacht – die Nächte*	*die Tochter – die Töchter*
die Frau – die Frauen	*die Oma – die Omas*	*die Toilette – die Toiletten*
die Freundin – die Freundinnen	*die Pflanze – die Pflanzen*	*die Tür – die Türen*

die Hand – die Hände	*die Sekunde – die Sekunden*	*die Wand – die Wände*
die Katze – die Katzen	*die Schwester – die Schwestern*	*die Woche – die Wochen*
die Lippe – die Lippen	*die Stadt – die Städte*	*die Wohnung – die Wohnungen*
die Maus – die Mäuse	*die Straße – die Straßen*	*die Zeit – die Zeiten*
das Auge – die Augen	*das Büro – die Büros*	*das Kleid – die Kleider*
das Auto – die Autos	*das Ei – die Eier*	*das Land – die Länder*
das Baby – die Babys	*das Fenster – die Fenster*	*das Licht – die Lichter*
das Bein – die Beine	*das Glas – die Gläser*	*das Mädchen – die Mädchen*
das Bett – die Betten	*das Haar – die Haare*	*das Ohr – die Ohren*
das Bild – die Bilder	*das Haus – die Häuser*	*das Rad – die Räder*
das Blatt – die Blätter	*das Hotel – die Hotels*	*das Schiff – die Schiffe*
das Boot – die Boote	*das Jahr – die Jahre*	*das Tuch – die Tücher*
das Buch – die Bücher	*das Kind – die Kinder*	*das Zimmer – die Zimmer*

Note that *das Wort* has two plural forms depending on meaning: *die **Worte*** = words used together in a phrase or sentence, *die **Wörter*** = isolated words (e.g. in a dictionary).

2.4 VERB AGREEMENT

Noun plurals in German occur with plural forms of verbs: e.g. *Der Mann **kommt*** vs. *Die Männer **kommen***. One important difference from English, however, is that **collective nouns** (i.e. singular nouns which are used to refer to a group or collection of people or things) always occur with a **singular verb** in German while English often allows a plural verb: e.g. *Seine **Familie** <u>war</u> sehr freundlich* vs. 'His family <u>were</u> very friendly'; *Die **Polizei** <u>hat</u> ihn verhaftet* vs. 'The police <u>have</u> arrested him.'

✎ EXERCISES

Vocabulary topic: *Essen*

1 Put the nouns in the following shopping list into the plural. (The gender of each noun is given in brackets):[5]

Tomate (f)	Apfel (m)	12 Ei (n)	Vollwertnudel (f)
Zwiebel (f)	Weintraube (f)	6 Brötchen (n)	2 Dose (f) Thunfisch
Kartoffel (f)	Erdbeere (f)	4 Joghurt (m/nt)	Kaffeefilter (m)
Champignon (m)	Pfirsich (m)	2 Pizza (f)	2 Kiste (f) Bier
Kraut (n)	Dattel (f)	Bonbon (m/nt)	4 Flasche (f) Wein
Gewürz (n)	Erdnuss (f)	Muesliriegel (m)	verschiedene Fruchtsaft (f)

[5] Units of measurement such as *Gramm, Kilo, Liter* (and also *Stück*) are always used in the singular after a numeral, e.g. *2 **Kilo** Orangen, 4 **Liter** Milch, 6 **Stück** Kuchen*.

2 Complete the following recipe by filling in the gaps using the appropriate plural forms of the nouns in brackets:

Couscous mit Gemüse[6] und ____ [Rosine]

1 Couscous in eine Schüssel geben. Das Wasser bis auf vier __ [Esslöffel] langsam dazugießen und den Couscous dabei mit einer Gabel durchrühren, bis er gleichmäßig feucht ist und keine __ [Klümpchen] bildet. __ [Rosine] im restlichen Wasser einweichen. Beide __ [Zutat] zugedeckt quellen lassen.

2 Couscous nach 30 __ [Minute] mit einer Gabel durchmischen, bis er wieder locker ist. In einem Topf knapp fingerhoch Wasser aufkochen. Die hälfte der Butter in __ [Stückchen] teilen und auf den Couscous legen. Bei schwächster Hitze eine Stunde dämpfen.

3 __ [Lauchzwiebel], __ [Paprikaschote] und __ [Zucchini] waschen und putzen. __ [Lauchzwiebel] mit dem saftigen Grün in etwa fingerdicke __ [Stück], __ [Schote] in __ [Streife], __ [Zucchini] in etwa fingerlange __ [Stift] schneiden.

4 Öl erhitzen, zerkleinertes Gemüse darin anbraten. Brühe zugießen. Abgetropfte __ [Kichererbse] und __ [Rosine] untermischen und erhitzen.

5 Während das Gemüse gart, __ [Mandel] grob hacken und in der restlichen Butter rösten. Joghurt mit der Pepperonicreme und etwas Salz verrühren.

6 Gemüse in die Mitte einer großen Platte geben und mit den __ [Mandel] bestreuen. Couscous in __ [Häufchen] um das Gemüse setzen. Joghurt dazu servieren.

Für 4 __ [Portion]. Pro Portion: 775 __ [Kalorie], 3242 __ [Joule], 11,1g __ [Ballaststoff], 53 mg Cholesterin. Dauert insgesamt ca. 1½ __ [Stunde].

Aus: Barbara Rias-Bucher, *Gesünder Leben – vegetarisch Essen.* ©1991 Verlag Zabert Sandmann.

---

[6] 'Vegetables' is plural in English but singular in German: *das Gemüse.*

✎ FURTHER EXERCISES

3 Complete the following crossword. All answers are in the plural (Umlauts are indicated by the letter *e* following the relevant vowel, e.g. *Männer* = maenner):

Kreutzworträtsel

Senkrecht

1 Leute, die aus der ehemaligen DDR kommen.

2 Das, was man an den Füßen trägt.

3 Man kauft sie, um die Nachrichten zu lesen.

4 Man isst sie manchmal zum Tee oder Kaffee.

Waagerecht

5 Stücke, die vom Brot abgeschnitten worden sind.

6 Man braucht sie, um eine abgeschlossene Tür aufmachen zu können.

7 Das, was man manchmal auf dem Kopf trägt.

For further exercises on noun plurals see Ch. 3, Ex. 2, Ch. 5, Ex. 3 and Revision Text 1, Ex. 1.

3 | Case[7]

Text

Deformiert Deutsch **das** Gesicht?

Die vielen Umlaute in ihr**er** Sprache machen Deutsche mürrisch und humorlos, *ä, ö* und *ü* zögen Mundwinkel und Laune nach unten. Das behauptet **ein** amerikanischer Psychologieprofessor.

5 LONDON – Professor David Myers vom Hope College in Michigan hat demnach bemerkt, dass sich **der** Mund bei **der** Aussprache deutscher Umlaute nach unten verzieht. **Dies** führe zu ein**em** miesepetrigen Gesichtsausdruck und aktiviere Muskeln, **die** „mit negativen Emotionen besetzt" seien. „**Das** kann **den** Gemütszustand ein**er** Person signifikant
10 beeinflussen", sagte Myers. „Es könnte **ein** guter Grund dafür sein, dass Deutsche **im** Ruf stehen, humorlos und mürrisch zu sein." Sogar ihr**e** „Probleme, sich zuweilen mit anderen Länder**n** in **der** Europäischen Union zu verständigen", ließen sich letztlich auf *ä, ö* und *ü* zurückführen.

Das Englische mit sein**en** vielen e- und a-Laute**n** lasse **die** Menschen
15 dagegen fröhlich und hilfsbereit werden. **Die** an **der** Royal Society in Edinburgh vorgestellte Theorie stieß **am** Freitag in Großbritannien auf großes Interesse. **Die** „Times" und **der** „Daily Telegraph" illustrierten **die** Ausführungen **am** Freitag auf ihr**en** Titelseiten mit Fotos ein**es** Mund**es**, **der** deutsche Umlaute ausspricht, und ein**es** missmutig dreinblickenden Gerhard
20 Schröder. **Die** „Daily Mail" fragte auf Deutsch: „Sprechen **Sie** grumpy (mürrisch)?" und listete deutsche Sprichwörter auf, bei **deren** Aussprache **man das** Gesicht besonders unvorteilhaft verziehe, etwa: „Unter **den** Blinden ist **der** Einäugige König." **Der** „Daily Star" imitierte in sein**er** Überschrift ein**en** deutsch**en** Akzent: „It's the vay ve talk zat makes us frown." (Unser**e**
25 Sprechweise lässt **uns** so finster aussehen.)

Ein**e** Stellungnahme **der** deutschen Botschaft in London erhielt keine **der** Zeitungen. „**Das** ist zu wissenschaftlich", sagte **ein** Sprecher.

Aus: *Der Spiegel* (*Online*), 25/8/00.

---

[7] This chapter deals with case endings on articles, pronouns and nouns. Endings on adjectives are more complex and will be dealt with separately in **Ch. 5**. A full list of article and adjective endings is given in **Appendix 2**.

mürrisch – grumpy	*die Ausführung* – observation
der Mundwinkel – corner of mouth	*missmutig dreinblickend* – morose looking
behaupten – to claim	*unvorteilhaft* – unattractive
die Aussprache – pronunciation	*der Einäugige* – one-eyed man
zich verziehen – to pull	*die Überschrift* – headline
miesepetrig – grumpy	*die Stellungnahme* – statement
Gemutszustand – emotional state	*die Botschaft* – embassy
zurückführen auf – to be attributed to	*wissenschaftlich* – scientific

⌕ Case shown in the text

3.1 USE OF CASE

In German, articles, pronouns, adjectives and some nouns have special endings depending on the case (nominative, accusative, genitive or dative), number (singular or plural) and gender (masculine, feminine, neuter) of the noun. Number and gender are integral features of the noun while **case** is assigned depending on the noun's relationship to other elements in the sentence: i) to express relationships between words in a sentence, e.g. subject versus object; ii) as a result of a particular word requiring a certain case, e.g. with prepositions.

3.1a Case expressing syntactic relationships between words

i) **Nominative** case is assigned to the **subject** of the sentence (i.e. the person or thing carrying out the action described by the verb): e.g. (with the verb underlined): *Der „Daily Star" imitierte* (23), *Die „Daily Mail" fragte auf Deutsch* (20), *Das Englische … lasse die Menschen* (14); and with two different subjects: *Die „Times" und der „Daily Telegraph" illustrierten* (17).[8]

In English, the subject usually precedes the verb, but this is not always the case in German (see **26.2a**, **26.8**): e.g. *Das behauptet ein amerikanischer Psychologieprofessor* (3–4). We know that 'an American psychology professor' is the subject because he is the one carrying out the action described by the verb: i.e. 'claiming'. Similarly, where the verb is *sein* (or *werden*) the nominative is used: *Unter den Blinden ist der Einäugige König* (22–23), *Es könnte ein guter Grund dafür sein* (10). In the latter example, 'it could be a good reason for it', *es* and *ein guter Grund* are both subjects of the verb, as they both refer to the same thing.[9]

With longer sentences consisting of two or more clauses (i.e. a part of a sentence containing a finite verb of its own), there will be a subject (in the nominative case) for each finite verb: e.g. *Professor David Myers vom Hope College in Michigan hat demnach bemerkt, dass sich der Mund bei der Aussprache deutscher Umlaute nach unten verzieht* (5–7).

[8] The subject of a **passive** sentence is also in the nominative: e.g. *Der Daily Star wird verkauft* 'the Daily Star is sold' (see **18.2**).

[9] Contrast sentences such as *Es gibt einen guten Grund dafür*, where the verb is not *sein* and the article is accusative.

ii) **Accusative** case is assigned to the **direct object** of the sentence (i.e. the person or thing directly affected by the action described by the verb): e.g. *Das kann **den** Gemütszustand einer Person signifikant beeinflussen* (9–10), *Die „Times" und der „Daily Telegraph" illustrierten **die** Ausführungen* (17–18), *Der „Daily Star" imitierte in seiner Überschrift **einen** deutschen Akzent* (23–24).

In English, direct objects usually follow the verb but this is not always the case in German (see **26.2b**, **26.6**): e.g. ***Eine** Stellungnahme … erhielt keine der Zeitungen* (26–27) shows that the object can come first.[10]

> [10] This example from the text is misleading at first sight, as *eine* is used for the nominative and the accusative. A more obvious example would be with a masculine singular: e.g. ***Den** Eindruck hatte ich auch* 'I had that impression too'.

iii) **Dative** case is assigned to the **indirect object** of the sentence, i.e. the recipient (usually a person) of the direct object (usually a thing). This is often expressed using 'to' in English. Consider the following examples (not in the text), in which the direct object is underlined and the indirect object is in bold print: e.g. *Er gab **dem** Lehrer einen Aufsatz* 'He gave **the teacher** an essay/He gave an essay **to the teacher**', *Er erklärte **seiner** Freundin das Problem* 'He explained the problem **to his girlfriend**'.

iv) **Genitive**: The use of the genitive in German is roughly equivalent to the use of the possessive *'s* in English (e.g. 'the man**'s** hat') or the use of the word *of* (e.g. 'her idea **of** a suitable partner'). The genitive tends to be used more in written and formal styles of spoken German rather than in everyday spoken language where it is often replaced by the preposition *von* (+ dative): e.g. *ein Freund **seines** Bruders* vs. *ein Freund **von** seinem Bruder*. As our text is a written report it includes quite a few genitives: e.g. *den Gemütszustand **einer** Person* (9), *eine Stellungnahme **der** deutschen Botschaft* (26), *keine **der** Zeitungen* (26–27), *Fotos **eines** Mundes* (18), ***eines** … Gerhard Schröder* (19–20), ***deren** Aussprache* (21). The last example is a relative pronoun meaning 'of which' or 'whose' (see **9.2c**).

Thus, to sum up, an example of a sentence with all cases present would be:

[***Der** Student*] *gab*	[***dem** Lehrer*]	[***den** Aufsatz*	***eines** Freundes*]
SUBJ. (NOM.)	IND. OBJ. (DAT.)	OBJ. (ACC.)	'OF' (GEN.)

'The student gave the teacher a friend's essay'.

3.1b Case required by particular words

Certain words, most commonly prepositions, require the following noun/article/pronoun to appear in a particular case, even though there seems to be no apparent reason for this in terms of subject–object relations. In the text there are seven prepositions, all of which take a particular case: *in* + dat.: *in **ihrer** Sprache* (2), *im Ruf* (11), *in **der** Europäischen Union* (12), *in **seiner** Überschrift* (23); *bei* + dat.: *bei **der** Aussprache* (6); *zu* +dat.: *zu **einem** miespetrigen Gesichtsausdruck* (7–8); *mit* + dat.: *mit **seinen** vielen … Lauten* (14); *an* + dat.: *an **der** Royal Society* (15), *am Freitag* (16, 18), *auf* + dat.: *auf **ihren** Titelseiten* (18); *unter* + dat.: *unter **den** Blinden* (22).[11] As case is unpredictable here it must be learnt together with the individual preposition (see **Tables 24.1** to **24.4** for a list of common prepositions with their case).

3.1c Scope of assigned case

Sometimes an accusative, dative or genitive object can consist of more than one noun (or pronoun), which means that their articles/pronouns **all** have to be marked with the appropriate case, even if some of them come much later in the sentence: e.g. *Fotos **eines** Mundes, der deutsche Umlaute ausspricht, und **eines** missmutig dreinblickenden Gerhard Schröder* (18-20); *Ich habe **den** Mann gesehen: **den** Freund von meiner Tochter* 'I saw the man: my daughter's boyfriend' (not in text). Similarly, if a preposition has scope over more than one noun, the related articles/pronouns must all have the same case ending: e.g. *Er hat sich mit **seiner** Mutter, **seinem** Vater und sogar **seinem** besten Freund gestritten* 'He had an argument with his mother, his father and even his best friend.' (not in text).

3.2 CASE ENDINGS

In German, case is shown on articles and pronouns. It is only shown on nouns in the genitive singular masculine and neuter (*-(e)s*)[12] and in the dative plural (*-n*)[13]. (For case on adjectives see **Tables 5.1–5.3** and for weak and adjectival nouns see **3.3**.) **Table 3.1** shows case endings on definite articles and **Table 3.2** shows case endings on indefinite articles. As you can see, the endings are very similar for both. Students are advised to learn these different case forms in the context of a whole phrase.

3.2a The definite article

Table 3.1 Forms of the definite article

	Masc.		Fem.		Neut.		Plural	
N		*der* Mann		*die* Frau		*das* Kind		*die* Kinder
A	*ich sehe*	*den* Mann	*ich sehe*	*die* Frau	*ich sehe*	*das* Kind	*ich sehe*	*die* Kinder
D	*ich sage*	*dem* Mann	*ich sage*	*der* Frau	*ich sage*	*dem* Kind	*ich sage*	*den* Kindern
G	*das Bild*	*des* Mannes	*das Bild*	*der* Frau	*das Bild*	*des* Kindes	*das Bild*	*der* Kinder

Other words which follow the pattern of **Table 3.1** are the demonstratives *dieser* 'this', *diese, dieses, diesen* etc.[14] and *jener* 'that', *jene, jenes* etc.; *jeder* 'each/every', *jede, jedes* etc., **welcher?** 'which?', *welche?, welches?* etc. and the **relative pronouns** which are identical to the definite articles (except for the genitive: e.g. *deren Aussprache*, and the dative plural, see **9.1**). *Viel* 'a lot/ many' and *wenig* 'few' have no ending in the singular but follow the same endings as the definite article in all the plural forms: e.g. *viel Zeit* vs. *viele, vielen, vieler Frauen*.

Some examples from the text are: nominative *der Mund* (6), *die „Times"* (17), *das Englische* (14), *die vielen Umlaute* (2); accusative *den Gemütszustand* (9), *das Gesicht* (22), *die Ausführungen* (17–18); dative *am Freitag* (18) [*dem* → *-m* after certain prepositions], *der Aussprache* (6), *den Blinden* (22), *Ländern* (12); genitive *der deutschen Botschaft* (26), *der Zeitungen* (26–27).

[14] *Dies* 'this', without an ending, is used to refer to a whole idea rather than a particular noun: *Dies führe zu einem miesepetrigen Gesichtsausdruck* (6–7) 'this (i.e. the pronunciation of German umlauts) leads to a grumpy look'. Similarly *das* is used to mean 'that' in a general sense: *Das kann den Gemützustand einer Person signifikant beeinflussen* (8–9) 'that can significantly influence a person's mood'.

3.2b The indefinite article

Table 3.2 Forms of the indefinite article

		Masc.		Fem.		Neut.
N		*ein* Mann		*eine* Frau		*ein* Kind
A	*ich sehe*	*einen* Mann	*ich sehe*	*eine* Frau	*ich sehe*	*ein* Kind
D	*ich sage*	*einem* Mann	*ich sage*	*einer* Frau	*ich sage*	*einem* Kind
G	*das Bild*	*eines* Mannes	*das Bild*	*einer* Frau	*das Bild*	*eines* Kindes

i) Other words following the same pattern as **Table 3.2** are *kein* 'not a/no' and the possessives *mein, dein, sein, unser, euer, ihr* (see **7.3**), although these also have plural forms, which the indefinite article does not have: e.g. *keine* (nom./acc.), *keinen* (dat.), *keiner* (gen.).[15]

Some examples from the text are: nominative *ein* Sprecher (27), *keine der Zeitungen* (26–27), *unsere Sprechweise* (24–25), *ihre Probleme* (11–12); accusative *einen deutschen Akzent* (23–24), *eine Stellungnahme* (26); dative *einem miesepetrigen Gesichtsausdruck* (7–8), *ihrer Sprache* (2), *seiner Überschrift* (23); genitive *eines Mundes* (18), *einer Person* (9).

[15] Personal pronouns, e.g. *ich, du* etc., have their own case forms and are dealt with in **7.1**. See 'Other points to note …' for the personal pronouns in the text.

ii) Indefinite articles used as pronouns. Sometimes a noun may be omitted but still understood, e.g. 'I've got two apples. Would you like **one**? [i.e. an apple]'. In this case, the indefinite article stands in for the noun and has the same endings as it would have had if the noun had been present: e.g. *Ich habe zwei Äpfel. Möchten Sie einen?* [< *einen Apfel*]. Exceptions are the **masc. nom. sg.** and the **neuter nom./acc. sg.**, which have the endings *-er* and *-(e)s* respectively: e.g. (not in text):

Hast du einen Apfel? – Ja, hier ist einer.   [NOT *hier ist ein*].

Ich habe frische Brötchen geholt. Möchtest du eines/eins?[16]   [i.e. a bread roll]

[16] 'One thing' is usually rendered by *eines/eins*: e.g. *Ein(e)s steht fest, …* 'One thing is certain, …'.

Other points to note in the text

- Adjective endings: *viel**en*** (2, 14), *amerikanisch**er*** (4), *deutsch**er*** (6), *miesepetrig**en*** (7), *negativ**en*** (8), *gut**er*** (10), *Europäisch**en*** (12), *groß**es*** (16), *deutsch**e*** (19, 21), *dreinblickend**en*** (19), *deutsch**en*** (24, 26) (see **Ch. 5**).
- Expanded attribute: *die an der Royal Society in Edinburgh vorgestell**te** Theorie* 'the theory put forward to the Royal Society in Edinburgh' (15–16) (see **5.3**).
- Adverbs: *signifikant* (9), *missmutig* (19), *unvorteilhaft* (22) (see **5.6**).
- Personal pronouns: *Sie* (20), *uns* (25) and impersonal *man* (22) (see **7.1**).
- Subjunctive in reported speech: Konjunktiv I: *führe* (7), *seien* (9), *lasse* (14), *verziehe* (22); Konjunktiv II: *zögen* (3), *ließen* (13) (see **Ch. 17**).
- Konjunktiv II as conditional: *könnte* (10) (see **16.2b**)

Discover more about case

3.3 CASE ON NOUNS

As a rule, case is only shown on nouns in the genitive singular masculine/neuter, e.g. *des Arbeiters, des Hauses*, and in the dative plural, e.g. *den Häusern*.[17] However, there are also certain types of noun which always have case endings: a) adjectival nouns; b) 'weak' nouns.

[17] The dative singular ending -e can be found in older texts, but it is now regarded as old-fashioned and is only used in set phrases: e.g. *zu Hause*.

3.3a Adjectival nouns

These are nouns derived from adjectives, e.g. *der Alte* 'the old man', *der Blinde* 'the blind man', and consequently take the same case (and gender and number) endings as **adjectives** (see **5.1–5.2** for adjective endings and **5.5** for adjectival nouns). There are some examples of adjectival nouns in our text: e.g. nominative *Deutsche* (11), *das Englische* (14), *der Einäugige* (23); accusative *Deutsche* (2); dative *den Blinden* (22), although the dative case marking is not visible in the last example as the nominative plural also ends in *-en*.

3.3b 'Weak' nouns

German has a small group of masculine[18] nouns which have the ending *-en* (*-n* after vowels and *-r* in an unstressed syllable) in all but the nominative singular form: e.g. *der Mensch – den Menschen – dem Menschen – des Menschen – die Menschen* etc. These nouns are traditionally known as 'weak' and often refer to male humans and animals. Some common examples are (in the accusative singular):

- Most masculines with a nom. sg. **ending in -e**: e.g. *den Affe-**n*** 'monkey/ape', *den Bursche-**n*** 'lad/fellow', *den Junge-**n*** 'boy', *den Löwe-**n*** 'lion', *den Postbote-**n*** 'postman'.
- Most masculines with a nom. sg. **ending in -ent/-ant/-ist**: e.g. *den Student-**en*** 'student', *den Polizist-**en*** 'policeman'.
- A small group of masculines with no ending in nom. sg.: e.g. *den Bär-**en*** 'bear', *den Mensch-**en*** 'person', *den Nachbar-**n*** 'neighbour'.[19]

[18] One neuter noun, *Herz* 'heart', has some weak endings; *das Herz, dem Herzen, des Herzen.*

[19] In colloquial German the weak endings are often dropped: e.g. *den Student/Polizist/Nachbar* etc.

The following variations are noteworthy:

Nom.	*der Herr*	*der Name*
Acc.	*den Herrn*	*den Namen*
Dat.	*dem Herrn*	*dem Namen*
Gen.	*des Herrn*	*des Namens*
All plural forms:	*die Herren*	*die Namen*

3.4 **VERBS TAKING A DATIVE OR GENITIVE OBJECT**

Some verbs always require their objects to be in the dative or, less commonly, the genitive. Some general rules can be given for this, but there are also a considerable number of verbs to which the rules do not apply, particularly with regard to dative objects, which are required by a relatively large group of verbs. This means that these verbs must be learnt together with their dative objects. **Table 3.3** lists some common examples.

3.4a   Verbs taking a dative object

These tend to correspond with English verbs taking 'to' before the object:[20]

einfallen: e.g. *Die Lösung **fällt** dem Student(en) **ein**.* 'The solution occurs to the student.'
erklären: e.g. *Ich **erkläre** dem Polizist(en), was passiert ist.* 'I explain to the policeman what happened.'
gehören: e.g. *Es **gehört** dem Chef.* 'It belongs to the boss.'
geschehen/passieren: e.g. *Es **geschieht/passiert** meinem Sohn.* 'It happens to my son.'
sagen[21]: e.g. *Ich **sage** dem Verkäufer, was ich möchte.* 'I say to the salesman what I'd like.'
vorkommen: e.g. *Es **kommt** dem Lehrer **vor**, als ob das Kind schläft.* 'It seems to the teacher that the child is asleep.'

Some of these take two objects at the same time: an accusative object (usually a thing) and a dative object (usually a person or animal): e.g. *Ich **zeige** dem Chef meinen Plan.* 'I show the boss my plan.' What all of these verbs have in common is that the speaker is conveying something (e.g. an object, a piece of information) to another person: e.g. *Ich **gab** dem Hund einen Ball.* 'I gave the dog a ball'; *Ich **schenkte** meiner Schwester einen Handy zum Geburtstag* 'I gave my sister a mobile phone for her birthday.'

[20] Adjectives used with 'to' also often take the dative: e.g. *dem Mann **behilflich*** 'helpful to the man'. Also: *ähnlich* 'similar to', *angenehm* 'pleasant to', *bekannt* 'known to', *dankbar* 'thankful to', *fremd* 'strange to', *klar* 'clear/obvious to', *lästig* 'troublesome to', *nahe* 'close to', *wichtig* 'important to'.

[21] Verbs of saying often take the dative: e.g. *Ich sage/erzähle/antworte/wiederspreche dem Lehrer.*

Table 3.3 Other common verbs taking a dative object

ich **antworte** *dem Lehrer*	'answer'	ich **helfe** *dem Kind*	'help'
ich **begegne** *dem Nachbarn*	'meet/run into'	ich **laufe** *dem Hund* **nach***	'run after/chase'
ich **danke** *dem Kellner*	'thank'	es **macht** *dem Vater* **Sorgen**	'it worries the father'
ich **drohe** *dem Kind*	'threaten'	es **macht** *dem Kind* **Spaß**	'the child enjoys it'
sie **fehlt** *ihrem Freund*	'her friend misses her'	ich **näherte mich** *dem Haus*	'approach'
ich **folge** *dem Auto*	'follow'	der Hut **passt** *dem Mann*	'suit/fit'
es **gefällt** *dem Chef*	'the boss likes it'	es **schadet** *dem Wald*	'harm/damage'
ich **gehorche** *meinem Vater*	'obey'	es **schmeckt** *mir*	'I find it tasty'
ich **gratuliere** *dem Ehepaar*	'congratulate'	ich **traue** *dem Arzt*	'trust'
es **gelingt** *dem Autor*	'the author succeeds'	es tut *dem Mann* **Leid**	'the man is sorry'
ich **glaube** *dem Arzt*	'believe'	es **tut** *dem Patienten* **weh**	'it hurts the patient'

* Verbs prefixed with *nach-, bei-, ent(gegen)-, wider-, zu-* take the dative.

3.4b   Verbs taking the genitive

These tend to correspond to English verbs taking 'of' before the object, e.g. *bedürfen* 'to be in
need **of**'; *sich schämen* 'to be ashamed **of**'; *sich vergewissern* 'to make sure **of**':[22]

*Sie bedürfen ein**es** Arzt**es***	You are in need of a doctor
*Er schämt sich sein**es** Benehmens*	He is ashamed of his behaviour
*Er vergewissert sich sein**es** Erfolgs*	He makes sure of his success

The use of the genitive here is restricted to more formal written language. In speech, prepositions
(or different verbs) would be used instead: e.g. *Sie **brauchen** einen Arzt, Er schämt sich **wegen**
seines Benehmens.*

> [22]   A few adjectives with 'of' take the genitive: *meines Fehlers* **bewusst** 'conscious of my mistake'.
>   Also: *gewiss* 'certain of', *müde* 'tired of', *schuldig* 'guilty of', *sicher* 'sure of'.

✎ EXERCISES

Vocabulary topic: *Emotionen*

1 Put the bracketed words into the correct case:

  1   Ich liebe [der Mann] [meine Schwester].
  2   Ich weiß, dass [der Junge] geweint hat.
  3   Sie hasst [der Chef].
  4   Schlecht gelaunt ist [mein Vater] nie!
  5   Er beneidet [der Freund] [das Nachbarmädchen].
  6   Fröhlich gab sie [die Kinder] [ein Kuss].
  7   Das ist [ein] von [die Nachbarn], nicht wahr? Er sieht sehr traurig aus.

    8 Ich habe [die Assistentin] erklärt, dass [der Chef] nicht sehr geduldig ist.

    9 Damit macht [der Junge] [sein Vater] sehr glücklich.

    10 Das Gesicht [der Lehrer] war rot vor Wut.

2 Put the underlined nouns into the plural and change the other words in the sentence as appropriate:

> *Example*: Leidenschaftlich gab sie dem <u>Mann</u> einen Kuss.
>
> *Answer*: Leidenschaftlich gab sie **den Männern** einen Kuss.

    1 Er hat Angst vor dem <u>Lehrer</u>.

    2 Sie schrie den <u>Hund</u> wütend an.

    3 Ich sagte der <u>Mutter</u>, dass das <u>Kind</u> böse war.

    4 Verärgert erklärte ich dem <u>Arbeiter</u> die Ursache des <u>Problems</u>.

    5 Warum muss die <u>Frau</u> immer über ihre Gefühle reden?

    6 Er macht seinem <u>Freund</u> Sorgen.

✎ FURTHER EXERCISES

3 Make sentences from the following words without changing the word order of the subjects and objects. Put the articles, adjectives, pronouns and nouns into the correct case and conjugate the verbs:

    1 ich / sagen / die / Kollegen / dass / ich / krank / sein (*past*)

    2 ich / fragen (*past*) / der / nett / Arzt / ob / er / ich / etwas / geben / können (*conditional*)

    3 der / schüchtern / Schüler / wollen antworten / der / streng / Lehrer / nicht (*past*)

    4 er / schenken / sein / Vater / ein / rot / Pullover / zu / Weihnachten (*perfect*)

    5 ich / versuchen zu helfen / meine / neu / Nachbarin (*perfect*)

    6 es / freuen / meine / Frau / sehr / wenn / Sie / sie / besuchen (*conditional*)

    7 mmm! / kaufen (*perfect*) du / frisch / Plätzchen? / ja / aber / ich / haben (*present*) / nur / ein / übrig

    8 er / folgen / eine / die / hübsch / Studentinnen / nach / Hause (*past*)

    9 schmecken / die / Kinder / der / neu / Saft? (*present*)

    10 du / müssen gehorchen / die / Eltern! (*present*)

    11 wir / suchen / ein / von / die / Gäste / er / heißen / Benno Andlinger (*present*)

    12 er / gratulieren / sein / alt / Onkel / zum / Geburtstag (*past*)

    13 ich / begegnen / eine / gut / Freundin / in / die / Stadt (*perfect*)

    14 wir / machen / ein / Ausflug / nach / Wien / es / gefallen / die / Schüler / dort / sehr (*perfect*).

    15 wer / erzählen / das / Kind / dieser / blöd / Witz? (*perfect*)

4 Make genitive constructions out of the following (more colloquial) sentences with *von*. Note that particularly 3, 6 and 7 sound much better in the genitive than with *von*:

    1 Das ist das Auto von einem Freund.

    2 Das ist die Frau von Peter.

    3 Es war die Idee von der Chefin.

4 Hast du die Bücher von Anna gesehen?

5 Was ist die Hauptstadt von Brasilien?

6 Ich bin mit dem Fortschritt von den Kindern sehr zufrieden.

7 Der Film handelt von der Untergang von der „Titanic".

5 Some of the following nouns are 'weak'. Add an ending only where appropriate:

1 Gestern war ich beim Nachbar_.

2 Wir zeigten dem Kunde_ unsere Ware.

3 Er gab dem Taxifahrer_ Trinkgeld.

4 Kennen Sie Herr_ Becker? Meinen Sie den Journalist_?

5 Das Kind zeichnete einen Löwe_, einen Tiger_, einen Elephant_, einen Bär_ und einen Hund.

6 Er sprach mit dem Kommissar_ und seinem Kollege_.

7 Das ist die Wohnung des Student_.

8 Wo ist das Büro des Professor_?

6 Complete the following text by using the correct gender, number and case forms of the articles/pronouns in bold print. The nouns in bold might also need changing. If you don't know the gender of a particular noun, look it up in the dictionary. For case after prepositions see **Ch. 24**.

Wer studiert, zieht aus – normalerweise. Nicht so, wenn die Uni in der Nähe **d__ Elternhaus** steht: Dann bleiben viele Studenten bei den Eltern wohnen, verlieren Zeit im Zug und verpassen oft gute Partys. So wie **d__** 23-jährige Florian Ludwig, er studiert Englisch und Geschichte auf Lehramt in Heidelberg und pendelt seit fünf Semestern mit Bus und Bahn vom Elternhaus in Karlsruhe zur 65 Kilometer entfernten Uni. Er spart so viel Geld, das ist ihm wichtig.[...]

Ein Viertel **d__** deutschen Studenten wohnen noch zu Hause, sagt Stefan Grob, Sprecher **d__** Deutschen **Studentenwerk** in Berlin. In Italien, **ein__** Land ohne Wohngeld und Bafög, leben über 70 Prozent noch bei den Eltern. In Nordeuropa hingegen kaum **ein__**; hier werden alle Studenten finanziell vom Staat unterstützt.

In Deutschland denken viele Studenten ähnlich wie Florian Ludwig: Geld ist **ein__** wichtiges Argument für **d__** Hotel Mama. "Viele Studenten sparen sich so **d__** Nebenjob, da die Kosten für Miete und Lebenshaltung wegfallen", sagt Grob.[...].

Durch den Schritt aus dem Elternhaus würden **d__** Studenten auch deutlich selbstständiger, sagt Studienberater Reiner Mund von der Technischen Universität Ilmenau in Thüringen. Geld sollte keine Rolle spielen: "Es gibt ja Bafög und Wohngeld." Wer weiterhin zu Hause wohne, verpasse oft **d__** Anschluss an die Kommilitonen und **d__** wahre Studentenleben. [...]. Spätestens nach der Hälfte **d__ Studium** sollte man aber **d__** Umzug wagen. "Dann hat man **d__** Aussiebe-Prüfungen hinter sich und weiß: Dabei bleibe ich"[...]. **D__** Umzug sei für **d__** gesamten Lebensweg wichtig, betont Studienberater Mund. "Unternehmen suchen heute hochflexible Leute, die auch mal **d__** Wohnort wechseln. Nesthocker haben es da schwer."

Aus: *Nesthocker: Warum Studenten aus dem Hotel Mama ausziehen sollten*, Spiegel Online, 20. Mai 2012. ©dapd.

For further exercises on case after prepositions see Ch. 24, Ex. 1 and Revision Text 2, Ex. 1. For general exercises on case see Revision Text 1, Ex. 2 and Revision Text 4, Ex. 1.

4 | Use of articles

Text

Vom Kneipier zum Bankier – Karriere trotz Lücken im Lebenslauf

Nicht immer verlaufen Biografien so glatt, dass sich daraus **der** perfekte
Lebenslauf basteln lässt: Orientierungslosigkeit nach **dem** Abi, **das**
abgebrochene Studium, **ein** halbes Jahr Nichtstun oder **der** schnell
5 gekündigte Job gehören bei vielen dazu. Doch **der** zukünftige Chef wird
nicht immer Lust haben, sich **die** Begründung dafür anzuhören.

   Der gelernte Bankkaufmann André **zum** Beispiel hat sich nach einigen
Jahren Bank **einen** Jugendtraum verwirklicht und seine eigene Kneipe
aufgemacht. Mit 37 macht er sich jetzt Gedanken über **eine** Rückkehr **zur**
10 Bank. Da wird **das** Schreiben **des** Lebenslaufs zu **einem** harten Stück
Arbeit: „Mir fehlen **im** Prinzip zehn Jahre, wo ich in **der** Gastronomie arbeite.
Was schreibe ich da? Selbständiger Kaufmann? Gastronomieberatung?
Oder irgendetwas, wo man kein Zeugnis **vom** Arbeitgeber vorweisen kann?"

   Von solchen kleinen Lügen hält Susanne Culo wenig. Sie ist Bewerber-
15 Trainerin bei **der** Kienbaum Personalberatung. Natürlich habe Andrés
Kneipenarbeit nicht viel mit **dem** Bankwesen zu tun, aber: „Er muss
begründen können, warum er es gemacht hat, muss vielleicht auch belegen,
dass er nebenher sein Interesse an **der** Bank oder **am** Finanzdienstleistungsbereich nie verloren hat. **Im** Bereich **der** Soft-Skills ist
20 **die** Dienstleistungsorientierung das, worauf man vielleicht herumreiten
sollte." Es gilt also erfinderisch zu sein, um darzulegen, inwieweit **die**
bisherigen Erfahrungen für **das** künftige Unternehmen nützlich sein könnten.
Das ist allemal besser als **der** Versuchung nachzugeben, **ein** wenig zu
tricksen, **die** Schulzeit einfach ein Jahr zu verlängern oder **einen** Job
25 anzugeben, den man nie hatte. Denn wenn **ein** solcher Schwindel auffliegt,
droht **der** Verlust **der** Arbeitsstelle.

Aus: Deutschlandfunk: *Campus & Karriere* [www.dradio.de], 26. April 2001.

der Kneipier – pub landlord	*der Bewerber* – applicant (for a job)
die Lücke – gap	*die Finanzdienstleistung* – financial services
der Lebenslauf – c.v.	*der Bereich* – sector
glatt – smoothly	*die Dienstleistung* – service
basteln – to make, work on	*die Orientierung* – direction, information
das Abitur, Abi – A-Levels	*herumreiten* – to harp on about, emphasize
kündigen – to give up your job	*erfinderisch* – inventive, imaginative
die Begründung – justification	*darlegen* – explain
die Rückkehr – return	*das Unternehmen* – company, business
selbständig – independent	*die Versuchung* – temptation
beraten – to advise	*auffliegen* – to get out, be exposed
das Zeugnis – certificate	*der Verlust* (+ gen.) – loss of

⚲ Use of articles in the text

4.1 SIMILAR USAGE IN GERMAN AND ENGLISH

By and large, definite and indefinite articles are used in much the same way in German as they are in English. Some examples from the text are:

- *dass sich daraus **der** perfekte Lebenslauf basteln lässt* (2–3) — that **the** perfect CV can be made out of it
- *sein Interesse an **der** Bank* (18) — his interest in **the** bank
- *besser als **der** Versuchung nachzugeben* (23) — better than giving in to **the** temptation
- ***einen** Job anzugeben, den man nie hatte* (24) — to put down **a** job that you never had
- *wenn **ein** solcher Schwindel auffliegt* (25) — if such **a** trick gets out …

There are, however, a few differences, some of which depend on the context and cannot be captured in terms of a hard-and-fast rule, others of which can be expressed in terms of tendencies, the most noticeable being: i) the **definite** article is used much more in German than in English; ii) the **indefinite** article is absent in certain constructions in German. These tendencies will be outlined in **4.2** and **4.3** below.

4.2 DEFINITE ARTICLE IN GERMAN VERSUS NO ARTICLE IN ENGLISH

4.2a With infinitival nouns
- *Da wird **das** <u>Schreiben</u> des Lebenslaufs zu einem harten Stück Arbeit* (10–11) — Writing the CV becomes hard work

4.2b With nouns denoting arts, science or vocational subjects[23]

[23] Yet this tends not to be the case with traditional school and university subjects: e.g. *Mathe, Physik, Geschichte* etc. or after the verbs *studieren, lernen* etc., e.g. *Er studiert Gastronomie.*

- *wo ich in **der** Gastronomie arbeite* (11) where I work in gastronomy
- *nicht viel mit **dem** Bankwesen zu tun* (16) not much to do with banking
- *im Bereich **der** Soft-Skills* (19) in the area of soft skills

4.2c After nouns following prepositions, where the article is in its contracted form

It is common to use a definite article after a preposition if the article can appear in its contracted form: e.g. *im, ins, am, vom, zum, zur* (see **24.1d**). This is particularly frequent in spoken German and in **less formal styles** of the written language. For instance, *vom Kneipier zum Bankier* (1) is a less formal alternative to *von Kneipier zu Bankier* 'from publican to banker'.

4.2d Instead of the possessive

German often uses a definite article when English would prefer a possessive: e.g. *Er hat eine Tätowierung auf **dem** Rücken* 'He has a tattoo on **his** back'. This is particularly the case with parts of the body and clothes, but can also be seen elsewhere. In our text there are a few occasions where a definite article may more naturally correspond to a possessive in English:

- *wo man kein Zeugnis vom Arbeitgeber vorweisen kann* (13) where you cannot produce references from **your** employer
- *inwieweit **die** bisherigen Erfahrungen … nützlich sein könnten* (21–22) to what extent **your** previous experience could be useful …
- ***die** Schulzeit … zu verlängern* (24) to extend **your** time in education

4.2e In some common set phrases with a preposition (cf. 4.2c above)

- *zum Beispiel* (7)[24] for example
- *im Prinzip* (11) in principle

[24] This is not an absolute rule, however: e.g. *zu Fuß* 'on foot'.

4.3 NO INDEFINITE ARTICLE IN GERMAN

i) One major difference between English and German with respect to the use of the indefinite article occurs with the names of **professions, religions** and **nationalities** where the indefinite article is present in English but not in German after the verbs *sein, werden, bleiben*: e.g. 'He's **an** Englishman' versus *Er ist Engländer*. There is an example of this in the text which refers to a profession: *Sie ist Bewerber-Trainerin* 'She is a job application trainer' (14–15). If, however, an **adjective** is used before the noun in question, the indefinite article is used: e.g. *Sie ist **eine** gute Bewerber-Trainerin*.[25]

ii) German usually has no indefinite article after *als* when it means 'as': e.g. *Als Kind war er immer krank* 'He was always ill as a child'.

[25] Line 1 of the text also contains an example of an omitted indefinite article: i.e. before *Karriere*, although this is probably due to the fact that it is a headline and German, like English, regularly drops articles in headlines, titles, advertisements etc.

Other points to note in the text

- Past participles used as adjectives: *abgebrochene* (4), *gekündigte* (5), *gelernte* (7).
- Use of the impersonal *man* meaning 'one' in lines 13, 20 and 25 (see **7.1b**).
- Reflexive pronoun (in the dative) used together with an accusative object: **sich** *die Begründung dafür anzuhören* (6), **sich** ... *einen Jugendtraum verwirklicht* (7–8), *macht er* **sich** *jetzt Gedanken* (9) (see **20.4**).
- Construction with *sich lassen* + infinitive (2–3) corresponding to a passive in English: '... that the perfect CV can be made of it' (see **18.6**).
- Infinitival nouns: *Nichtstun* (4), *das Schreiben* (10) (see **27.1e**).
- Nouns in *-er* denoting occupations: *Arbeitgeber* (13), *Bewerber* (14), *Trainerin* (15), with an additional suffix *-in* denoting female; but note *Kneipier* (1) and *Bankier* (1) which, unusually, end in *-ier* (see **27.1a**).
- Noun compounds: *Lebenslauf* (3, 10), *Bankkaufmann* (7), *Jugendtraum* (8), *Gastronomieberatung* (12), *Arbeitgeber* (13), *Bewerber-Trainerin* (15), *Personalberatung* (15), *Kneipenarbeit* (16), *Bankwesen* (16), *Finanzdienstleistungsbereich* (19), *Dienstleistungsorientierung* (20), *Schulzeit* (24), *Arbeitsstelle* (26) (see **27.4**).

Discover more about the use of articles

4.4 PREFERENCE FOR DEFINITE ARTICLE IN GERMAN

As mentioned in **4.1–4.2** above, the definite article is used in many more contexts in German than it is in English. The most common of these are outlined below:

4.4a Days, months, seasons

Er kommt am Montag/im April[26]	He's coming on Monday/in April
*Mir gefällt **der** Herbst besser als **der** Sommer*	I like autumn better than summer

[26] Yet the article is not needed if no preposition is used: e.g. *Januar ist der erste Monat des Jahres.*

4.4b Meals

*Habe ich **das** Frühstück verpasst?*	Have I missed breakfast?
Was gibt es zum Abendessen?	What's for dinner?

4.4c Lakes, mountains and planets

*Sie bestiegen **den** Mount Everest*	They climbed Mount Everest
***Der** Luganer See ist sehr schön*	Lake Lugano is very beautiful

4.4d Street names

*Er wohnt in **der** Steinfurterstrasse*	He lives in Steinfurt street
*Ich warte auf **dem** Berliner Platz*	I'll wait on Berlin Square

4.4e Feminine and plural names of countries and regions[27]

*Er kommt aus **der** Türkei*	He comes from Turkey
*Wir fahren in **die** Schweiz*	We're going to Switzerland

By contrast, the more common neuter countries, e.g. *Deutschland, England, Frankreich, Spanien* etc. do not have an article, unless they are preceded by an **adjective**: e.g. *das vereinigte Deutschland* 'unified Germany'.

²⁷ Plural examples are *Die Niederlande* 'The Netherlands', *Die USA* 'the USA' (= *die Staaten*). With the small number of masculine countries the definite article is optional: e.g. *Er wohnt im* (or *in*) *Iran.*

4.4f Institutions and buildings

Er geht in die Schule/Kirche/Uni — He goes to school/church/university/
ins Gefängnis/in den Kindergarten — prison/nursery

4.4g Names of languages

The article is used particularly when referring to translating from one into another, or where a genitive is needed. Here, the noun declines like an adjective.

eine Übersetzung aus dem Deutschen — a translation from German to French
ins Französische
die Wichtigkeit des Englischen — the importance of English

In most other contexts, the article is not used and the noun has no ending: e.g. *Er spricht/lernt Deutsch; Er sagte es auf Deutsch.*

4.4h Some abstract nouns

The use of the definite article before abstract nouns is extremely variable and context-dependent. It tends to be preferred before nouns that are frequently used and very familiar to the speaker (unless the sentence is a generalisation or saying/idiom). It also tends to be preferred after a preposition (but, again, this is not always the case):

Das Alter spielt keine Rolle — Age doesn't matter
Sie würde alles für die Schönheit machen — She would do anything for beauty

Abstract nouns that commonly appear with the definite article are infinitival nouns (see **4.2a**) and, yet to a lesser extent, nouns denoting arts, science or vocational subjects (see **4.2b**).

4.4i Nouns in the genitive or dative when the case is to be made explicit

This is particularly common in the **genitive**, especially the genitive of feminine and plural nouns, where the definite article is the only way of expressing that case:

die Bedürfnisse der Kinder — the needs of children
die Probleme der Gesellschaft — the problems of society

4.4j In colloquial German, before people's names

Hast du den Peter gesehen? — Have you seen Peter?
Der Schumacher hat gewonnen — Schumacher has won

In standard German, proper names are only preceded by articles when they are qualified by an adjective: e.g. *Kennst du Peter?* vs. *Kennst du den jungen Peter?*

4.4k   In some common phrases with prepositions

*Er geht in **die** Stadt/wohnt in **der** Stadt*   He goes to town/lives in town
*Er lag **im** Bett/fiel aus **dem** Bett*   He lay in bed/fell out of bed
*Es hat sich mit **der** Zeit verbessert*   It's improved with time
Was möchtest du zum Geburtstag?   What would you like for your birthday?

4.5   NO DEFINITE ARTICLE IN GERMAN

In German there is no definite article with the names of **musical instruments** after the verbs *spielen, lernen* etc.: e.g. *Er spielt Klavier* vs. 'He plays **the** piano'. This is also the case with many other leisure activities when the noun is the direct object: e.g. *Sie liest Zeitung* 'She reads **the** newspaper', *Ich höre gern Radio* 'I like listening to **the** radio'.

✎ EXERCISES

Vocabulary topic: *Finanzwesen*

1 Translate the capitalised articles into German (or omit the article entirely, if appropriate):

 1 Ihr Bruder ist A Bankangestellter und hat 5.000 Euro auf ihr Sparkonto überwiesen.
 2 Mein Freund ist A erfolgreicher Steuerberater und kann dir mit THE Steuererklärung helfen.
 3 Der Kunde ist A Deutscher und will wissen, was THE Wechselkurs ist.
 4 Wann haben THE Polen THE Euro als Währung eingeführt?
 5 Ich suche A Hypothek mit niedrigen Zinsen.
 6 Ich bin A Kollege von Klaus. Wir arbeiten beide bei THE Europäischen Zentralbank.
 7 Als A Student kann man A Kredit aufnehmen, der THE Studiengebühren deckt.
 8 Ich will Geld abheben. Wo ist THE nächste Geldautomat?
 9 Du brauchst A Versicherungsberater.
 10 Ich möchte A Scheck einlösen. Das sind meine Spesen von THE Arbeit.
 11 „Was macht dein Sohn beruflich?" „Er ist jetzt A Bankdirektor. Schon als A Kind hat er sein Sparschweinchen immer geliebt."
 12 Da ich A Europäer bin darf ich mit A Kreditkarte bezahlen. Studenten aus Übersee müssen bar bezahlen, aber sie müssen nicht THE ganzen Betrag auf einmal begleichen. Sie können A Anzahlung von 200 Euro machen.

✎ FURTHER EXERCISES

2 Fill in the gaps with the DEFINITE article only where appropriate. Where present, use the contracted forms of the articles after prepositions, e.g. *am, im, zum, zur*:

 1 Er isst immer ein gekochtes Ei zu __ Frühstück.
 2 In __ Sommer wird es in __ Griechenland bis zu __ vierzig Grad.
 3 Wir fahren in __ Herbst in __ USA.

4 Er wohnt in __ Nordrhein-Westfalen.

5 „Ich suche __ Gescherweg." „Fahren sie __ Hammerstraße entlang bis zu __ großen Kreisverkehr und nehmen Sie __ dritte Straße links".

6 Jedes Jahr verbringt er __ Urlaub an __ Bodensee.

7 Er hat Probleme mit __ Gesundheit.

8 Er liebt __ Leben. Für ihn ist __ Alter kein Hindernis.

9 __ Alter vor __ Schönheit!

10 Ich interessiere mich sehr für __ Musik und spiele __ Gitarre und __ Querflöte.

11 „Was hat dir in __ Schule am besten gefallen?" „__ Physik."

12 Ich studiere __ Betriebswirtschaft an __ Universität.

13 Wir werden es schon schaffen. Es ist nur eine Frage __ Zeit.

14 „Kommt er aus __ Polen?" „Nein, aus __ ehemaligen Jugoslawien".

15 „Kommst du an __ Montag?" „Nein, __ Montag ist schwierig. __ Dienstag wäre besser."

5 | Adjectives

Text

Ich hatte Angst vor meiner Frau!

*Dass Männer ihre Partnerin schlagen, ist **traurige** Wirklichkeit. Dass*
*es fast genauso häufig auch umgekehrt passiert, ein **großes** Tabu. Ein*
*Mann erzählt, wie er zum Opfer **häuslicher** Gewalt wurde.*

5 Ein Fahrradunfall, sagte Jochen Willberg, wenn Kollegen nach der Wunde
über seiner Augenbraue fragten. Was hätte er auch erzählen sollen: Ach, das
ist von der Handtasche, mit der meine Freundin gestern auf mich
eingeprügelt hat? Als er vom Arzt kam, küsste sie ihn, versprach, dass es nie
mehr so weit kommen würde. Er legte einen Eisbeutel auf den mit drei
10 Stichen **genähten** Riss und versuchte, ihr zu glauben. Wie jedes Mal.
Geredet hat der 38-Jährige mit niemandem. Es fällt ihm heute noch nicht
leicht, über seine Erlebnisse zu sprechen, obwohl er seit vier Jahren von
der Frau getrennt ist, die ihm das angetan hat.
    An sich ist der IT-Spezialist kein Opfertyp, weder charakterlich noch
15 optisch. Ein **ruhiger** Mann, **nüchterne** Art, **nettes** Lächeln, 1,80 Meter groß,
kein Muskelprotz, doch auch kein Schwächling. Er selbst aber hatte **lange**
Zeit jeden Respekt vor sich verloren. [...].
    Dass Männer von Frauen verprügelt werden, war für Jochen Willberg,
der seinen **richtigen** Namen nicht nennen möchte, kein Thema, bis seine
20 Freundin Nicole zum **ersten** Mal auf ihn eindrosch. Verständlich. Immerhin
geht es um ein Problem, das weder in der Politik noch bei der Polizei wirklich
zur Kenntnis genommen wird und auch in der Öffentlichkeit als Tabu gilt.
Denn wenn von **häuslicher** Gewalt die Rede ist, sind die Rollen klar verteilt:
Männer als Angreifer, Frauen als Leidtragende. Dabei zeigen
25 Untersuchungen, dass dieses Bild an der Realität vorbeigeht [...]. Laut einer
Studie der **evangelischen** Kirche sind Männer meist die Täter, wenn es um
grobe, **körperliche** Angriffe geht. Bei **leichten** Attacken, worunter auch
Ohrfeigen, Treten und das Werfen mit Gegenständen zählt, gibt es kaum
geschlechterspezifische Unterschiede. Und geht es um **psychische**
30 Nötigung oder Mobbing, sind Frauen in der Mehrheit. [...].

Aus: *Freundin*, September 2012 (S. 127–128).

häusliche Gewalt – domestic violence	*verteilt* – distributed
einprügeln – to lay into someone	*der Angreifer* – attacker
der Stich – stitch	*der Leidtragende* – sufferer
das Opfer – victim	*der Täter* – culprit
nüchtern – sober, sensible	*grob* – rough
der Muskelprotz – muscle man	*der Angriff* – attack
der Schwächling – weakling	*die Ohrfeige* – slap
verprügeln – to beat up	*treten* – to kick
eindreschen auf – to lay into	*die Nötigung* – coercion
zur Kenntnis nehmen – to take notice of	*der Mobbing* – bullying

⌕ Adjectives in the text

5.1 USE OF ADJECTIVE ENDINGS

In German, adjectives used **before** nouns require a special ending depending on the **gender** of the following noun (masculine, feminine or neuter), the **case** of the noun (nominative, accusative, genitive or dative), the **number** of the noun (singular or plural) and which type of element precedes the adjective (e.g. a definite or indefinite article, a pronoun with or without an ending): e.g. *der kleine Mann*, with an ending, versus *der Mann ist klein*, where the adjective is used predicatively (i.e. it follows the verb) and therefore has no ending. Consider the following examples taken from the text:

i) **Nominative.** Masculine is shown by *-er*, feminine and plurals by *-e*, neuter by *-es*. These are known as 'strong' endings.

Masc. Sg.:	*ein ruhiger Mann* (15)	a quiet man
Fem. Sg.:	*lange Zeit* (16–17)	long time
Neut. Sg.:	*ein großes Tabu* (3)	a big taboo
All plurals:	*grobe, körperliche Angriffe* (27)	rough physical attacks[28]

[28] This is accusative in the text, although the nominative would have the same form.

However, if these endings are contained in a preceding element which is not another adjective (e.g. articles *der, die, das*; pronouns *dieser, dieses, meine, seine* etc.), the default adjective ending *-e* is used for all singulars and *-en* for all plurals. These are known as 'weak' endings. Contrast the examples above with the following.

Masc. Sg.:	*der ruhige Mann*	the quiet man
Fem. Sg.:	*die lange Zeit*	the long time
Neut. Sg.:	*dieses große Tabu*	this big taboo
Plurals:	*seine groben körperlichen Angriffe*	his rough physical attacks

Thus, a general principle operates whereby gender, case and number are shown either by the adjective or by the element preceding it, but not by both (except for feminine singulars), e.g. *ein ruhiger Mann, der ruhige Mann*, but not **der ruhiger Mann*.

ii) Accusative. Masculine singulars are always shown by *-en*. Otherwise the accusative adjective endings are identical to the nominative ones.

| Masc. Sg.: | *seinen richtigen Namen* (19) | his correct name |
| | *auf den … genähten Riss* (9–10) | on the … stitched-up gash |

iii) Dative. Masculine and neuter are shown by *-em*, feminine by *-er*, plurals by *-en*:

| Fem. Sg.: | *von häuslicher Gewalt* (23) | from domestic violence |
| Plural: | *bei leichten Attacken* (27) | with minor attacks |

When preceded by an element containing these endings (e.g. *dem, einem, der, dieser*), the 'weak' ending *-en* is used. Thus, *von häuslicher Gewalt* would become e.g. *von der häuslichen Gewalt*. An example of a weak dative ending from the text is:

| Neut. Sg.: | *zum ersten Mal* (20) | for the first time |

iv) Genitive. Masculine and neuter are shown by *-en*, feminine and plurals by *-er*:

| Fem. Sg.: | *Opfer häuslicher Gewalt* (4) | victim of domestic violence |

When preceded by an element containing the genitive endings *-es* and *-er* (e.g. *des, eines, der, einer*), the 'weak' adjective ending is *-en*, as in the dative.

| Fem. Sg.: | *Studie der evangelischen Kirche* (26) | study of the Protestant church |

In practice, genitive and dative endings with *-en* occur much more frequently than those with the strong endings *-em* and *-er*.

Other points to note in the text

- Weak masculine noun: **Namen** (19) (see **3.3b**).
- Conditionals: *dass es nie mehr so weit kommen* **würde** 'that it would not go that far any more' (8–9) and conditional perfects: *Was* **hätte** *er auch erzählen* **sollen** 'What should he have said' (6), *nicht nennen* **möchte** 'would not like to name' (19) (see **Ch. 16**).
- Passives: *Dass Männer von Frauen* **verprügelt werden** 'that men are beaten by women' (18), *ein Problem, das … zur Kenntnis* **genommen wird** 'a problem that is being taken notice of' (21–22), and the *sein*-passive: **sind** *die Rollen klar* **verteilt** 'the roles are clearly distributed' (23) (see **Ch. 18**).
- Relative pronouns: *Handtasche,* **mit der** *meine Freundin … auf mich eingeprügelt hat* 'handbag with which my girlfriend .. beat me' (7–8); *von der Frau…,* **die** *ihm das angetan hat* 'of the woman who did that to him' (13), *Willberg,* **der** *seinen… Namen nicht nennen möchte* 'Willberg, who does not want to give his name' (18–19), *ein Problem,* **das** *…zur Kenntnis genommen wird* 'a problem that is being taken notice of' (21–22) (see **Ch. 9**).

Discover more about adjectives

5.2 **SUMMARY OF ADJECTIVE ENDINGS**

Below is a summary of adjective endings in German. It is advisable to learn these by heart together with an accompanying noun (and, where appropriate, article):[29]

> [29] A full set of article and adjective endings within the context of a whole sentence is given in **Appendix 2**.

Table 5.1 Strong endings (where gender, number and case are shown fully)

	Masc.	*Fem.*	*Neut.*	*Plural*
N	*kleinER Mann*	*kleinE Frau*	*kleinES Kind*	*kleinE Kinder*
A	*kleinEN Mann*	*kleinE Frau*	*kleinES Kind*	*kleinE Kinder*
D	*kleinEM Mann*	*kleinER Frau*	*kleinEM Kind*	*kleinEN Kindern*
G	*kleinEN Mannes*	*kleinER Frau*	*kleinEN Kindes*	*kleinER Kinder*

The strong endings in **Table 5.1** are used after elements **without an ending**, e.g. *ein, kein, mein, viel, wenig*; and when **no article or pronoun** precedes the adjective: e.g. *kleine Kinder, zwei kleine Kinder*.

Table 5.2 Weak endings (using a default *-e* or *-en*)

	Masc.	*Fem.*	*Neut.*	*Plural*
N	*der kleinE Mann*	*die kleinE Frau*	*das kleinE Kind*	*die kleinEN Kinder*
A	*den kleinEN Mann*	*die kleinE Frau*	*das kleinE Kind*	*die kleinEN Kinder*
D	*dem kleinEN Mann*	*der kleinEN Frau*	*dem kleinEN Kind*	*den kleinEN Kindern*
G	*des kleinEN Mannes*	*der kleinEN Frau*	*des kleinEN Kindes*	*der kleinEN Kinder*

The weak endings in **Table 5.2** are used after elements **with an ending**, e.g. *der, die, das, dies-er/-e/-es/-em/-er/-en, ein-er/-e/-es/-em/-er/-en, kein- er/-e/-es/-em/-er/-en, mein-er/-e/-es/-em/-er/-en, all-e/-er/-em/-en*.[30]

This means that when using the indefinite article *ein* (and similar forms like *kein* and the possessives *mein, dein, sein, ihr* etc.), both the strong and the weak endings are used depending on whether the article has an ending or not (see **Table 5.3**).

> [30] Despite having an ending, the plurals *einige* 'some', *mehrere* 'several', *viele* 'many', *wenige* 'few' and *andere* 'others' are exceptions to the above rules in that they have no influence on the following adjective: i.e. the adjective takes a strong ending as if the preceding word was not there, e.g. *viele kleine Kinder* 'a lot of small children', *das Geschrei vieler kleiner Kinder* 'the screaming of many small children'.

Table 5.3 Endings after all forms of *ein* (mixed strong and weak)

	Masc.	Fem.	Neut.
N	*ein kleinER Mann*	*eine kleinE Frau*	*ein kleinES Kind*
A	*einen kleinEN Mann*	*eine kleinE Frau*	*ein kleinES Kind*
D	*einem kleinEN Mann*	*einer kleinEN Frau*	*einem kleinEN Kind*
G	*eines kleinEN Mannes*	*einer kleinEN Frau*	*eines kleinEN Kindes*

A few examples of common exceptions to the above rules are:

- Adjectives ending in a vowel other than -*e* have no ending: e.g. *ein **lila** Rock, ein **sexy** Mann*.[31]
- Adjectives derived from names of towns and numerals always end in -*er*, irrespective of gender, number and case: e.g. *die **Berliner** Philharmonie, in den **sechziger** Jahren*.
- The first element of hyphenated adjectives has no ending: e.g. *die **österreichisch**-ungarische Monarchie* 'the Austro-Hungarian monarchy.'

[31] Adjectives ending in -*e* drop the -*e* before adding the endings, e.g. *böse: ein böser Mann*.

5.3 ADJECTIVAL PHRASES BEFORE NOUNS

In written German it is common to place whole phrases which end in an adjective *before* the noun, particularly in quality newspapers and literary texts, e.g. *der **vor ihm stehende** Mann* 'the man standing in front of him' (literally 'the standing in front of him man'), where the adjective is derived from the present participle *stehend* and, like all adjectives before nouns, takes the necessary ending. These phrases are known as **expanded attributes** (or 'extended attributes') and can sometimes be very long, particularly when used to create a particular effect in literary texts, e.g. *die **in dieser Landschaft und Natur und Architektur existierenden und sich von Jahr zu Jahr kopflos multiplizierenden** schwachsinnigen Bewohner* 'the idiotic inhabitants existing in this landscape and nature and architecture, and mindlessly multiplying from year to year' (Thomas Bernhard: *Die Ursache*).

In our text there is one example of this: *Er legte einen Eisbeutel auf den **mit drei Stichen genähten** Riss* 'He put an ice pack on the gash **which had been sewn up with three stitches**' (9–10), where the adjective is derived from the past participle *genäht*. Note that the final adjective(s) of the phrase(s) must take the usual ending: e.g. compare *auf den **großen** Riss* 'on the large gash'.

5.4 OMITTED NOUNS

Adjectives with endings are usually used before nouns but are also needed when the noun is omitted but understood, e.g. *Was für ein Auto hast du? Ein groß**es** oder ein klein**es**?* 'What sort of car do you have? A large one or a small one?' *Ist es ein neuer Film? Nein, ein alter.* 'Is it a new film? No, an old one.'

5.5 ADJECTIVAL NOUNS

It is common in German to use adjectives as nouns (adjectival nouns), particularly when referring to the appearance, characteristics or state of a person, e.g. *der Alte* 'the old man', similarly *der Deutsche, der Arbeitslose, der Unglückliche*, all of which begin with capital letters. Sometimes the adjectival nouns may be derived from present or past participles, *e.g. der Geliebte* ('the lover', literally 'the loved' from *geliebt*, past participle of *lieben*). In all these cases one must still use the appropriate adjective endings:

Der Deutsche kommt	*Ich mag den Deutschen nicht*
Ein Deutscher kommt	*Die Frau des Deutschen kommt*

When referring to unspecified *things* rather than people, *etwas* (or, in the negative, *nichts*) is used, followed by the neuter form of the adjective, e.g. *etwas Gutes* 'something good', *nichts Schwieriges* 'nothing difficult':

Ich habe etwas Gutes gefunden	*Er kam mit etwas Gutem nach Hause*

Similarly, expressions such as 'the nice thing', 'the bad thing' are rendered by *das* + the adjectival noun in *-e*: e.g. *Das Schlimme war, dass ich meinen Koffer verloren habe* 'The bad thing was that I lost my suitcase', *Das war für mich das Interessante daran* 'That was the interesting thing for me'.

There are two examples of adjectival nouns in our text, one of which is derived from a present participle in *-end*:

der 38-Jährige (11)	the 38-year-old
Frauen als Leidtragende (24)	women as sufferers

5.6 ADVERBS

German adverbs are usually identical to their related adjectives, e.g. *Er ist sehr langsam* (adjective 'slow'), *Er spricht sehr langsam* (adverb 'slowly'). From the text: *Dass es … häufig … passiert* (2–3) 'that it happens frequently'. The difference appears when used before nouns, as adverbs, unlike adjectives, do not have an ending: e.g. *eine schreckliche Familie* 'a terrible family' versus *eine schrecklich nette Familie* 'a terribly nice family'.

✎ EXERCISES

Vocabulary topic: *Europa: ihre Produkte und ihre Sprachen*

1 Fill in the gaps below with the appropriate adjective endings:

deutsch_ Bier	der englisch_ Tee	diese schwedisch_ Fleischklöße
holländisch_ Käse	ein schottisch_ Lachs	welcher österreichisch_ Wein?
spanisch_ Oliven	keine belgisch_ Pralinen	
das frisch_ französisch_ Brot	mein griechisch_ Schafskäse	

2 Fill in the gaps below with the appropriate adjective endings, paying particular attention to the CASE of the noun:

   1 Frankreich ist für seinen gut_ Wein sehr bekannt.

   2 Italien ist ein sehr schön_ Land und erwirtschaftet einen groß_ Teil seines heutig_ Bruttonationalprodukts durch Tourismus.

   3 Schweden freut sich über den europaweit_ Erfolg seines riesig_ Möbelgeschäfts.

   4 Deutschland produziert weltberühmt_ Autos von sehr hoh_ Qualität.[32]

   5 Er kam mit einem sehr schick_ italienisch_ Anzug nach Hause.

   6 Er gab ihr zwei klein_ Flaschen teuer_ französisch_ Parfums zum vierzigst_ Geburtstag.

[32] The adjective *hoch* changes to *hoh-* before adding an ending.

3 Put the capitalised adjectives into the correct form:

Deutsch lernen – warum?

Deutsch wird als Muttersprache in mehr EUROPÄISCH Ländern gesprochen als Englisch, Französisch, Spanisch oder Italienisch [...]. Deutsch ist insbesondere, nach Englisch, die WICHTIGST Sprache, um sich als JUNG Mensch auf den Gebieten Biologie, Chemie, Pharmazie, Elektrotechnik und Elektronik, Maschinenbau, Fahrzeugbau, Diplomatie, Finanzen, Sport, Tourismus und im Bildungswesen zu qualifizieren. Die DEUTSCH Sprache wird dabei auch für die Bezeichnung und Erklärung vieler NEU, TECHNISCH Entwicklungen verwendet. Nach einer Studie, die 1994 von der DEUTSCH-AMERIKANISCH Handelskammer durchgeführt wurde, gaben 65% der BEFRAGT Unternehmen an, dass die Zweisprachigkeit Englisch/Deutsch für sie ein WICHTIG Einstellungskriterium sei. [...].

   Die ENGLISCH Sprache wird ständig dominanter, nicht nur durch den WELTWEIT Einfluss der AMERIKANISCH Supermacht und die Geschichte des BRITISCH Commonwealth, sondern auch durch die Verbreitung des Internets. Dabei wird es aber für ENGLISCH Muttersprachler immer wichtiger, eine ANDER Sprache zu lernen, um die VERSCHIEDEN Ausprägungen und FEIN KULTURELL Unterschiede innerhalb der EIGEN Sprache zu verstehen. Zwar mag die Übersetzung ins Englische in vielen Zusammenhängen einen UNIVERSELL Kontaktpunkt schaffen, gleichzeitig verlieren sich aber auf diese Weise SPRACHLICH Bedeutungen und Untertöne.

   Deutsch ist die MEISTVERBREITET und MEISTGESPROCHEN Sprache Europas, und Deutschkenntnisse können daher ihre Reise durch Europa wesentlich erleichtern. In den Touristenzentren von Italien, Frankreich, Spanien, Portugal, der Türkei und Griechenland können sie sich oft besser auf Deutsch verständigen als auf Englisch. Ein Grund hierfür ist, dass viele Südeuropäer in den SECHZIG und SIEBZIG Jahren als Gastarbeiter nach Deutschland, Österreich und in die Schweiz kamen. Ein weiterer Grund liegt darin, dass Reisen ans Mittelmeer in Deutschland eine LANG Tradition haben, so dass die LOKAL Tourismusindustrie sich an die DEUTSCHSPRACHIG Gäste angepasst hat. Wenn Sie also bemerken sollten, dass Englisch an ihrem Urlaubsort nicht verstanden wird, versuchen Sie es auf Deutsch [...]. Lernen sie Deutsch, um ihre Reise durch Mitteleuropa zu einem INTENSIV und PERSÖNLICH Erlebnis zu machen!

Aus: www.wirtschaftsdeutsch.com/warum-deutsch-lernen.htm 13. Februar 2012.

✎ FURTHER EXERCISES

4 Complete the following text by filling in the gaps using the appropriate adjective ending where needed. (Note: if it is an adverb it does not need an ending):

Als Gregor Samsa eines Morgens aus unruhig_ Träumen erwachte, fand er sich in seinem Bett zu einem ungeheuer_ Ungeziefer verwandelt. Er lag auf seinem panzerartig_ hart_ Rücken und sah, wenn er den Kopf ein wenig hob, seinen gewölbt_, braun_, von bogenförmig_ Versteifungen geteilt_ Bauch, auf dessen Höhe sich die Bettdecke, zum gänzlich_ Niedergleiten bereit, kaum noch erhalten konnte. Seine viel_, im Vergleich zu seinem sonstig_ Umfang kläglich_ dünn_ Beine flimmerten ihm hilflos vor den Augen.

»Was ist mit mir geschehen?«, dachte er. Es war kein Traum. Sein Zimmer, ein richtig_, nur etwas zu klein_ Menschenzimmer, lag ruhig zwischen den vier wohlbekannt_ Wänden. Über dem Tisch, auf dem eine auseinandergepackt_ Musterkollektion von Tuchwaren ausgebreitet war – Samsa war Reisender – hing das Bild, das er vor kurzem aus einer illustriert_ Zeitschrift ausgeschnitten und in einem hübsch_, vergoldet_ Rahmen untergebracht hatte. Es stellte eine Dame dar, die mit einem Pelzhut und einer Pelzboa versehen, aufrecht dasaß und einen schwer_ Pelzmuff, in dem ihr ganz_ Unterarm verschwunden war, dem Beschauer entgegenhob. Gregors Blick richtete sich dann zum Fenster, und das trüb_ Wetter – man hörte Regentropfen auf das Fensterblech aufschlagen – machte ihn melancholisch.

Aus: Franz Kafka, *Die Verwandlung.* Aufl. 1984. Fischer Taschenbuch Verlag.

5 Put the underlined nouns into the plural and change the other words accordingly, paying particular attention to the adjective endings. Replace *ein-* with *zwei*:

1 Mein schönes altes <u>Haus</u> hat *ein* besonders großes <u>Schlafzimmer</u>.
2 Das schwarze <u>Hemd</u> mit dem weißen <u>Streifen</u> hing im Kleiderschrank.
3 Guter <u>Wein</u> ist selten billig. Nimm diesen *einen* französischen, zum Beispiel.
4 Diese frischgepflückte <u>Blume</u> ist für meine neue <u>Freundin</u>.
5 Sie ist trotz des verspäteten <u>Zuges</u> relativ früh nach Hause gekommen.

6 a Find the four expanded attributes in the text in question 4 above.

6 b Make expanded attributes out of the phrases following the comma, paying particular attention to the ending that they will take:

EXAMPLE: Der Mann, der von der Hitze rot geworden ist.
ANSWER: Der von der Hitze rot geworden**e** Mann.

1 Seine Mutter, die vor zwei Tagen achtzig geworden ist.
2 Ein Schriftsteller, der von mehreren Akademikern viel gelobt wird.
3 Ein Gesetz, das von den Deutschen eingeführt wurde.
4 Sie bieten vier Arbeitsplätze an, die von der Gemeinde finanziert werden.
5 Sie haben keinen Kandidaten gefunden, der für die Stelle geeignet ist.

7 Replace the underlined words with the appropriate adjectival noun (inserting **etwas** where necessary):

EXAMPLE: **a)** Der <u>Mann</u> lag im Bett [krank].   **b)** Ich habe <u>ein Kleid</u> gekauft [neu].

ANSWER: Der **Kranke** lag im Bett.   Ich habe **etwas Neues** gekauft.

1 Hier kommt die <u>Frau</u>. [unfreundlich]

2 Sie spielte mit dem <u>Kind</u>. [klein]

3 Der Chef feuerte den <u>Mann</u>. [angestellt]

4 Sie war die Freundin des <u>Mannes</u>. [gestorben]

5 Wir müssen für die <u>Menschen</u> mehr spenden. [arm]

6 Ich habe <u>ein Buch</u> gelesen. [interessant]

7 Ich muss dir leider <u>eine Sache</u> mitteilen. [traurig]

8 Translate the following sentences into German, paying particular attention to the adjectives and adverbs:

1 He has an unusually large nose.

2 What an incredibly dirty room!

3 She has a tastefully decorated flat.

4 It was an unpleasantly hot day.

For further exercises on adjective endings see Revision Text 1, Ex. 3 and for general exercises on article and adjective endings see Revision Texts 2 (Ex. 2), 3 (Ex. 1) and 4 (Ex. 3).

6 | Comparatives and superlatives

Text

> *KK*: Ich habe mich mal gefragt, ob die Freundin eigentlich immer **kleiner** als der Freund sein muss, und ob (wenn es so sein sollte) es irgendwelche Probleme dabei gibt.
>
> *Leco*: Also wenn die Freundin gleich groß oder 1–2cm **größer** ist, geht das
> 5 noch, aber was ich manchmal auf der Straße sehe – da muss ich mir das Lachen verkneifen. Will jetzt nicht intolerant sein, aber es sieht einfach doof aus, wenn da so ein Zwerg neben einer großen Frau läuft, Arm in Arm [...].
>
> *Minochisena*: Was ist das bitte für eine Frage? Wenn sich zwei Menschen gefunden haben und sie sich lieben, was spielt es für eine Rolle, wer
> 10 **größer** und wer **kleiner** ist? Habt ihr sonst nichts zu tun?
>
> *Enteca:* Meiner Meinung nach muss es nicht sein, aber irgendwie sieht es doch **cooler** aus. Dann hat das Mädel jemanden, der rein optisch so aussieht, als wäre er **stärker** als sie, und ich denke, Frauen schauen auch darauf, ob ein Mann in der Lage ist, sie zu beschützen. Hab damit mit
> 15 1,86m nicht so sehr die Probleme. Gibt wenige Menschen, die **größer** sind als ich.
>
> *ManiacKiller*: Finde ich schon. Meine Freundin ist auch **kleiner** als ich. Bin zwar nicht der **größte** Bursche mit 1,94m, aber trotzdem ...
>
> *Salamanduar*: Also um ehrlich zu sein bei mir schon. Das hat rein gar nichts
> 20 mit Dominanz oder so zu tun, ich steh halt nun mal auf **kleinere**, **zierlichere** Frauen [...].
>
> *Spann3r*: Es gibt kein Gesetz, was vorschreibt, wer **größer**, wer **älter** oder wer **schlauer** sein muss. Ich finde, das ist jedem selbst überlassen! Wenn man sich liebt, spielt sowas keine Rolle.

Aus: Raidrush Forum [board.raidrush.ws/], 8/11/08.

verkneifen – to repress	*zwar* – it's true that
doof – stupid	*aber trotzdem* – but still
der Zwerg- dwarf	*stehen auf etwas* – to like, fancy sth.
eine Rolle spielen – to play a role, to matter	*zierlich* – petite, dainty
das Mädel – girl	*vorschreiben* – to prescribe, stipulate
in der Lage sein – to be in a position to	*schlau* – clever, smart
beschützen – to protect	*überlassen* (+ dat.) – to be up to (s.o.)

Comparatives and superlatives in the text

6.1 COMPARATIVES

The comparative form of the adjective/adverb is used when comparing two or more things: e.g. *Er ist **kleiner** als ich* 'He's **smaller** than me'. German comparatives are formed by adding *-er* (or *-r* after words ending in *-e*) to the adjective/adverb and, with certain words, umlauting the preceding stressed vowel. Examples from the text are:

klein-er 'smaller' (1, 10, 17, 20), *cool-er* 'cooler' (12), *zierlich-er* 'more dainty' (20), *schlau-er* 'smarter' (23).
With umlautable vowels: *groß – größ-er* 'big – bigger' (4, 10, 15, 22), *stark – stärk-er* 'strong – stronger' (13), *alt – ält-er* 'old – older' (22) (see **6.3**).

Note that comparatives take the same endings as ordinary adjectives when they appear in the noun phrase: e.g. *kleiner-e, zierlicher-e Frauen* 'smaller, daintier women' (20).

6.2 SUPERLATIVES

The superlative is used to express the most extreme degree of the adjective: e.g. *der **kleinste** Hund* 'the **smallest** dog', and is formed by adding *-st* (or *-est* after *-d, -t, -s, -ß, -sch, -z* and, optionally, after long vowels/diphthongs) to the adjective. Adjectives which umlaut their vowels in the comparative also do in the superlative form.

There is one example of a superlative in our text: *der **größte** Bursche* 'the biggest (here meaning "tallest") bloke/lad' (18). Because it appears in the noun phrase, here following a definite article, it has an adjective ending (*-e*). It is usual for superlatives to follow definite articles, so they commonly have an adjective ending. (For superlatives as adverbs see **6.4**.)

Other points to note in the text

- The placing of elements after the verbal bracket, as an afterthought or for emphasis in the spoken language: *Wenn da so ein Zwerg neben einer großen Frau läuft, **Arm in Arm*** 'when such a dwarf is walking next to a tall woman, arm in arm' (7) (see **26.5**).
- Omission of *dass*, which allows main clause word order: *Ich denke Frauen schauen auch darauf*, instead of *Ich denke, dass Frauen auch darauf schauen* 'I think women are also looking' (13–14), *Ich finde, das ist jedem selbst überlassen* instead of *Ich finde, dass das jedem selbst überlassen ist* 'I think that's up to the individuals themselves' (23).
- Dropping of first person *-e* in the present tense in colloquial speech: *Hab* (14), *ich steh* (20) (see footnote in **10.2a**).
- Dropping of pronouns, also a feature of colloquial speech: *Will* instead of *ich will* (6), *Hab* instead of *ich habe* (14), *Gibt* instead of *Es gibt* (15), *Bin* instead of *ich bin* (17), *Finde ich* instead of *Das finde ich* (17).
- Use of *was* as a relative pronoun in colloquial speech instead of the standard *das*: *Es gibt kein Gesetz, **was** vorschreibt* 'there's no law **that** stipulates' (22) (see **Ch. 9**).

Discover more about comparatives and superlatives

6.3 UMLAUT

Not all adjectives/adverbs with umlautable vowels have umlaut in the comparative and superlative: e.g. *groß – größer – größt* versus *froh* 'happy' *– froher – frohest*, but it is always the case that, if umlaut is present, it appears in **both** the comparative **and** the superlative. Here are some common examples that do have umlaut, many of which have the vowel *a*:

alt – älter – ältest	'old'	*schwach – schwächer – schwächst*	'weak'
arg – ärger – ärgst	'bad'	*stark – stärker – stärkst*	'strong'
arm – ärmer – ärmst	'poor'	*warm – wärmer – wärmst*	'warm'
hart – härter – härtest	'hard'	*dumm – dümmer – dümmst*	'dumb'
kalt – kälter – kältest	'cold'	*jung – jünger – jüngst*	'young'
krank – kränker – kränkst	'ill'	*klug – klüger – klügst*	'clever'
lang – länger – längst	'long'	*kurz – kürzer – kürzest*	'short'
scharf – schärfer – schärfst	'sharp'	*grob – gröber – gröbst*	'rough'

Some adjectives have alternative forms with and without umlaut:

bang –	*banger – bangst*	'afraid'	*schmal –*	*schmaler – schmalst*	'narrow'
	bänger – bängst			*schmäler – schmälst*	
blass –	*blasser – blassest*	'pale'	*krumm –*	*krummer – krummst*	'bent'
	blässer – blässest			*krümmer – krümmst*	
glatt –	*glatter – glattest*	'smooth'	*fromm –*	*frommer – frommst*	'pious'
	glätter – glättest			*frömmer – frömmst*	
nass –	*nasser – nassest*	'wet'	*gesund –*	*gesunder – gesundest*	'healthy'
	nässer – nässest			*gesünder – gesündest*	

6.4 SUPERLATIVES WITH *AM ... -STEN*

When a superlative is used after a verb, i.e. as a predicative adjective (see (i)) or, more often, as an **adverb** (see (ii)), a special ending *-en* is added and the superlative is preceded by *am*. This is compulsory with adverbs (i.e. those superlatives occurring with verbs other than *sein* and *werden*):

i) *Der Fahrer ist schnell* → *Der Fahrer ist **der schnellste** or ... ist **am schnellsten**.*[33]
   'The driver is fast' → 'The driver is **the fastest** or ... is **fastest**'

ii) *Er __fährt__ schnell* → *Er __fährt__ **am schnellsten*** [NOT **Er fährt der schnellste*].
   'He drives fast' → He drives **the fastest**'

---

[33] The *am ... -sten* alternative is not possible if a qualifying statement follows: e.g. *Er ist **der** schnellste __der Rennfahrer__* 'He's the fastest of the racing drivers' NOT **Er ist am schnellsten der Rennfahrer.*

6.5 IRREGULAR FORMS

Some adjectives and adverbs (which, incidentally, are very frequently used in the comparative and superlative) are irregular. Consider the following examples:

groß	'big'	*größer*	*größt*	[after verb: *am größten*]
gut	'good'	*besser*	*best*	[after verb: *am besten*]
hoch	'high'	*höher*	*höchst*	[after verb: *am höchsten*]
nah	'near'	*näher*	*nächst*	[after verb: *am nächsten*]
viel	'many'	*mehr*	*meist*	[after verb: *am meisten*]
gern	'gladly'	*lieber*	*am liebsten*	[adverb only]

Note that *mehr* 'more' (and *weniger* 'fewer', the comparative of *wenig* 'few') never take adjective endings: e.g. *Hier gibt es mehr/weniger Leute.*

6.6 COMMON CONSTRUCTIONS WITH COMPARATIVES AND SUPERLATIVES

i) '-er **than**' (e.g. 'bigger than you'). 'Than' is translated as *als* in German and is usually followed by a noun/pronoun in the **nominative** case[34]: e.g. *Ich bin größer als <u>du</u>; Du bist schneller als <u>ich</u>* (literally: 'you are quicker than I'). There are four examples of this construction in our text (lines 1, 16, 18 and 20). By contrast, a sentence such as 'I am **as** big **as** you' is rendered as: *Ich bin **so** groß **wie** du.*[35]

ii) '-er **and** -er' (e.g. 'bigger and bigger'). The most common translation of this construction is with ***immer*** + comparative: e.g. *Er wird **immer** dicker* 'He's getting fatt**er** and fatt**er**'.

iii) '**the** -er ... **the** -er' (e.g. 'the bigger the better'). Expressions such as '<u>the</u> sooner you come, <u>the</u> better' are rendered by *je* + comparative...***desto*** + comparative: ***Je** früher du kommst **desto** besser*; and with 2 full clauses: ***Je mehr** Zeit ich mit ihm verbringe, **desto mehr** mag ich ihn* 'The more time I spend with him, the more I like him.'

iv) '**the** -est **of all**'. The superlative can be stressed by prefixing it with *aller-* to render the meaning 'of all': e.g. *Der See ist der **allergrößte*** 'That lake is the biggest of all'. Otherwise 'of' is translated using the genitive or *von*: e.g. *Sie ist die fleißigste **der** (or **von den**) Studenten.* 'She's the most hardworking of the students.'

v) '**the** -est **thing**'. In constructions such as 'the hardest thing is', 'the nicest thing about it was', the superlative is used as a noun, and is therefore capitalised: e.g. ***Das Beste** war die Musik* 'the best thing was the music'. These nouns are always neuter.

[34] Unless the **verb** requires use of another case: e.g. *Ich <u>helfe</u> ihm lieber als seinem Bruder.*

[35] In colloquial German, particularly in the south and in Austria, *als* and *wie* are often confused: e.g. *Er ist kleiner **wie** sein Sohn* 'He is smaller than his son'.

EXERCISES

Vocabulary topic: *Maße*

1 Make sentences out of the following words using the comparative form of the adjective. Your answers should be factually correct, so you may need to change the word order:

Example: [klein] ein Baby, ein Heranwachsender

Answer: Ein Baby ist kleiner als ein Heranwachsender

1 [tief] ein Teich, eine Pfütze
2 [hoch] das Rathaus, der Fernsehturm in Berlin
3 [breit] eine Gasse, eine Autobahn
4 [schlank] ein Supermodel, die durchschnittliche Frau
5 [dick] ein Rennreiter, ein Sumo-Ringer
6 [schmal] ein Doppelbett, ein Einzelbett
7 [niedrig] die Preise bei Aldi, die Preise bei anderen Supermärkten

2 Take the first noun from your answers above and add the superlative form of the adjective to describe it. Use the definite article:

Example: Ein Baby ist kleiner als ein Heranwachsender.

Answer: Das Baby ist das kleinste.

3 Put the adjectives in bold into a) the comparative, b) the superlative:

1 Er trägt den **langen** Mantel.
2 Gefällt dir der **kurze** Rock?
3 Hast du das **kleine** Kind gesehen?
4 Welche Weintrauben nimmst du? Die **großen** schmecken am besten.
5 Ich möchte die **dünne** Scheibe, bitte.

FURTHER EXERCISES

4 Put the following adjectives into EITHER the comparative OR the superlative depending on the context of the sentence. Remember to use the correct adjective endings if they appear in the noun phrase:

1 Mein Bruder ist JUNG als ich.
2 Ich bin der ALT in der Familie.
3 Man merkt, dass Klaus ALT wird. Er wird immer LANGSAM.
4 Er ist der GUT Fußballspieler in Deutschland.
5 Je REICH er wird, desto ARROGANT wird er.
6 Normalerweise ist Deutschland im Sommer WARM und im Winter KALT als England.
7 Er hält sich für den KLUG Burschen in der Klasse.
8 Das ist der HOCH von den Bergen.
9 Welchen Wein möchten Sie? Den BILLIG, bitte.
10 Der Geruch wird immer STARK.

5 Put the following adjectives into the superlative and decide whether to use the *-st* or the *am … -sten* form. Sometimes both are possible:

Example: Diese Blumen sind **schön**.

Answers: a) Diese Blumen sind **die schönsten**; b) Diese Blumen sind **am schönsten**.

1 Dieses Warenhaus ist **teuer**.

2 Klaus spielt nicht schlecht, aber Hermann spielt **gut**.

3 Wo verbringst du **gern** deinen Urlaub?

4 Wer kann **laut** singen?

5 Das war der **nasse** Tag des Jahres.

7 | Personal pronouns and possessives

Text

Chanel07: Aus welchen Gründen würde **man** Lehrer(in) werden wollen?

mia68: "Wirkliche Gründe" – damit ist in <u>meinen</u> Augen so ein Empfinden wie eine Art "Berufung" gemeint [...]. **Es** geht darum, nicht nur Wissen, sondern so etwas wie eine Art "Haltung zum Leben" zu vermitteln. Und die
5 Bereitschaft, auch selbst immer mehr und weiter lernen zu wollen; von und mit den Menschen, mit denen **man** da zu tun hat. [...].

pepsi40: ... weil **man** den Umgang mit Kindern mag. ... weil **man** die Vielfältigkeit in diesem Beruf liebt? Keine Ahnung. **Ich** hab 5 Jahre im Elternbeirat mitgewirkt. Respekt, wenn heute noch irgendwer Lehrer
10 werden möchte, bei den Eltern ...

→ *Kommentar von kristall08*: Die Eltern sind allerdings echt ein Argument gegen den Beruf.
→ *Kommentar von pepsi40*: Das darfst **du** laut sagen ... schade nur, dass **ich** im Laufe der 5 Jahre einige motivierte Lehrer sah, die immer mehr
15 wegen der Eltern resignierten ...

eizzim: Warum Lehrer werden? Um die Kinder zu quälen, so wie **du** mal gequält wurdest.

parademix: **Ich** kenne viele Leute, die das machen wegen der Sicherheit, dem Geld und den Ferien. **Sie** sind dann extrem deprimiert und wirklich
20 schlechte Lehrer. Ein Lehrer muss in den Ferien arbeiten. Das ist den meisten anderen Berufen im Urlaub erspart. Die Beweggründe, die ein Mensch haben sollte, wären wohl: Umgang mit Kindern/Jugendlichen zu mögen, sich beim Lehren wohl zu fühlen. Die Idee des Lehrens sollte ein Ideal sein. Einzusehen, dass **es** nicht um sich geht, sondern um die
25 Schüler. [...] **Wir** Lehrer entscheiden das Schicksal tausender Schüler in <u>ihrem</u> Berufsleben. Wer sich nicht absolut sicher ist, dass dieser Beruf der richtige für **ihn/sie** ist, sollte **ihn** nicht annehmen. Außerdem sollte **es** klar sein, den Schülern nicht die eigene Meinung oder das eigene Weltbild näher zu bringen, das ist nicht Sinn der Sache, **man** kann **ihnen** Tipps
30 geben, ja. Aber Kinder müssen immer die Chance haben sich <u>ihre</u> eigenen Gedanken zu jedem Thema zu machen, ohne jegliche Vorurteile.

Aus: Forum *Gute Frage* [www.gutefrage.net], 15/1/09.

das Empfinden – feeling
die Berufung – calling, vocation
die Haltung – attitude
der Umgang – contact
die Vielfältigkeit – variety
der Elternbeirat – parents' association

quälen – to torture
der Beweggrund – motive
einsehen – to realise
das Schicksal – fate
der Sinn – sense, point
das Vorurteil – prejudice

Personal pronouns and possessives in the text

7.1 PERSONAL PRONOUNS

7.1a Personal pronouns and case

Personal pronouns are the pronouns used to refer to persons and things: e.g. 'I', 'you', 'he', 'she', 'it'. In English, some of these pronouns have different forms depending on whether they appear as the subject or the object of the sentence: e.g. subj.: '**I** love John' vs. obj.: 'John loves **me**'. The same principle applies in German, yet here there is an additional difference between the direct object pronoun, which is in the **accusative**, and the indirect object pronoun, which is in the **dative** (see **Table 7.1**). These accusative and dative forms are also used after prepositions and other elements which require a particular case. Examples of personal pronouns in the text appear in bold print.

Table 7.1 Personal pronouns

Subject (nom.)		Object (acc.)	Indirect object (dat.)
ich	'I'	Er liebt **mich**	Er sagt **mir**
du*	'you'	Er liebt **dich**	Er sagt **dir**
er	'he'	Er liebt **ihn**	Er sagt **ihm**
sie	'she'	Er liebt **sie**	Er sagt **ihr**
es	'it'	Er liebt **es**	Er sagt **ihm**
wir	'we'	Er liebt **uns**	Er sagt **uns**
ihr*	'you'	Er liebt **euch**	Er sagt **euch**
sie	'they'	Er liebt **sie**	Er sagt **ihnen**
Sie*	'you'	Er liebt **Sie**	Er sagt **Ihnen**

* German has three different words for *you* depending on the number of people addressed and the speaker's relationship towards them. **Du** (*dich, dir*) is the informal singular form. It is used: i) to address a person who the speaker is on friendly terms with;[36] ii) to address children (up to about 14–15); iii) among young adults (e.g. students) who wish to be informal. **Ihr** (*euch*) is the plural form of *du*, which is used to address two or more people who would normally be addressed as *du*. **Sie** (*Ihnen*), which is always written with a capital letter, is the polite form used to address (adult) strangers and people who are acquaintances but not on familiar terms with the speaker (e.g. work colleagues). It is used for singular **and** plural addressees.

36 But it can also be used to show contempt, if it is used with a stranger or someone who would normally be addressed more politely.

Examples of personal pronouns used in the text are:

Subject (nom.): *Ich hab* (8), *dass **ich** im Laufe der 5 Jahre* (14); *Das darfst **du** laut sagen* (13), *so wie **du** mal gequält wurdest* (16); ***Wir** Lehrer* (25); ***Sie** sind dann extrem deprimiert* (= 'they') (19)
Object (acc.): *der Richtige für **ihn*** (27), *der Richtige für **sie*** (= 'her') (27)
Indirect object (dat.): *Man kann **ihnen** Tipps geben* (= 'them') (29)

Note that the form used for 'you' is informal, as the text is taken from an internet forum, and the participants are using an informal style of language.

7.1b *man*

In addition, German has a general 'impersonal' pronoun, *man* (accusative: *einen*, dative: *einem*), which corresponds to English 'one' but is used much more frequently than English 'one', as can be seen by its occurrences in our text (lines 1, 6, 7, 29). As English 'one' is considered rather formal, it is usually avoided in the spoken language and 'you', 'they', 'people', 'someone' or a passive construction are used to translate *man*: e.g. *Aus welchen Gründen würde **man** Lehrer(in) werden wollen?* 'What reasons would **you** (or **people**) have for becoming a teacher?' (1); ***Man** kann ihnen Tipps geben* '**You** can give them tips' (or 'They **can be given** tips') (29–30). This means that when English 'you' is used to mean 'people in general', it must be translated by *man* (acc. *einen*, dat. *einem*) and not *du*.[37] The possessive form of *man* is *sein*, even when referring to women: e.g. *Man erlebt **seine** Schwangerschaft jedesmal anders* 'One experiences one's (*literally* 'his') pregnancy differently every time.[38]

37 In more formal English, a passive construction is often preferred to 'you', 'people', 'they' etc.: e.g. *Man sagt oft, dass …* 'It is often said that …'.
38 This has often been criticised by feminist linguists (see Senta Trömel-Plötz, *Frauensprache – Sprache der Veränderung*, Fischer Taschenbuch-Verlag, 1982).

7.2 TRANSLATION OF 'IT'

In English, non-human nouns are usually expressed using the pronoun 'it': e.g. 'Did you read the book?' 'Yes, **it** was interesting'. In German, however, every noun has a gender, which means that the **choice of pronoun depends on the gender of the word**: e.g. *der Film* takes the masculine singular pronoun (and its different case forms depending on the context) while *die Musik* takes the feminine singular pronoun. (The plural pronoun is the same for all genders.) Consider the following examples:

Hast du den Film gesehen?	Did you see the film?
*Ja, **er** war sehr gut, aber ich fand **ihn** ein bisschen zu lang.*	Yes, **it** was very good but I found **it** a bit too long
*Das war eine Wespe. Has du **sie** gesehen?*	That was a wasp. Did you see **it**?
*Gesehen? Ja, **sie** hat mich gestochen!*	See **it**? Yes, **it** stung me!

There is an example of this in our text: *Wer sich nicht absolut sicher ist, dass dieser Beruf der Richtige für ihn/sie ist, sollte **ihn** nicht verüben* 'Whoever isn't absolutely certain that this career is the right one for him/her should not follow **it**' (*ihn* = ***der** Beruf*) (26–27).

'It' is translated as *es* with neuter nouns, e.g. *Das Buch hat mir gefallen. **Es** war sehr interessant*, and when 'it' does not refer to a specific noun but is used more generally (i.e. to refer to a whole idea, or a situation): e.g. ***Es** geht darum, nicht nur Wissen ... zu vermitteln* 'It's not just about imparting knowledge' (3–4); *Außerdem sollte **es** klar sein* 'Besides, **it** should be clear' (27–28).[39]

> [39] It can also be used when the noun (or something standing in for the noun) is mentioned later, after the verb: e.g. *Es war ein sehr guter Film*; *Ja **es** war ein guter*; *Der Ring – es ist meiner*.

7.3 POSSESSIVES

Possessives (see **Table 7.2**) are used to indicate possession in constructions such as '**my** friend', '**your** bike'. As with personal pronouns, there are three forms for 'your' in German, depending on whether the addressee would be *du*, *ihr* or *Sie*. All possessives take the **same endings as the indefinite article** (see **Table 7.3**; compare with **Table 3.2**).

Table 7.2 Possessives

Singular		Plural	
mein	'my'	*unser*	'our'
dein	'your' (informal sg.)	*euer**	'your' (informal pl.)
sein	'his'	*ihr*	'their'
ihr	'her'	*Ihr*	'your' (polite sg. and pl.)
sein	'its'		

* This tends to become *eur-* when an ending is added: e.g. *eure Wohnung*.

Table 7.3 Forms of the possessives

	Masc.	Fem.	Neut.	Plural
N	*mein Mann*	*meine Frau*	*mein Kind*	*meine Kinder*
A	*meinen Mann*	*meine Frau*	*mein Kind*	*meine Kinder*
D	*meinem Mann*	*meiner Frau*	*meinem Kind*	*meinen Kindern*
G	*meines Mannes*	*meiner Frau*	*meines Kindes*	*meiner Kinder*

Examples of possessives in the text are underlined. They are in the accusative: *ihre eigenen Gedanken ... zu machen* 'to have their own thoughts' (30–31), and dative: *in meinen Augen* 'in my eyes' (2), *in ihrem Berufsleben* 'in their career' (25–26).

Possessives can also be used as pronouns, standing in for nouns that would usually follow but have been omitted. In this case, the possessives would take the form that they normally would if the noun were present, e.g. (not in text) *In ihrem Berufsleben haben Sie viel Erfolg, aber in*

meinem *(Berufsleben) habe ich nur Schwierigkeiten* 'In their career they are very successful but in **mine** I only have difficulties'. This is the case for all possessives except the masc. nom. sg. and the neuter nom./acc. sg. which take *-er* and *-(e)s* respectively:

Ist das dein Schlüssel? –	Is that your key? -
*Ja es ist **meiner**.*	Yes, it's **mine**
Du hast dein Bier ausgetrunken –	You've drunk your beer –
*Willst du auch **meines** haben?*[40]	Do you want **mine** too?

Proper nouns, e.g. names, have a special possessive form with *-s*, as in English. However, there is no apostrophe: *Herberts Freundin* 'Herbert's girlfriend'.

[40] *Meines, deines, seines* etc. are usually pronounced (and often written) *meins, deins, seins* etc.

Other points to note in the text

- Dropping of first person *-e* in the present tense in colloquial speech: *ich hab* (8) (see **10.2a**).
- Relative clauses: *Menschen, mit denen man da zu tun hat* (6), *motivierte Lehrer [...], die immer mehr wegen der Eltern resignierten* (14–15), *die Beweggründe, die ein Mensch haben sollte* (21–22), *Ich kenne viele Leute, die das machen wegen der Sicherheit, dem Geld und den Ferien* (18–19). Here the verb has not gone to the end, as it reflects colloquial speech (see **Ch. 9**).
- Demonstratives: *bei den Eltern* (10) meaning 'with **those** parents', *dieser Beruf* (26), *diesem Beruf* (8) (see **Ch. 8**).
- Passive: *so wie du mal gequält wurdest* (16–17) (see **Ch. 18**).
- Konjunktiv II as conditional: *würde* (1), *wären* (22), *sollte* (22, 23, 27) (see **16.3**).
- Infinitive with *um ... zu: Um die Kinder zu quälen* '(in order) to torture the children' (16) (see **21.2**).

Discover more about personal pronouns and possessives

7.4 GENITIVE FORMS

Personal pronouns also have genitive forms: e.g. *meiner, deiner, seiner* etc., but these are considered archaic and only very rarely used. The only genitive forms which are still in general use are taken from the demonstrative pronoun: *dessen* (plural: *deren*) and usually render English 'of it' ('of them'): e.g. *Er war **dessen** nicht bewusst* 'He was not aware **of it**.'

7.5 PREPOSITIONS WITH NON-HUMAN PRONOUNS

If a preposition occurs with a personal pronoun meaning 'it' or 'they/them' referring to a non-human noun, *da-* (*dar-* before a vowel) + preposition may be used as an alternative to the usual personal pronouns. In fact, it is used very frequently:

Kennst du den Film? Was hältst du von ihm	
or ***davon**?*	'... What do you think of **it**?'
Die Ohrringe? Ich habe 30 Euro für sie bezahlt	
or ***dafür***[41]	'... I paid 30 euros for **them**'

[41] With animals, particularly pets, the same personal pronouns are used as for humans (as is the case in English): e.g. *Das ist mein Hund. Ich gehe jetzt mit ihm spazieren*, not **damit* 'with **it**'.

Da(r)- + preposition is **obligatory** i) when the alternative pronoun would be *es*, e.g. with neuter nouns: *Das Buch – Was hast du dafür* (not **für es*) *bezahlt?*; ii) when 'it' refers to a general idea or abstract entity rather than to a specific concrete noun: e.g. *Ich muss heute Überstunden machen – ich bin damit nicht zufrieden* 'I have to work overtime today – I'm not happy **about it**' (i.e. about the situation in general).

7.6 DEMONSTRATIVES (*DER, DIE, DAS* ETC.) USED AS PERSONAL PRONOUNS

In colloquial spoken German it is very common to use demonstrative pronouns (see **8.2**) instead of the third person forms of the personal pronouns (i.e. instead of *er, sie, es* and plural *sie*, whether referring to people or things). In this case they often appear at the beginning of the clause:

*Klaus? Ja, **der** gefällt mir ganz gut.*	Klaus? Yes, I quite like **him**.
*Ute? **Die** kann ich überhaupt nicht leiden.*	Ute? I can't stand **her** at all.
*Datteln? Von **denen** kriege ich Durchfall.*	Dates? **They** give me diarrhoea.

7.7 *DESSEN* AND *DEREN* AS POSSESSIVES

The genitive forms of the demonstrative pronouns, *dessen* (masc./neut. sg.) and *deren* (fem. sg./ and all pl.), may be used instead of the ordinary possessives *sein* and *ihr* in cases where ambiguity is possible. In other words, *dessen* means 'his' or 'its' and *deren* means 'her' or 'their'. For instance, if two or more nouns are mentioned which could be connected to the possessive, the use of *dessen/deren* makes it clear that it is **the last noun mentioned** that the possessive refers to:

Klaus kam mit Fritz und seiner Frau.	Klaus came with Fritz and his wife [*seiner* probably refers to Fritz but, theoretically, could refer to Klaus].
*Klaus kam mit Fritz und **dessen** Frau.*	[This makes it clear that it is Fritz's wife].

7.8 THE POSSESSIVE DATIVE

In some constructions, particularly when referring to parts of the body, it is more common to use a dative to express possession rather than an ordinary possessive: e.g. *Ich wasche **mir** die Haare* 'I wash my hair', *Du putzt **dir** die Zähne* 'You clean your teeth', *Er hat **sich** das Bein gebrochen* 'He broke his leg'. In these cases, a dative reflexive pronoun is used (see **20.4**) and a definite article (literally 'I wash to myself the hair' etc.). This construction can also be used with non-reflexives when someone else is performing the action. Dative object pronouns are used: e.g. *Ich wasche **ihm** das Gesicht* 'I wash his face', *Ich trockne **dem** Kind die Haare* 'I dry the child's hair'.

✎ EXERCISES

Vocabulary topic: *Computer, Internet und Soziale Medien*

1 Fill in the appropriate personal pronouns:

1 Hast __ (*you*) die Fotos von __ (*me*) auf Facebook gepostet? Zwanzig Leute haben __ (*them*) schon empfohlen.

2 __ (*we*) chatten regelmäßig im Rock-Chatraum. Die Chat-Teilnehmer kontaktieren __ (*us*), wenn sie Fragen über E-Gitarren haben.

3 __ (*you*, polite) müssen zuerst einloggen und dann auf die Homepage gehen. Dort finden __ (*you*) einen Link zum Leserforum, der __ (*you*) zeigen wird, welche aktuelle Themen besprochen werden.

4 __ (*you*, informal plural) verbringt viel zu viel Zeit am Computer. Es ist nicht gut für __ (*you*). __ (*one*) darf nicht mehr als eine Stunde vor dem Bildschirm sitzen.

5 __ (*he*) hat für __ (*me*) zehn Lieder von i-Tunes gratis heruntergeladen, und die meisten davon gefallen __ (*me*) sehr gut.

6 „Was ist mit dem Drucker los? __ (*it*) geht nicht." „__ (*you*) musst __ (*it*) an den Computer anschließen. Soll ich __ (*you*) dabei helfen?"

2 Fill in the appropriate personal pronouns and possessives:

1 Ich muss mit __ (*them*) über __ (*their*) Website reden. Das Layout ist überhaupt nicht anwenderfreundlich.

2 __ (*his*) Internetverbindung funktioniert zur Zeit nicht. Statt __ (*him*) zu emailen, kannst du __ (*me*) einfach texten und ich werde __ (*him*) die Nachricht weitergeben.

3 __ (*my*) Kollegin twittert die ganze Zeit. Ich habe __ (*her*) Tweets gelesen, aber ich finde __ (*them*) nicht besonders interessant.

4 Ich habe __ (*your*, informal sg.) Blog gelesen. __ (*it*) war sehr lustig.

5 __ (*our*) Tochter will Informatik studieren. __ (*she*) interessiert sich für Web-Design und elektronische Datenverarbeitung, aber Programmieren gefällt (*her*) nicht.

6 Können __ (*you*, polite) die Dateien von der Website auf __ (*your*) Festplatte downloaden?

7 __ (*you*, informal plural) müsst __ (*your*) Passwort eingeben, sonst lassen __ (*they*) __ (*you*) nicht uploaden.

8 __ (*my*) Laptop hat nicht genug Speicher und ist deshalb so langsam. Darf ich __ (*yours*) mal borgen? __ (*yours*) ist viel schneller.

9 Marion bekommt sehr viele SMS von __ (*her*) Freundin und __ (*her*) Mann.

10 „__ (*our*) System in der Arbeit ist eine Katastrophe. __ (*we*) bekommen jeden Tag Werbe-Emails, die __ (*us*) zum Wahnsinn treiben." „Echt? __ (*ours*) funktioniert sehr gut. __ (*they*) haben unseren Spamfilter sehr effektiv eingestellt."

✎ FURTHER EXERCISES

3 Form possessive phrases using the following nouns, first using the possessive + noun, then using the possessive as a pronoun:

Example: Die Limonade – ich.
Answers: i) Das ist **meine Limonade**; ii) Das ist **meine**.

1 Der Lippenstift – ich.

2 Das Zimmer – du.

3 Die Schuhe – er.

4 Der Wagen – wir.

5 Die Bücher – ihr.

6 Die Ohrringe – sie ('she').

7 Das Baby – sie ('they').

8 Der Kaffee – Sie.

4 Replace the nouns in bold print with the appropriate German word for 'it' (or 'they/them' in the plural):

1 Die Tür steht offen. – Ja, er hat **die Tür** nicht zumachen wollen.

2 Wo sind deine Handschuhe? – Ich habe **die Handschuhe** verloren.

3 Schmeckt dir der Tee nicht? – Nein, **der Tee** ist kalt geworden.

4 Der Kuchen ist lecker. – Danke, ich habe **den Kuchen** selbst gebacken.

5 **Der Rock** war ein teurer Rock.

6 **Der Wagen** ist meiner.

7 Ich habe das Auto von meinem Bekannten gekauft. Er hat nur 5000 Euro für **das Auto** verlangt.

8 Hier sind deine Pommes. Möchtest du Ketchup auf **die Pommes** haben?

9 Er ist nicht sehr begeistert von **der Idee**.

10 Ich habe meinen Schlüssel verloren. – Hast du **den Schlüssel** irgendwo gesehen?

5 Translate the following sentences into English, paying particular attention to the translation of *man* (acc. *einen*, dat. *einem*):

1 Man darf hier nicht rauchen.

2 Man hat eben eine neue Brücke gebaut.

3 Das kann einem wirklich auf die Nerven gehen.

4 Man hält die Deutschen für sehr fleißig.

5 Das Wetter hier kann einen ziemlich deprimieren.

For further exercises on personal pronouns and possessives see Revision Text 4, Ex. 2 and for exercises on demonstratives used as personal pronouns see Ch. 8, Ex. 4.

8 | Demonstratives

Das verflixte **dieses** Jahres

*"Wir haben zum 1. Januar **diesen** Jahres die Steuern gesenkt", verkündet die Regierung stolz. **Das** ist natürlich erfreulich, auch wenn es leider nicht richtig ist; denn diese Aussage enthält einen Fehler. **Der** ist allerdings so*
5 *weit verbreitet, dass er kaum noch auffällt. Auch die Presse hat ihn gefressen. Journalisten rechnen immer mit dem schlimmsten Fall, nur nicht mit dem zweiten.*

Munter singend läuft das Rotkäppchen durch den Wald, in der Hand den Korb mit Kuchen und Wein für die Großmutter. Da erscheint der Wolf
10 und spricht: "Hallo, mein Kind, so spät noch unterwegs?" – "Grüß dich, Wolf!", ruft das Rotkäppchen furchtlos, "wie geht's?" – "Phantastisch!", sagt der Wolf, "ich habe mir Anfang **diesen** Jahres einen roten Sportwagen gekauft, **der** ist einsame Spitze! Wenn du willst, kann ich dich ein Stück mitnehmen!" – "Einen Sportwagen? Ich glaub dir kein Wort!" – "Doch, doch,
15 er steht gleich dort drüben zwischen den dunklen, finsteren Tannen, hähä." – "**Der** ist doch bestimmt geklaut!", sagt das Rotkäppchen. Der Wolf hebt feierlich die Pfote: "Ich schwör bei deiner roten Kappe, ich habe ihn gekauft! Das heißt, vorläufig noch geleast, aber spätestens im Sommer **diesen** Jahres gehört er mir. Was ist, Bock auf eine Spritztour?" – "Nein danke",
20 erwidert das Rotkäppchen, "ich gehe lieber zu Fuß." Und naseweis fügt es hinzu: "Übrigens heißt es 'zu Anfang und im Sommer **dieses** Jahres'." Damit springt es singend davon. Der Wolf denkt verächtlich: "Blöde Göre! Ob ich dich im Sommer **diesen** Jahres oder im Sommer **dieses** Jahres fresse, worin liegt da der Unterschied? Fressen werde ich dich so oder so!"

Aus: Bastian Sick [www.spiegel.de/kultur/zwiebelfisch/0,1518,281668,00.html], 1/2004.

verflixt – damned, dratted	*die Tanne* – fir tree
die Steuern (pl.) – tax	*klauen* – to steal, pinch
verbreitet – widespread	*feierlich* – solemnly
auffallen – to be noticed	*leasen* – to hire
der Fall – case	*Bock haben auf etwas* – to fancy sth.
der zweite (Fall) – genitive	*naseweis* – cheekily
Rotkäppchen – Little Red Riding Hood	*die Göre* – brat
furchtlos – without fear	*verächtlich* – disdainful
einsame spitze – top class	*so oder so* – anyway

⌕ **Demonstratives in the text**

8.1 DEMONSTRATIVES BEFORE NOUNS

Demonstratives are used to point out a specific person or thing, differentiating it from other similar members of its class: e.g. 'this man', 'that table'. In German, the most commonly used demonstrative has the same form as the definite article (see **Table 3.1**): e.g. *der Mann* 'that man', *die Frau* 'that woman', *das Kind* 'that child'. It is usually used to mean 'that', but can also be used in contexts where English would use 'this': e.g. *Mmm, der Wein ist lecker* 'Mmm, this wine is lovely'.[42] Because these demonstratives look like definite articles they are difficult to recognise in a written text: e.g. *der Mann* could mean 'the man' or 'that man', but in the spoken language the demonstratives are stressed and therefore identifiable.[43]

In addition to the demonstrative meaning 'that', there is also a form that usually means 'this': *dies-*, which also declines for gender, number and case. In our text, it appears in the genitive case before a noun: *im Sommer dieses Jahres* 'in the summer of this year' (21). The writer points out, however, that many people use an incorrect ending in this construction, as if the demonstrative were an adjective: **Anfang diesen Jahres* 'beginning of this year' (12), and in his Red Riding Hood story, the girl corrects the wolf's bad grammar (21). **Table 8.1** sets out all the gender, case and number forms of *dies-*.

> [42] *Jener* is also a demonstrative meaning 'that' and takes the same endings as *dies-* (see **Table 8.1**). However, it is much less commonly used than *der, die, das*.
>
> [43] One indication of demonstrative rather than article status is the use of the full form rather than the contracted form: e.g. *zur Zeit* 'at the time/moment' vs. *zu der Zeit* 'at **that** time/moment' (see **24.1d**).

Table 8.1 *Dies-*

	Masc.	Fem.	Neut.	Plural
N	*dieser Mann*	*diese Frau*	*dieses Kind*	*diese Kinder*
A	*diesen Mann*	*diese Frau*	*dieses Kind*	*diese Kinder*
D	*diesem Mann*	*dieser Frau*	*diesem Kind*	*diesen Kindern*
G	*dieses Mannes*	*dieser Frau*	*dieses Kindes*	*dieser Kinder*

8.2 DEMONSTRATIVE PRONOUNS

Sometimes demonstratives can be used in place of a noun which is omitted but understood. In this case the demonstrative has the same gender and number as the omitted noun (and also the appropriate case): e.g. *Welchen Saft möchten Sie? – Ich möchte den, bitte.* 'Which juice would you like? – I'd like **this one/that one**, please' [< *ich möchte den Saft*].[44] Here are some more examples:

Der Wein:	*Der schmeckt gut*	That one tastes good (wine)
	Ich trinke den gern	I like drinking that one
	Mit dem bin ich zufrieden	I'm pleased with that one

Die Torte:	***Die** ist lecker*	That one is delicious (cake)
	*Ein Stück von **der**, bitte*	A piece of that one, please
Das Bier	***Das** ist zu stark*	That one is too strong (beer)
Die Tomaten:	***Die** sind frisch*	Those ones are fresh (tomatoes)
	*Ein paar von **denen***	A few of those ones

[44] English '**the one** who/that ...' is usually translated by *derjenige, der* ..., which behaves like a definite article + adjective as far as endings are concerned, but is written as one word: e.g. *derjenige, der; diejenige, die; dasjenige, das; mit demjenigen, der* etc.: e.g. *Klaus? Ist das derjenige, der jetzt in Afrika wohnt?* 'Klaus? Is that **the one** who now lives in Africa?'

Note that the dative plural form *denen* is different from the equivalent definite article form, which is *den*: *Ein paar von **den** Tomaten* vs. *Ein paar von **denen***.

Dies- can also be used as a pronoun and takes the same endings as it would if the noun was present (see **Table 8.1**): e.g. *der Wein: **Dieser** schmeckt gut, Ich find **diesen** besser, Mit **diesem** bin ich zufrieden; die Tomaten: **Diese** sind frisch, Ein Paar von **diesen***.

In our text there are three instances of *der* being used as a demonstrative pronoun:

***Der** ist allerdings so weit verbreitet* (4–5)	It is so widely used, however
***Der** ist einsame Spitze!* (13)	It's in a class of its own!
***Der** ist doch bestimmt geklaut!* (16)	It's bound to be stolen!

The first example refers to the noun *der Fehler* and the second two to *der Wagen*. Note, however, that the English equivalent here is 'it' rather than 'that one'. In less formal German, it is common to use the demonstrative pronouns *der, die, das* instead of the personal pronouns *er, sie, es* to mean 'it' (or 'he/she' if referring to people). For example, when referring to a masculine noun such as *der Wagen*, one could either say *Ich mag ihn nicht* or, more colloquially, *Ich mag **den** nicht* 'I don't like it'.

8.3 *DAS*

When 'this' and 'that' refer not to particular nouns but to whole ideas, *das* is used. In fact, because of this function, it is the most frequently used demonstrative of all: *Das ist natürlich erfreulich* 'of course that's good news' (3). Similarly, *das* is used when the noun (or something standing in for the noun) is mentioned later: e.g. (not in text) *Das ist mein Freund, Karl* 'This is my friend, Karl', *Das ist er* 'That's him'.

Other points to note in the text

- Personal pronouns meaning 'it': *Er steht gleich dort drüben* 'It (*der Wagen*) is standing right over there' (15), *Ich habe **ihn** gekauft* 'I bought it' (*den Wagen*) (17), *... gehört **er** mir* ' ... it belongs to me' (19) (see **7.2**).
- Words omitted for stylistic effect in speech: e.g. *Bock auf eine Spritztour* 'fancy a spin?', instead of *Hast du Bock ... ?* (19).
- Future tense: *Fressen **werde** ich dich* 'I will eat you' (24) versus present used for future: *Spätestens im Sommer ... **gehört** er mir* 'It will belong to me in the summer, at the latest' (18–19) (see **Ch. 15**).

- Subordinating conjunctions: *wenn* (3), *dass* (5), *ob* (23) versus co-ordinating conjunction *denn* (4) (see **25.1**).

Discover more about demonstratives

8.4 GENITIVE FORMS OF DEMONSTRATIVE PRONOUN *DER*

The demonstrative pronoun *der* also has the genitive forms **dessen** (for masculine and neuter singulars) and **deren** (for feminine singulars and all plurals), which mean 'of that'/'of those'. These are less commonly used than the other case forms and are mainly restricted to the written language: e.g. *Die Anzahl **deren**, die in den letzten zwei Jahren nach Deutschland gekommen sind.* 'The number **of those** who have come to Germany in the last two years'.

8.5 SEMANTIC DIFFICULTIES WITH 'THIS' AND 'THAT'

Often, *dieser, diese, dieses* etc. corresponds to English 'this' (see **8.1**). However, sometimes it is used when English would prefer 'that': e.g. *Ich war zu **dieser** Zeit sehr glücklich* 'I was very happy at that time'. *Dieser* is used quite often, but is much less common than *der*, particularly when used as a **demonstrative pronoun** (e.g. *Ich möchte **den*** is more common than *Ich möchte **diesen***).

When referring to a particular **idea** (rather than to a single noun) that has just been mentioned in the previous sentence, *dies* is sometimes used, e.g. at the beginning of the text in **Ch. 11**: *Überlege dir, wie du zu Anfang der Präsentation die Aufmerksamkeit der Zuhörer gewinnen kannst. **Dies** kann in Form einer Frage, eines Zitats oder eines Videos erfolgen* 'Consider how you can gain the attention of the listeners at the beginning of your presentation. **This** can be in the form of a question, a quotation or a video'. On the whole, however, *das* is used more frequently than *dies* to refer to an idea (see **8.3** above).

8.6 *DA* + PREPOSITION

When demonstrative pronouns occur with prepositions, *da-* + preposition (*dar-* before vowels) is often used as an alternative to the ordinary pronoun, as long as it is referring to things and not to people:

- *Von dem weiß ich überhaupt nichts/*   I don't know anything about that
  ***Davon** weiß ich überhaupt nichts*
- *Nein, mit dem bin ich nicht zufrieden/*   No, I'm not happy about that
  *Nein, **damit** bin ich nicht zufrieden*

On the whole, *da-* tends to be used when referring to general ideas rather than to concrete objects which are stressed: e.g. *Mit welchem <u>Messer</u> kann man am besten Fleisch schneiden? Mit **dem** oder mit **dem**?* 'Which knife can you cut the meat best with? That one or that one?' vs. *Was halten Sie von der <u>Situation</u>? – Ich bin **damit** überhaupt nicht zufrieden.* 'What do you think of the situation? – I'm not at all happy about that.'

Less commonly, *dies* with a preposition becomes *hier-*. This is primarily used in formal styles of German: e.g. **Hiermit** *bestätige ich…* 'I hereby confirm…'. Mostly, a preposition + 'this' is translated as *da(r-)* + preposition: e.g. 'Do you know anything about this?' *Weißt du etwas* **davon**?

✎ EXERCISES

Vocabulary topic: *Kleidung*

1 Fill in the gaps with the appropriate form of the demonstrative, first using **der** and then using **dieser**:

Example: Ich muss d_ Hemd bügeln.
Answers: i) Ich muss das Hemd bügeln; ii) Ich muss dieses Hemd bügeln.

1 D_ Rock darfst du nicht anziehen. Er ist viel zu kurz.
2 Die Schuhe passen sehr gut zu d_ Hose.
3 D_ schwarze Mantel ist sehr schön.
4 Kannst du mit d_ hohen Schuhen überhaupt gehen?
5 Die Farbe d_ Pullis gefällt mir nicht.
6 Die Löcher in d_ Socken werden immer größer!

2 Answer the following questions using the appropriate form of the demonstrative pronoun, first using **der** and then using **dieser**:

Example: Welches Kleid gefällt dir am besten?
Answers: i) Das da; ii) Dieses da.

1 Welche Jacke willst du anziehen?
2 Welcher Schal ist wärmer?
3 Zu welchen Handschuhen passt mein Mantel am besten?
4 Welchen Hut hat er getragen?
5 Von welcher Weste hat sie gesprochen?
6 Von welchen Stiefeln sind die Absätze zu hoch?
7 Welcher Schuh hat ein Loch drin?
8 Welche Krawatte soll ich anziehen?

✎ FURTHER EXERCISES

3 Fill in the gaps with the appropriate form of the demonstrative *der*:

1 D_ Kaffee trinke ich am liebsten.
2 Gehen wir ins Kino? – Ja, d_ ist eine gute Idee.
3 D_ ist mein Freund Robert.
4 Robert ist d_, der früher bei Siemens gearbeitet hat. (= *the one who*)
5 Was ist mit d_ passiert, der nach Australien ausgewandert ist? (= *the one who*)

6 Er wollte mit mir über die politische Situation in Uganda reden, aber ich verstehe nichts von d_ (*or* _von).

7 Es ist höchste Zeit, dass er eine richtige Arbeit sucht, aber an d_ (*or* _an) denkt er nie.

4 Replace the personal pronouns in bold print with demonstrative pronouns and move them to the beginning of the clause, as is common in colloquial spoken German. Remember the 'verb second rule' (see 26.1a(ii)):

Example: Was hältst du von Katrin? – Ich finde sie sehr sympathisch.

Answer: Was hältst du von Katrin? – Die finde ich sehr sympathisch.

1 Wie geht's Klaus? – Ich weiß es nicht. Ich habe **ihn** seit langem nicht gesehen.

2 Wo ist Oskar? – **Er** ist im Urlaub.

3 Hast du auch ein Geschenk von deinen Eltern bekommen? – Ja, ich habe **von ihnen** diese Uhr gekriegt.

4 Was hast du Astrid zum Geburtstag geschenkt? – Ich habe **ihr** eine CD gegeben.

5 Warum will Tobias nicht ins Fischrestaurant gehen? – Fisch und Meeresfrüchte schmecken **ihm** überhaupt nicht.

9 | Relative pronouns

Der Prüfungstraum

Jeder, **der** mit der Maturitätsprüfung seine Gymnasialstudien abgeschlossen hat, klagt über die Hartnäckigkeit, mit **welcher** der Angsttraum, dass er durchgefallen sei, die Klasse wiederholen müsse u.
5 dgl. ihn verfolgt. Für den Besitzer eines akademischen Grades ersetzt sich dieser typische Traum durch einen anderen, **der** ihm vorhält, dass er beim Rigorosum nicht bestanden habe, und gegen **den** er vergeblich noch im Schlaf einwendet, dass er ja schon seit Jahren praktiziere, Privatdozent sei oder Kanzleileiter. Es sind die unauslöslichen Erinnerungen an die Strafen,
10 **die** wir in der Kindheit für verübte Untaten erlitten haben, **die** sich so an den beiden Knotenpunkten unserer Studien, an dem »*dies irae, dies illa*« der strengen Prüfungen in unserem Inneren wieder geregt haben. [...]. Eine weitere Erklärung der Prüfungsträume danke ich einer Bemerkung von Seite eines kundigen Kollegen, **der** einmal in einer wissenschaftlichen
15 Unterhaltung hervorhob, dass seines Wissens der Maturatraum nur bei Personen vorkomme, **die** diese Prüfung bestanden haben, niemals bei solchen, **die** an ihr gescheitert sind. Der ängstliche Prüfungstraum, **der**, wie sich immer mehr bestätigt, dann auftritt, wenn man vom nächsten Tage eine verantwortliche Leistung und die Möglichkeit einer Blamage erwartet,
20 würde also eine Gelegenheit aus der Vergangenheit herausgesucht haben, bei **welcher** sich die große Angst als unberechtigt erwies und durch den Ausgang widerlegt wurde. Es wäre dies ein sehr auffälliges Beispiel von Missverständnis des Trauminhalts durch die wache Instanz. Die als Empörung gegen den Traum aufgefasste Einrede: Aber ich bin ja schon
25 Doktor u. dgl., wäre in Wirklichkeit der Trost, **den** der Traum spendet und **der** also lauten würde: Fürchte dich doch nicht vor morgen; denke daran, welche Angst du vor der Maturitätsprüfung gehabt hast, und es ist dir doch nichts geschehen.

Aus: Sigmund Freud, *Die Traumdeutung.* © Fischer TaschenbuchVerlag, 1991.

die Maturitätsprüfung/	*die Bemerkung* – observation
also: *die Matura* – A Levels (in Austria)	*kundig* – knowledgeable, expert
das Gymnasialstudium – secondary school studies	*hervorheben* – to highlight
abschließen – to complete	*scheitern an* – to fail
die Hartnäckigkeit – persistence	*bestätigen* – to confirm
durchfallen – to fail (an exam)	*auftreten* – to occur, arise
u. dgl. (abbrev. of *und dergleichen*) – and similar	*die Leistung* – performance
der akademische Grad – university degree	*die Blamage* – disgrace
jmdm. vorhalten – to reproach someone	*sich erweisen als* – to turn out as
das Rigorosum – PhD viva	*unberechtigt* – unjustified
bestehen – to pass (an exam)	*der Ausgang* – outcome
vergeblich – in vain	*auffällig* – conspicuous, noticeable
einwenden – to object	*die wache Instanz* – analysis
der Privatdozent – lecturer	when awake
der Kanzleileiter – head of office	*widerlegen* – to prove wrong
unauslöslich – indelible	*die Empörung* – outrage
der Untat – atrocity	*die Einrede* – objection
dies irae, dies illa – that day, the day of wrath	*der Trost* – consolation

⌕ Relative pronouns in the text

9.1 THE FORM OF RELATIVE PRONOUNS

9.1a The relatives *der, die, das*

Relative pronouns in German correspond to the use of English 'who', 'which' and 'that' after a noun or pronoun: e.g. 'the <u>man</u> **who** lives next door', 'the <u>car</u> **which/that**[45] I just bought'. In German, the relative pronoun is often identical to the **definite article**, agreeing in gender and number with the preceding noun that it is referring to: e.g. <u>*der Mann*</u>, *der auf den Bus wartet* 'the man **who** waits for the bus'. It can also appear in all four cases depending on the context, but the nominative is the most common. **Table 9.1** lists all forms of the relative pronoun, underlining those that differ from the definite article. Note that relative pronouns are identical to demonstrative pronouns (see **8.2**).

---

[45] English learners of German are often tempted to use the conjunction *dass* instead of a relative pronoun, as it also means 'that'. However, if in English 'that' could also mean 'which' or 'who', then it must be translated using a relative pronoun in German: e.g. *das Auto,* **das** (not **dass*) *ich kaufte* 'the car that/which I bought'.

Table 9.1 Relative pronouns

	Masc.	Fem.	Neut.	Plural
N	der Mann, **der**	die Frau, **die**	das Kind, **das**	die Kinder, **die**
A	der Mann, **den**	die Frau, **die**	das Kind, **das**	die Kinder, **die**
D	der Mann, **dem**	die Frau, **der**	das Kind, **dem**	die Kinder, **denen**
G	der Mann, **dessen**	der Frau, **deren**	das Kind, **dessen**	die Kinder, **deren**

Examples from the text are in the nominative (see (a)) and accusative (see (b)):

(a) _Jeder_, **der** ... _abgeschlossen hat_ (2–3)   everyone **who** has finished ...

einen _anderen_, **der** _ihm vorhält_ (6)   another one **which** reproaches him

Kollegen, **der** _einmal ... hervorhob_ (14–15)   colleague **who** once highlighted ...

bei _Personen_ ..., **die** ... _bestanden haben_ (16)   to people **who** have passed ...

der ... _Prüfungstraum_, **der** ... _auftritt_ (17–18)   the ... dream of exams **that** occurs ...

bei _solchen_, **die** ... _gescheitert sind_ (17)   with those **who** have failed ...

der Trost ..., **der** _also lauten würde_ (25–26)   the consolation ... **that** would say ...

(b) der _Trost_, **den** _der Traum spendet_ (24–25)   the consolation **that** the dream gives

Strafen, **die** _wir ... erlitten haben_ (8–9)   punishments **that** we have suffered ...

We can see from these examples that the relative pronouns are always preceded by a comma and send the following finite verb to the end of the clause.

9.1b Relative pronouns with prepositions

When a relative pronoun is used with a preposition, e.g. 'the man **who** she works <u>with</u>', the preposition always precedes the relative pronoun, as in formal English: 'the man <u>with</u> **whom** she works', e.g. _der Mann <u>mit</u> dem sie arbeitet._[46] The relative pronoun appears in the case required by the preposition. There is one example of this in the text: _einen anderen ..., <u>gegen</u> den er ... einwendet_ (6–7) 'another one **that** he objects <u>to</u>'

[46] In less formal styles of English, the relative pronoun may be omitted, e.g. 'the man she works with'. This is not possible in German. Similarly, English constructions of the type 'the man waiting for the bus', where the relative pronoun 'who' and the finite verb 'is' are omitted, must be translated using a relative pronoun in German: _der Mann, der auf den Bus wartet._

9.2 WELCHER

A more formal alternative to the relative pronouns given above is _welcher_, which has the same endings as the relatives _der, die, das_ etc., except that it does not occur in the genitive (see **Table 9.2**).

Table 9.2 Forms of _welcher_

	Masc.	Fem.	Neut.	Plural
N	welcher	welche	welches	welche
A	welchen	welche	welches	welche
D	welchem	welcher	welchem	welchen

It is often used as an alternative to *der* etc. to avoid repetition: *die Hartnäckigkeit, mit **welcher** der Angsttraum …* 'the persistence with **which** the nightmare …' (3–4) [instead of *mit **der** der Angsttraum…*], although *der … der* would not be incorrect. Often it is simply used as a more formal variant of *der* and can be found particularly after prepositions: e.g. *eine Gelegenheit … , bei **welcher** sich die große Angst als unberechtigt erwies* 'an occasion on **which** the great anxiety turned out to be unjustified' (20–21).

Other points to note in the text

- Weak masculine noun: *eines kündigen **Kollegen*** (14) (see **3.3b**).
- Extended attribute: *die **als Empörung gegen den Traum aufgefasste** Einrede* (23–24) (see **5.3**).
- Imperative: ***fürchte** dich doch nicht* (26), ***denke** daran* (26) (see **Ch. 11**).
- *Konjunktiv I* in reported speech: *durchgefallen **sei*** (4), *wiederholen **müsse*** (4), *bestanden **habe*** (7), *praktiziere* (8), *sei* (8), *vorkomme* (16) (see **Ch. 17**).
- *Konjunktiv II* in reported speech: ***würde** … ausgesucht haben* (20), *wäre* (22, 25), *lauten **würde*** (26) (see **17.4**).
- Use of reflexive instead of passive: *ersetzt **sich*** (5).
- Use of the older dative singular -e: *vom nächsten **Tage*** (18) (see footnote in 3.3).

Discover more about relative pronouns

9.3 RELATIVE PRONOUNS IN THE DATIVE AND GENITIVE

9.3a Dative

If the relative pronoun is an **indirect object** or occurs with a preposition or verb taking the dative, it appears in its dative form (***dem*** for masculine and neuter singulars, ***der*** for feminine singulars and ***denen*** for all plurals):

*Der Polizist, **dem** ich alles erklärt habe*	The policeman who(m) I explained it all to
*Die alte Dame, **der** du geholfen hast*	The old lady who(m) you helped

9.3b Genitive ('whose')

Genitive relative pronouns are the German equivalent of English 'whose' (or, with inanimate objects, 'of which'). If the preceding noun referred to is masculine or neuter singular ***dessen*** is used, and if it is feminine or plural ***deren*** is used:

*Der Mann, **dessen** Auto vor der Tür steht*	The man whose car is in front of the door
*Die Frau, **deren** Sohn eben geheiratet hat*	The woman whose son just got married
*Die Nachbarn, auf **deren** Hund ich aufpasse*	The neighbours whose dog I look after

9.4 USE OF *WAS*

The relative pronoun *was* is used when no particular noun precedes it, i.e. it refers back to indefinite expressions such as *das, etwas, nichts, vieles* etc. (see (i)) or to a whole clause (see (ii)):

i) *Das, **was** ich immer sage*   **What** I always say (literally 'that which')

  *Ich habe etwas gefunden, **was** dich*   I've found something **that** will

  interessieren wird   interest you

ii) *Er gibt sein Studium auf, **was** meiner*   He's giving up his studies, **which**

  Meinung nach ein Fehler ist   in my opinion is a mistake

9.5 USE OF *WO(R)*- WITH PREPOSITIONS

If a construction with *was* needs a preposition, *was* becomes *wo-* (*wor-* before a vowel) and the preposition is added to the end: e.g. *Er gibt sein Studium auf, **wo**mit ich nicht einverstanden bin* 'He is giving up his studies, **which** I don't agree with', *Das ist etwas, **wor**an ich immer denke* 'That's something **which** I always think about.'

✎ EXERCISES

Vocabulary topic: *Psychologie*

1 Fill in the gaps with the appropriate relative pronouns:

1 Er hat viele Ängste, __ er überwinden muss.

2 Das ist ein Angsttraum, __ oft bei Personen vorkommt, __ unter Stress stehen.

3 Er redet von einem Kontrollzwang, __ er nicht nur in der Arbeit sondern auch zu Hause hat.

4 Das ist ein Verhalten, __ für unsichere Menschen typisch ist.

5 Das sind persönliche Fähigkeiten, mit __ man das Leben besser organisieren kann.

6 Die Behandlung ist in den meisten Fällen effektiv, __ natürlich sehr gut ist.

7 Die Patientin, __ der Psychologe geholfen hat, kommt jetzt viel besser zurecht.

8 Der Spezialist, __ viele Leute gelobt haben, hat kognitive Verhaltenstherapie vorgeschrieben.

9 Über meine Zwangsstörung habe ich vieles gelernt, __ mir helfen könnte.

10 Der junge Mann, __ ich ein Buch über Wut-Management geliehen habe, hat mich verprügelt.

2 Turn the following sentences into nouns described by a relative clause by moving the underlined words to the beginning (putting them into the nominative case), inserting the correct preposition + relative pronoun and changing the word order:

Example: Ich arbeite seit einem Jahr an seinem Selbstwertgefühl.

Answer: **Sein Selbstwertgefühl, an dem** ich seit einem Jahr arbeite.

1 Er hat Selbstbehauptungstraining von seinem Chef bekommen.

2 Sie verlässt sich zu sehr auf ihre Anti-Depressiva.

3 Er hat mehr als genug von der Neurose seiner Frau.

4 Ich kann nichts mit dem Persönlichkeitstest anfangen.

5 Die Papiere <u>des Psychiaters</u> liegen auf dem Tisch.

6 Die Vorschläge <u>meiner Beraterin</u> haben mir sehr geholfen.

7 Der Autor beschäftigt sich viel mit <u>der Vergangenheitsbewältigung</u>.

8 Sie haben lange auf <u>den Eheberater</u> gewartet.

9 Ich weiß nicht viel über <u>die Psychotherapie</u>.

10 Er leidet seit langem an <u>schweren Depressionen</u>.

3 Join the phrases together using either *was* or *wo(r)* + preposition where appropriate:

Example: Er fühlt sich viel selbstbewusster. Das ist natürlich super.

Answer: Er fühlt sich viel selbstbewusster, **was** natürlich super ist.

1 Meine Tochter ist sehr ängstlich. Das ist echt ein Problem.

2 Mein Patient hat einen Minderwertigkeitskomplex. Wir müssen daran arbeiten.

3 Er hat irgendeine Psychose aber lässt sich nicht helfen. Die Ärzte können nicht damit umgehen.

4 Mein Kollege is asozial. Das macht meine Arbeit sehr schwierig.

5 Mein Mann ist von Natur aus Optimist. Ich bin dafür sehr dankbar.

✎ FURTHER EXERCISES

4 Translate the following love poem into German, paying attention to the relative pronouns (and adding commas where necessary). Capitalise the first word of each line, as in the original, and use the *du* form.

You have beautiful eyes
Which light up when you speak.
Eyes that you can look into my heart with
And see something that I want to keep secret.

And your mouth which is always smiling,
Which I always want to kiss,
Which I always come back to
In my thoughts.

But your big heart that forgives all faults,
In which I feel at home,
That is what I think about the most.
The best thing about you.

Author unknown

<u>Vocabulary help</u>: *aufleuchten* 'to light up'; *jemandem ins Herz schauen* 'to look into s.o.'s heart', *geheimhalten* 'to keep secret', *die Schuld* 'fault', *das Beste an jemandem* 'the best thing about s.o.'

10 | Present tense

Text

<u>Anglizismen – ein Problem für die deutsche Sprache?</u>

Noch **sprechen** 100 Millionen Menschen auf der Erde Deutsch. Aber viele,
vielleicht sogar die meisten, nur recht widerwillig. Der moderne Modell-
Germane **joggt, jumpt, trekkt, walkt, skatet** oder **biket, hat** fun und feelings,
5 moods und moments, sorrows und emotions, und **scheint** vor nichts auf
Erden solche Angst zu haben, als seine eigene Sprache zu benutzen –
Deutsch zu sprechen **ist** vielen Deutschen ganz offensichtlich lästig oder
peinlich. Dass Musik, sofern gesungen, im deutschen Radio fast nur noch auf
English **stattfindet, ist** schon so normal geworden, dass es niemandem mehr
10 **auffällt.** Und andere Kommunikationskanäle **holen** mit großem Tempo **auf.**
Was **sagt** der ZDF-Reporter bei der Übertragung der letzten Sonnenfinsternis,
als der Mond zum ersten Mal die Sonne **berührt**: first contact. Eben hat der
first contact stattgefunden. [...].

Diese indirekte Bitte an das Ausland, Deutsch erst gar nicht zu erlernen, **hat**
15 ihren Gegenpart in der perversen Lust der Deutschen selber, das Deutsch, das
sie noch **können**, möglichst gründlich wieder zu vergessen. Wie
selbstverständlich **scheinen** viele Menschen, die Deutsch als Muttersprache
haben, heute das Englische als ihre Leit- und Kommandosprache aufzufassen.
Das **fängt** mit einem angel-shop im Erzgebirge (Laden für Weihnachtszubehör)
20 oder einer alten Dame **an**, die auf dem Bahnhof nach dem Eis-Zug **fragt** (so
gesehen auf dem Hauptbahnhof in München), und **hört** bei Jugendlichen **auf**,
die den deutschen Ausdruck turteln ohne nachzudenken auf die Gehweise von
Schildkröten **beziehen.**

Der Gipfel dieser Anbiederung an den angelsächsischen Kulturkreis **ist**
25 erreicht, wenn deutsche Politiker deutsche Wähler mit englischen
Werbesprüchen zu gewinnen **suchen**: „Vote Yellow" (so die FDP bei der
Kommunalwahl NRW), „Law and order is a Labour issue" (SPD-Plakat bei der
Wahl zur Bürgerschaft in Hamburg), „Welcome today, welcome tomorrow"
(Wahlkampflied der CDU in Niedersachsen) usw. Hier **scheint** die bekannte
30 Einschätzung von Churchill, dass man die Deutschen entweder an der Gurgel
oder an den Füßen habe, eine weitere Bestätigung zu finden.

Aus einem Artikel von Prof. Dr. Walter Krämer. © *Forschung und Lehre*, 10/2000.

widerwillig – reluctantly		*der Gegenpart* – counterpart
lästig – irritating		*Leit- und Kommando-* – control and command
peinlich – embarrassing		*das Zubehör* – accessories
stattfinden – to happen, take place		*der Eiszug* – (meaning *ICE*) Inter City Express train
auffallen (+ dat.) – to stand out		*turteln* – whisper sweet nothings
aufholen – to catch up		*die Schildkröte* – turtle
die Übertragung – broadcast		*die Anbiederung* – idolisation
die Sonnenfinsternis – solar eclipse		*die Einschätzung* – assessment, evaluation
die Bitte – request		*die Gurgel* – throat

The present tense in the text

10.1 USAGE

As in English, the present tense in German is primarily used to refer to present time, e.g. *sprechen* (line 2 of text), habitual actions: e.g. *joggt, jumpt, trekkt* etc. (4) or in general statements which are not linked to any particular time: e.g. *fängt … an, hört … auf* (19–21). One particular narrative technique is to use the present tense to refer to past events, which can create a feeling of immediacy, excitement or humour: e.g. *Was **sagt** der ZDF-Reporter … , als der Mond zum ersten Mal die Sonne berührt?* 'What **does** the ZDF reporter **say** as the moon first **touches** the sun?' (11–12).

There is no special progressive form of the present in German. Thus, 'they speak' and 'they are speaking' are both rendered by *sie sprechen*.[47]

[47] If, however, a speaker/writer of German feels that it is important to emphasise the progressive aspect in a particular context, the following alternatives may be used: e.g. 'I'm writing an essay' → *Ich schreibe **eben** (or **gerade**) einen Aufsatz* OR *Ich bin **eben/gerade dabei**, einen Aufsatz zu schreiben*. In addition, where no object is present, *beim* + infinitival noun is possible: e.g. *Ich bin **beim Schreiben**.* These constructions can also be used in tenses other than the present: e.g. *Ich telefonierte gerade; Ich **war** beim Lesen; Ich **bin** eben dabei **gewesen**, meine Mutter anzurufen* 'I was just ringing my mother'.

10.2 FORMATION

10.2a Regular verbs

The present tense is formed using the present tense stem (the infinitive minus *-en*) with the following endings:

-e	-en	e.g. *sagen*	*ich **sage**[48]*	*wir **sagen***
-st	-t	(Stem: *sag-*)	*du **sagst***	*ihr **sagt***
-t	-en		*er/sie/es **sagt*** (11)	*sie/Sie **sagen***

[48] In spoken German (and in writing imitating dialogue), *-e* is often dropped, especially in more colloquial speech, e.g. *ich sag', ich denk', ich find'.*

This text uses the third person singular (i.e. the *er/sie/es*-form): *joggt, jumpt, trekkt, skatet, biket* (4), *scheint* (5, 29), *berührt* (12), and the third person plural (*sie*-form): *sprechen* (2), *können* (16), *scheinen* (17), *haben* (18), *suchen* (26).

Points to note:

- For ease of pronunciation, if the stem of the verb ends in *-d, -t* or a consonant + *n* or *m*, *-e-* is added before the endings *-st* and *-t*, e.g. *stattfinden* becomes *stattfind-e-t* (9).
- The *du*-form ending *-st* becomes *-t* after *s, ß, z* and *x*, e.g. *reisen – du reis-t*.
- *-en* appears as *-n* when the infinitive of the verb has *-n*, e.g. *tun, klingeln*.

10.2b Separable verbs

Separable prefixes are sent to the end of the clause when the verb is in the present tense. Examples in the text are **auf**holen (10), **an**fangen (19–20), **auf**hören (21). The separable verbs **statt**finden (9) and **auf**fallen (10) appear with their prefixes attached because the verbs themselves have been sent to the end of the clause following *dass*. (See **Ch. 19** for more information on separable verbs.)

10.2c Irregular verbs

Some of the verbs which are irregular in the past tense are also irregular in the present, particularly in the *du-* and *er/sie/es*-forms (see **10.4**). Examples from the text are *fängt … an* from *anfangen* (19–20), *auffällt* from *auffallen* (10). *Haben* and *sein* are also irregular: **hat** (4, 14), **ist** (7, 9, 24).

Other points to note in the text

- Perfect tense: *ist… geworden* (9), *hat… stattgefunden* (12–13) (see **Ch. 13**).
- *Konjunktiv I*: *habe* (31) (see **Ch. 17**).
- *Sein*-passive: *ist … erreicht* (24–25) (see **18.5**).
- Prepositions with different usage from English equivalents: *auf* (2, 5, 20, 22) *in* (8), *mit* (10), *bei* (11, 26, 27), *zu* (12, 28), *an* (14, 24, 30, 31), *nach* (20) (see **24.5–24.6**).

Discover more about the present tense

10.3 USAGE

In some cases, German uses a present tense where English would not:

i) To refer to the **future**, particularly where it is clear from the context that the future is meant and no ambiguity with the present can arise: e.g. *Ich **komme** um 2 Uhr* 'I'll come at 2 o'clock', *Wir **treffen** uns vor dem Kino* 'We'll meet in front of the cinema'.

ii) To refer to an action or event **beginning in the past** which is still **continuing into the present**. This would be expressed using a perfect tense in English: e.g. *Ich **wohne** hier seit vier Jahren* 'I've been living here for four years (and still am)'. These constructions are usually used with *seit* (or *seitdem* followed by a clause) 'since' and *schon* 'already': e.g. *Ich **bin** seit Januar verheiratet* 'I've been married since January', *Seitdem er die neue Arbeit **hat**, geht er sehr selten aus* 'Since he's had the new job he rarely goes out'.

iii) To indicate present relevance, even when speaking in the **past** (or perfect) tense. For instance, in English the past tense tends to be used after another past to keep the tenses consistent. Thus 'I <u>knew</u> that he **was** over forty' can be used to refer to the present (i.e. he is over forty now), as it would be ungrammatical to say *'I knew that he **is** over forty'. In German, however, a present is used here: *Ich <u>wusste</u>, dass er über vierzig **ist**.*

10.4 IRREGULAR PRESENT FORMS

Verbs with a vowel change in the *du-* and *er/sie/es*-forms of the present are:[49]

e – i	*brechen –* **brichst, bricht,** *(fr)essen –* **(fr)isst, (fr)isst,** *gelten –* **gilt,** *helfen –* **hilfst, hilft,** *messen –* **misst, misst,** *sprechen –* **sprichst, spricht** *(and with long e: geben –* **gibst, gibt,** *nehmen –* **nimmst, nimmt,** *treten –* **trittst, tritt).**
e – ie	*lesen –* **liest, liest,** *stehlen –* **stiehlst, stiehlt.**
a(u) – ä(u)	Most verbs in -a- and -au- with an irregular past tense. Some examples are: *fallen –* **fällst, fällt,** *fangen –* **fängst, fängt,** *halten –* **hältst, hält,** *schlafen –* **schläfst, schläft,** *wachsen –* **wächst, wächst,** *laufen –* **läufst, läuft.**

Table 10.1 lists some other irregular present tense forms.

[49] For more information, see **Appendix 1** for a full list of common irregular verbs.

Table 10.1 Other common irregular verbs

	ich	*du*	*er/sie/es*	*wir*	*ihr*	*sie/Sie*
haben	*habe*	*hast*	*hat*	*haben*	*habt*	*haben*
sein	*bin*	*bist*	*ist*	*sind*	*seid*	*sind*
werden	*werde*	*wirst*	*wird*	*werden*	*werdet*	*werden*
dürfen	*darf*	*darfst*	*darf*	*dürfen*	*dürft*	*dürfen*
können	*kann*	*kannst*	*kann*	*können*	*könnt*	*können*
mögen	*mag*	*magst*	*mag*	*mögen*	*mögt*	*mögen*
müssen	*muss*	*musst*	*muss*	*müssen*	*müsst*	*müssen*
sollen	*soll*	*sollst*	*soll*	*sollen*	*sollt*	*sollen*
wollen	*will*	*willst*	*will*	*wollen*	*wollt*	*wollen*
wissen	*weiß*	*weißt*	*weiß*	*wissen*	*wisst*	*wissen*

10.5 DERIVED VERBS

Verbs with prefixes follow the same pattern as the verbs from which they are derived: i.e. if the basic verb is irregular, the derived verb will also be irregular: e.g. *fallen – fällt* → *auffallen – auffällt, einfallen – einfällt, umfallen – umfällt* etc.

10.6 PRESENT PARTICIPLES

Present participles in German are formed by taking the infinitive of the verb and adding -*d*, e.g. *lachend* 'laugh**ing**', *weinend* 'cry**ing**', and are mainly used as adjectives: e.g. *der* **kommende** *Montag* 'this **coming** Monday', *eine* **rauchende** *Frau* 'a smoking woman' (particularly in expanded attributes, see **5.3**) and adverbs: e.g. *Er saß* **schweigend** 'He sat there **saying nothing**'. By contrast, English present participles are used in many verbal constructions: e.g. 'I was working', 'He's the man reading a newspaper', 'He left the house, saying that he'd be late', where German would have a simple finite verb (see **25.5**).

✎ EXERCISES

Vocabulary topic: *Sprache*

1 Put the verbs in square brackets into the present tense. If they are separable (see **Ch. 19**), show where the prefix goes:

a **1**   Du [können] gut Englisch.
  2   Stefan [finden] Russisch sehr schwierig, aber es [gefallen] ihm trotzdem.
  3   Wie [aussprechen] man „Chrysantheme"?
  4   Bettina [lesen] einen französischen Roman.
  5   Ich [denken], die Grammatik und der Wortschatz [sein] relativ einfach, aber die Aussprache [sein] sehr schwer.

b Anglizismen – ein Problem für die deutsche Sprache (*Contd. from above*).

Es [sein] vor allem diese „linguistic submissiveness" (so die Londoner *Times*), die die in Deutschland grassierende Anglizitis über ihre Gefahr für die Sprache als solche zu einer so peinlichen und würdelosen Affäre [machen] – man [sich fühlen] angeschleimt und ausländischen Gästen gegenüber oft beschämt. („[Sein] ich hier in Chicago oder wo?" – Kommentar eines polnischen Gastwissenschaftlers auf dem „airport" Düsseldorf). Denn anders als die Englisch-Englisch-über-alles Lobby hierzulande gerne [glauben] und immer wieder als Begründung für das Fliehen aus der Muttersprache [anführen], [werden] ebendiese sprachliche Selbstaufgabe andernorts keineswegs als das Zeichnen weltoffenen Kosmopolitentums verstanden, als das viele Deutsche es so gerne sähen. Man [denken] ganz im Gegenteil an Churchill und [sich aufwappnen] für den Moment, wo man die Deutschen wieder an der Gurgel [haben]. Nicht umsonst [heißen] ein altes Sprichwort under Reisenden: Trau nur dem, der sich selbst [vertrauen], und mit diesem peinlichen Anbiedern an das Englische [einsetzen] wir für alle Welt ein unübersehbares Misstrauensvotum gegen unsere eigene Sprache und Kultur.

2 Complete these *Zungenbrecher* (tongue-twisters) by filling in the gaps using the present tense of the given verbs, remembering to show where any separable prefixes go. Read your answers out loud:

  1   Fritz __ [fischen] frische Fische.
  2   Hinter Hermann Hannes Haus __ [raushängen] hundert Hemden.

3 Welch schlecht berechtigtes Vermächtnis __ [entwachsen] dem
    schwächlichen Gedächtnis.

4 Max, wenn du Wachsmasken __ [mögen], dann mach Wachsmasken!

5 Wenn der Benz __ [bremsen], __ [brennen] das Benz-Bremmslicht.

6 Tuten __ [tun] der Nachtwächter. Und wenn er genug getutet hat, __ [reintun]
    er seine Tute wieder in den Tutkasten.

7 Wer gegen Aluminium minimal immun __ [sein], __ [besitzen]
    Aluminiumminimalimmunität.

8 Der Schweizer Schweißer __ [schwitzen] und __ [schweißen].

✎ FURTHER EXERCISES

3 Complete these German jokes by putting the verbs into the present (and moving prefixes
where appropriate):

1 Ein älteres Ehepaar __ [gehen] zum ersten Mal in die Oper. Neben einer kleinen Mahlzeit
__ [mitbringen] es auch zwei Flaschen Apfelsaft. Am Eingang __ [fragen] die
Platzanweiserin: „__ [wollen] Sie ein Opernglas?" __ [antworten] der Mann: „Nein, danke,
wir __ [trinken] aus der Flasche."

2 Susanne __ [sitzen] mit ihrer Freundin bei leckerer Torte im Café und __ [meinen]: „__
[wissen] du was, Beate?, ich habe in der letzten Woche 82 Kilo verloren." – „Quatsch, das
__ [glauben] du doch selber nicht! Wie __ [sollen] das denn gehen?" – „Ganz einfach: Ich
habe meinen Mann vor die Tür gesetzt!"

3 __ [fragen] der Arzt seinen Patienten: „__ [sprechen] Sie im Schlaf?" – „Nein, ich
__ [sprechen], wenn andere __ [schlafen]" – „Wieso das denn?" Antwort: „Ich __ [sein]
Lehrer!"

4 „So, dann Sie __ [müssen] mich begleiten", __ [befehlen] der Polizist. Darauf der
Straßenmusikant: „Aber gerne, Herr Wachtmeister! Was __ [singen] Sie denn?"

5 „Mutti", __ [sagen] der kleine Erwin, „hier __ [stehen], dass das Theater Statisten sucht.
Was __ [sein] denn das?" – „Statisten __ [sein] Leute, die nur __ [herumstehen] und nichts
zu sagen __ [haben]." – „Aber Mutti, das wäre doch etwas für Papi!"

6 Bei einem Klassentreffen __ [fragen] der Lehrer einen seiner ehemaligen Schüler: „Na, du
__ [sein] doch der Karl? Wie __ [gehen] es dir, __ [sein] du verheiratet?" „Ja, ich __ [haben]
acht Kinder." – „So, du warst schon immer sehr fleißig, aber aufgepasst hast du nie!"

7 Die kleine Veronika __ [laufen] zum Infostand im Kaufhaus: „Sie, wenn eine aufgeregte
Frau __ [kommen], die ihr Kind verloren hat, dann richten Sie aus, ich __ [sein] in der
Spielzeugabteilung."

4 Change the perfect tense forms in bold into the present only where appropriate (i.e. if the
sentence is ungrammatical):

1 Ich **habe** sehr gern bei der Firma **gearbeitet**.

2 Er **hat** seit Februar in Berlin **gewohnt**.

3 Sie **sind** um drei Uhr in die Stadt **gefahren**.

4 Wir **sind** seit vier Jahren zusammen **gewesen**.

5 Seitdem ich meine neue Wohnung **gehabt habe**, bin ich viel glücklicher.

5 Complete the following crossword by filling in the gaps in the clues (umlauts are indicated by placing *e* after the vowel in question, e.g. *für* = fuer):

Kreutzworträtsel

Senkrecht

1 Man __ einen Ball.

2 Ich __ die vorbeigehenden Menschen.

3 Er __ sehr leise.

4 Er __ die Katze der alten Frau.

Waagerecht

3 Du __ das Boot.

5 Es __ sehr stark.

6 Das Bild __ an der Wand.

For further exercises on the present tense see Revision Text 3, Ex. 1.

11 | Imperative

Tipps für eine gute Präsentation

- **Überlege** dir, wie du zu Anfang der Präsentation die Aufmerksamkeit der Zuhörer gewinnen kannst. Dies kann in Form einer Frage, eines Zitats oder eines Videos erfolgen.

5 - **Nenne** zu Beginn deines Vortrags deine Ziele. Warum hältst du diese Präsentation? Was willst du bezwecken? [...]. **Stelle** deine Intention klar **heraus**.

- **Beziehe** das Publikum mit **ein**. **Stelle** deinen Zuhörern Fragen, **biete** ihnen die Möglichkeit sich zu beteiligen und **richte** deine Präsentation speziell auf dieses Publikum **aus**.

10 - **Bringe** etwas **mit**. Präsentierst du dein Hobby Bergsteigen, dann **zeige** doch einen Teil deiner Ausrüstung. Das veranschaulicht die theoretischen Ausführungen ungemein.

- **Führe** einfache Beispiele **an**. Auf diese Weise kannst du die komplexesten und kompliziertesten Sachverhalte erklären. [...]

15 - **Gehe** immer auf Fragen der Zuhörer **ein**. Das zeigt, dass du sie ernst nimmst und dich sicher mit dem jeweiligen Themengebiet auskennst.

- Blickkontakt <u>halten</u>: jeden im Raum kurz <u>anschauen</u> und dann den Blick weiter <u>schweifen lassen</u>. So fühlen sich alle angesprochen und sind motiviert, weiter zuzuhören.

20 - [Falls du eine PowerPoint-Präsentation verwendest]: **Schreibe** die Folien nicht zu voll: nicht mehr als sieben Zeilen pro Folie. **Bedenke**, dass die Bilder und Schriftzeichen auf der Folie nicht zu klein sein sollten. **Achte** auf einen Kontrast zwischen Hintergrund- und Schriftfarbe. Gut eignet sich beispielsweise ein blauer Hintergrund mit weißer oder gelber Schrift. **Achte**
25 darauf, dass du dich während des Vortrags nicht ständig umdrehst, um auf die Folien zu schauen.

©2012 Studieren im Netz [www.studieren-im-netz.org/im-studium/studieren/praesentieren].

sich (dat.) *überlegen* – to consider	*veranschaulichen* – to illustrate
die Aufmerksamkeit – attention	*die Ausführung* – exposition, explanation
das Zitat – quotation	*der Sachverhalt* – facts
das Ziel – aim	*eingehen auf* – to go into, give time to
bezwecken – to aim at	*jeweilig* – respective
herausstellen – to underline	*schweifen* – to wander
einbeziehen – to include	*die Folie* – slide
sich beteiligen – to participate	*die Zeile* – line
ausrichten auf – to gear towards	*achten auf* – to watch out for
das Bergsteigen – mountaineering	*das Schriftzeichen* – character
die Ausrüstung – equipment	*sich eignen* – to be suitable

⌕ The imperative in the text

11.1 USAGE

The imperative mood is used to express a command: e.g. 'Come **here**!', '**Put** that down!', '**Take** a seat!' In German, there are three different forms of the imperative depending on whom the speaker is addressing: i) the informal singular form for a person who would be addressed as *du*, e.g. **Komm** *her!* ii) the informal plural form for people addressed as *ihr*, e.g. **Kommt** *her!* iii) the polite form for people (singular and plural) who would be addressed as *Sie*, e.g. **Nehmen Sie** *Platz*. As our text is aimed at young students, the *du*-imperative is used rather than the more formal *Sie*-imperative, and it is written as if talking to one person (hence the singular form).

In addition to these direct imperatives there is also an indirect one which is not linked to any of the 'you' forms but is used more generally, for example on public signs, in instruction manuals and recipes, and takes the **infinitive** form of the verb, e.g. *Nicht* **rauchen** 'No smoking', *Zwiebel* **schneiden** 'Cut the onions'. This is very common in the written language and there are also some examples in our text (underlined).

11.2 FORMATION OF THE 'DU'-IMPERATIVE

The form of the imperative used in the text is the informal singular (*du*) form which is made up from the present tense stem of the verb (the infinitive minus -*en*; see **10.2a**) plus the ending -*e*, e.g. *überlege* (2), *nenne* (5), *stelle* (6), *biete* (7), *zeige* (10), *schreibe* (20), *bedenke* (21), *achte* (22, 24).[50] Note, however, the following:

- The -*e* is often dropped in spoken German and less formal written German, e.g. *zeig'*, *schreib'*.[51]
- As in the present tense, separable prefixes are sent to the end of the clause in the imperative: *stelle ... heraus* (6), *beziehe ... ein* (7), *richte ... aus* (8–9), *bringe ... mit* (10), *führe ... an* (13), *gehe ... ein* (15).
- As in the present tense, reflexive pronouns follow the verb form: *überlege* **dir** (2) (dative reflexive, see **Ch. 20** for reflexive verbs).

- Verbs with a stem vowel change from -e- to -i- or -ie- in the present tense show the same change in the imperative. Examples are (not in text): *gib* 'give', *nimm* 'take', *iss* 'eat', *hilf* 'help', *lies* 'read' (see **10.4**). The ending -e is never added to verbs with a vowel change.

> 50 Except in the case of *sein*, which never has -e: e.g. **Sei** *ruhig!* 'Be quiet!'
>
> 51 Stems ending in -d and -t retain the -e, e.g. *biete*, along with stems which would be difficult to pronounce without it, e.g. *Leugne es nicht!* 'Don't deny it!' (*leugn* is impossible).

11.3 THE INFINITIVAL IMPERATIVE

In written German, it is common to see an infinitive being used as an imperative. It can also be used in the spoken language but this is less usual, as the infinitival imperative is a less direct, more general way of giving instructions. Where it is used, the infinitive appears at the **end** of the clause. There are three examples in our text (underlined): *Blickkontakt* <u>halten</u>: *jeden im Raum kurz* <u>anschauen</u> *und dann den Blick weiter* <u>schweifen lassen</u>.[52] '<u>Maintain</u> eye contact: briefly <u>look</u> at each person in the room and then <u>let</u> your eyes wander' (17–18).

> 52 This is a double infinitive construction (see **21.3**).

11.4 OTHER IMPERATIVES

The **informal plural** (*ihr*) and **polite** (*Sie*) imperatives are less problematic than the *du*-imperative as they simply use their present tense forms (see **10.2**), with a following pronoun in the case of *Sie*:

informal pl. (*ihr*):		formal sg. and pl. (*Sie*):	
kommt		*kommen Sie*[53]	
nehmt		*nehmen Sie*	
arbeitet		*arbeiten Sie*	
setzt euch		*setzen Sie sich*	

> 53 A similar construction can be made with the *wir*-form of the present, meaning 'let's ..': e.g. *Gehen wir* 'Let's go', *Legen wir uns hin* 'Let's lie down'.

Other points to note in the text

- Genitives: *die Aufmerksamkeit **der** Zuhörer* (2), *in Form **einer** Frage, **eines** Zitats oder **eines** Videos* (3), *einen Teil **deiner** Ausrüstung* (11), *während **des** Vortrags* (25) (see **3.1a(iv)**).
- Superlatives: *komplexes**ten*** (13), *kompliziertes**ten*** (14) (see **6.2**).
- Reflexive verbs: *Überlege **dir*** 'consider' (2), ***sich** zu beteiligen* 'to participate' (8), *dass du ...**dich** auskennst* 'that you are knowledgeable' (15–16), *so fühlen **sich** alle ...* 'so everyone feels ...' (18), *gut eignet **sich*** 'what is suitable/works well' (23), *dass du **dich** ... umdrehst* 'that you turn around' (25) (see **Ch. 20**).
- Use of infinitives with *zu*: *die Möglichkeit sich **zu beteiligen*** (8), *motiviert, weiter **zuzuhören*** (18–19), *um ... zu*: ***um** auf die Folien **zu** schauen* (26) and 'bare': ***gewinnen** kannst* (3), *kann ...*

erfolgen (3–4), *willst bezwecken* (6), *kannst du... erklären* (13–14), *schweifen lassen* (18), *sein sollten* (22) (see **Ch. 21**).

- Fronting for emphasis: *Auf diese Weise kannst du* '**In this way** you can' (13), *Gut eignet sich ... ein blauer Hintergrund* '**What works well** is ... a blue background' (23) (see **26.4**).

✎ EXERCISES

Change the following questions into imperatives, using the correct form of address. Some verbs have -<u>e</u> in the <u>du-</u> form in more formal German and drop the -<u>e</u> in less formal German. For these verbs, give two answers:

Examples: Kannst du etwas mitbringen?   Könnt ihr etwas mitbringen?
Answers: **Bringe/bring** etwas mit!   **Bringt** etwas mit!

1 Kannst du heute Abend mitkommen?
2 Willst du mir einen Kuss geben?
3 Könnt ihr brav zu Hause bleiben?
4 Können Sie mir Bescheid sagen?
5 Könnt ihr euer Zimmer aufräumen?
6 Würden Sie mich entschuldigen, bitte?
7 Willst du dein Gemüse essen?
8 Kannst du das noch einmal sagen?

9 Willst du deinen Regenschirm mitnehmen?
10 Willst du dir die Hände waschen?
11 Willst du dich ausruhen?
12 Kannst du dir die Situation vorstellen?
13 Wollen wir ins Kino gehen?
14 Wollen wir uns setzen?
15 Darf man den Rasen nicht betreten?

12 | Past tense

Text

Nackte Übermacht – Allein unter Deutschen

Neue Runde im Handtuchkrieg: Die britische Boulevardpresse hat ihre Lieblingsfeinde wiederentdeckt – die deutschen Touristen. Bayerische Volksmusik, Schnitzel zum Abendessen und rundherum nur nackte
5 Deutsche. Für zwei Briten **entwickelte** sich der Kanarenurlaub zum Alptraum. Jetzt wollen die beiden ihr Geld zurück.

London – Lange hatten sich die beiden Briten Dick und Angie Emery, beide 40, auf ihre Sommerferien gefreut – und dann das: Ihr Hotel **war** voller Deutscher. Ein gefundenes Fressen für die Boulevardpresse auf der Insel.
10 „Urlaub in der Hölle", **titelte** das Massenblatt „The Sun" am Donnerstag „exklusiv" und in großer Aufmachung. Zu ihrem Schrecken **mussten** die beiden Briten feststellen, dass in dem Hotel auf Fuerteventura nur deutsch gesprochen **wurde**. Vor der Speisekarte **rätselten** sie, was mit „Schnitzel" gemeint sein könnte. Der Fernseher auf ihrem Zimmer **war** nur auf
15 deutsche Sender programmiert. Und abends **gab** es bayerische Volksmusik.

Doch das Schlimmste: „Viele Gäste **sonnten** sich nackt – und das **war** nicht gerade ein schöner Anblick." Mit Schrecken **erinnerte** sich Angie: „Wir **waren** geradezu umzingelt. Sie **waren** einfach überall." Schon im
20 Morgengrauen hatten sich die Deutschen die besten Liegen mit ihren Handtüchern gesichert. Für Dick, inzwischen wieder zurück in Birmingham, ist die Sache klar: „Wir wollen unser Geld zurück."

Aus: *Der Spiegel* (*Online*), 17/8/00.

---

die Übermacht – superior strength
das Handtuch – towel
die Boulevardpresse – tabloid press
sich entwickeln – to develop
der Alptraum – nightmare
das gefundene Fressen – godsend
die Hölle – Hell

die Aufmachung – presentation, layout
rätseln – to puzzle over
sich sonnen – to sunbathe
der Anblick – sight
umzingelt – surrounded
im Morgengrauen – at dawn
die Liege – lounger, deckchair

⌕ The past tense in the text

12.1 USAGE

In German, the past tense, also known as the 'simple past', 'imperfect' or 'preterite', is usually used to refer to events in the past, particularly when narrating a story, and is mostly associated with the **written language** (e.g. novels and newspaper reports[54] etc. referring to past events). On the other hand, in spoken German it is more common to use the perfect tense to refer to past events (see **Ch. 13**).

As there are no special progressive forms of tenses in German, a sentence such as e.g. *Viele Gäste* **sonnten** *sich nackt* (17) could mean 'many guests sunbathed naked' or 'many guests **were sunbathing** naked' (see footnote in **10.1**). Usually it is apparent from the whole context which version is required. Similarly, English expressions such as 'used to' and 'would', as in 'I would visit him every day', which refer to repeated or habitual actions are often rendered by simply using the past tense in German: e.g. *Sie sonnten sich nackt* could mean 'they used to sunbathe naked' or 'they would sunbathe naked'.[55]

---

[54] Although in newspaper reports it is usual to have the first sentence in the perfect tense and the rest in the past (see lines 2–3 of text).

[55] Habitual 'would' should not be confused with conditional 'would', as in 'I would go if I could' (German *Ich* **würde** *gehen, wenn ich könnte*, see **Ch. 16**).

12.2 FORMATION

12.2a Regular verbs

The past tense of regular verbs is formed using the present tense stem (= infinitive minus -*en*; see **10.2a**) plus the past tense ending -*te*. This gives the **past tense stem**. In the plurals and the *du* and *Sie* forms, further personal endings are added to the past tense stem:

te	te-*n*	e.g. *sagen*	*ich* **sagte**[56]	*wir* **sagten**
te-*st*	te-*t*	(Past stem: *sagte*) *du* **sagtest**		*ihr* **sagtet**
te	te-*n*		*er/sie/es* **sagte**	*sie/Sie* **sagten**

---

[56] For ease of pronunciation, if the stem of the verb ends in -*d*, -*t* or a consonant + *n* or *m*, -*e*- is added before the past tense ending, e.g. *arbeiten* – *arbeit-e-te*.

This text uses the third person singular (*er/sie/es*-form), e.g. *entwickelte* (5), *titelte* (10), *erinnerte* (18), and the third person plural (*sie*-form), e.g. *rätselten* (13), *sonnten* (17).

12.2b Irregular verbs

Most commonly used verbs in German are irregular, which means that their past tense stem differs from that of regular verbs. Examples from the text are **war**, **waren** from *sein* (8, 14, 17, 19), **mussten** from *müssen* (11), **gab** from *geben* (15) and **wurde** from *werden* (13) which, here, forms a past passive construction (see **Ch. 18**).

The irregular past tense stems take the following endings:

--	*-en*	e.g. *war*	ich **war**		wir **waren**
-st	*-t*		du **warst**		ihr **wart**
--	*-en*		er/sie/es **war**		sie/Sie **waren**

Other points to note in the text

- Genitive plural ending: *voller Deutscher* (8–9) (see **5.1(iv)**).
- Pluperfect: *hatten sich... gefreut* (7–8), *hatten sich ... gesichert* (20–21) (see **Ch. 14**).
- *Konjunktiv II* as conditional: *könnte* 'could' (14) (see **16.2b**).
- Reflexive verbs: *entwickelte sich* (5), *hatten sich ... gefreut* (7–8), *sonnten sich* (17), *erinnerte sich* (18), *hatten sich ... gesichert* (20–21) (see **Ch. 20**)

Discover more about the past tense

12.3 IRREGULAR VERBS

12.3a Irregular past stems

Some of the most commonly used German verbs are irregular in the past tense, which means that their irregular stems have to be learned as exceptions to the general past tense rule. In addition to these, there are other verbs whose irregularities are more systematic in that the vowel change pattern used to mark the past tense is shared by certain other verbs. This second type of verb is often referred to as 'strong' and these are best learnt in groups according to their vowel changes.

Learn the past tense stems in bold print in **Table 12.1** and **Table 12.2**. These serve as the *ich-* and the *er/sie/es-* forms. For the other personal forms, add the endings given in **12.2b**, e.g. *du gingst, wir gingen*. **Table 12.1** contains frequently used irregular verbs (and strong verbs which do not follow a systematic pattern common to many other verbs). **Table 12.2** contains relatively systematic strong verbs. Note that the corresponding past participles are also listed here, as they usually (but not always) follow the same pattern as the past tense forms and are therefore best learnt together with the past tense. Note that a subset of strong verbs have a vowel change in their past form only, with the past participle following the form of the infinitive – see the last three groups in **Table 12.2**. (For a comprehensive alphabetical list of common irregular and strong verbs with their English translations, see **Appendix 1**.)

Table 12.1 Frequently occurring irregular verbs

bringen – **brachte** – gebracht	lüge – **log** – gelogen
denken – **dachte** – gedacht	mögen – **mochte** – gemocht
dürfen – **durfte** – gedurft	müssen – **musste** – gemusst
fangen – **fing** – gefangen	nennen – **nannte** – genannt
gehen – **ging** – gegangen	rennen – **rannte** – gerannt
haben – **hatte** – gehabt	rufen – **rief** – gerufen
hangen – **hing*** – gehangen	sein – **war** – gewesen
heißen – **hieß** – geheißen	sitzen – **saß** – gesessen
kennen – **kannte** – gekannt	stehen – **stand** – gestanden
kommen – **kam** – gekommen	tun – **tat** – getan
können – **konnte** – gekonnt	werden – **wurde** – geworden
laufen – **lief** – gelaufen	wissen – **wusste** – gewusst

* Only when intransitive: e.g. *Das Bild **hing** an der Wand*. When used transitively (i.e. with a direct object), *hängen* is regular: e.g. *Ich **hängte** das Bild an die Wand*.

Table 12.2 Frequently occurring strong verb patterns

ei – **ie** – ie	bleiben – **blieb** – geblieben	schreien – **schrie** – geschrie(e)n	
	leihen – **lieh** – geliehen	schweigen – **schwieg** – geschwiegen	
	reiben – **rieb** – gerieben	steigen – **stieg** – gestiegen	
	scheiden – **schied** – geschieden	treiben – **trieb** – getrieben	
	scheinen – **schien** – geschienen	vermeiden – **vermied** – vermieden	
	schreiben – **schrieb** – geschrieben	weisen – **wies** – gewiesen	
ei – **i** – i	beißen – **biss** – gebissen	schleichen – **schlich** – geschlichen	
	gleiten – **glitt** – geglitten	schmeißen – **schmiss** – geschmissen	
	leiden – **litt** – gelitten	schneiden – **schnitt** – geschnitten	
	reißen – **riss** – gerissen	schreiten – **schritt** – geschritten	
	reiten – **ritt** – geritten	streichen – **strich** – gestrichen	
	scheißen – **schiss** – geschissen	streiten – **stritt** – gestritten	
e – **a** – o	befehlen – **befahl** – befohlen	sprechen – **sprach** – gesprochen	
	brechen – **brach** – gebrochen	stehlen – **stahl** – gestohlen	
	erschrecken – **erschrak** – erschrocken	sterben – **starb** – gestorben	
	helfen – **half** – geholfen	treffen – **traf** – getroffen	
	nehmen – **nahm** – genommen	verderben – **verdarb** – verdorben	
		werfen – **warf** – geworfen	
i – **a** – u	binden – **band** – gebunden	sinken – **sank** – gesunken	
	dringen – **drang** – gedrungen	springen – **sprang** – gesprungen	
	finden – **fand** – gefunden	stinken – **stank** – gestunken	
	gelingen – **gelang** – gelungen	trinken – **trank** – getrunken	
	klingen – **klang** – geklungen	zwingen – **zwang** – gezwungen	
	singen – **sang** – gesungen		
i – **a** – o	beginnen – **begann** – begonnen	schwimmen – **schwamm** – geschwommen	
	gewinnen – **gewann** – gewonnen	spinnen – **spann** – gesponnen	

ie – o – o	biegen – **bog** – gebogen	riechen – **roch** – gerochen
	fliegen – **flog** – geflogen	schieben – **schob** – geschoben
	fliehen – **floh** – geflohen	schießen – **schoss** – geschossen
	fließen – **floss** – geflossen	schließen – **schloss** – geschlossen
	genießen – **genoss** – genossen	verlieren – **verlor** – verloren
	gießen – **goss** – gegossen	wiegen – **wog** – gewogen
	kriechen – **kroch** – gekrochen	ziehen – **zog** – gezogen
e – a – e	geben – **gab** – gegeben	essen – **aß** – gegessen
	lesen – **las** – gelesen	fressen – **fraß** – gefressen
	sehen – **sah** – gesehen	messen – **maß** – gemessen
	treten – **trat** – getreten	
a – ie – a	blasen – **blies** – geblasen	fallen – **fiel** – gefallen
	braten – **briet** – gebraten	halten – **hielt** – gehalten
	schlafen – **schlief** – geschlafen	lassen – **ließ** – gelassen
a – u – a	fahren – **fuhr** – gefahren	tragen – **trug** – getragen
	schlagen – **schlug** – geschlagen	wachsen – **wuchs** – gewachsen

12.3b Derived verbs

Verbs with prefixes (separable and inseparable) which are derived from irregular verbs follow the same past tense patterns as the original irregular verb. Some common examples are:

from **kommen**: *ankommen, bekommen, auskommen, mitkommen, umkommen*
from **fallen**: *auffallen, ausfallen, einfallen, gefallen, umfallen*
from **sprechen**: *aussprechen, besprechen, entsprechen, versprechen*
from **stehen**: *aufstehen, bestehen, entstehen, gestehen, verstehen*

12.3c Separable verbs

As is the case in the present tense, separable prefixes are sent to the end of the clause when the verb is in the past tense: e.g. *ankommen: Er **kam** heute morgen **an** 'He arrived this morning' (see **Ch. 19**). This applies to both regular and irregular verbs.

✎ EXERCISES

Vocabulary topic: *Urlaub*

1 The following sentences are in the present tense. Put them into the past:

   1 Andreas und Ute buchen ihren Urlaub.   **6** Ich kaufe mehr als 50 Ansichtskarten.

   2 Wir reservieren ein Hotelzimmer.   **7** Die Kinder spielen gern am Strand.

   3 Er übernachtet in einer billigen Pension.   **8** Der Urlaub dauert zwei Wochen.

   4 Du willst ein Zimmer mit Bad und Dusche.   **9** Wir wandern auf die Alm.

   5 Ihr amüsiert euch auf dem Campingplatz.   **10** Wir frühstücken auf dem Balkon.

2 Put the bracketed infinitives into the past, bearing in mind that many of these are irregular verbs. If the verbs are separable (see **Ch. 19**), show where the prefixes go:

   1 Er [haben] nicht viel Geld übrig.

2 Die Kinder [schwimmen] im Meer.

3 Meine Eltern [fliegen] nach Griechenland.

4 Wir [ankommen] um halb elf am Flughafen.

5 Wir [essen] lieber im Restaurant als im Hotel.

6 Die Jugendherberge [kosten] viel weniger als das Hotel.

7 Der Tourist [aufnehmen] alles mit der Videokamera.

8 Die Reiseleiter [sein] alle sehr freundlich.

9 Der Bus [abreisen] um 16 Uhr.

10 Wir [ansehen] uns die schönsten Städte.

✎ **FURTHER EXERCISES**

3 Complete the following crossword. All answers are in the past tense and are near synonyms of the clues:

Kreutzworträtsel

Senkrecht

1 sprach

2 entdeckten

3 guckte

4 soffen

Waagerecht

4 rügten

5 erwiderte

6 kamen zum Ende

4 Complete the following text by putting the bracketed infinitives into the appropriate form of the past tense. If there are separable prefixes, show where they go:

Das salomonische Urteil

Damals [kommen] zwei Dirnen und [treten] vor den König. Die eine [sagen]: Bitte, Herr, ich und diese Frau wohnen im gleichen Haus, und ich habe dort in ihrem Beisein geboren. Am dritten Tag nach meiner Niederkunft [gebären] auch diese Frau. Wir [sein] beisammen; kein Fremder [sein] bei uns im Haus, nur wir beide [sein] dort. Nun [sterben] der Sohn dieser Frau während der Nacht; denn sie hatte ihn im Schlaf erdrückt. Sie [aufstehen] mitten in der Nacht, [wegnehmen] mir mein Kind, während deine Magd [schlafen], und [legen] es an ihre Seite. Ihr totes Kind aber [legen] sie an meine Seite. Als ich am Morgen [aufstehen], um mein Kind zu stillen, [sein] es tot. Als ich es aber am Morgen genau [ansehen], [sein] das nicht mein Kind, das ich geboren hatte. Da [rufen] die andere Frau: Nein, mein Kind lebt, und dein Kind ist tot. Doch die erste [entgegnen]: Nein, dein Kind ist tot, und mein Kind lebt. So [streiten] sie vor dem König. Da [beginnen] der König: Diese sagt: Mein Kind lebt, und dein Kind ist tot! und jene sagt: Nein, dein Kind ist tot und mein Kind lebt. Und der König [fortfahren]: Holt mir ein

Schwert! Man [bringen] es vor den König. Nun [entscheiden] er: Schneidet das lebende Kind entzwei, und gebt eine Hälfte der einen und eine Hälfte der anderen! Doch nun [bitten] die Mutter des lebenden Kindes den König – es [regen] sich nämlich in ihr die mütterliche Liebe zu ihrem Kind: Bitte, Herr, gebt ihr das lebende Kind, und tötet es nicht! Doch die andere [rufen]: Es soll weder mir noch dir gehören. Zerteilt es! Da [befehlen] der König: Gebt jener das lebende Kind, und tötet es nicht; denn sie ist seine Mutter. Ganz Israel [hören] von dem Urteil, das der König gefällt hatte, und sie [aufschauen] mit Ehrfurcht zu ihm; denn sie [erkennen], dass die Weisheit Gottes in ihm [sein], wenn er Recht [sprechen].

Aus der Bibel: *1 Könige 3*, 16 –28. Einheitsübersetzung der Heiligen Schrift. © Katholische Bibelanstalt, Stuttgart, 1980.

5 Write a paragraph describing what you did yesterday, using the past.

For further exercises on the past tense see Revision Text 3, Ex. 2.

13 | Perfect tense

Kommissar Kress: **Hat** er Sie eigentlich noch **angerufen** gestern Nacht – der Florian Balsam?

Weigelt: Nein, warum sollte er?

Kress: **Sind** Sie, nachdem Sie mit Ihrer Frau gestern Nacht nach Hause
5   **gekommen sind**, nochmal **weggefahren**?

Weigelt: Ist Ihnen diese Art der Routine nicht langweilig, Herr Kress?

Kress: **Sind** Sie nochmal **weggefahren**?

Weigelt: Nein, **bin** ich nicht.

Kress: **Habe** ich Ihnen schon **gesagt**, dass wir die hunderttausend bei
10   Balsams Eltern **gefunden haben**? Das Geld von Richard Lotke aus dem Einbruch.

Weigelt : Nein, das **haben** Sie mir nicht **gesagt**.

Kress: Und was fangen Sie jetzt an … mit der Unschuld von Florian Balsam? Sie wussten, dass er schuldig ist. Seit wann wissen Sie es, Herr Weigelt?

15 Weigelt: Jetzt ist es ein Verhör, nicht wahr?

Kress: Ja, das ist es.

Weigelt: Dann **sind** Sie taktisch sehr schlecht **vorgegangen**, Herr Kress.

Kress: Was **ist** gestern Nacht **passiert**, Herr Weigelt?

Weigelt: Ihre Fragen werden dadurch nicht besser, dass Sie sie wiederholen.

20 Kress: Was **ist** gestern Abend, als Sie den Freispruch **gefeiert haben** – Sie, ihre Frau, Florian Balsam und Hubert Schatz – was **ist** da **vorgefallen**?

Weigelt: Nichts. Absolut nichts.

Kress: Herr Weigelt, **hat** Florian Balsam Sie in der Nacht noch **angerufen**?

Weigelt: Nein. Ich sagte Ihnen das bereits.

25 Kress: Ich frage Sie noch mal. **Sind** Sie noch **weggefahren** in der Nacht?

Weigelt: Nein.

Kress: Herr Weigelt, **sind** Sie von Florian Balsam in der Nacht noch **angerufen worden**?

Weigelt: Nein.

30 Kress: Sie lügen. Und ich kann Ihnen das beweisen.

Weigelt: Der Telefoncomputer im Hoten Einberger, nicht wahr?

Frau Weigelt: (*kommt herein*): Guten Abend.

Kress: Guten abend, Frau Weigelt. Stimmt das, dass Ihr Mann gestern Nacht nochmal **weggefahren ist**?

35 Frau Weigelt: Ja.

Aus: *Der Alte* [Deutscher TV-Krimi]. © 1988 Volker Vogeler (Drehbuch). Folge: *Der Freispruch*.

> *der Einbruch* – burglary
> *die Unschuld* – innocence
> *das Verhör* – interrogation
> *vorgehen* – to act, proceed
>
> *der Freispruch* – acquittal
> *vorfallen* – to happen
> *bereits* – already
> *beweisen* – to prove

⌕ The perfect tense in the text

13.1 USAGE

The perfect tense in German is usually used to refer to events in the past. Some of these may have relevance to the present, e.g. *Schau! Ich **habe** diesen Wein **gekauft*** 'look, I've bought this wine' (and it's still here to be drunk), others may be completed actions in the past which would be expressed using the past tense rather than the perfect in English, e.g. *Was **ist** gestern Nacht passiert?* (line 18) 'what <u>happened</u> last night?', NOT *'what <u>has happened</u> last night?' This means that events in the past can be expressed in German either by using the past tense (see **Ch. 12**) or the perfect. The main difference in usage is that **the perfect is mainly used in spoken German** (and forms of writing which imitate speech: e.g. dialogues, hence the extensive use of the perfect in the chosen text) while the past is usually used in written narratives (see the news report in the previous chapter).[57]

> [57] The preference of the perfect over the past is most striking in southern Germany, Austria and Switzerland, where the past is rarely used in speech (apart from with very common verbs (see Further notes: i), and even these often appear in the perfect). In northern and central Germany the past can be used in speech, yet it is much less frequent than the perfect. One example of the past being used in northern/central speech is in the narration of a series of events, e.g. *Ich **stand** auf, **ging** in die Küche und **machte** mir einen Kaffee* 'I **got** up, **went** into the kitchen and **made** myself a coffee' (although the perfect would not be incorrect here either).

Further notes:

i)   Very common verbs such as *haben, sein, sagen, wissen* and the modal verbs *dürfen, können, mögen, müssen, sollen, wollen*[58] often appear in the **past** rather than the perfect, even in the spoken language: *Nein, warum **sollte** er?* 'No, why **should** he?' (3), *Sie **wussten**, dass er schuldig ist* 'You **knew** he was guilty' (24), *Ich **sagte** Ihnen das bereits* 'I already **told** you that' (24).

ii) In expressions with *seit/seitdem* 'for, since' German uses a **present** tense where English would use a perfect: *Seit wann **wissen** Sie es, Herr Weigelt?* 'since when **have** you **known**, Herr Weigelt?' (14) (see **10.3(ii)**).

> [58] When modal verbs (and *lassen* 'to let') occur in the perfect tense with another verb, two infinitives are used instead of a past participle: e.g. *Ich bin weggefahren* 'I left', vs. *Ich habe wegfahren **wollen*** 'I wanted to leave', *Ich habe es ihn **machen** lassen* 'I let him do it'. *Haben* is used with all modals, irrespective of the verb with which they co-occur (see **21.4b**).

13.2 FORMATION

13.2a Parts of verbs used

The perfect tense is formed using the present tense of the auxiliary verb **haben** or **sein** plus the **past participle** of the main verb:[59]

ich **habe gesagt** (9)	ich **bin gekommen**
du **hast gesagt**	du **bist gekommen**
er/sie/es **hat gesagt**	er/sie/es **ist gekommen**
wir **haben gesagt**	wir **sind gekommen**
ihr **habt gesagt**	ihr **seid gekommen**
sie/Sie **haben gesagt** (12)	sie/Sie **sind gekommen** (5)

From the text we see that the past participle usually appears at the end of the clause: *weggefahren* (7), *gesagt* (9, 12), *vorgegangen* (17), *passiert* (18), *vorgefallen* (21), *angerufen* (23), *worden* (28), unless the auxiliary verb has been sent to the end because of a subordinating conjunction or relative pronoun: *gekommen* **sind** (5), *gefunden* **haben** (10), *gefeiert* **haben** (20), *weggefahren* **ist** (34), or some other element has been moved to the end for special emphasis: e.g. *gestern Nacht* (1) (see 'Other points to note in the text').[60]

---

[59] For the future perfect: e.g. *Er* **wird** *es* **gesagt haben**, and the conditional perfect: *Er* **hätte** *es* **gesagt**, see **15.4** and **16.3** respectively.

[60] Further occurrences of *haben/sein* following the past participle can be found in the future perfect: e.g. *Er* **wird** *es gemacht* <u>haben</u> (see **15.4**) and with modals: e.g. *Er* **muss** *es gemacht* <u>haben</u> (see **21.5a**).

13.2b Formation of regular past participles

Regular past participles are formed by adding *ge-* and *-t*[61] to the present tense stem (the infinitive minus *-en*; see **10.2a**): e.g. *sagen* → **ge**-*sag*-**t** (9, 12), *feiern* → **ge**-*feiert* (20). If the stem is not stressed on the first syllable (i.e. if it begins with an inseparable prefix, e.g. *be-, ent- er-, ge-, ver-*, or ends in *-ier*), *ge-* is dropped: e.g. *passieren* → *passiert* (18), NOT *gepassiert.

---

[61] or *-et* after *t, d* or a consonant + *n* or *m*: e.g. *landen* – **gelandet**, *öffnen* – **geöffnet**.

13.2c Irregular past participles

As is the case in the past tense, most commonly used verbs have irregular past participles,[62] hence their relatively high rate of occurrence in the text. Most irregular past participles end in *-en* and many have a vowel change in the stem: *gekommen* (5), *gefunden* (10) from *finden*. The past participle of *werden* is *geworden*, yet it appears in this text as *worden* (28) as it is used in a passive construction (see **18.7**). Irregular participles are best learnt together with their corresponding past tense forms, as they are often (but not always) very similar. See **12.3a** for the past participles of common irregular and strong verbs.

---

[62] Note, however, that *haben* has a regular participle: *gehabt*.

13.2d Past participles of separable verbs

Separable prefixes **precede** ge- in past participles. Many of the irregular participles in this text are from separable verbs: _weggefahren_ (5, 7, 25, 34), _angerufen_ (1, 23, 28), _vorgegangen_ (17), _vorgefallen_ (21) (see **Ch. 19**).

13.2e Choice of auxiliary: _haben_ or _sein_?

Most verbs take _haben_ in the perfect tense, which means that those which take _sein_ must be learned as exceptions, although the group is quite large. Verbs taking _sein_ are **intransitive** (i.e. they do not occur with an accusative object), and the factors that determine which intransitive verbs take _sein_ are set out in **13.3** below. In the text we have three common intransitive verbs taking _sein_: **kommen** (5), **passieren** (18), **werden** (28) and three verbs which are derived from common intransitives taking _sein_: **wegfahren** (5, 7, 25, 34) from _fahren_, **vorgehen** (17) from _gehen_, **vorfallen** (21) from _fallen_.

> ### Other points to note in the text
>
> - Present tense used i) after _seit_: _Seit wann **wissen** Sie es?_ 'Since when have you known this' (14); ii) after a past tense: _Sie wussten, dass er schuldig ist_ 'They knew that he was guilty' (14) (see **10.3(ii), 10.3(iii)**).
> - Questions with i) Subject-verb inversion: _**hat** er_ (1), _**ist** ihnen diese Art_ (6), _**sind** Sie_ (4, 7, 25, 28), _**habe** ich_ (9), _**hat** Florian Balsam_ (23), _**stimmt** das_ (33); ii) interrogatives: _warum_ (3), _was_ (13, 18, 20, 21), _seit wann_ (14) (see **Ch. 23**).
> - Omission of the demonstrative pronoun _das_: _Nein, bin ich nicht_ (instead of _Nein, **das** bin ich nicht_) 'No I did not (do that)', (8), which is a feature of spoken German.
> - Expressions of time placed at the end of the clause (after the past participle) for emphasis: _gestern Nacht_ (1), _in der Nacht_ (25) (see **26.7**). This emphasis can be understood within the context: i.e. something happened on the previous night (a murder).

Discover more about the perfect tense

13.3 VERBS TAKING _SEIN_

13.3a Verbs which always take _sein_

All verbs taking _sein_ in the perfect tense are **intransitive**, i.e. do not occur with a direct (accusative) object, and can roughly be divided into two main categories. The first category consists of verbs denoting **movement from A to B**: e.g. _Er **ist** nach Hause **gegangen**_ 'He has gone/ walked home'. Other examples are: _ist **gefahren**_ 'has gone, driven', _ist **geflogen**_ 'has flown', _ist **gerannt**_ 'has run', _ist **gelaufen**_ 'has run', _ist **geklettert**_ 'has climbed', _ist **gekrabbelt**_ 'has crawled', _ist **gefallen**_ 'has fallen', _ist **gestürzt**_ 'has fallen, plunged', _ist **gerast**_ 'has raced', _ist **gekommen**_ 'has come', _ist **gefolgt**_ 'has followed'.

The second category consists of verbs denoting a **change of state**: e.g. _Er **ist** alt **geworden**_ 'He has become old'. Other examples are: _ist **geboren**_ 'has been born', _ist **gestorben**_ 'has died', _ist **gewachsen**_ 'has grown', _ist **geschrumpft**_ 'has shrunk', _ist **verwelkt**_ 'has wilted', _ist **gebrochen**_ 'has been broken', _ist **aufgewacht**_ 'has woken up', _ist **eingeschlafen**_ 'has fallen asleep', _ist **aufgestanden**_ 'has got up', _ist **erschienen**_ 'has appeared', _ist **verschwunden**_ 'has disappeared'.

In addition there are some common verbs taking *sein* which are difficult to classify, among them the verb *sein* itself:[63] e.g. *ist gewesen* 'has been', *ist geblieben* 'has stayed', *ist passiert/geschehen* 'has happened', *ist gelungen* 'has succeeded'.

> [63] In southern varieties of German (including Swiss and Austrian), verbs denoting position occur with *sein*: e.g. *Er ist gestanden/gesessen/gelegen* 'He has been standing/sitting/lying'.

13.3b Verbs that take *sein* or *haben* depending on the following object

If a verb which would usually take *sein* is used **transitively** (i.e. with a direct object in the accusative), *haben* will be used in the perfect, as this is the case with all transitive verbs. Similarly, **reflexive** verbs always take *haben*. Consider the following examples with the accusative objects underlined:

*Er **ist** nach Frankreich gefahren*	He went/drove/travelled to France
*Er **hat** den neuen Wagen gefahren*	He drove the new car
*Er **ist** vom Dach gestürzt*	He fell/plunged from the roof
*Er **hat** sich in die Arbeit gestürzt*	He threw/plunged himself into his work

13.3c Derived verbs

Intransitive verbs derived (usually by the addition of prefixes) from verbs taking *sein* usually take *sein* themselves:[64]

e.g. *ist gekommen:*   *ist angekommen, ist vorgekommen, ist entkommen, ist verkommen*
        ist gefallen: *ist aufgefallen, ist eingefallen, ist verfallen, ist zerfallen*

> [64] A verb taking *haben* may occasionally have a corresponding prefixed form which expresses movement or a change of state. In this case, the prefixed verb takes *sein*: e.g. *Er hat vor dem Haus **gestanden*** 'he stood in front of the house' vs. *Er **ist** früh **aufgestanden*** 'He got up early'.

✎ EXERCISES

Vocabulary topic: *Reisen und Verkehrsmittel*

1 The following sentences are in the present tense. Put them into the perfect:

1	Wir warten auf den Bus.	**5**	Wir verkaufen unser altes Motorrad.
2	Der Zug hat Verspätung.	**6**	Sie treffen sich am Bahnhof.
3	Ich brauche eine Rückfahrkarte.	**7**	Wir sitzen im Nichtrauchercoupé.
4	Kauft ihr ein neues Auto?	**8**	Siehst du die Straßenbahn?

2 Fill in the gaps with the appropriate forms of *haben* or *sein*:

1 Wir __ um 8 Uhr am Flughafen angekommen.

2 Ich __ zu schnell gefahren.

3 Der Taxifahrer __ plötzlich gebremst.

4 Der Bus __ noch nicht da gewesen.

5 Ich __ bei der Bushaltestelle gestanden.

6 __ du dein Fahrrad verloren?

7 Ich __ heute mein neues Auto gefahren.

8 Das Flugzeug __ schon abgeflogen.

9 Sein Bruder __ eine Harley-Davidson gefahren.

10 Meine Eltern __ gestern mit dem Boot abgereist.

11 Das Kind __ seinen Opa in seinem alten Wohnwagen besucht.

12 Wie __ du dorthin gekommen? Ich __ zu Fuß gegangen.

✎ FURTHER EXERCISES

3 Put the following past tense forms into the perfect:

1 Der Junge **lief** nach Hause.

2 Die Teekanne **fiel** zum Boden und **brach**.

3 Du **brachst** das Weinglas.

4 Die Kinder **blieben** in ihrem Zimmer und **spielten**.

5 Wir **flogen** mit KLM nach Amsterdam.

6 Er **flog** heute zum ersten Mal sein Modellflugzeug, aber leider **stürzte** es **ab**.

7 Der Schüler **schlug** einen Mitschüler ins Gesicht.

8 Der Lehrer **kam** ins Zimmer **herein**.

9 Ich **legte** mich aufs Bett **hin**.

10 Der Dieb **brach** in das Haus **ein**.

4 The following text is an extract from a novel. Decide whether the past tense or the perfect would be most appropriate to use with each of the bracketed verbs, bearing in mind that some of the text is narrative and some is dialogue. Where you decide to use the perfect, take care where to place the past participle:

«Du kennst doch die Geschichte, die vor vier Jahren im Institute [stattfinden]?»

«Welche Geschichte?»

«Nun, die gewisse!»

«Nur beiläufig. Ich weiß bloß, dass es damals wegen irgendwelcher Schweinereien einen großen Skandal [geben] und dass eine ganze Anzahl deswegen strafweise entlassen werden [müssen].»

«Ja, das meine ich. Ich [erfahren] Näheres darüber einmal auf Urlaub von einem aus jener Klasse. Sie [haben] einen hübschen Burschen unter sich, in den viele von ihnen verliebt [sein]. Das kennst du ja, denn das kommt alle Jahre vor. Die aber [treiben] damals die Sache zu weit.»

«Wieso?»

«Nun, … wie…?! Frag doch nicht so dumm! Und dasselbe tut Reiting mit Basini!»

Törleß [verstehen], worum es sich zwischen den beiden [handeln], und er [fühlen] in seiner Kehle ein Würgen, als ob Sand darinnen wäre.

«Das hätte ich nicht von Reiting gedacht.» Er [wissen] nichts Besseres zu sagen. Beineberg [zucken] die Achseln.

«Er glaubt, uns betrügen zu können.»

«Ist er verliebt?»

«Gar keine Spur. So ein Narr ist er nicht. Es unterhält ihn, höchstens reizt es ihn sinnlich.»

«Und Basini?»

«Der…? [Auffallen] dir nicht, wie frech er in der letzten Zeit [werden]? Von mir [lassen] er kaum mehr etwas sagen. Immer [heißen] es nur Reiting und wieder Reiting, – als ob der sein persönlicher Schutzheiliger wäre. Es ist besser, [denken] er sich wahrscheinlich, von dem einen sich alles gefallen zu lassen als von jedem etwas. Und Reiting wird ihm [versprechen], ihn zu schützen, wenn er ihm in allem zu Willen ist. Aber sie sollen sich [irren], und ich werde es Basini noch austreiben!»

«Wie [kommen] du darauf?»

«Ich [nachgehen] ihnen einmal.»

Aus: Robert Musil, *Die Verwirrungen des Zöglings Törleß.* © Rowohlt Verlag, 1978.

14 | Pluperfect tense

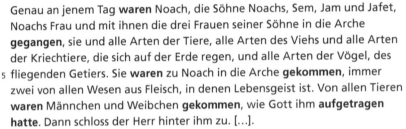

Genau an jenem Tag **waren** Noach, die Söhne Noachs, Sem, Jam und Jafet, Noachs Frau und mit ihnen die drei Frauen seiner Söhne in die Arche **gegangen**, sie und alle Arten der Tiere, alle Arten des Viehs und alle Arten der Kriechtiere, die sich auf der Erde regen, und alle Arten der Vögel, des
5 fliegenden Getiers. Sie **waren** zu Noach in die Arche **gekommen**, immer zwei von allen Wesen aus Fleisch, in denen Lebensgeist ist. Von allen Tieren **waren** Männchen und Weibchen **gekommen**, wie Gott ihm **aufgetragen hatte**. Dann schloss der Herr hinter ihm zu. [...].
   Die Flut auf der Erde dauerte vierzig Tage. Das Wasser stieg und hob
10 die Arche immer höher über die Erde. Das Wasser schwoll an und stieg immer mehr auf der Erde, die Arche aber trieb auf dem Wasser dahin. Das Wasser **war** auf der Erde gewaltig **angeschwollen** und bedeckte alle hohen Berge, die es unter dem ganzen Himmel gibt. Das Wasser **war** fünfzehn Ellen über die Berge hinaus **angeschwollen** und **hatte** sie **zugedeckt**. Da
15 verendeten alle Wesen aus Fleisch, die sich auf der Erde **geregt hatten**, Vögel, Vieh und sonstige Tiere, alles, wovon die Erde **gewimmelt hatte**, und auch alle Menschen. Alles, was auf der Erde durch die Nase Lebensgeist atmete, kam um. Gott vertilgte also alle Wesen auf dem Erdboden, Menschen, Vieh, Kriechtiere und die Vögel des Himmels; sie alle wurden
20 vom Erdboden vertilgt. Übrig blieb nur Noach und was mit ihm in der Arche war. Das Wasser aber schwoll hundertfünfzig Tage lang auf der Erde an.

Aus der Bibel: *Genesis 7, 13–24*. Einheitsübersetzung der Heiligen Schrift, ©, Katholische Bibelanstalt, Stuttgart 1980.

die Arche – ark	*das Wesen* – the being	*treiben* – to float
das Vieh – livestock	*der Lebensgeist* – spirit of life	*die Elle* – cubit
das Kriechtier – reptile	*Männchen/Weibchen* – male/female	*umkommen* – to die
sich regen – to move	*auftragen* (+ dat.) – to command	*wimmeln* – to teem
das Getier – creatures	*anschwellen* – to swell	*vertilgen* – to destroy

⌕ **The pluperfect in the text**

14.1 USAGE

The pluperfect in German is used much in the same way as the pluperfect in English: i.e. to indicate that a particular event is one step further into the past than the past events related to it, i.e. it **had** (already) happened: e.g. *Der Mann, der mich **eingeladen hatte**, begrüßte mich sehr herzlich* 'the man who **had invited** me greeted me heartily'. The chosen text from the Bible contains a mixture of verbs in the past tense, which is commonly used in written narratives, and in the pluperfect, the latter of which indicates that these events occurred prior to those denoted by the past: e.g. *Von allen Tieren **waren** Männchen und Weibchen **gekommen**, wie Gott ihm **aufgetragen hatte**. Dann <u>schloss</u> der Herr hinter ihm zu.* 'And male and female of all flesh **had gone** in, as God **had commanded** him: and the Lord <u>shut</u> him in' (6–8).[65]

> [65] In English, the pluperfect progressive (e.g. 'I **had been** doing my homework when he arrived') is often used to refer to an action in the past which had not been completed (contrast the completed action in the ordinary pluperfect 'I **had done** my homework'). As German does not have progressive forms and the German pluperfect is only used to refer to completed actions in the past, English progressive pluperfects cannot be translated by the pluperfect in German. Instead, the **past** is used: e.g. 'I **had been cooking** when he arrived' → *Ich **kochte** (gerade) als er ankam* (see footnote in **10.1**). Similarly: 'I **had been living** there for five years → *Ich **wohnte** dort seit fünf Jahren*.

14.2 FORMATION

The pluperfect tense is formed using the **past tense** of the auxiliary verb *haben* or *sein*[66] plus the **past participle** of the main verb. (Details on the formation of past participles are dealt with in **13.2b–d**):

*ich **hatte gesagt***	*ich **war gekommen***
*du **hattest gesagt***	*du **warst gekommen***
*er/sie/es **hatte gesagt***	*er/sie/es **war gekommen***
*wir **hatten gesagt***	*wir **waren gekommen***
*ihr **hattet gesagt***	*ihr **wart gekommen***
*sie/Sie **hatten gesagt***	*sie/Sie **waren gekommen*** (5, 7)

From the text we see that the past participle usually appears at the end of the clause, as it does in the perfect: *waren ... gegangen* (1–3), *waren ... gekommen* (5, 7), *war ... angeschwollen* (12, 13–14), *hatte ... zugedeckt* (14), unless the auxiliary verb appears at the end because of a subordinating conjunction or relative pronoun: *aufgetragen hatte* (7–8), *geregt hatten* (15), *gewimmelt hatte* (16).

> [66] Verbs that take *sein* in the perfect also do so in the pluperfect: e.g. **waren** ... *gegangen* (1–3), **waren** ... *gekommen* (5, 7), **war** ... *angeschwollen* (12, 13–14). These are dealt with in **13.3**.

Other points to note in the text

- Genitives: *Noachs* (1), *seiner Söhne* (2), *alle Arten **der** Tiere ... **des** Viehs* (3), *... **der** Kriechtiere* (4), *alle Arten **der** Vögel ... **des** fliegenden Getiers* (4–5) (see **3.1a(iv)**).
- Relative pronouns: ***die** ... regen* (4), *in **denen** ... ist* (6), ***die** es ... gibt* (13), ***die** ... geregt hatten* (15), ***wovon** ... gewimmelt hatte* (16), ***was** ... atmete* (17–18) (see **Ch. 9**).
- Present tense used after past and pluperfect: *regen* (4), *ist* (6), *gibt* (13) (see **10.3(iii)**).
- Past passive: ***wurden...vertilgt*** (19–20) (see **Ch. 18**).

✎ EXERCISES

Vocabulary topic: *Wetter und Natur*

1 Put the bracketed verbs into the pluperfect, paying attention to the position of the past participle:

   1 Der Rasen stand unter Wasser, da es vier Tage lang [regnen].

   2 Am vorigen Tag [schneien] es und die Felder waren alle weiß.

   3 Die Sonne [untergehen] und es wurde kühler.

   4 Es [geben] einen Sturm und zwei Bäume [umfallen] und blockierten die Straße.

   5 Es [sein] in letzter Zeit am Meer sehr windig, deshalb wollte ich dort nicht Fahrrad fahren.

   6 Man sah an den Beulen auf dem Autodach, dass es in der Nacht sehr stark [hageln].

2 Put the sentences in Chapter 13, Exercises 2 and 3 into the pluperfect.

3 Translate the following sentences into German, paying particular attention to whether the pluperfect or the past tense is needed:

   1 I had driven home in the fog.

   2 I had been driving home from work when the thunderstorm started.

   3 It had been quite warm and the ice had melted.

   4 I had been sunbathing in the garden when the telephone rang.

   5 It had been cloudy all day.

15 | Future tense

<u>Die Unterscheidung zwischen TV und Internet ist obsolet</u>

Die heutigen Zahlen ermöglichen einen Blick in die Zukunft. Während bei den dinosaurierhaften „Über 50jährigen" das Verhältnis von Fernsehnutzung (300 Minuten) zu Internetnutzung (34 Minuten) bei 10:1 liegt, ist das Verhältnis bei
5 den 14–29jährigen ausgeglichen (147 Minuten zu 146 Minuten). Neben TV und PC konkurrieren Smartphones, Tabletts und Spielkonsolen um die Gunst der User. So erodiert die Fernsehnutzung – wenigstens, wenn man es mit den heutigen Maßstäben misst. Aber sind die wirklich noch zeitgemäß? Diese Messungen fokussieren sich sehr stark auf die Endgeräte. Aber: Wenn ich mir
10 einen Film im Netz ansehe, gucke ich dann fern oder gucke ich dann Internet? Eigentlich ist es irrelevant, wo ich den Content konsumiere, was wichtig ist, ist der Content selbst und seine medienadäquate Umsetzung.

Konvergenz lautet das Buzzword. Analysten rechnen damit, dass bis 2015 weltweit 500 Millionen Fernseher onlinefähig **sein werden**. Das **werden** 47
15 Prozent aller ausgelieferten TV Geräte **sein**. Die rituelle Trennung zwischen TV und Internet wird also zunehmend obsolet. Ob wir bewegte Bilder terrestrisch, über Kabel oder übers Netz empfangen, ist in der postdigitalen Gesellschaft egal […]. **Kommen werden** die Bilder wohl tatsächlich weitgehend übers Netz. Laut einer IHS Screen Digest Untersuchung **wird** in den Big 5 EU-Staaten bis
20 zum Jahre 2015 die Gesamtnutzungsdauer von Onlinevideos von 10 Milliarden Stunden auf mehr als 20 Milliarden Stunden **steigen**. Oder anders ausgedrückt, 90 Prozent des Internet-Traffics **wird** Video-Content **sein**.

Smart TVs **werden** dabei eher das Lean-Back-Bedürfnis der Zuschauer **bedienen**. Momentan gehen die Geräte noch genau an diesem Bedürfnis
25 vorbei. Sie versuchen Social Media, Internet, VoD und lineares TV unter einen Hut zu bringen – aber ganz ehrlich: Will man über einen Riesen-Fernseher surfen oder twittern? Nein, wir **werden** das TV-Gerät auch in Zukunft für das **nutzen**, für was wir es lieben: zum gucken. Den Rest erledigen wir über eine Second Screen.

das Verhältnis – relation(ship)	*onlinefähig* – can be used online
ausgeglichen – evened out	*die Gesamtnutzung* – total usage
die Gunst – favour	*die Dauer* – length of time
der Maßstab – measurement	*das Bedürfnis* – need
zeitgemäß – up-to-date	*bedienen* – to serve
das Endgerät – equipment used	*der Zuschauer* – viewer
medienadäquate Umseztung – implementation	*unter einen Hut* – all together, reconciled
using the most appropriate media	*erledigen* – to deal with it

The future tense in the text

15.1 USAGE

The future tense is primarily used to refer to future time, particularly when making promises or predictions, hence the abundant use of future forms in the chosen text, which is predicting how our TV viewing will change over the coming years: e.g. *dass bis 2015 weltweit 500 Millionen Fernseher onlinefähig **sein werden*** Cthat by 2015, 500 million TVs will have an online function' (13–14), *Das **werden** 47 Prozent aller ... Geräte **sein**,* 'That will be 47 percent of all ... sets' (14–15), ***Kommen werden** die Bilder wohl tatsächlich weitgehend übers Netz* 'Certainly the pictures will come to us extensively through the net' (18), *90 Prozent des Internet-Traffics **wird** Video-Content **sein*** '90 percent of internet traffic will be video content' (22), *Nein, wir **werden** das TV-Gerät ... **nutzen*** 'No, we will use the TV set' (27–28).

15.2 FORMATION

The future tense is formed using the present tense of the auxiliary verb ***werden*** plus the **infinitive** of the main verb:

*ich **werde fernsehen***	*wir **werden fernsehen***
*du **wirst fernsehen***	*ihr **werdet fernsehen***
*er/sie/es **wird fernsehen***	*sie/Sie **werden fernsehen***

From the text we see that the infinitive goes to the end of the clause: *sein* (15, 22), *steigen* (21), *bedienen* (24), *nutzen* (28), unless the auxiliary verb has been sent to the end: *sein **werden*** (14) or the verbs have been fronted for stylistic reasons: *Kommen **werden*** (18). If the future occurs with a modal verb plus an infinitive, the two infinitives go to the end: e.g. *Ich werde online **fernsehen** müssen* 'I will have to watch TV online' (not in text).

Other points to note in the text

- Genitives: *47 Prozent **aller** ausgelieferten TV Geräte* '47 percent **of** all TVs delivered' (14–15), *90 Prozent **des** Internet-Traffics* '90 percent **of** the internet traffic' (22), *das Lean-Back-Bedürfnis **der** Zuschauer* 'the viewers' need to lean back' (23) (see **Ch. 3**).

- Da + preposition before following clause: *Analysten rechnen damit, dass ...*'Analysts reckon that ...' (13) (see **24.6b**).
- Demonstratives: *diese* (8), *diesem* (24), *die* (8), *das* (27) (see **Ch. 8**).
- Subordinating conjunctions: *während* (2), *wenn* (7, 9), *dass* (13), *ob* (16) (see **25.1**).
- Interrogatives used as subordinating conjunctions: *wo* (11), *was* (11) (see **25.2**).

Discover more about the future tense

15.3 USAGE

15.3a Expressing probability

As in English, the future tense in German is often used to express a supposition or probability which is not necessarily associated with future time: e.g. *Er ist nicht zu Hause – er **wird** noch in der Arbeit **sein*** 'He's not at home – he**'ll** still **be** at work'. Here it is clear from the context that we are dealing with the present, not the future (i.e. he **is** probably still at work).

15.3b Use of present to express future

German uses the future tense much less often than English to refer to future time, unless the speaker/writer is making a promise or prediction (see text). Wherever possible, the present is used instead: e.g. *Ich **komme** morgen um vier Uhr* 'I'll come/I'm coming tomorrow at four', although the future would not be grammatically incorrect here. There is also an example of present tense usage in our text: *Den Rest **erledigen** wir über eine Second Screen* 'We'll deal with the rest via a second screen' (28–29). Only if the use of the present would create ambiguity (i.e. if it was not clear from the context whether present or future time was meant) would it be replaced by the future.

15.4 FUTURE PERFECT

To refer to completed actions in the future, German has a future perfect tense similar to that of English: e.g. *Ich **werde** es bis nächste Woche **gelesen haben*** 'I **will have read** it by next week'. The future perfect is formed using the present tense of the auxiliary verb *werden* plus the perfect tense of the main verb. For example, below are the German equivalents of 'will have worked' and 'will have gone':

*ich werde **gearbeitet haben***	*ich werde **gegangen sein***
*du wirst **gearbeitet haben***	*du wirst **gegangen sein***
*er/sie/es wird **gearbeitet haben***	*er/sie/es wird **gegangen sein***
*wir werden **gearbeitet haben***	*wir werden **gegangen sein***
*ihr werdet **gearbeitet haben***	*ihr werdet **gegangen sein***
*sie/Sie werden **gearbeitet haben***	*wir werden **gegangen sein***

As with the simple future tense, the future perfect may also be used to express an assumption: e.g. *Er **wird** sie gestern **angerufen haben*** 'He will have phoned her yesterday'.

✎ EXERCISES

Vocabulary topic: *Politik*

1 Put the following present tense forms into the future:

   1 Welche Partei **ist** nächstes Jahr an der Macht?

   2 Es **gibt** wahrscheinlich eine Koalition.

   3 Welchen Kandidaten **wählst** du?

   4 Die nächste Wahl **findet** im Juni dieses Jahres **statt**.

   5 Alle Parteien **unterstützen** das Verhältniswahlrecht.

   6 In welchem Wahlkreis **seid** ihr nächstes Jahr?

   7 Ich **schreibe** dem Innenminister.

   8 Er **wird** wahrscheinlich Außenminister.

   9 Der Abgeordnete **vertritt** seine Wähler.

  10 Die Politiker, die an die Macht **kommen**, sind die, die dem Publikum **zuhören**.

2 Put the following verbs into the future perfect:

   1 Die Regierung **reduziert** ihre Ausgaben.

   2 Die Linken **investieren** mehr in das Schulwesen.

   3 Der Bundeskanzler **tritt zurück**.

   4 Die Rechten **lösen sich auf**.

   5 Er **ist** Mitglied des Europaparlaments.

✎ FURTHER EXERCISES

3 The present tense is commonly used to refer to future time. Determine which of the bracketed verbs can be put into the present (referring to the future) and which need to be in the future tense. Explain the reasons for your choice:

   1 Wir [treffen] uns morgen um drei Uhr.

   2 Wann [fahren] ihr nach Spanien?

   3 Wir wollen heute Nachmittag im Wald spazierengehen. Ich glaube, es [sein] schön.

   4 Schau! Es kommen graue Wolken. Es [regnen].

   5 Der Zug [ankommen] um 18 Uhr.

   6 Morgen [schneien] es.

   7 Was [machen] du morgen Abend?

   8 Was [machen] er?

4 The future tense is often used to express a supposition. Change the following sentences into suppositions by putting them into the future (or future perfect where appropriate) and adding *wahrscheinlich* after the finite verb (or, where there is one, the accusative object):

  Example: Johannes **ist** zu Hause

  Answer: Johannes **wird wahrscheinlich** zu Hause **sein**.

1 Klaus **arbeitet** noch.
2 Ruf ihn nicht zu früh an. Er **schläft** noch.
3 Peter **hat** es schon **gemacht**.
4 Die Nachbarn **sind** schon **abgereist**.
5 Er **hat** es seiner Frau **erzählt**.

16 | Conditional

Was würden Sie tun, wenn Sie viel Geld gewinnen?

hrotto: Dann **würde** ich **warten** bis ich wieder aufwache, gggggg

fernweh: Ich **würde** es wahrscheinlich wie hrotto **machen**. [...]. Also ich glaube als Normalverdiener **hätte** man schon einige Ideen, was man mit viel Geld
5 **machen würde**. Ich fürchte aber, dass man sich über diese Anschaffungen gar nicht so **freuen würde** wie man glaubt. Davon träumen ist doch oft schöner als sie besitzen.

Gitti195: Wenn ich **gewinnen würde**, dann **würde** ich mich einmal **hinsetzen** und in aller Ruhe **nachdenken**. Es ist leicht aus dem Vollen zu schöpfen und
10 dann passiert: wie gewonnen, so zerronnen. Davon träumen ist vielleicht wirklich schöner.

Despina: Ich **würde** auch erstmal **überlegen**, **hinsetzen**, mich **zwicken**, um wach zu werden. Eigentlich fällt mir nicht viel ein - die Wohnung **würde** ich sicherlich **wechseln**, hinaus ins Grüne **ziehen**, vielleicht ein bissl Urlaub
15 **machen**, meinem Mann sein Lieblingswunschauto **kaufen** und dann ..... fällt mir nichts mehr ein. Die Gesundheit gibts nicht um viel Geld, **würde** mir aber mein Leben auf irgendeine Art sicherlich leichter **machen**.

Der Richter: **Hätte** ich das große Glück einmal viel Geld zu gewinnen,dann **wäre** es für mich eine Selbstverständlichkeit in erster Linie jenen Menschen zu
20 helfen, die bisher an der Schattenseite stehen mussten, sprich vom großen Wohlstand bisher nichts verspürten. In zweiter Linie **würde** ich dem geringeren Teil meiner Familie was zukommen **lassen** und mir einige kleine Wünsche **erfüllen**.

wolke62: Wenn das Wörtchen "wenn" nicht **wäre** ;-) Deshalb **würde** ich mich
25 erst dann entscheiden was ich damit mache, "wenn" ich viel Geld gewonnen habe.

hrotto: Wenn ich viel Geld **gewinnen würde**, **wäre** ich sehr verwundert, weil ich kein Spieler bin. LOL

Aus dem Forum: Finanzen, 07/2007 [www.webheimat.at/], © Communitor.

die Anschaffung – purchase
besitzen – to possess
aus dem Vollen schöpfen – to draw on plentiful resources
zerinnen – to melt away
zwicken – to pinch, nip

ein bissl – a bit (Austrian version of *bisschen*)
sich (dat.) *einfallen* – to come to mind
die Schattenseite – the dark side
der Wohlstand – prosperity
zukommen lassen (+ dat.) – to give, send to
der Wunsch – wish

⸮ The conditional in the text

16.1 USAGE

The conditional is primarily used to refer to hypothetical situations and to indicate that something does not correspond to reality. It usually corresponds to English 'would + verb', e.g. *Dann **würde** ich **warten*** 'Then I **would wait**' (2), and often co-occurs in a sentence with words meaning 'if' (e.g. *wenn* 'if', *als ob* 'as if'): *Wenn ich **gewinnen würde*** 'If I would win/If I won' (8).[67] Alternatively, instead of using the word *wenn*, the finite verb of the conditional can be brought to the beginning of the sentence to convey the same idea: ***Hätte** ich das große Glück* 'If I was really lucky' (18). There are many examples of this construction in our text, as the members of the forum are talking about a hypothetical situation: what they **would do** if they won a lot of money.

[67] Like the English conditional, it can also be used in polite requests: e.g. ***Würden** Sie mich **begleiten?*** 'Would you accompany me?'

16.2 FORMATION

16.2a The conditional with *würde* + infinitive

The conditional tense is formed by taking the past tense form of the auxiliary verb *werden* and adding an umlaut (*wurde → würde*, otherwise known as the *Konjunktiv II* form, see **16.2b**) plus the **infinitive** of the main verb:

ich **würde gewinnen** (8, 27)	wir **würden gewinnen**
du **würdest gewinnen**	ihr **würdet gewinnen**
er/sie/es **würde gewinnen**	sie/Sie **würden gewinnen**

Further examples from the text are: *Ich **würde** es wahrscheinlich wie h̲rotto **machen*** '(I) would probably do the same as hrotto' (3), *dass man sich über diese Anschaffungen gar nicht so **freuen würde*** 'that one wouldn't really be so happy with these purchases' (5–6), *dann **würde** ich mich einmal **hinsetzen** und in aller Ruhe **nachdenken*** 'then I would just sit down and take time to think about it' (8–9), *die Wohnung **würde** ich sicherlich **wechseln*** 'I would definitely change my flat' (13–14), ***würde** mir aber mein Leben auf irgendeine Art sicherlich leichter **machen*** '(It) would surely make my life easier somehow' (16–17), ***würde** ich dem geringeren Teil meiner Familie was zukommen **lassen*** 'I would give certain members of my family something' (21–22), *deshalb **würde** ich mich erst dann **entscheiden*** 'therefore I would only decide' (24–25).

Note that *würde* can be followed by more than one infinitive, if the speaker is listing actions: *Ich **würde** auch erstmal **überlegen**, **hinsetzen**, mich **zwicken*** 'I would also think about it, sit down, pinch myself at first' (12).

16.2b The conditional expressed using the *Konjunktiv II*

For regular verbs and some common irregular verbs there is an alternative form of the conditional, known as the *Konjunktiv II*, which is formed as follows:

- For regular verbs, the *Konjunktiv II* is identical to the **past tense** indicative (see **12.2a**): e.g. *ich machte, du machtest* etc.
- For irregular verbs, take the **past tense stem** (**12.2b**) of the verb, which is used in the *ich* and *er/sie/es* forms, **add -e** (if the stem does not already end in *-e*) and **umlaut** the vowel where possible: e.g. *ich war → wär-e, ich kam → käm-e, ich ging → ging-e, ich hatte → hätte*. This *Konjunktiv II* stem then needs the following personal endings (which are the same as the personal endings in the ordinary past tense indicative):

-	-n
-st	-t
-	-n

e.g. *sein*   *ich **wäre***   *wir **wären***

Konj. II stem: *wäre*   *du **wärest**[68]*   *ihr **wäret***

(line 24 in text)   *er/sie/es **wäre***   *sie/Sie **wären***

In practice, only very common verbs have a frequently used *Konjunktiv II* form (see **Table 16.1**).

[68] In spoken German the *-e-* is often dropped before *-st* and *-t*.

Table 16.1 *The Konjunktiv II of common verbs*

	ich	*du*	*er/sie/es*	*wir*	*ihr*	*sie/Sie*
haben	hätte	hättest	hätte	hätten	hättet	hätten
sein	wäre	wärest	wäre	wären	wäret	wären
werden	würde	würdest	würde	würden	würdet	würden
dürfen	dürfte	dürftest	dürfte	dürften	dürftet	dürften
können	könnte	könntest	könnte	könnten	könntet	könnten
mögen	möchte	möchtest	möchte	möchten	möchtet	möchten
müssen	müsste	müsstest	müsste	müssten	müsstet	müssten
sollen*	sollte	solltest	sollte	sollten	solltet	sollten
wissen	wüsste	wüsstest	wüsste	wüssten	wüsstet	wüssten
wollen*	wollte	wolltest	wollte	wollten	wolltet	wollten

* *Sollen* and *wollen* never have umlaut. Thus, their *Konjuntiv II* form is identical to the past tense.

In **written** German, the *Konjunktiv II* forms are used quite often in the conditional, particularly with **regular** verbs and with the **common** verbs listed in **Table 16.1**. There are also some other irregular verbs which can be used in their *Konjunktiv II* form in the written language: *geben* (*gäbe*), *gehen* (*ginge*), *kommen* (*käme*), *tun* (*täte*). In more formal registers of writing, we can also add *fahren* (*führe*), *lassen* (*liesse*), *halten* (*hielte*), *sitzen* (*säße*), *stehen* (*stünde*).

In **spoken** German the **würde + infinitive** construction is preferred for all regular verbs and most irregular verbs, except for the very common ones given in **Table 16.1**. In addition, the verbs *kommen* (*käme*), *tun* (*täte*) and *gehen* (*ginge*[69]) may be used in the *Konjunktiv II* but less frequently than the *werden + infinitive* alternative: e.g. *Es wäre schön, wenn du* **kämest** (more commonly: *Es wäre schön, wenn du* **kommen würdest**).[70]

[69] Especially in the phrase *Wenn es nach mir ginge* 'If it were up to me'.

[70] In colloquial German one may hear a *Konjunktiv II* form of *brauchen*: **bräuchte**, which is becoming increasingly acceptable.

Our text is taken from an internet forum, which reflects a relatively informal style of language. Most occurrences of the conditional appear with *würde + infinitive*, as we would expect in the spoken language, and the four examples of *Konjunktiv II* forms used are from the very frequent verbs *haben* and *sein*: *als Normalverdiener* **hätte** *man schon einige Ideen* 'As a normal earner one **would** indeed **have** some ideas' (4), *Hätte ich das große Glück* 'If I **was/were** really lucky' (18), *Wenn das Wörtchen "wenn" nicht* **wäre** 'If there **wasn't/weren't** an "if"' (24), **wäre** *ich sehr verwundert* 'I **would be** very surprised' (27).

Other points to note in the text

- Features of colloquial language: *nix* 'nothing' (16), LOL (28), reduction of *etwas to was* 'something' (22), regionalisms: *ein bissl* 'a bit' (14), contraction of *gibt es to gibts* 'there's' (16), omission of subject pronoun: *würde ... mein Leben ... leichter machen*, instead of *es würde ...* 'It would make my life easier' (16–17).
- Demonstrative *jener*, in the dative case because of *helfen*: **jenen** *Menschen zu helfen* 'to help **those** people' (19–20) (see first footnote in **8.1**).
- Verbs with accusative and dative object, where the dative is a person: *Eigentlich fällt* **mir nicht** *viel ein* 'Actually I can't think of much' (13), **meinem Mann sein Lieblingswunschauto** *kaufen* 'buy my husband the car he wants most' (15), *würde* **mir mein Leben** *... leichter machen* 'would make my life easier' (16–17), *würde ich* **dem geringeren Teil** *meiner Familie was zukommen lassen* 'would give something to certain members of my family' (21–22), **mir einige kleine Wünsche** *erfüllen* 'fulfil a few small wishes of mine' (22–23) (see **3.1aiii**).
- Diminutive noun: *das Wörtchen* 'the little word' (24) (see **27.1g**).
- Word play on the conjunction *wenn*, which can mean 'if' or 'when'. In line 24 it means 'if': **Wenn das Wörtchen "wenn" nicht wäre**, literally: 'If that little word "if" did not exist' (24), and in lines 25–26 it means 'when': **"wenn"** *ich viel Geld gewonnen habe* '"When" I have won a lot of money'.

Discover more about the conditional

16.3 THE CONDITIONAL PERFECT

The conditional perfect is used when talking hypothetically about completed actions. It corresponds to English 'would have' plus past participle: e.g. *Ich **hätte** es **gemacht*** 'I **would have done** it'. This tense is formed using the *Konjunktiv II* form of the auxiliary verb *haben* or *sein* plus the past participle of the main verb. The distribution of *haben* and *sein* is the same as for the ordinary perfect tense (see **13.3**):

- ich **hätte gesagt**   'would have said'
- du **hättest gesagt**
- er/sie/es **hätte gesagt**
- wir **hätten gesagt**
- ihr **hättet gesagt**
- sie/Sie **hätten gesagt**

- ich **wäre gekommen**   'would have come'
- du **wärst gekommen**
- er/sie/es **wäre gekommen**
- wir **wären gekommen**
- ihr **wäret gekommen**
- sie/Sie **wären gekommen**

Note that it is quite common to have a **modal** verb (*dürfen, können, mögen, müssen, sollen, wollen*) used with another verb in the conditional perfect to express meanings such as 'could have ...', 'should have ...' etc. Where this occurs, **two infinitives** are used instead of past participles, as is the case with the ordinary perfect (see **21.4b**, **21.5b**). All modals take *haben*, irrespective of the verb with which they co-occur:

*Ich **hätte** das nicht **sagen sollen***	I **shouldn't have said** that
*Sie **hätten** länger **bleiben können***	They **could have stayed** longer

If *hätte* appears in a **subordinate** clause where it would normally be sent to the end, it cannot follow a double infinitive construction but is sent to the position immediately before the two infinitives: e.g. *Ich dachte, dass ich es vielleicht diesmal nicht **hätte** sagen sollen* 'I thought that I perhaps shouldn't have said it this time'.

16.4 FURTHER EXAMPLES OF CONDITIONALS IN 'IF' (*WENN*) CLAUSES

One problematic aspect of 'if' clauses for speakers of English is that 'if' is followed not by a conditional in English but a past tense form, even though the *meaning* is conditional: e.g. 'If I **had** more time'. This is not possible in German, as the verb must be in the conditional: *Wenn ich mehr Zeit **hätte***. Below are some examples of 'if' clauses, both in the conditional and conditional perfect, as used in everyday spoken German. Students are advised to learn these patterns by heart:

Conditional

*Wenn wir das Geld **gewinnen würden**, **würden** wir in Urlaub **fahren***	If we **won** the money we **would go** on holiday
*Wenn er richtig krank **wäre**, **würde** er ins Bett **gehen***	If he **was/were** really ill he **would go** to bed
*Wenn du Lust **hättest**, **könntest** du mich anrufen*	If you **wanted** to you **could** ring me

- *Wenn ich samstags arbeiten **müsste**,*   If I **had to** work on Saturdays
  würde** ich meine Stelle **aufgeben   I **would give up** my job

Conditional Perfect

- *Wenn[71] wir das Geld **gewonnen hätten**,*   If we **had won** the money
  wären** wir in Urlaub **gefahren   we **would have gone** on holiday
- *Wenn er richtig krank **gewesen wäre**,*   If he **had been** really ill
  wäre** er ins Bett **gegangen   he **would have gone** to bed
- *Wenn du Lust **gehabt hättest**,*   If you **had wanted** to
  hättest** du mich **anrufen können   you **could have rung** me
- *Wenn ich samstags **hätte arbeiten müssen**,[72]*   If I **had had to** work on Saturdays
  hätte** ich meine Stelle **aufgegeben   I **would have given up** my job

---

[71] Alternatives without *wenn*: **Hätten** *wir das Geld gewonnen;* **Wäre** *er richtig krank gewesen;*
Hättest *du Lust gehabt;* **Hätte** *ich samstags arbeiten müssen.*

[72] See **16.3** for the position of *hätte* after a subordinating conjunction like *wenn*.

✎ EXERCISES

Vocabulary topic: *Im Garten*

1 Put the bracketed verbs into the simple conditional ('would …'), using either *würde* + infinitive
or the *Konjunktiv II* as appropriate:

Examples: i) Jörg [mähen] den Rasen; ii) Jörg [haben] einen Rasenmäher.

Answers: i) Jörg **würde** den Rasen **mähen**; ii) Jörg **hätte** einen Rasenmäher.

1 Ich [gießen] die Blumen.

2 Er [eingraben] die neuen Pflanzen.

3 Wir [mögen] auf der Terasse frühstücken.

4 Es [sein] schön beim Brunnen zu sitzen.

5 Ich [finden] es schwierig, den großen Busch zurückzuschneiden.

6 Wir [müssen] eigentlich den Rosenstrauch düngen.

7 Der Baum [verlieren] im Winter seine Blätter.

8 [Können] du Unkraut jäten? Ich [haben] eine Schaufel.

9 Ich [sollen] einen richtigen Komposthaufen machen.

10 [Wissen] du zufällig, wo der Rechen sein [können]?

2 The following sentences are in the past tense. Put them into the conditional perfect ('would
have …'):

Example: Jörg **mähte** den Rasen.

Answer: Jörg **hätte** den Rasen **gemäht**.

1 Der Gärtner **machte** es besser.

2 Ich **kaufte** eine Regentonne, aber sie war zu groß zu transportieren.

3 Ein guter Spaten **war** zu teuer. Deshalb habe ich die Schaufel genommen.

4 Ich **sollte** den Gartenzaun streichen, aber es war zu viel Arbeit.

5 Rhododendren haben eigentlich sehr kleine Wurzeln. Du **konntest** sie in einen Topf pflanzen.

6 Eine schöne Elster **flog** in den Garten, aber die Katze hat sie weggescheucht.

3 Make 'wenn clauses' out of the following sentences, using the simple conditional (or *Konjunktiv II* where appropriate) and translate your answers into English:

Example: Jörg mäht den Rasen. Sein Garten sieht schöner aus.

Answer: **Wenn** Jörg den Rasen **mähen würde**, **würde** sein Garten schöner **aussehen**.
'If Jörg mowed the lawn his garden would look nicer.'

1 Es regnet nicht. Die Erde ist sehr trocken.

2 Sie haben Geld. Sie kaufen einen Wintergarten.

3 Ich habe ein Glashaus. Ich kann Tomaten ziehen.

4 Das Wetter ist besser. Die Kletterpflanzen wachsen höher.

5 Du gibst mir den Gartenschlauch. Ich spritze den Rasen.

6 Wir pflanzen jetzt die Zwiebeln. Die Krokusse und Narzissen kommen im Frühling.

7 Der Blumenstock verwelkt. Ich muss ihn umtopfen.

8 Du willst mir helfen. Du kannst den Gartenschuppen aufbauen.

4 Take your answers to 3 above and put them into the conditional perfect. Then translate them into English:

Example: Wenn Jörg den Rasen mähen würde, würde sein Garten schöner aussehen.

Answer: Wenn Jörg den Rasen **gemäht hätte**, **hätte** sein Garten schöner **ausgesehen**.
'If Jörg **had** mowed the lawn his garden would **have looked** nicer.'

For more exercises on modal verbs in the conditional perfect ('could have', 'should have' etc.) see Ch. 21, Ex. 4.

17 | Subjunctive in reported speech

Text

Regierung begrüßt Obamas Einsatz für Homo-Ehe

*Außenminister Westerwelle lobt im Namen der Bundesregierung US-Präsident Obamas Vorstoß zur gesetzlichen Anerkennung der gleichgeschlechtlichen Ehe. Dies **entspreche** auch der deutschen Politik.*

5 Außenminister Guido Westerwelle […], der selbst seit September 2010 mit dem Sportrechte-Manager Michael Mronz verheiratet ist, sprach von einem "mutigen Schritt". Auf Englisch fügte er hinzu: "It's okay to marry gay." […].
  Obamas Plädoyer für die Eheschließung zwischen Homosexuellen inspiriert auch die Linksfraktion im Bundestag. Der Präsident **habe** "ein
10 international vernehmbares Signal **gesendet**, das auch der deutsche Bundestag erhören sollte", sagte die Lesben- und Schwulenpolitische Sprecherin der Fraktion, Barbara Höll. Die Diskriminierung von Lesben und Schwulen **sei** nicht mehr zeitgemäß. Höll forderte, "dass alle Abgeordneten frei von Fraktions- und Koalitionszwängen über die
15 Eheöffnung im Bundestag abstimmen". Dann **könne** Homosexuellen die Eheschließung "zügig" ermöglicht werden.
  Gleichgeschlechtliche Paare können in Deutschland eine eingetragene Lebenspartnerschaft, umgangssprachlich "Homo-Ehe", eingehen, die aber nicht in allen rechtlichen Fragen der Ehe gleichgestellt ist.
20   Auch der Grünen-Politiker Volker Beck verlangte auch in Deutschland ein Ende von Diskriminierungen im Steuer- und Adoptionsrecht für Homosexuelle Paare. "Es ist an der Zeit, dass auch Angela Merkel öffentlich bekennt: It's ok to marry gay", mahnte Beck. Obama **sei** genauso für die Öffnung der Ehe wie der neue französische Präsident Francois Hollande.
25 Der britische Premier David Cameron **habe** die Öffnung der Ehe sogar zu einem konservativen Projekt **gemacht**, erklärte Beck. Beck bescheinigte dem US-Präsidenten Mut, denn in den USA **würden** Fragen der Sexualmoral deutlich konservativer diskutiert als hierzulande […].
  Obama hatte sich am Mittwoch in einem Interview mit dem
30 Fernsehsender ABC erstmals offen für eine Legalisierung gleichgeschlechtlicher Ehen ausgesprochen. "Für mich persönlich ist es wichtig, voranzugehen und zu betonen, dass gleichgeschlechtliche Paare heiraten können sollten", sagte der Präsident. Er ergänzte, sein Meinungswandel **sei** nicht zuletzt durch gleichgeschlechtliche Eltern im
35 Bekanntenkreis seiner Töchter **erfolgt**, die Benachteiligungen erleiden **müssten**.

Aus: [http://article.wn.com/], © dapd. 10/05/2012.

> *der Einsatz* – commitment
> *der Außenminister* – foreign minister
> *loben* – to praise
> *der Vorstoß* – advance
> *die Anerkennung* – recognition
> *gleichgeschlechtlich* – same-sex
> *entsprechen* (+ dat.) – to correspond to
> *der Plädoyer* – plea
> *vernehmbar* – audible
> *zeitgemäß* – up-to-date
>
> *zügig* – speedy/speedily
> *ermöglichen* – to make possible
> *eingetragen* – registered
> *verlangen* – to demand
> *bescheinigen* – to confirm
> *betonen* – to stress
> *ergänzen* – to add
> *der Meinungswandel* – change of opinion
> *erfolgen* – occur, come about
> *die Benachteiligung* – discrimination

⌕ The subjunctive in the text

17.1 USAGE

The subjunctive mood, particularly the form of the subjunctive in German known as the *Konjunktiv I*, is used to indicate reported speech: it signals that someone other than the writer of the text has made a particular statement, e.g. the use of the subjunctive in *Dies* **entspreche** *auch der deutschen Politik* 'this also corresponds to German policy' (line 4) makes it clear that the foreign minister Westerwelle made this statement, not the writer of the report. The subjunctive is primarily a feature of the **written language** – it is used extensively in newspaper reports and in literary texts – and tends to be avoided in spoken German, where the indicative is preferred. The subjunctive can be used in the present tense: e.g. *Dies* **entspreche** ... , the perfect tense: *Der Präsident* **habe** *ein international vernehmbares Signal* **gesendet** 'the President has sent a signal to be heard internationally' (9–10) and, less commonly, in the future tense (e.g. **werde** plus infinitive).

17.2 FORMATION

The *Konjunktiv I* is formed by using the present tense stem (**10.2a**): e.g. *mach-, komm-, woll-, müss-,*[73] plus the personal endings given in the box below. Unlike the indicative present tense, there are no irregularities in the *Konjunktiv I*: e.g. indicative *ich gebe, du gibst* vs. subjunctive *ich gebe, du gebest*.

-e	-en
-est	-et
-e	-en

e.g. *können:*
[könn-]

ich **könne**	*wir* **können**
(*du* **könnest**	*ihr* **könnet**)[74]
er/sie/es **könne** (15)	*sie/Sie* **können**

---

[73] Infinitives ending in *-eln* drop e and *n*: e.g. *lächeln → er lächl-e.*

[74] In practice, the *du* and *ihr* forms of the *Konjunktiv I* are rarely used with verbs other than *sein*, as they are felt to be rather stilted.

One can change a **perfect** indicative into its subjunctive equivalent by using the *Konjunktiv I* forms of the appropriate auxiliary verb *haben* or *sein*. Note that *sein* does not have *-e* in the singular:

senden:	*ich* **habe** *gesendet*	*wir* **haben** *gesendet*
(10)	*du* **habest** *gesendet*	*ihr* **habet** *gesendet*
	er/sie/es **habe** *gesendet*	*sie/Sie* **haben** *gesendet*
sein:	*ich* **sei** *gewesen*	*wir* **seien** *gewesen*
(not in text)	*du* **sei(e)st** *gewesen*	*ihr* **seiet** *gewesen*
	er/sie/es **sei** *gewesen*	*sie/Sie* **seien** *gewesen*

Similarly, the **future** (and **passive**) auxiliary *werden* also has a regular *Konjunktiv I* form:

ich **werde** *gehen*	*wir* **werden** *gehen*
du **werdest** *gehen*	*ihr* **werdet** *gehen*
er **werde** *gehen*	*sie* **werden** *gehen*

17.3 USE OF PARTICULAR TENSE FORMS IN WRITTEN GERMAN

It is customary when reporting an utterance to keep to the same tense as originally used by the speaker. For instance, if someone says *Ich* **brauche** *viel Geld*, the **present** subjunctive is used when reporting the utterance, even if the preceding verb, e.g. *sagen, berichten*, is in the past: *Er sagte, er* **brauche** *viel Geld* (or *er sagte,* **dass** *er viel Geld brauche*). By contrast, English uses the past tense after verbs in the past: 'he said (that) he **needed** a lot of money'. Examples of present subjunctives in the text are given below, with the original utterance in square brackets:

- *Dies* **entspreche** *auch der deutschen Politik* (4)
  [„*Dies* **entspricht** *auch der deutschen Politik*"]
  'This corresponds to German policy'
- *Die Diskriminierung von Lesben und Schwulen* **sei** *nicht mehr zeitgemäß* (12–13)
  [„*Die Diskriminierung von Lesben und Schwulen* **ist** *nicht mehr zeitgemäß*"]
  'Discrimination against lesbians and gays is out of date'
- *Dann* **könne** *Homosexuellen die Eheschließung zügig ermöglicht werden* (15–16)
  [*Dann* **kann** *Homosexuellen die Eheschließung zügig ermöglicht werden*]
  'Then, for gay people, the wedding **can** be made possible quickly'

When the original utterance refers to the **past** (i.e. when the past, perfect or pluperfect tense is used), the reported speech is given in the **perfect subjunctive**, e.g. *Ich* **brauchte** *damals nicht viel Geld* → (*Er sagte*), *er* **habe** *damals nicht viel Geld gebraucht*. Examples of perfect subjunctives in the text are:

- *Der Präsident* **habe** *ein international vernehmbares Signal* **gesendet** (9–10)
  'The president has sent a signal to be heard internationally'
- *David Cameron* **habe** *die Öffnung der Ehe sogar zu einem konservativen Projekt* **gemacht** (25–26)
  'David Cameron has even made the opening up of marriage into a Conservative project'

- *Sein Meinungswandel **sei** nicht zuletzt durch gleichgeschlechtliche Eltern im Bekanntenkreis seiner Töchter **erfolgt*** (33–35)
  'His change of opinion came about not least because of same-sex parents in his daughters' circle of friends'

These uses of the perfect subjunctive suggest that the original speaker used some sort of past tense, e.g.:

- „*Der Präsident **hat** … **gesendet**"* or „*Der Präsident **hatte** … **gesendet**"*
- „*David Cameron **hat** …**gemacht**"* or „*David Cameron **machte** …*"
- „*Mein Meinungswandel **ist** … **erfolgt**"* or „*Mein Meinungswandel **erfolgte** …*"

The use of tenses in the subjunctive is summarised in **Table 17.1**.[75]

---

[75] For the use of ***würden*** and ***müssten*** in the text, see **17.4**.

Table 17.1 Tenses used in the *Konjunktiv I*

Original utterance	*Reported speech*
Present	Present subjunctive
Past Perfect Pluperfect	Perfect subjunctive
Future	Future subjunctive

Other points to note in the text

- Modals with a bare infinitive: *erhören **sollte*** 'should listen to' (11); ***könne** …ermöglicht werden* 'can be made possible' (15); ***können** eine … Homo-Ehe … eingehen* 'can enter into a gay marriage' (17–18); *dass gleichgeschlechtliche Paare heiraten **können sollten*** 'that same-sex couples SHOULD be able to get married' (32–33); *die Benachteiligungen erleiden **müssten*** 'who have to suffer discrimination' (35–36) (see **21.3–21.5**).
- Verbs taking the dative: *entspreche … **der** deutschen Politik* ‚'correspond to German policy' (4); the accusative and dative: *Beck bescheinigte **dem** US-Präsidenten **Mut*** 'Beck confirmed the US President's courage' (26–27); and adjectives taking the dative: ***der** Ehe gleichgestellt* 'equal to marriage' (19) (see **3.4a**).
- Weak masculine nouns: *im Name**n*** (2); *dem US-Präsident**en*** (27) (see **3.3b**).

Discover more about the subjunctive

17.4 USE OF THE *KONJUNKTIV II*

17.4a Written German

When replacing an original verb by its subjunctive equivalent in reported speech there is a danger that the subjunctive form may be identical to the original indicative, particularly in the case of plurals ending in -*en*, e.g. *Sie **müssen** Benachteiligungen leiden* 'they have to suffer discrimination', where *müssen* could be indicative or subjunctive. In order to make it clear that a subjunctive is being used for the reported speech it is necessary to take a different form of the subjunctive, commonly known as the *Konjunktiv II*, which is formed by taking the **past tense** stem of the verb (e.g. *mach**te***) and, for most irregular verbs, adding umlaut (e.g. *hätte, wäre, könnte, müsste*) (see **16.2b** for the formation of the *Konjunktiv II*).

Thus, the plural *müssen* in a sentence like „ *Sie **müssen** leiden*" would be replaced by *müssten* in reported speech. Contrast:

> „*Ich **muss** leiden*" → *Er sagte, er **müsse** leiden*[76]
>
> „*Sie **müssen** leiden*" → *Sie sagten, sie **müssten** leiden*

[76] Such sentences are possible with or without *dass*. If *dass* is used, the finite verb is sent to the end of the clause, e.g. *Er sagte, dass er große Sympathie **habe*** (see **26.1b** for word order).

Other examples are:

- „*Wir können es machen*" → *sie sagten, sie **könnten** es machen*
- „*Wir werden es machen*" → *sie sagten, sie **würden** es machen*
- „*Wir wissen nichts davon*" → *sie sagten, sie **wüssten** nichts davon*

And with regular verbs, whose *Konjunktiv II* form looks like an ordinary past tense:

- „*Wir arbeiten jetzt daran*" → *sie sagten, sie **arbeiteten** jetzt daran*
- „*Wir machen eine Pause*" → *sie sagten, sie **machten** eine Pause*

In our text, there are two examples of *Konjunktiv II* forms being used instead of the *Konjunktiv I* in order to make the distinction between indicative and subjunctive clear:

- *Eltern … , die Benachteiligungen erleiden **müssten*** (34–36)
  'parents … who have to suffer discrimination'
  (originally „*Eltern … , die Benachteiligungen erleiden **müssen***")
- *denn in den USA **würden** Fragen der Sexualmoral … diskutiert* (27–28)
  'because in the US questions of sexual morality are discussed … '
  (originally „*denn in den USA **werden** Fragen der Sexualmoral … diskutiert*")

The use of *Konjunktiv II* in writing is restricted to regular verbs and very common irregular ones (i.e. those discussed in **16.2b**). Other irregular verbs have *würde* (pl. *würden*) plus the infinitive as their *Konjunktiv II* equivalent:

- „*Wir sprechen nie darüber*" → *Sie sagten, sie **würden** nie darüber **sprechen***
  'They said they never talk about it'
- „*Wir stehen zu unserer Meinung*" → *Sie sagten, sie **würden** zu ihrer Meinung **stehen**[77]*
  'They said they are sticking to their opinion'

When the original utterance refers to the **past** and, according to the rules in **17.3** above, is replaced by a perfect subjunctive, the auxiliary *haben* may need to be replaced by *hätten* to avoid ambiguity with the indicative:

- „*Ich sprach nie darüber*" → *Er sagte, er **habe** nie darüber gesprochen* (KI)
- „*Wir sprachen nie darüber*" → *Sie sagten, sie **hätten** nie darüber gesprochen* (KII)

[77] *stünden* is also possible, but many speakers find it rather old-fashioned and stilted.

17.4b Spoken German

As mentioned in **17.1** above, the *Konjunktiv I* tends to be avoided in the spoken language unless a more formal register is required. In everyday colloquial German, the original indicative is simply used in reported speech, e.g. *Er sagte, er **ist** krank*. If, however, the speaker wants to use the subjunctive to indicate reported speech, particularly if s/he does not agree with or doubts the validity of the original statement, the ***Konjunktiv II*** is used instead:

i) It is used with **very common verbs** such as the modals *dürfen, können, mögen, müssen, sollen, wollen* and also *haben, sein, werden*, when used either as main verbs or auxiliaries:

- „*Ich **bin** krank*" →
  Er sagte, er ist krank (Indicative)
  *Er sagte, er **wäre** krank* (Subjunctive)

- „*Ich **muss** gehen*" →
  Er sagte, er muss gehen (Ind.)
  *Er sagte, er **müsste** gehen* (Subj.)

- „*Es **wird** regnen*" →
  Er sagte, es wird regnen (Ind.)
  *Er sagte, es **würde** regnen* (Subj.)

- „*Ich **habe** es gemacht*" →
  Er sagte, er hat es gemacht (Ind.)
  *Er sagte, er **hätte** es gemacht* (Subj.)

- „*Wir **blieben** zu Hause*" →
  Sie sagten, sie blieben zu Hause (Ind.)
  *Sie sagten, sie **wären** zu Hause geblieben* (Subj.)

- „*Ich **war** sehr zufrieden*" →
  Er sagte, er war sehr zufrieden (Ind.)
  *Er sagte, er **wäre** sehr zufrieden gewesen* (Subj.)[78]

[78] The formal *Konjunktiv I* forms of the last three examples are *Er **habe** es gemacht, Sie **seien** zu Hause geblieben* and *Er **sei** zufrieden gewesen* as the original statements are in the perfect or past tense, which requires a perfect subjunctive equivalent. Thus, it is the auxiliaries *haben* and *sein* that are put into the *Konjunktiv II*, not the main verbs themselves, e.g. *machen, bleiben*.

ii) With other verbs, i.e. all regular verbs and those irregular ones not belonging to the very common group discussed in **17.4b(i)** above, *würde(-st, -t, -n)* plus the infinitive is used (when the original utterance is in the present):[79]

- *„Ich arbeite morgen"* →   *Er sagte, er arbeitet morgen* (Ind.)
  *Er sagte, er **würde** morgen **arbeiten*** (Subj.)
- *„Wir bleiben zu Hause"* →   *Sie sagten, sie bleiben zu Hause* (Ind.)
  *Sie sagten, sie **würden** zu Hause **bleiben*** (Subj.)

---

[79] The *Konjunktiv II* of the verbs *kommen, tun* and, particularly, *wissen* (*käme, täte, wüsste*) are sometimes heard in spoken German, alongside their alternatives with *würde*, e.g. *Er sagte, er **wüsste** nichts davon.*

17.4c   Degree of formality

Although a generalisation can be made that, to indicate reported speech, the *Konjunktiv I* is used in written German and the *Konjunktiv II* is used in the spoken language (except when the *Konjunktiv II* is used to disambiguate a form, as described in **17.4a**), less formal written texts may use more instances of the *Konjunktiv II* and, conversely, speakers in a formal situation may use the *Konjunktiv I*. Indeed, in some texts they may be used interchangeably. In our text, the *Konjunktiv I* is preferred, as it is from a quality newspaper.

✎ EXERCISES

Vocabulary topic: *Sport*

1 Imagine you are writing a sports report for a quality newspaper:

a) Put the following quotations into reported speech, using the appropriate form of the *Konjunktiv I* (Remember to change the punctuation and pronouns where necessary):

Example: Der Stürmer sagte: „Ich habe besonders schlecht gespielt"
Answer: Der Stürmer sagte, <u>er</u> habe besonders schlecht gespielt.

1   Das Formel 1 Team teilte mit: „Der Ferrari-Fahrer kann voraussichtlich aus dem Krankenhaus entlassen werden." Die Ärzte stellten nach eingehenden Untersuchungen fest: „Kein medizinischer Eingriff ist nötig."

2   Der jüngere der beiden Brüder sagte: „Ich will diesen Kampf unbedingt und ich hoffe, dass ich bald diese Chance bekomme." Er sagte: „Ich warte auf große Kämpfe. Zu 70 Prozent bin ich zufrieden, 30 Prozent muss ich mir noch erarbeiten."

3   „Wenn der Vertrag unter Dach und Fach ist", ergänzte der Trainer, „kommt Schmidt bereits in der nächsten Woche mit ins Trainingslager nach Österreich."

4   „Es kann nicht sein", betonte der Kapitän, „dass es nur als Pflichtübung gilt, in der Nationalmannschaft zu spielen. Jeder muss es wollen. Es muss eine Ehre sein."

5   Die dreimalige Olympiasiegerin sagte: „Ich bin froh, das ich es versucht habe. Ich werde nichts in Zweifel ziehen, jetzt liegt alles hinter mir."

6   „Als ich über die Ziellinie lief, kamen jahrelang angestaute Gefühle auf", jubelte die Siegerin. „Seit ich neun bin, träumte ich davon, im Olympia-Team zu stehen. Jetzt ist der Traum wahr."

7   „Eigentlich hatte ich gar nicht so recht mit diesem Sieg gerechnet, weil ich diese Rallye nicht kannte", erklärte der 32 Jahre alte Finne. „Daher freue ich mich umsomehr darüber."

b) Put the following sentences into reported speech, using *Konjunktiv I*, or *Konjunktiv II* when necessary:

Example: Der Stürmer sagte: „Wir haben besonders schlecht gespielt."[80]

Answer: Der Stürmer sagte, sie hätten besonders schlecht gespielt.

1   Der Trainer sagte am Sonntag: „Wir haben uns am Wochenende mit Beck und Ajax so weit geeinigt, dass man davon ausgehen kann, er kommt zu uns."

2   Deichmanns Anwalt Michael Exner kommentierte: „Heinz Deichmann soll sich erst einmal in Ruhe auf Sydney vorbereiten, dann sehen wir weiter."

3   Der Vorsitzender des DLV-Bundesausschusses Leistungssport, sagte: „Natürlich fehlen die großen Reißer. Aber wir haben eine sehr ausgeglichene Mannschaft, wobei die Frauen gegenüber dem letzten Jahr deutlich im Aufwind sind. Bei den Männern muss man sehen. Der erste Tag war nie der Tag der Deutschen. Die big points werden sicher morgen kommen."

4   Maatz fügte hinzu: „Nach einer EM oder großen Turnieren gab es immer einen Schnitt. Einige hören aus Altersgründen auf, andere fallen durch das Sieb. Wenn ein neuer Trainer kommt, hat man andere Vorstellungen."

5   „Die Australier rechnen zu 90 Prozent damit, dass sie zum Endspiel nach Spanien reisen müssen und nicht gegen die USA im heimischen National Tennis Centre in Melbourne antreten können", berichtete die australische Presseagentur APA.

6   Der Coach meinte: „Die MetroStars werden die Entscheidung treffen. Der Müller hat da nur noch wenig zu sagen […] Ich glaube, dass er die falsche Einstellung hat. Es dreht sich hier nicht alles um den einen Stürmer, das hat es nie getan." Der Coach erklärte: „Wir hatten einige Fragen an den Spieler zu seiner Verletzung und seiner Einstellung zur Mannschaft. Alle haben ihre Meinung gesagt."

---

[80] In German, a colon is placed before the direct speech when the preceding verb is a verb of saying.

---

2   Imagine that you are telling a friend what someone has said. Use the less formal *Konjunktiv II* to indicate reported speech:

Example: Klaus sagte: „Ich bin mit dem neuen Kapitän nicht zufrieden."

Answer: Klaus sagte, er wäre mit dem neuen Kapitän nicht zufrieden.

1   Paul sagte: „Ich spiele lieber Squash als Tennis."

2   Mein Bruder sagte: „Matthäus hat zwei Tore innerhalb fünf Minuten geschossen."

3   Meine Freundin meinte: „Ich interessiere mich überhaupt nicht für Autorennen."

4   Benno sagte: „Der Schiedsrichter zeigte ihm die gelbe Karte."

5   Unsere Gegner drohten uns: „Wir werden euch mit fünf zu null schlagen."

6 Anton sagte: „Ich muss mich beeilen. Ich gehe gleich ins Fußballstadion."

7 Sabine sagte: „Ich weiß nicht, ob er gewonnen hat."

8 Mein Schilehrer sagte: „Man muss beim Schifahren immer auf der Piste bleiben, sonst kann ein Unfall passieren."

9 Mein Vater sagte: „Es gibt nichts schöneres als Pferderennen!"

10 Ulrike sagte: „Ich wollte mit ihm Badminton spielen, aber er hatte keine Zeit."

✎ FURTHER EXERCISES

3 Put the highlighted indicatives into the appropriate form of the subjunctive to indicate reported speech in a written text:

In diesem Augenblick erst zog Katharina die beiden Ausgaben der ZEITUNG aus der Tasche und fragte, ob der Staat – so drückte sie es aus – nichts tun **kann**, um sie gegen diesen Schmutz zu schützen und ihre verlorene Ehre wiederherzustellen. Sie **weiß** inzwischen sehr wohl, dass ihre Vernehmung durchaus gerechtfertigt **ist**, wenn ihr auch dieses »Bis-ins-letzte-Lebensdetail-Gehen« nicht **einleuchtet**, aber es **ist** ihr unbegreiflich, wie Einzelheiten aus der Vernehmung [...] **haben** zur Kenntnis der ZEITUNG gelangen können. Hier griff Staatsanwalt Hach ein und sagte, ... [b]eleidigende und möglicherweise verleumderische Details der Berichterstattung **kann** sie zum Gegenstand einer Privatklage machen, und – falls sich **herausstellt**, dass es »undichte Stellen« innerhalb der untersuchenden Behörde **gibt**, so **wird** diese, darauf **kann** sie sich verlassen, Anzeige gegen Unbekannt erheben und ihr zu ihrem Recht verhelfen [...]

   [Blorna] teilte Hach mit, dass Katharinas Mutter wahrscheinlich infolge eines Besuchs von Tötges von der ZEITUNG unerwartet **starb**. Hach war milder als am Morgen, bat Katharina, die ihm gewiss nicht **grollt**, wozu sie auch keinen Grund **hat**, sein persönliches Beileid auszusprechen. Im Übrigen **steht** er jederzeit zur Verfügung. Er **ist** zwar jetzt sehr beschäftigt mit den Vernehmungen von Götten, **wird** sich aber freimachen; im Übrigen **ergab** sich aus den Vernehmungen Göttens bisher nichts Belastendes für Katharina. Er **sprach** mit großer Zuneigung und fair von ihr und über sie. Eine Besuchserlaubnis **ist** allerdings nicht zu erwarten, da keine Verwandtschaft **vorliegt** und die Definition »Verlobte« sich bestimmt als zu vage herausstellen und nicht stichhaltig sein würde [...].

   Natürlich konfrontierte Katharina Dr. Heinen mit der Ausgabe der ZEITUNG, in der das Tötges-Interview erwähnt und ihre Mutter zitiert wurde, sie teilte aber keineswegs Dr. Heinens Empörung über das Interview, sondern meinte, diese Leute **sind** Mörder und Rufmörder, sie **verachtet** das natürlich, aber offfenbar **ist** es doch geradezu die Pflicht dieser Art Zeitungsleute, unschuldige Menschen um Ehre, Ruf und Gesundheit zu bringen.

Aus: Heinrich Böll, *Die verlorene Ehre der Katharina Blum*, © Verlag Kiepenheuer & Witsch, Köln, 1974.

4 Write a quality newspaper report putting the direct speech into reported speech by changing the verb forms in bold print and dropping the inverted commas:

Jede zweite Frau fühlt sich zu fett

Berlin – In einer Umfrage des Forsa-Instituts im Auftrag der Zeitschrift *Brigitte* und des Bundesgesundheitsministeriums sollten die Ernährungsgewohnheiten der Frauen erfragt werden. Die Ergebnisse der Umfrage präsentierte die stellvertretende Chefredakteurin Tania Miglietti in Berlin.

Was gilt überhaupt als Diät? „Jede zweite Frau in Deutschland möchte weniger wiegen. 44 Prozent der Frauen zwischen 20 und 60 Jahren **wollen** kalorienbewusst essen. Fast die Hälfte der befragten Frauen **hat angegeben**, schon einmal eine Diät gemacht zu haben", sagte Miglietti. „Allerdings **werden** 88 Prozent so genannte *Formula-Diäten*, also das Ersetzen einer Mahlzeit durch einen Drink, nicht als Diät angesehen. Auch eine Mahlzeit ausfallen zu lassen, **wird** von 80 Prozent nicht als Abmagerungskur empfunden."

Der Griff zur Tüte: Miglietti erklärte, dass „jede siebte Frau zur Gruppe der *unkritischen Pflichtesserinnen* **gehört**. Diese *Trash-Fress-Frauen* **greifen** häufig zu Fertiggerichten oder **beschäftigen** sich neben dem Essen noch mit anderen Dingen. Vor allem junge Singles im Alter von 20 bis 30 Jahren **gehören** zu dieser Gruppe."

„43 Prozent der Frauen **essen** beim Fernsehen, 42 Prozent **lassen** sich vom leckeren Anblick der Speisen verleiten", erklärte die Journalistin. „80 Prozent der Frauen **haben angegeben**, gesundheitsbewusst zu kochen. Demgegenüber **haben** allerdings 54 Prozent **erklärt**, sie **benutzen** auch Halbfertig- oder Fertigprodukte wie Soßenpulver. 62 Prozent **müssen** immer Salziges oder Süßes zum Knabbern zu Hause haben. Ein entspanntes Verhältnis zum Essen **haben** nur 40 Prozent der 20- bis 60-Jährigen. Sie **sind** auch eher mit ihrem Gewicht zufrieden."

Adapted from *Der Spiegel* (online), 4/12/00.

For further exercises on the subjunctive, see Revision Text 3, Ex. 3.

18 | Passive

<u>Ein Date oder nicht? Der Name ist wichtig</u>

Sorry, "Sarah": Beim Ranking der Single-Vornamen schneidest du leider
nicht so toll ab. **Festgestellt wurde** das im Rahmen einer Studie des
Datingportals eDarling: Bestimmte Vornamen, so fand man heraus, **wurden**
5 deutlich seltener **angeklickt** als andere. Woran das genau liegt, ist schwer
zu sagen – vermutlich spielt die persönliche Erfahrung eine wichtige Rolle.
Wer in der Schule schon von einem nervigen "Holger" **bedrängt wurde**, <u>ist</u>
vielleicht auch von seinem Namensvetter <u>abgeschreckt</u>. Männer würden
vermutlich ihrerseits dem Profil von "Edeltraut" weniger Beachtung
10 schenken, wenn sie nur einen Klick weiter mit "Paris" Kontakt aufnehmen
können. Die Vornamen-Tendenz zeigte sich völlig unabhängig davon, ob ein
attraktives Profilbild vorlag oder nicht – denn das konnten die Teilnehmer
nicht sehen.

Im Bildungsbereich ist der Einfluss des Vornamens schon länger
15 bekannt – Lehrer gaben beispielsweise zu, bei Kindern mit den Vornamen
"Kevin" oder "Chantalle" sofort Vorurteile aufzubauen, und den betreffenden
Schülern wenig Intelligenz zusprachen. Nun zeigt sich, dass der Vorname
auch bei der Partnerwahl zumindest ein größerer Faktor ist.

Für die Studie **wurden** die Klickraten ausgewählter Vornamen von
20 Kunden des Dating-Portals **verglichen**. Partnervorschläge bei eDarling
enthalten grundsätzlich nur den Vornamen, das Alter und den Wohnort eines
registrierten Nutzers – weitere Informationen gibt es erst nach dem Klick.
Daher <u>ließ sich</u> (unter Berücksichtigung der Faktoren Alter und Wohnort)
schnell erkennen, welche Vornamen am häufigsten **ignoriert**
25 **wurden**.

Ist das fair? Natürlich nicht. Aber jeder von uns hat nun einmal sofort eine
Assoziation zu einem Vornamen, ob nun negativ oder positiv. Entscheidend
ist, dass man sich dessen bewusst ist, und nicht vielleicht den perfekten
Partner verpasst, weil sich "Fridolin" für uns nicht so sexy anhört.
30 Schließlich hindert uns ja niemand daran, einen ansprechenderen
Kosenamen zu finden. Also, nur Mut, "Maximilian", "Michael" und "Andreas"
(auch bekannt als "Platz 18 bis 20")! Wir würden euch eine Chance geben!!

Top 10 Frauennamen: *Hannah, Lena, Katharina, Claudia, Sophie,
Susanne, Ines, Cornelia, Katrin, Marie*. Top 10 Männernamen: *Felix, Paul,*
35 *Lukas, Jens, Luca, Tim, Jan, Christian, Niklas, Torsten.*

Aus: *Brigitte*, Juli 2011 [www.brigitte.de/].

gut abschneiden – to do well	*vergleichen* – to compare
feststellen – to confirm	*der Vorschlag* – suggestion
bedrängen – to pester	*der Nutzer* – user
der Namensvetter – person of same name	*die Berücksichtigung* – consideration
abschrecken – to scare off	*entscheidend* – crucial
die Beachtung – attention	*ansprechend* – attractive
das Vorurteil – bias, prejudice	*der Kosename* – pet name
zusprechen – to award, attribute	*nur Mut!* – don't lose heart

♀ The passive in the text

18.1 USAGE

The passive voice is used to shift the emphasis away from the agent (i.e. the 'doer') of the action described by the verb to the **recipient** of the action. Thus, an ordinary 'active' sentence like *Clara und Lisa fragte den Lehrer* 'Clara and Lisa asked the teacher' becomes <u>*Der Lehrer*</u> **wurde** *(von Clara und Lisa)* **gefragt** '<u>The teacher</u> **was asked** (by Clara and Lisa)' in the passive.

Passives are often used when a speaker/writer does not want to specify the agent. For instance, in our chosen text the aim of the writer is to inform us about a study investigating how first names influence the choice of partners in online dating. The emphasis is not on **who** did the study but on the outcomes: e.g. *Festgestellt wurde* das 'that was confirmed' (3), *Bestimmte Vornamen* **wurden** ... **angeklickt** 'Certain first names were ... clicked' (4–5), *Für die Studie* **wurden** *die Klickraten* ... **verglichen** 'For the study, the click rates ... were compared' (19–20). This 'agentless passive' is the most frequently used passive in German and is more common in the **written** language than in speech.

18.2 CASE FORMS OF PASSIVE SUBJECTS

We can see by the first example given in **18.1** above, *Clara und Lisa fragten den Lehrer* → *Der Lehrer wurde von Clara und Lisa gefragt*, that the recipient of the action (*den Lehrer* in the accusative) becomes the **subject** of the passive sentence, which is shown by making it nominative in German: *Der Lehrer wurde ...*, and the finite verb (in this case *werden*) agrees with the new subject: it is now singular. In our text, the subjects of the passive sentences are also in the nominative: e.g. *Bestimmte Vornamen* **wurden** ... **angeklickt** 'Certain first names were ... clicked' (4–5), *Wer* ... *bedrängt wurde* 'who was pestered ...' (7).

18.3 FORMATION

The passive can be used in all the main tenses (although some are more common than others). It is formed using the appropriate tense of the auxiliary verb **werden** plus the **past participle** of the main verb.[81] Below are examples of the present and past passive, the latter of which is used in our text, as it is reporting on a study that has already taken place:

ich **werde** *oft* **gefragt** 'I <u>am</u> often <u>asked</u>'   *ich* **wurde** *oft* **gefragt** 'I <u>was</u> often <u>asked</u>'

du **wirst** oft **gefragt**	*du* **wurdest** oft **gefragt**
er/sie/es **wird** oft **gefragt**	*er/sie/es* **wurde** oft **gefragt**
wir **werden** oft **gefragt**	*wir* **wurden** oft **gefragt**
ihr **werdet** oft **gefragt**	*ihr* **wurdet** oft **gefragt**
sie/Sie **werden** oft **gefragt**	*sie/Sie* **wurden** oft **gefragt**

The text mainly uses the third person singular, e.g. *festgestellt* **wurde** (3), *bedrängt* **wurde** (7), and the third person plural forms, e.g. **wurden** *angeklickt* (4–5), **wurden** *verglichen* (19–20), *ignoriert* **wurden** (24–25).

> [81] For the formation of past participles see **13.2b-d**.

18.4 THE AGENT

Some passive sentences may specify an agent: e.g. 'He was asked <u>by the girl</u>'. In German, the direct agent of the action is usually introduced by *von* (+ dat.): *Er wurde* **von** *dem Mädchen gefragt*. This usually refers to **people**, as in our text: e.g. *Wer in der Schule schon* **von** *einem nervigen "Holger" bedrängt wurde* 'Who was pestered at school **by** an irritating "Holger"' (7).

Less commonly, the agent might be an inanimate object or a more abstract concept, e.g. 'inflation', 'bad weather', 'the current situation', in which case *durch* is used: e.g. *Die Wirtschaft wird* **durch** *die Inflation geschwächt* 'the economy is weakened by/through inflation' (not in text). As can be seen from the translation, if English can use 'through', this indicates the use of *durch* in German.

Although *von* is usually used with human agents, it can be used with an inanimate object if this object is seen as being the **direct** agent of the action. Contrast the following sentences (not in text):

- *Die Katze wurde* **von** *einem Auto überfahren* — The cat was run over by a car
- *Die Katze wurde* **durch** *fahrlässiges Fahren getötet* — The cat was killed by/through careless driving

18.5 THE *SEIN*-PASSIVE

Usually, when one talks of 'the passive' in German one is referring to the *werden* + past participle constructions outlined above. There is, however, another type of passive which is formed using the auxiliary verb *sein* plus the past participle and, consequently, is known as the '*sein*-passive'. The difference between the *werden*-passive and the *sein*-passive is that the former indicates an **action**, which is often shown using an *-ing* form in English, while the latter describes a **state**:

Das Brot **wird** *geschnitten*	The bread is being cut (i.e. at this moment)
Das Brot **ist** *geschnitten*[82]	The bread is cut (i.e. has already been cut)
Das Auto **wurde** *repariert*	The car was being repaired
Das Auto **war** *repariert*	The car was repaired

> [82] In the *sein*-passive, the past participle functions like an **adjective**. Thus *Das Brot ist geschnitten* is grammatically equivalent to *Das Brot ist frisch*.

There is an example of the *sein*-passive in our text: ... *ist vielleicht auch von seinem Namensvetter abgeschreckt* '... **is** perhaps **put off** by someone with the same name' (7–8).

18.6 *SICH LASSEN* + INFINITIVE WITH A PASSIVE MEANING

When used reflexively and with a bare infinitive, the verb *lassen* can be used to express a passive meaning, even though the grammatical construction is not a passive. For example, in our text the sentence *Daher ließ sich ... schnell erkennen, welche Vornamen am häufigsten ignoriert wurden* can be translated with a passive in English: 'Consequently, it could quickly **be identified** which first names were most often ignored' (23–25).

Other points to note in the text

- Genitive: *der* Single-Vornamen (2), *einer* Studie (3), *des* Datingportal**s** (3–4, 20), *des* Vornamen**s** (14), ausgewählt**er** Vornamen (19), ein**es** registriert**en** Nutzer**s** (22), *der* Faktoren (23) (see **3.1a(iv)**), and genitive form of demonstrative: *dessen* bewusst 'aware of that' (28) (see **8.4**).
- Comparatives: *selt**ener*** (5), *läng**er*** (14), *größ**er*** (18), *weit**er*** (22); *ansprechend**er*** (30) and superlative: *häufig**st*** (see **Ch. 6**).
- Conditional: *Männer* **würden** ... *dem Profil von "Edeltraut" weniger Beachtung* **schenken** 'Men would pay less attention to "Edeltraut's" profile' (9–10), *Wir* **würden** *euch eine Chance* **geben** 'We would give you a chance' (32) (see **16.1–16.2**).

Discover more about the passive

18.7 OTHER TENSES OF THE PASSIVE

The perfect and pluperfect tenses also have passive equivalents,[83] which are formed using the **perfect** and **pluperfect** tenses of *werden* respectively, plus the past participle of the main verb. Note that *geworden* is shortened to *worden* to avoid having to pronounce two participles beginning with *ge-*:

Perfect: 'I have been asked'	*Ich **bin** (du bist/er ist/wir sind/ihr seid/sie sind)* ***gefragt worden***
Pluperfect: 'I had been asked'	*Ich **war** (du warst/er war/wir waren/ihr wart/sie waren)* ***gefragt worden***

The tenses are used in the passive in the same way as in the active: e.g. the perfect passive is used mainly in **spoken** German to refer to the past while the past passive is used mainly in **written** German, hence its frequency of occurrence in our text.

[83] The future passive (e.g. *Ich **werde** gefragt **werden** '*I will be asked') is rarely used, as the present is usually preferred when referring to the future. Future perfect, conditional and conditional perfect passives also exist (e.g. *Ich **werde** gefragt **worden sein*** 'I will have been asked', *Ich **würde** gefragt **werden*** 'I would be asked'; *Ich **wäre** gefragt **worden*** 'I would've been asked') though, in practice, they are not frequently used.

18.8 MODAL VERBS WITH A PASSIVE

The passive can also be used with modals, in which case *werden* appears in the infinitive: e.g. *Es muss sofort gemacht werden* 'It must be done immediately'.

18.9 *ZU* + INFINITIVE WITH A PASSIVE MEANING

When *zu* plus an infinitive occurs with the verbs *sein* and *bleiben* it often has a passive meaning. Consider the following examples:

Diese Kriterien sind zu erfüllen	These criteria are to be fulfilled
Das Problem bleibt noch zu besprechen	The problem remains to be discussed
Der Aufsatz ist bis nächste Woche abzugeben	The essay is to be handed in by next week

18.10 THE USE OF *ES* WITH A PASSIVE

If the passive is used in a general statement not referring to any specific person or thing, the sentence can appear without a proper subject: e.g. 'There was a lot of smoking going on', where the emphasis is on the action of the verb and not on who was actually doing the smoking or what was being smoked. In English, such sentences often begin with 'there', which has a very general meaning. In German, the equivalent is *es*: *Es wurde viel geraucht*, and the verb is in the third person singular. If other words appear at the beginning of the sentence, however, *es* is omitted: e.g. *Auf der Fete wurde viel geraucht* 'there was a lot of smoking (going on) at the party'.

Es can also occur when there **is** a proper subject in the sentence, but only when the subject **follows** the verb, thereby allowing *es* to appear at the beginning of the sentence: e.g. *Es wurden viele Zigaretten geraucht* is an alternative to *Viele Zigaretten wurden geraucht*. We can see by the plural verb form that the verb agrees with the subject where present, not with *es*.

18.11 VERBS TAKING THE DATIVE OR A PREPOSITIONAL OBJECT

We saw in **18.2** above that subjects of passive sentences are in the nominative case: e.g. *Clara und Lisa fragten den Lehrer* becomes *Der Lehrer wurde … gefragt* in the passive. However, if a verb takes a dative object, or a prepositional object, then these **remain the same** when the sentence is passive: e.g. *Clara und Lisa antworteten dem Lehrer* does not become **Der Lehrer wurde … geantwortet* but *Dem Lehrer wurde … geantwortet* 'The teacher was answered …'.

Similarly, *Clara und Lisa sprachen mit dem Lehrer* becomes *Mit dem Lehrer wurde … gesprochen* in the passive 'The teacher was spoken to …', and the whole prepositional phrase (preposition plus whatever case it takes) remains unchanged.

18.12 THE PASSIVE IN SPOKEN GERMAN

The passive is used much **less frequently** in spoken German than in the written language. This may cause problems for English learners of German, as the passive is used extensively both in written and in spoken English. Often an English passive is best translated as an ordinary active sentence in German, particularly where an agent is present: e.g. 'I was treated badly by my boss' → *Mein Chef hat mich schlecht behandelt*. If the agent is not present speakers will either use the passive ('I was treated badly' → *Ich wurde schlecht behandelt*) or, very often, an active construction with *man* 'one' as the subject: ***Man** hat mich schlecht behandelt* (see **7.1b**).

✎ **EXERCISES**

Vocabulary topic: *Schule*

1 Put the bracketed verbs into the present passive:

   1 Musik oft als Wahlfach [nemen].
   2 Die Hausarbeit muss bis Montag [abgeben].
   3 Fragen können während der Gruppenarbeit [stellen].
   4 Das Klassenzimmer [aufräumen].
   5 Wie viele Fächer hier [unterrichten]?

2 Put the bracketed verbs into the appropriate tense of the passive:

   1 Der Unterricht [stören, *past*].
   2 Die Prüfungen [verschieben, *perfect*].
   3 Dieses Thema schon drei Mal [besprechen, *pluperfect*], aber trotzdem fanden es die Schüler sehr schwierig zu verstehen.
   4 Die Übungen nicht [machen, *perfect*].
   5 Keine Taschenrechner dürfen [benutzen, *present*].
   6 Die Schüler nächsten Monat in diesem Fach [prüfen, *future*].

3 Put the active sentences below into the passive and pay attention to the following: i) Do not change the TENSE of the original sentence; ii) Decide whether the AGENT should be preceded by *von* or *durch*. If the agent is *man*, it should be omitted:

Example: Der Schüler fragte den Lehrer, wer Bismarck war.
Answer: Der Lehrer **wurde von** dem Schüler **gefragt**, wer Bismarck war.

   1 Die Schüler beleidigten den Lehrer.
   2 Der Klassensprecher hat das Problem erwähnt.
   3 Der Sportlehrer hatte Klaus für die Fußballmannschaft der Schule ausgewählt.
   4 Das schlechte Wetter ruinierte das Hockeyturnier.
   5 Das Geräusch des Rasenmähers hat die Konzentration der Prüfungskandidaten gestört.
   6 Der Direktor wird den Unruhestifter aus der Schule herausschmeißen.
   7 Die Lehrer zwangen Peter wegen seiner schlechten Noten sitzenzubleiben.
   8 Die Prüfer haben sechs Auszeichnungen erteilt.
   9 Die Organisatoren hatten den Schüleraustausch wegen Mangel an Interesse gestrichen.
   10 Man kann ihn wegen Schwänzerei der Schule verweisen.

4 Identify the passives in the following text and say whether they are *werden* passives, *sein* passives or *zu* + infinitive passives:

   • Der Religionsunterricht ist in den öffentlichen Schulen mit Ausnahme der bekenntnisfreien Schulen ordentliches Lehrfach. Unbeschadet des staatlichen Aufsichtsrechtes wird der

Religionsunterricht in Übereinstimmung mit den Grundsätzen der Religionsgemeinschaften erteilt. Kein Lehrer darf gegen seinen Willen verpflichtet werden, Religionsunterricht zu erteilen.

- Das Recht zur Errichtung von privaten Schulen wird gewährleistet. Private Schulen als Ersatz für öffentliche Schulen bedürfen der Genehmigung des Staates und unterstehen den Landesgesetzen. Die Genehmigung ist zu erteilen, wenn die privaten Schulen in ihren Lehrzielen und Einrichtungen sowie in der wissenschaftlichen Ausbildung ihrer Lehrkräfte nicht hinter den öffentlichen Schulen zurückstehen und eine Sonderung der Schüler nach den Besitzverhältnissen der Eltern nicht gefördert wird. Die Genehmigung ist zu versagen, wenn die wirtschaftliche und rechtliche Stellung der Lehrkräfte nicht genügend gesichert ist.
- Eine private Volksschule ist nur zuzulassen, wenn die Unterrichtsverwaltung ein besonderes pädagogisches Interesse anerkennt oder, auf Antrag von Erziehungsberechtigten, wenn sie als Gemeinschaftsschule, als Bekenntnis- oder Weltanschauungsschule errichtet werden soll und eine öffentliche Volksschule dieser Art in der Gemeinde nicht besteht.

Aus dem Grundgesetz für die Bundesrepublik Deutschland, 1993, Artikel 7, Schulwesen [§3–5].

✎ FURTHER EXERCISES

5 Put the active sentences below into the passive, moving the underlined nouns/pronouns to the beginning of the passive sentence with their accompanying articles, pronouns, prepositions etc. Bear in mind that SOME of these must be put into the nominative while others must stay unchanged. Omit the agent.

Example: Er rechnete nicht mit der <u>Frage</u>.
Answer: <u>Mit der Frage</u> **wurde** nicht **gerechnet**.

1 Man hat meinem <u>Sohn</u> bedroht.
2 Jemand hat mitten in der Nacht meinen <u>Mann</u> angerufen.
3 Bei uns in der Firma nehmen sie auf <u>keinen</u> Rücksicht.
4 Man redet oft über <u>Geld</u>, aber es gibt wichtigere Dinge im Leben.
5 Jemand folgte meiner <u>Freundin</u> nach Hause.
6 Sie hatten die <u>Nachbarn</u> nicht eingeladen.
7 Sie haben den <u>Angestellten</u> nichts gesagt.
8 Man spielt nicht mit <u>Elektrizität</u> herum!
9 Schau, man hat <u>mir</u> diese leckeren Pralinen geschenkt!
10 Man hatte den <u>Brief</u> noch nicht weggeschickt.

6 **a)** Rewrite your answers to question 2 above using *man* instead of the passive.
   b) Translate the following sentences into German using *man*:

Example: He was seen → ***Man** sah ihn* (OR ***Man** hat ihn gesehen*).

1 My handbag has been stolen!
2 What can be done?

3 I was given a cheque.

4 He is often described as arrogant.

7 Put the following sentences into the *sein*-passive (present tense) to express a state. Where this is not grammatically possible (i.e. where the verb cannot describe a state), use a *werden*-passive in the perfect. Translate your answers into English:

Example: Jemand hat den Tisch gedeckt.
Answer: Der Tisch **ist gedeckt**. 'The table is set'.

1 Jemand hat die Tasse gebrochen.

2 Jemand hat den Nagel gebogen.

3 Jemand hat meinen Bruder gesehen.

4 Jemand hat Maria eben geküsst.

5 Jemand hat das Kind angezogen.

6 Jemand hat die Zeitung gelesen.

8 Match up the inventions in the left column with the correct inventors in the right column, making a passive sentence for each, using the tense given:

Example: der Dieselmotor (*past*)
Answer: Der Dieselmotor **wurde** von Rudolf Diesel **erfunden**.

1 der Dieselmotor (*past*)	Michael Faraday
2 das Flugzeug (*past*)	Carl Benz
3 die Atombombe (*past*)	Johannes Gutenberg
4 das Dynamo (*past*)	Daniel Gabriel Fahrenheit
5 der Personenaufzug (*perfect*)	Robert Oppenheimer
6 die Glühbirne (*perfect*)	Rudolf Diesel
7 das Automobil (*perfect*)	Alessandro Volta
8 das Thermometer (*perfect*)	Guglielmo Marconi
9 die Buchdruckerkunst (*pluperfect*)	Orville und Wilbur Wright
10 die Fotografie (*pluperfect*)	E. A. Edison und J. Swan
11 der Rundfunk (*pluperfect*)	Benjamin Franklin
12 der Sportschuh (*past*)	Louis-Jacques Daguerre
13 die Batterie (*past*)	Charles Goodyear
14 der Computer (*past*)	Elisha A. Otis
15 das Gummi (*perfect*)	Adolf (Adi) Dassler
16 der Blitzableiter (*perfect*)	Konrad Zuse

19 | Separable verbs

Text

Das Lied vom Anstreicher Hitler

Der Anstreicher Hitler
Sagte: Liebe Leute, **laßt**[84] mich **ran**!
Und er nahm einen Kübel frische Tünche
5 Und **strich** das deutsche Haus neu **an**.
Das ganze deutsche Haus neu **an**.

Der Anstreicher Hitler
Sagte: Diesen Neubau hat's im Nu!
Und die Löcher und die Risse und die Sprünge
10 Das **strich** er einfach alles **zu**.
Die ganze Scheiße **strich** er **zu**.

O Anstreicher Hitler
Warum warst du kein Maurer? Dein Haus
Wenn die Tünche in den Regen kommt
15 **Kommt** der Dreck drunter wieder **raus**.
Kommt das ganze Scheißhaus wieder **raus**.

Der Anstreicher Hitler
Hatte bis auf Farbe nichts studiert
Und als man ihn nun eben **ranließ**
20 Da hat er alles **ange**schmiert.
Ganz Deutschland hat er **ange**schmiert.

---

[84] now spelt *lasst*.

Aus: Bertolt Brecht *Gedichte III*, © Suhrkamp, 1961.

der Anstreicher – painter and decorator	*der Riss/ der Sprung* – crack
jemanden ranlassen – to give s.o. a go	*zustreichen* – to paint over
anstreichen – to paint	*der Maurer* – bricklayer
die Tünche – whitewash	*der Dreck* – dirt
der Neubau – newbuild	*anschmieren* – to smear
hat's im Nu – will be done in a jiffy	(metaphorically – to con)

⌕ **Separable verbs in the text**

19.1 POSITION OF PREFIX

German has a special class of verbs known as **separable**, as their prefixes are separated from the verb in certain grammatical constructions. For instance, when the verb is finite (i.e. when it indicates a certain tense, person and number) its prefix is sent to the end of the clause. Thus, the infinitive *ranlassen* becomes *lasst ... ran* in line 3 of the text. Similarly: *anstreichen* → *strich ... an* (5, 6), *zustreichen* → *strich ... zu* (10, 11), *rauskommen* → *kommt ... raus* (15, 16).[85] If the finite verb has itself been sent to the end, due to the presence of a subordinating conjunction, for example, the prefix and verb come together again: *als ... ranließ* (19). In the past participle, *ge-* appears between the separable prefix and the verb stem: *angeschmiert* (20, 21) and, similarly, in a '*zu* + infinitive' construction the *zu* is placed between prefix and verb: e.g. *rauszukommen*, *anzuschmieren* (not in text).

> [85] Note that, in longer sentences containing two or more clauses, the prefix goes to the end of its clause, not to the end of the sentence: e.g. *Ich strich das Zimmer **an** und putzte die Fenster.*

Other points to note in the text

- Imperative in *ihr*-form: *lasst* (3). [older spelling *laßt*] (see **11.4**).
- Use of *wenn* and *als*: *wenn* with present tense (14), *als* with past (19) (see **25.3a**).
- Colloquial usage: *heranlassen* → *ranlassen* (3), *herauskommen* → *rauskommen* (15, 16), *hat es* → *hat's* (8), *darunter* → *drunter* (15).

Discover more about separable verbs

19.2 SEPARABLE VERSUS INSEPARABLE

19.2a Separable verbs

Separable verbs are recognised by the fact that their prefixes are usually identical to **prepositions**, e.g. *an, aus, mit, um, vor, zu*,[86] or variants thereof. Variants can be formed by prefixing prepositions with *her-*, e.g. *heran, heraus* (which in the text are shortened to the more colloquial *ran* and *raus*); *hin-: hinein, hinaus, hinüber*,[87] and *da(r)-*, e.g. *davon-, dazu-, daraus-*. Often, the meaning of the preposition is recognisable within the verb: e.g. *ausgehen* 'to go **out**', *aufschauen* 'to look **up**', *mitkommen* 'to come **with** (someone)', but this is not always the case: e.g. *umkommen* does not mean 'to come around' but 'to die'. In speech, separable prefixes are always stressed (indicated here by underlining): e.g. *<u>an</u>kommen, <u>mit</u>machen*.

There are also several separable verbs whose prefixes are not prepositional: e.g. *fernsehen* 'to watch TV', *kennenlernen* 'to get to know', *stattfinden* 'to take place', *vollstopfen* 'to cram full'.

> [86] Note that *in* has the prefix equivalent *ein-*, e.g. *einsteigen* 'to climb in'.
>
> [87] Often *her* is used to indicate movement towards the speaker while *hin* indicates movement away from the speaker: e.g. *Er kam in mein Zimmer **herein*** vs. *er ging aus dem Zimmer **hinaus**. Her-* and *hin-* can also be used on their own as separable prefixes: e.g. *hinlegen* 'to lie down', *herkommen* 'to come here'.

19.2b Inseparable verbs

By contrast, inseparable prefixes are not usually prepositional (but see **19.2c** below). They are: *be-, ent-, er-, ge-, ver-, zer* and are unstressed: e.g. *be<u>spre</u>chen* 'to discuss', *ent<u>spre</u>chen* 'to correspond to', *er<u>kennen</u>* 'to recognise', *ge<u>stehen</u>* 'to admit', *ver<u>stehen</u>* 'to understand', *zer<u>stören</u>* 'to destroy'. They are never separated from the verb, e.g. *Ich verstehe das*, and do not admit *ge-* in the past participle, e.g. *Ich habe es besprochen/erkannt/verstanden/zerstört* (see **27.3a** for their meanings).

19.2c Prefixes which may be separable or inseparable

Less commonly, a prefix can be separable or inseparable depending on the verb to which it attaches: e.g. ***durch**kommen* 'to get through' (*Ich komme durch*) vs. *durch<u>denk</u>en* 'to think through' (*Ich durchdenke es*); *sich **<u>um</u>**drehen* 'to turn around' (*Ich drehe mich um*) vs. *um<u>armen</u>* 'to hug' (*Ich umarme dich*). Sometimes the verbs may look identical and differ only in meaning (indicated by the placing of stress): e.g. ***<u>über</u>**ziehen* 'to put on' (*Ich **ziehe** mir einen warmen Pulli **über*** 'I put on a warm jumper') vs. *über<u>zieh</u>en* 'to cover' (*Ich **überziehe** das Bett mit einer frischen Decke* 'I cover the bed with a fresh blanket').

19.3 COMMON SEPARABLE PREFIXES

Below is a list of the most frequently used separable prefixes and some of the meanings usually associated with them:

ab-	'away/off'	*Ich fahre **ab***	Im setting off
an-	'on'	*Ich ziehe einen Mantel **an***	I put on a coat
auf-	'up'	*Ich stehe **auf***	I get up
	'open'	*Ich mache die Tür **auf***	I open the door
aus-	'out'	*Ich gehe **aus***	I go out
	'off'	*Ich ziehe den Mantel **aus***	I take the coat off
ein-	'in'	*Er bricht **ein***	He's breaking in
mit-	'with/along'	*Komm **mit**!*	Come along
	'too'	*Er spielt **mit***	He's playing with (us)/too
nach-	'after'	*Er läuft ihr **nach***	He's running after her
vor-	'in front/ahead'	*Er dringt ständig **vor***	He's always pushing ahead
weg-	'away'	*Geh **weg**!, Sie liefen **weg***	Go away! They ran away
zu-	'towards'	*Er kam auf mich **zu***	He came towards me
	'shut'	*Ich machte die Tür **zu***	I shut the door

✎ EXERCISES

Vocabulary topic: *Wohnen*

1 Complete the following sentences by inserting the correct form of the bracketed separable verbs into the correct place. All sentences are in the present tense:

1 Wir [einziehen] am Samstag in unser neues Haus.

2 Ich [umziehen] heute.

3   Wann [ausziehen] du?

4   Die Männer [anstreichen] gerade das Wohnzimmer.

5   Die Gäste [sich hinsetzen] am Tisch.

6   Ich versuche aus dem Küchenfenster zu [hinausschauen], aber es ist zu schmutzig.

7   Wir [vorhaben] die neuen Gardinen zu [aufhängen].

8   [Aufdrehen] du den Wasserhahn?

2   Put your answers to question 1 into the perfect tense, paying particular attention to the form of the past participle.

3   Complete the following sentences by inserting the correct form of the bracketed verbs into the correct place, using the tenses given. Note that some of the bracketed verbs are separable and others are inseparable:

1   Er war müde und [sich hinlegen, *past*] aufs Sofa.

2   Als er ins Badezimmer [hereinkommen, *past*], saß sie schon im Bad.

3   Ich [ersetzen, *present*] diesen alten Teppich.

4   Wir [einrichten, *present*] eine neue Küche.

5   [Wegreißen, *perfect*] du die alte Tapete?

6   Die Katze [zerreißen, *perfect*] meine neue Bettdecke.

7   Wenn du das Fenster [aufmachen, *present*], können wir das Schlafzimmer ein bisschen lüften.

8   Der Maurer versucht die Wand zu [verputzen].

9   Ich habe keine Zeit dieses Geschirr zu [abtrocknen].

10 Man [herrichten, *perfect*] das Zimmer noch nicht.

11 [Ausschalten, *imperative: 'du'-form*] den Fernseher!

12 Er [überziehen, *present*] den Esstisch mit einer bunten Tischdecke.

20 | Reflexive verbs

Text

Lass mich raus aus der Erasmus-Blase!

*Über 30.000 deutsche Studenten absolvierten im vergangenen Jahr ein
Erasmus-Semester im europäischen Ausland. Doch häufig haben
Hochschüler in der Ferne dabei mehr Kontakt zu anderen*
5 *Austauschstudenten als zu einheimischen Kommilitonen. [...]. "Man bleibt in
einer Blase", sagt Jule Türke vom International Office der Universität
Frankfurt am Main. Das **lässt sich** jedoch leicht **vermeiden**. Erasmus-
Experten verschiedener deutscher Unis wissen Rat:*

Schon vor der Abreise sollte man sich darüber informieren, welche
10 Projekte es an der Wunsch-Universität gibt, um Erasmus-Studenten die
Integration zu erleichtern. "Viele Unis bieten zum Beispiel ein Buddy-
Programm an", sagt Verena Wagner von der Erasmus-Beratung der
Universität Konstanz. Dabei hilft ein einheimischer "Kumpel" einem oder
mehreren Auslandsstudenten, **sich** an der Uni oder im Alltag
15 **zurechtzufinden**. "Über den Buddy **lassen sich** dann auch gut andere
Einheimische **kennenlernen**." Häufig schlügen Universitäten von <u>sich</u> aus
eine Teilnahme am Buddy-Programm vor, ansonsten **lohne** es **sich**,
nachzufragen.

Dazu sollte man **sich** informieren, wie viele Kurse des gewünschten
20 Studienfaches auch für Austauschstudenten geöffnet sind. "Wenn Erasmus-
Studenten nur an speziellen Seminaren teilnehmen können, bleiben sie
zwangsläufig unter <u>sich</u>", sagt Wagner, die selbst in Stockholm ein
Auslandssemester absolvierte. Daher sollte man **sich** für eine Uni
entscheiden, bei der Erasmus-Studenten reguläre Kurse mit
25 Einheimischen besuchen können. [...]

Ist man an der Uni angekommen, steht meist eine Orientierungswoche
speziell für Erasmus-Studenten an. "Dabei lernt man die anderen Ausländer
kennen", sagt Türke. Alle sind neu, suchen Kontakt, man hat die gleichen
Probleme – es ist bequem, in dieser Gruppe zu bleiben. "Da muss man früh
30 entgegensteuern", rät Türke. "Also nicht immer nur mit anderen Erasmus-
Studenten in die Mensa gehen, sondern auch mal Einheimische fragen." In
der Theatergruppe, dem Uni-Chor oder Sportkursen lernt man schnell
Einheimische kennen – für diese Angebote sollte man **sich** aber bereits in
der ersten Woche **anmelden**, bevor sie überfüllt sind. [...]

35 Das Internetportal Couchsurfing sei eine gute Gelegenheit, noch mehr
von dem Erasmus-Land zu sehen, empfiehlt Inga Rosemann. "Generell
sollte man im Auslandssemester so viel reisen wie möglich und nicht nur
zwischen Uni und Wohnung pendeln." Für größere Trips **biete** es **sich an**,

einen Monat länger im Ausland zu verweilen. "Für solche Reisen ist eine
40 Erasmus-Gruppe aber wiederum sehr nett." Insgesamt sei es wichtig, eine
Balance zwischen dem Kontakt mit anderen Austauschlern und
Einheimischen zu schaffen. "Man sollte das Semester nicht in der Blase
verbringen, aber man muss **sich** deswegen auch nicht komplett von den
anderen Austauschstudenten **abschotten**."

Aus: *Spiegel Online (Unispiegel)*, 16/04/12, von Samuel Acker, © dapd.

absolvieren – to complete one's studies	*zwangsläufig* – inevitably
der Kommilitone – classmate	*entgegensteuern* – to steer away from
der Austauschstudent – exchange student	*sich anmelden* – to apply
die Blase – bubble	*pendeln* – to commute
sich zurechtfinden – to find one's way	*verweilen* – to stay somewhere
der Einheimische – native	*sich abschotten* – to seal oneself off

⌕ Reflexive verbs in the text

20.1 REFLEXIVE PRONOUNS

A reflexive verb is a verb whose direct object is a **reflexive pronoun**: e.g. *Ich wasche **mich** '*I wash **myself**'. A reflexive pronoun always refers to the same person/thing as the subject (i.e. 'I' and 'myself' are the same person). The reflexive pronouns in German are as follows:

sich entscheiden (23–24)	*ich entscheide **mich***	*wir entscheiden **uns***
'to decide'	*du entscheidest **dich***	*ihr entscheidet **euch***
	*er/sie/es entscheidet **sich***	*sie/Sie entscheiden **sich***

Reflexive pronouns usually follow the same word order as direct objects: i.e. they most commonly occur immediately after the subject and verb: *Das lässt **sich** (7), ansonsten lohne es **sich** (17), daher sollte man **sich** ... entscheiden* (23–24), *für größere Trips biete es **sich** an* (38), *man muss **sich** ... abschotten* (43–44); although sometimes the subject can be moved to later in the sentence, particularly when it is a noun rather than a pronoun: *Über den Buddy lassen **sich** dann auch gut andere Einheimische kennenlernen* (15–16).

20.2 VERBS USED REFLEXIVELY WITH A PASSIVE MEANING

Sometimes, a verb that is not usually a reflexive verb can be used with a reflexive pronoun to express a passive meaning. This is very common with the verb *lassen* 'to let', which when used reflexively and with another infinitive expresses the meaning 'can be done'. There are two examples of this in our text: *Das **lässt sich** jedoch leicht **vermeiden** '*However that **can** easily **be avoided**' (7), *... **lassen sich** dann auch gut andere Einheimische **kennenlernen** '*... you can also get to know other native students well' (15–16) (literally 'other native students **can** also **be got to know** well').

Another example of a verb being used reflexively with a passive meaning is *anbieten* in line 38: *Für größere Trips* **biete** *es* **sich an**, *einen Monat länger ... zu verweilen* 'For larger trips a further month's stay is offered' (literally 'For larger trips **it is offered** to stay a further month').

20.3 REFLEXIVE PRONOUNS USED ON THEIR OWN

Often a reflexive pronoun is used to express the concept of 'oneself', without being linked to a reflexive verb. This is particularly the case after prepositions, as our text demonstrates: *Häufig schlügen Universitäten von <u>sich</u> aus eine Teilnahme am Buddy-Programm vor* 'Frequently universities suggested participation in a buddy programme <u>themselves</u>' (16–17).[88] Similarly: ... *bleiben sie zwangsläufig unter <u>sich</u>* 'they inevitably keep to <u>themselves</u>' (21–22). Note that this last pronoun refers to the Erasmus students as a group rather than the individual self. Another way of translating the reflexive pronoun when it refers to more than one person is 'each other': e.g. 'they spend time with each other'.

[88] Contrast a sentence like 'they'll do it themselves' → *Sie machen es selbst/selber*, where there is no preposition and '-self' is rendered by *selbst/selber* rather than by a reflexive pronoun.

Other points to note in the text

- *Konjunktiv I* to indicate reported speech: *ansonsten* **lohne** *es* **sich** *nachzufragen* 'otherwise it is worth asking' (17–18), *Couchsurfing* **sei** *eine gute Gelegenheit* '"Couchsurfing" is a good opportunity' (35), *Für größere Trips* **biete** *es sich an* 'for larger trips it is offered' (38), *Insgesamt* **sei** *es wichtig* 'All in all it is important' (40) (see **17.1–17.3**).
- *Konjunktiv II* to indicate reported speech, where the Konjunktiv I form would look like an indicative: *Häufig* **schlügen** *Universitäten von sich aus eine Teilnahme am Buddy-Programm vor* (instead of *schlagen ... vor*) 'Frequently universities suggest ... ' (16–17) (see **17.4**).
- Compound words with a hyphen: *Erasmus-Blase* (1), *Erasmus-Semester* (3), *Erasmus-Experten* (7–8), *Erasmus-Studenten* (10, 20–21, 24, 27, 30–31), *Wunsch-Üniversität* (10), *Buddy-Programm* (11–12, 17), *Erasmus-Beratung* (12), *Uni-Chor* (32), *Erasmus-Land* (36), *Erasmus-Gruppe* (40) (see **27.4a**).
- Modal verbs: *sollte ... informieren* (9, 19), *teilnehmen* **können** (21), **sollte** *entscheiden* (23–24), *besuchen* **können** (25), **muss** *... entgegensteuern* (29–30), *sollte ... anmelden* (33–34), *sollte ... reisen* (37), *sollte ... verbringen* (42–43), *muss ... abschotten* (43–44) (see **21.3–21.4**).

Discover more about reflexive verbs

20.4 DIFFICULTIES WITH REFLEXIVES

For English learners one of the most difficult aspects of reflexive verbs in German is that they often do not correspond to English reflexives. Thus, while *Ich wasche mich* corresponds to the English reflexive 'I wash myself',[89] *Ich erinnere mich* 'I remember' is not reflexive in English. This means that reflexive verbs in German must simply be learnt as such. A selection of common verbs which are often used reflexively is given in **Table 20.1** below as a starting point. Note that those verbs marked with an asterisk are 'true reflexives' which can only be used with a reflexive pronoun. The others, although very often used reflexively, can also be used with other objects, e.g.:

[89] The option of omitting the reflexive pronoun with some verbs in English is not possible in German: e.g. 'I wash myself' or 'I wash' is always *Ich wasche* **mich** with the pronoun.

Ich wasche **mich** – *wasche* **mein Auto**	I wash (myself) – wash my car
Ich ziehe **mich** *an – ziehe* **mein Baby** *an*	I dress (myself) – dress my baby
Ich ärgere **mich** – *ärgere* **meine Mutter**	I'm annoyed – annoy my mother
Ich amüsiere **mich** – *amüsiere* **meine Freunde**	I enjoy myself – entertain my friends

A further complication arises from the fact that some reflexive verbs take a **dative** reflexive pronoun instead of the more common accusative reflexive given above. The dative pronouns differ from the accusatives only in the *ich*- and *du*-form:

e.g. *sich vorstellen*[90]	*ich stelle* **mir** *vor*	*wir stellen uns vor*
'to picture, imagine'	*du stellst* **dir** *vor*	*ihr stellt euch vor*
	er stellt sich vor	*sie/Sie stellen sich vor*

In **Table 20.1** the difference between the accusative and dative reflexives is made explicit by using the first person *ich*-form in the examples.[91]

[90] Not to be confused with *sich vorstellen* + accusative, meaning 'to introduce oneself', e.g. *Darf ich* **mich** *vorstellen?* 'May I introduce myself'.

[91] A major difference between accusative and dative reflexive pronouns is that the former cannot co-occur with an accusative object while the latter can: e.g. *Ich stelle* **mir** <u>*etwas Schlimmes*</u> *vor* 'I'm imagining something bad'.

Table 20.1 Verbs commonly used reflexively

ACCUSATIVE			
ich amüsiere mich	I enjoy myself	*ich fühle mich*	I feel
ich ärgere mich	I get annoyed	*ich interessiere mich für*	I'm interested in
*ich bedanke mich**	I thank	*ich irre mich**	I am wrong
*ich beeile mich**	I rush/hurry	*ich langweile mich*	I am bored
*ich benehme mich**	I behave (myself)	*ich lege mich hin*	I lie down
ich bewege mich	I move	*ich rasiere mich*	I shave
ich drehe mich um	I turn around	*ich schäme mich**	I'm ashamed
ich dusche mich	I have a shower	*ich setze mich*	I sit down
ich erinnere mich	I remember	*ich verstecke mich*	I hide
ich frage mich	I wonder	*ich wasche mich*[†]	I wash (myself)
*ich freue mich**	I am pleased	*ich ziehe mich an/*	I get dressed/
*ich freue mich auf**	I look forward to	*aus/um*	undressed/changed

DATIVE			
*ich bilde mir ein**	I imagine (wrongly)	*ich stelle mir vor**	I imagine
*ich nehme mir vor**	I plan/intend to	*ich widerspreche mir*	I contradict myself
*Ich überlege mir (etwas)**	I think (sth.) over	*ich tue mir weh*	I hurt myself

* 'True' reflexive

† But if a body part is mentioned, the possessive dative is used: e.g. *Ich wasche* **mir** *die Hände* (see **7.8**).

Another verb which can occur quite frequently with a dative reflexive pronoun is *kaufen* 'to buy', which is not reflexive as such, but when it occurs with the reflexive pronoun it expresses the meaning 'to buy oneself (something)': e.g. *Ich kaufe **mir** ein neues Kleid* 'I'm buying **myself** a new dress'.

✎ EXERCISES

Vocabulary topic: *Körper und Gesundheit*

1 Replace the subjects in bold print with those given in brackets, changing the reflexive pronouns and verb forms where necessary. All reflexive pronouns are in the accusative:

Example: **Andreas** fühlt sich nicht gut. [ich]
Answer: **Ich fühle mich** nicht gut.

   1 **Ich** bemühe mich sehr das Rauchen aufzugeben. [er]
   2 **Die Kinder** haben sich erkältet. [du]
   3 **Dein Freund** hat sich mit dem Whiskeytrinken krank gemacht. [wir]
   4 Als **sie** schwanger war, hat **sie** sich jeden Morgen übergeben. [ich]
   5 **Ich** hatte vor zwei Wochen eine Grippe, aber jetzt habe **ich** mich erholt. [die Kinder]
   6 **Du** musst dich warm anziehen, sonst bekommst **du** einen Schnupfen. [ihr]

2 Make proper sentences from the following, using the correct verb forms and changing word order where necessary. Decide whether the reflexive pronoun in brackets should be in the accusative or dative:

   1 Habt ihr [sich putzen] die Zähne?
   2 Ich werde [sich duschen] und die Haare [sich waschen].
   3 Du hast einen Unfall gehabt? Hast du [sich wehtun]?
   4 Du bist ganz schmutzig. Hast du heute nicht [sich waschen]?
   5 Ich habe das Bein [sich brechen].
   6 Ich muss [sich beeilen]. Ich habe einen Arzttermin.
   7 Sie müssen ärztlich [sich untersuchen lassen].
   8 Er hat aufgehört [sich rasieren]. Der Stoppelbart passt ihm sehr gut.
   9 Wir beide [sich schämen] wegen unseres Gewichts.
  10 Hast du das Handgelenk [sich verstauchen]?

✎ FURTHER EXERCISES

3 Some (but not all!) of the sentences below are ungrammatical due to missing reflexive pronouns. Add the appropriate pronouns in the correct place only where necessary:

   1 Interessierst du für Fußball?
   2 Er arbeitet für eine andere Firma.
   3 Ich freue sehr auf die Sommerferien.
   4 Erinnert ihr an letzten Silvester?

5 Ich habe vergessen, wieviel ich für das Auto bezahlt habe.

6 Nein, das stimmt nicht. Sie müssen geirrt haben.

7 Er langweilt zu Hause.

8 Kannst du vorstellen, wie ich gefühlt habe?

9 Er hat erzählt, dass ihn seine Frau verlassen habe.

10 Wir wollten irgendwo hinsetzen, aber es gab keinen Platz.

21 | Infinitives and modal verbs

Text

Vielleicht haben triviale Gespräche vor allem die Funktion, dass man von sich selbst **reden** <u>kann</u>; daher auch die nicht enden <u>wollenden</u> Themen wie Krankheit, Kinder, Reisen, Erfolg, wie auch die unzähligen, einem wichtig erscheinenden täglichen Begebenheiten. Da man ja nicht beständig über
5 sich selbst **reden** <u>kann</u>, ohne in den Verdacht **zu geraten**, langweilig **zu sein**, <u>muss</u> man – **um** nur über sich selbst reden **zu können** – auch bereit **sein**, anderen **zuzuhören**, wenn sie nur über sich selbst reden. Private Treffen und oftmals auch Treffen von Vereinigungen und Gruppen sind kleine Märkte, wo man sein Bedürfnis, über sich **zu reden** und den Wunsch,
10 angehört **zu werden**, gegen das gleiche Bedürfnis anderer austauscht. Die meisten respektieren dieses gegenseitige Arrangement. Die, die dies nicht tun und mehr über sich selbst **reden** <u>wollen</u>, als sie bereit sind, anderen **zuzuhören** sind „Spielverderber"; sie sind unbeliebt und <u>müssen</u> sich, um toleriert **zu werden**, minderwertige Gesellschaft **aussuchen**.
15   Man <u>kann</u> das Bedürfnis vieler Menschen, über sich selbst **zu reden** und auch angehört **zu werden**, kaum **überschätzen**. Wäre dieses Bedürfnis nur bei sehr narzissistischen, ganz von sich absorbierten Personen vorhanden, <u>so könnte</u> man es leicht **verstehen**. Aber wir finden es auch beim Durchschnittsmenschen, und die Gründe dafür wurzeln in unserer Kultur.
20 Der moderne Mensch ist ein Massenmensch, er ist in hohem Maße „sozialisiert", aber er ist sehr vereinsamt […]. Der Mensch hat sich von den anderen entfremdet und befindet sich in einem Dilemma: Er hat vor nahem Kontakt mit anderen Angst, und er hat genau so Angst, allein **zu sein** und keinen Kontakt **zu haben**. Es ist die Aufgabe der trivialen Unterhaltung, die
25 Frage **zu beantworten**: Wie <u>kann</u> ich alleine bleiben, ohne einsam **zu sein**? Das Reden wird zur Sucht. Während ich rede, weiß ich, dass ich existiere, dass ich kein Niemand bin, dass ich eine Vergangenheit, einen Beruf, eine Familie habe. Indem ich über all das rede, bestätige ich mich selbst. Ich brauche aber jemanden, der mir zuhört. Hätte ich nur mich, würde ich
30 verrückt **werden**; der Zuhörer verhilft mir zur Illusion eines Dialogs, wo es sich in Wirklichkeit um einen Monolog handelt.

Aus: Erich Fromm, *Vom Haben zum Sein: Wege und Irrwege der Selbsterfahrung.* Hrsg. von Rainer Funk.
© Rainer Funk, 1989.

unzählig – countless	*überschätzen* – to overestimate
die Begebenheit – event	*vorhanden sein* – to be present
beständig – constantly	*der Durchschnittsmensch* – average person
der Verdacht – suspicion	*wurzeln in* – to be rooted in
die Vereinigung – organisation	*in hohem Maße* – to a great extent
das Bedürfnis – need	*vereinsamt* – lonely
austauschen – to exchange	*sich entfremden* – to become alienated
der Spielverderber – kill-joy	*die Aufgabe* – task
unbeliebt – unpopular	*die Unterhaltung* – conversation
minderwertig – inferior	*bestätigen* – to confirm

⌕ Infinitives in the text

21.1 INFINITIVES WITH *ZU*

The infinitive is the form of the verb, usually ending in *-en*, which is always given in dictionaries: e.g. *machen, kommen, gehen*. It most commonly occurs in a clause with *zu* (known as an 'infinitive clause') which is dependent on a preceding (or, less frequently, following) clause with a finite verb: e.g. *Ich habe heute keine Zeit, <u>mit dir ins Kino **zu gehen**</u>* 'I don't have time **to go** to the cinema with you today'. As can be seen from this example, *zu* immediately precedes the infinitive, which comes at the end of the clause.[92] If there are two infinitives, *zu* precedes the last one: e.g. *Ich habe Lust schwimmen **zu gehen*** 'I want **to go** swimming'. Examples of *zu* + infinitive from the text are:

• *bereit sein, anderen **zuzuhören** (7)*	to be prepared **to listen** to others
• *sein Bedürfnis, über sich **zu reden** (9)*	his need **to talk** about himself
• *den Wunsch angehört **zu werden** (10)*	the wish **to be** listened to
• *Es ist die Aufgabe der trivialen Unterhaltung, die Frage **zu beantworten** (24–25)[93]*	It is the task of trivial conversation **to answer** the question

[92] Separable verbs have *zu* between the prefix and main verb: e.g. *... mit dir **mitzukommen*** (see **19.1**).

[93] In older texts such as this, a comma is always used before an infinitive clause. This is no longer compulsory.

As can be seen from the above examples, *zu* + infinitive usually corresponds to English 'to + verb'. However, after *ohne* 'without' and certain nouns, zu + infinitive corresponds to an '-ing' form in English:[94]

• *ohne in den Verdacht **zu geraten**, langweilig **zu sein** (5–6)*	without **arousing** suspicion of **being** boring
• *ohne einsam **zu sein** (25)*	without **being** lonely

- *Angst, allein **zu sein** und keinen Kontakt*   fear of **being** alone and **having**
  __zu haben__ (23–24)   no contact

Note that *zu* + infinitive can also be used with a passive meaning: e.g. *Das Problem bleibt noch **zu besprechen*** (not in text) 'The problem remains to be discussed' (see **18.9**).

> 94   *Zu* + infinitive can only be used for English 'to' and '-ing' when the subject of the infinitive clause is the same as the preceding subject, otherwise a different clause with a finite verb must be used. Contrast 'I tried to ring her' *Ich versuchte sie anzurufen* with 'I asked <u>him</u> to ring her' *Ich fragte ihn, ob er sie anrufen könnte* (lit. 'I asked him if he could ring her'; 'he' being the subject of the second clause). Similarly with modals: 'I wanted to come' *Ich wollte kommen* vs. 'I wanted <u>you</u> to come' *Ich wollte, dass du kommst*.

21.2 INFINITIVES WITH *UM ... ZU*

When *zu* + infinitive expresses a purpose (i.e. if it can be rendered by 'in order to ...' in English) the infinitive clause begins with *um*:[95]

- ***um** nur über sich selbst reden **zu können*** (6)   **(in order) to be able to** just talk about oneself
- ***um** toleriert **zu werden*** (13–14)   **(in order) to be** tolerated

> 95   *Um ... zu* is also used after adjectives qualified by *zu* or *genug*: e.g. *Ich bin zu müde um auszugehen* 'I'm too tired to go out' (although *um* is sometimes omitted in the spoken language).

21.3 INFINITIVES WITH MODAL VERBS

Modal verbs are unusual in that when they occur with another verb it is always a bare infinitive (i.e. without *zu*): e.g. *Ich **will** es <u>machen</u>* 'I **want** <u>to do</u> it' (not **Ich will es zu machen*).[96] There are six modal verbs in German: *dürfen* 'to be allowed to/may', *können* 'to be able to/can', *mögen* 'to like to', *müssen* 'to have to/must', *sollen* 'to be supposed to/should' and *wollen* 'to want to', three of which appear in this text (underlined):

- *dass man von sich selbst <u>reden</u> **kann*** (2, 5)   that one **can** <u>talk</u> about oneself
- *die nicht <u>enden</u> **wollenden** Themen* (2)   the subjects that don't **want** <u>to end</u>
- *man **kann** das Bedürfnis [...] kaum <u>überschätzen</u>* (15–16)   one **can** hardly <u>overestimate</u> the need
- *so **könnte** man es leicht <u>verstehen</u>* (18)   then one **could** easily <u>understand</u> it
- ***muss** man [...] auch bereit <u>sein</u>* (6–7)   one **must** also <u>be</u> prepared
- *die, die [...] mehr über sich selbst <u>reden</u> **wollen*** (11–12)   those who **want** <u>to talk</u> more about themselves

The 'bare' infinitive *werden* in lines 29–30 is not dependent on a modal verb but is used as part of a conditional construction: *würde ich verrückt werden* 'I would become mad' (see **16.2a**).

[96] A few other verbs can also occur with a bare infinitive: verbs of perception such as *sehen, hören, fühlen,* some verbs of motion such as *fahren, gehen, kommen* and the verbs *lassen* and *bleiben*: e.g. *Ich hörte ihn kommen* 'I heard him coming', *sie lassen ihn warten* 'they are keeping him waiting'.

Other points to note in the text

- Use of genitive: *anderer* (10), *vieler Menschen* (15), *der trivialen Unterhaltung* (24), *eines Dialogs* (30) (see **3.1a(iv)**).
- Verbs taking a dative object: *einem wichtig erscheinenden* (3–4), *anderen zuzuhören* (7, 13), *verhilft mir* (30) (see **3.4a**).
- Extended attributes: *die nicht enden wollenden Themen* 'the topics that never want to end' (2), *die unzähligen, einem wichtig erscheinenden täglichen Begebenheiten* 'the countless daily events that seem important to people' (3–4), *bei ... ganz von sich absorbierten Personen* 'with ... people who are completely absorbed in themselves' (17) (see **5.3**).
- Use of *man* (1, 4, 6, 9, 15) and in its dative form *einem* (3) (see **7.1b**).
- Relative pronouns: *jemanden, der* (29); and with scope over two verbs, *Die, die dies nicht tun und mehr über sich selbst reden wollen* (11–12) (see **Ch. 9**).
- Conditional clauses with *wenn* omitted: *Wäre ... so könnte ...* (16–18), *Hätte ..., würde ...* (29) (see **16.4**).
- Reflexive pronouns: *sich* (9, 13, 17, 21, 31); *sich* emphasised by adding *selbst* '-self' (2, 5, 6, 7, 12, 15); *mich* (29), *mich selbst* (28) (see **Ch. 20**).

Discover more about modal verbs

21.4 THE FORMS OF THE MODALS

21.4a Formation of modal verbs

As modal verbs are very frequently used, students are advised to learn all their forms, many of which are irregular (indicated in bold print in **Table 21.1**).

Table 21.1 Modal verbs

	Present		Past stem*	Past participle†	Konj. II stem
dürfen 'may/ be allowed'	ich **darf** du **darfst** er **darf**	wir dürfen ihr dürft sie dürfen	durfte	gedurft	dürfte
können 'be able/ can'	ich **kann** du **kannst** er **kann**	wir können ihr könnt sie können	konnte	gekonnt	könnte
mögen 'like'	ich **mag** du **magst** er **mag**	wir mögen ihr mögt sie mögen	**mochte**	**gemocht**	**möchte**
müssen 'have to/ must'	ich **muss** du **musst** er **muss**	wir müssen ihr müsst sie müssen	musste	gemusst	müsste
sollen 'supposed to/ should'	ich **soll** du **sollst** er **soll**	wir sollen ihr sollt sie sollen	sollte	gesollt	sollte (no umlaut)
wollen 'want'	ich **will** du **willst** er **will**	wir wollen ihr wollt sie wollen	wollte	gewollt	wollte (no umlaut)

* The personal endings must then be added to the past and *Konjunktiv II* stems: e.g. *ich durfte, du durftest, er/sie/ es durfte, wir durften, ihr durftet, sie/Sie durften; ich könnte, du könntest* etc. (see **12.2b**).

† All modal verbs take *haben* as their perfect and pluperfect auxiliary.

21.4b Double infinitives with modals

In all perfect, pluperfect and future tenses, the modal verb appears in its **infinitive** form <u>after</u> the infinitive of the co-occuring verb:[97]

*Er wird wahrscheinlich <u>mitkommen</u> **wollen***	He'll probably want to come too.
*Ich habe es nicht <u>machen</u> **können***	I haven't been able to do it.
*Wir hätten zu Hause <u>bleiben</u> **sollen***	We should have stayed at home.

> [97] This also applies to *lassen* and verbs of perception such as *sehen* and *hören* when used together with another verb: e.g. *Ich habe mein Auto <u>reparieren</u> **lassen*** 'I have had my car repaired', *Er hat mich <u>kommen</u> **sehen*** 'He saw me coming' (but not to *gehen, fahren, bleiben* etc.).

This is particularly striking in the perfect, pluperfect and conditional perfect, as we would normally expect a past participle here (e.g. **Ich habe es nicht machen gekonnt*, which is completely ungrammatical). The past participles of modal verbs are only used when there is no co-occuring verb: e.g. *Ich habe es nicht* **gewollt** 'I didn't want it'; and as modals are much more often used together with another verb than they are on their own, the past participles of modals are relatively infrequent.

When a double infinitive construction appears in a **subordinate** clause (see **26.1b(i)**), the finite auxiliary verbs are sent not to the end of the clause, as would normally be the case, but to the position **immediately before the two infinitives**:

*Ich meine, <u>dass</u> er wahrscheinlich **wird** mitkommen wollen.*

<u>Obwohl</u> *ich es nicht **habe** machen können.*

*Ich wusste, <u>dass</u> wir zu Hause **hätten** bleiben sollen.*

21.5 OTHER TENSES FREQUENTLY USED WITH MODALS

In addition to ordinary present and past constructions: e.g. *Ich **will** kommen, Ich **wollte** kommen*, and the future and perfect constructions mentioned in **21.4b** above: e.g. *Er **wird** nicht kommen wollen, Er **hat** nicht kommen **wollen***, modals are commonly used in the following ways:

21.5a With a verb in the perfect tense (infinitive of *haben/sein* + past participle):

This is often used to express a **supposition**:

*Er **kann** es nicht <u>gemacht haben</u>*	He can't have done it.
*Er **könnte** der Mörder <u>gewesen sein</u>*	He could have been the murderer.
*Sie **müssen** schon <u>weggefahren sein</u>*	They must have already left.

21.5b In the conditional perfect

Here, it is the modal verb that is in the conditional perfect, which means that *haben* is always used as the auxiliary, irrespective of the co-occurring verb. This type of construction is used extremely frequently, so students are advised to learn these patterns by heart:

*Das **hättest** du nicht <u>machen</u> **sollen**!*	You shouldn't have done that!
*Wir **hätten** früher <u>kommen</u> **können***	We could have come earlier.

Note that 'could have' expresses a supposition when translated as *könnte* + perfect tense (see **21.5a**) while in the conditional perfect it means 'would have been able to'. This is also true of the other modals when used in this way: e.g. *Er **müsste** es schon gemacht haben* 'He should have done it already' (i.e. 'I'm assuming that he has done it') vs. *Er **hätte** es machen **müssen*** 'He should have done it' (i.e. 'He had to do it but didn't').

21.6 SEMANTIC DIFFICULTIES WITH MODALS

In particular contexts, modal verbs may have meanings that differ from the basic meanings given in **21.4a**. Some of these are particularly problematic for English learners of German:

- In English, 'can' is often used instead of 'may' when asking for permission: e.g. *Can I use your car?* This is usually translated not by *können* but by *dürfen*: **Darf** *ich dein Auto benutzen?* Similarly 'can't' is translated by *nicht dürfen* when refusing permission: *Hier **darfst** du nicht rauchen* 'You can't smoke here' (i.e. 'you're not allowed').[98]
- 'Must/have to' is usually translated by *müssen*: e.g. *Ich muss gehen*, yet when it is negative (i.e. 'must not'), *dürfen* is used: e.g. *Das **darfst** du nicht machen* 'You mustn't do that'. If *müssen* is used negatively: e.g. *Das **musst** du nicht machen*, it means 'don't **have to**': 'You don't have to do that'.
- *Sollen* usually means 'to be supposed/meant to': e.g. *Es **soll** eine Überraschung sein* 'It's supposed to be a surprise'. It also means 'supposed to' in the sense of 'it is said that': e.g. *Er **soll** seine Frau verlassen haben* 'He is supposed to have left his wife' (= 'it is said that he's left his

wife'). When used in the past/*Konjunktiv II*, *sollte* means 'should/ought to' and is very similar in meaning to *müssen*: e.g. *Ich **sollte** gehen* 'I should/ought to go'.

- *Wollen* usually means 'to want to', but when used with *eben* or *gerade* it has the meaning 'to be about to': e.g. *Ich wollte dich **eben/gerade** anrufen* 'I was just about to phone you'.

- The *Konjunktiv II* forms *könnte* and *dürfte* are often used to express possibility and probability respectively: i.e. *könnte* means 'could/may/might' and *dürfte* means 'is likely': e.g. *Klaus **könnte** jetzt zu Hause sein* 'Klaus could/may/might be at home now' vs. *Klaus **dürfte** jetzt zu Hause sein* 'Klaus is probably/likely to be at home now'. Similarly, *müsste* is used to mean 'ought to' when expressing probability: *Ja, Klaus **müsste** jetzt zu Hause sein* 'Yes, Klaus should be at home now'.

- The English expression 'can't help + -ing' (e.g. 'I couldn't help laughing') is commonly translated using *einfach müssen*: e.g. *Ich **musste einfach** lachen*. However, when the *-ing* form is absent, e.g. 'I can't help it', *können* is used: *Ich **kann** nichts dafür*.

- *Mögen* usually means 'to like' but it is sometimes used to mean 'may' in contexts where the speaker then goes on to qualify what was said, usually putting the other side of the argument: e.g. *Das **mag** wohl sein, aber …* 'That may well be, but …'.

- *Lassen* (*ich lasse, du/er/sie/es lässt, wir lassen, ihr lässt, sie/Sie lassen*; past *ließ*) is not technically a modal verb but it behaves like one in that it often occurs together with the infinitive form of other verbs. It usually means 'to let' *Er **ließ** den Hund auf dem Rasen spielen* 'He let the dog play on the lawn'; but it can also mean 'to have/get something done' *Ich **lasse** mir die Haare schneiden* 'I'm having my hair cut'; or 'to make' (= 'to cause to'): *Es **lässt** mich denken* 'It makes me think'.

[98] If 'can' is used with a passive meaning, e.g. 'It **can** be done', German often renders this using *sich lassen* + infinitive: *Das lässt sich machen*. Similarly, *Diese Kartoffeln lassen sich gut schälen* 'These potatoes are easy to peel' (= 'These potatoes can be peeled easily'). See **18.6**.

✎ EXERCISES

Vocabulary topic: *Vokabular aus der Berichterstattung*

1 Where needed, insert **zu** or **um … zu** in the correct position in the sentence. Where an infinitive clause is not possible (in three cases), rewrite it as a proper finite clause:

   1 Nach offiziellen Angaben sei es zu spät gewesen den Opfern des Flugzeugabsturzes helfen.
   2 Sicherheitsbeamte haben es geschafft einen Banküberfall verhindern.
   3 Aufständische sind sofort auf Konfrontationskurs gegangen ihren Plan durchführen.
   4 Der Finanzminister will die Benzinpreise erhöhen mehr Geld in den Straßenbau investieren können.
   5 Der Soldat hat versucht sich mit der deutschen Botschaft in Kontakt setzen Näheres über seine Kamaraden erfahren.
   6 Der Außenminister will mit den anderen EU-Ländern zusammenarbeiten. Er will sie alle bald zu einer Vereinbarung kommen.

7 Auf Anordnung des Verteidigungsministers musste der Kampf gegen den Terrorismus fortgeführt werden, obwohl keine Spur der vermuteten Massenvernichtungswaffen finden war.

8 Laut Berichten aus dem betroffenen Gebiet ist es noch zu früh festlegen, genau wie viele Menschen beim Erdbeben und der darauffolgenden Flutwelle ums Leben kamen, aber es ist befürchtet, dass mehr als zwanzigtausend Menschen umgekommen sind.

9 Während des Hochwassers hatten viele Pendler Schwierigkeiten in zur Arbeit fahren. Sie wollten die Überschwemmungsgebiete vermeiden und benutzten deshalb die Nebenstraßen, aber die meisten konnten nicht durchkommen und lange Staus haben sich gebildet.

10 Die Polizei hat eine Rufnummer veröffentlicht mögliche Zeugen des Autounfalls erreichen.

11 Der Polizeichef behauptet, er brauche mehr Hinweise aus der Bevölkerung diesen Mordfall lösen. Er und seine Kollegen brauchten auch mehr Zeit Spuren nachgehen und Beweise sammeln.

12 Der Attentäter hatte die Absicht das Landesgericht in die Luft sprengen, aber seinen Plan ausführen musste er den Sprengstoff hineinschmuggeln, und er konnte das nicht machen ohne erwischt werden.

13 Die Bundeskanzlerin hatte keine Zeit an der Pressekonferenz teilnehmen. Sie musste sofort nach Brüssel reisen.

14 Manche Leute wollen wir in Deutschland die Todesstrafe einführen Kriminelle von größeren Straftaten wie Vergewältigung und Mord abschrecken.

15 Die Gewerkschaft ruft ihre Mitglieder auf streiken, bessere Arbeitsverhältnisse fordern, aber die Mehrheit will das Risiko nicht eingehen, ihre Arbeit verlieren.

16 Der Angeklagte wurde des Mordes schuldig gesprochen und wurde zu einer lebenslänglichen Gefängnisstrafe verurteilt. Die Frau des Ermordeten sagte, der Mörder habe es verdient seine Freiheit verlieren und von der Gesellschaft ausgeschlossen werden.

17 Die Regierung will wir eine höhere Einkommensteuer zahlen unsere Renten sichern. Gleichzeitig steigt das Rentenalter, so dass wir länger arbeiten müssen. Es ist nicht fassen!

2 Translate the verbs in brackets into German, using the tense forms given, insert them into the correct position in the sentence and change and move the co-occuring verbs as appropriate.

1 Die Direktoren des großen Konzerns bauen vierhundert Arbeitsplätze ab. (*wanted*, past)

2 Die Pressefreiheit wird gewährleistet. (*had to*, past)

3 Der Rockstar verklagt die Reporter gegen Verleumdung. (*could*, conditional)

4 Die Einwanderungsbehörde schränkt die Zahl der Einwanderer ein. (*must*, present)

5 Laut dem Bildungsminister werden die Studiengebühren nicht erhöht. (*must*, present)

6 Die Regierung führt ein neues Gesetz gegen das Rauchen in der Öffentlichkeit ein. (*should*, past)

7 Der Täter ist brutal vorgegangen. (*is said/supposed to*, present)

8 Beim Banküberfall öffneten die Räuber den Tresor. (*lassen, past*)

3 Go back to question 2 above and put the bracketed verbs into the perfect tense (except for no. 7, which does not work in the pefect).

✎ FURTHER EXERCISES

4 Translate the following sentences into German:

1 I would like four bread rolls.

2 Can I smoke here?

3 Do you have to work today?

4 You mustn't forget your keys.

5 You don't have to wait for me.

6 He's supposed to be quite rich. (= 'it is said that')

7 I was supposed to ring him but I forgot.

8 Where's Peter? He could be at his girlfriend's.

9 He would have to come at five thirty.

10 I was just about to make a cup of tea.

11 You should have phoned me yesterday.

12 He could have stayed longer but he didn't want to.

13 Who has drunk my beer? It could have been Peter.

14 I wouldn't have been able to go.

15 They wouldn't have wanted to come anyway.

16 Normally I wouldn't have had to work on a Saturday, but my colleague was ill.

For further exercises on infinitives see Revision Text 4, Ex. 3.

22 | Negation

Kein Tanz an Karfreitag

TRIER. Karfreitag gilt als höchster protestantischer, Ostersonntag als
wichtigster katholischer Feiertag. 1952, zu einer Zeit, als
Tanzveranstaltungen noch deutlicher hörbar waren, wurde das österliche
5 Tanzverbot erlassen. Das ist von Bundesland zu Bundesland
unterschiedlich ausgeprägt. [...]

Simon, hochgewachsen mit kurzen braunen Haaren, tanzt gerne. Selbst
wenn er religiös wäre, wollte er sich den Spaß hieran **nicht** nehmen
lassen.[...]. Der 21-Jährige ist zwar katholisch, aber "**nicht** wirklich gläubig".
10 Er findet das Tanzverbot "einfach antiquiert. Vor allem in einem Land, in
dem viele Religionen zusammenleben, muss man **nicht** alle zusammen
einschränken, nur weil eine Religion die vorherrschende ist". Simon hat
auch **kein** Verständnis dafür, dass die Kirche, die junge Menschen braucht,
um weiter bestehen zu können, sich ins eigene Fleisch schneide, wenn sie
15 den jungen Leuten das Tanzen verbiete.

Zwei junge Frauen vor der Großraumdiskothek A1 finden das
Tanzverbot dagegen gut – weil "die Auferstehung von Jesus gefeiert wird,
ist das richtig so", sagt die 20-jährige Julia. Ihre gleichaltrige Freundin
Jessica sieht das ähnlich. Doch dass beide an Ostern **nicht** tanzen werden,
20 ist noch längst **nicht** ausgemacht: Man sei bei einer Freundin zum
Geburtstag eingeladen, gut möglich, dass dort auch getanzt werde.

Soweit es sich im privaten Rahmen bewegen sollte, würden die
Gastgeberin und ihre Freunde **nicht** gegen das Tanzverbot verstoßen.
Denn das umfasst ausschließlich öffentliche Veranstaltungen, betont das
25 Rathaus. Allerdings **nicht** nur solche, auf denen getanzt wird: Wie ein
Sprecher der Stadt auf Anfrage gegenüber *16vor* konkretisierte, sind laut
Landesfeiertagsgesetz an Karfreitag und Ostersonntag auch andere
öffentliche Unterhaltungsveranstaltungen wie Sport oder Turnen **nicht**
erlaubt. [...]
30 Verboten sind auch Veranstaltungsformate wie "Silent Dancing", erläutert
man im Rathaus. Denn es handele sich schließlich **nicht** um ein
Musikverbot, sondern um ein Verbot, öffentlich Tanzbewegungen zu
vollziehen. Nachfrage beim zuständigen Ordnungsdezernenten Thomas
Egger, ob er eine solche Regelung noch für zeitgemäß halte? "Die
35 Verwaltung ist an Recht und Gesetz gebunden. Auf die eigene Meinung
oder Bewertung der Verwaltung, ob eine Regelung sinnvoll ist oder **nicht**,
kommt es daher **nicht** an."

Aus: *16vor* [www.16vor.de/], 3/04/12.

Karfreitag – Good Friday	*verstoßen* – to infringe, violate
die Veranstaltung – event	*umfassen* – to cover, encompass
österlich – Easter	*ausschließlich* – exclusively
das Tanzverbot – dancing ban	*öffentlich* – public
erlassen – to pass, issue	*die Unterhaltung* – entertainment
ausgeprägt – distinctive	*das Turnen* – gymnastics
gläubig – religious	*erläutern* – to explain
einschränken – to restrict	*vollziehen* – to carry out, perform
vorherrschend – dominant	*zuständig* – responsible
sich ins eigene Fleisch schneiden –	*die Ordnung/Regelung* – ruling
(fig.) to shoot oneself in the foot	*der Dezernent* – councillor
verbieten – to prohibit, ban	*zeitgemäß* – up-to-date
die Auferstehung – resurrection	*die Verwaltung* – administration
ausgemacht – arranged, agreed	*ankommen auf* – to depend on

⌕ Negation in the text

There are various ways of negating a sentence in German, the most common being the use of *nicht* and *kein*.

22.1 *NICHT* 'NOT'

22.1a The position of *nicht*

Most sentences in German are made negative by the use of *nicht*. The position of *nicht* can cause problems for English learners, as it very much depends on the nature of the other elements in the sentence. The following rules are given as a rough guide, although they are often broken when a shift of emphasis is required (see **22.3b**).

i) *Nicht* **usually appears at the end of a clause**: e.g. *Ich liebe dich **nicht**, Ich kenne den Mann **nicht***. If there is already an element occupying that end position (e.g. an infinitive, past participle, separable prefix or finite verb sent to the end), then *nicht* precedes that element:

- *wollte er sich den Spaß hieran **nicht** nehmen lassen* (8–9)
  'he would **not** want to let the fun of this be taken away from him'
- *dass beide an Ostern **nicht** tanzen werden* (19)
  'that both of them will **not** dance at Easter'
- *Auf die eigene Meinung ... kommt es daher **nicht** an* (35–37)
  'therefore it does **not** depend on one's own opinion ...'

This 'end of clause' rule does not apply when the main verb is *sein* or *werden*. In these cases *nicht* precedes the main noun or pronoun: e.g. *Es ist **nicht** die eigene Meinung* 'It's **not** one's own opinion', *Es ist **nicht** meine* 'It's **not** mine'.

ii) If the sentence contains an **adjective** or **adverb** to be negated (including expressions of quantity, e.g. *sehr, wirklich, oft, viel*), then *nicht* precedes it:

- *aber **nicht** <u>wirklich gläubig</u>* (9)   'but **not** <u>really religious</u>'
- *ist noch längst **nicht** <u>ausgemacht</u>*[99] (20) 'is **not** at all yet <u>agreed</u>'
- *sind ... auch andere ... Veranstaltungen*   'other ... events are also **not** <u>allowed</u>'
  ***nicht** <u>erlaubt</u>* (26–29)

iii) *Nicht* usually precedes **pronouns that are stressed**, e.g. *alle, jeder, solche, viele* etc. (but not personal pronouns *mich, dich, ihn* etc., which are usually unstressed):

- *man muss **nicht** <u>alle</u> ... einschränken* (11–12) 'one need **not** restrict <u>everyone</u>'
- ***nicht nur** <u>solche</u>, auf denen getanzt*   '**not only** <u>such ones</u> where there's
  wird (25)[100] dancing'

iv) If the sentence contains a **phrase beginning with a preposition** required by a verb, *nicht* tends to be placed before that phrase:[101]

- *würden die Gastgeberin und ihre Freunde*   'the hostess and her friends would
  ***nicht** <u>gegen das Tanzverbot</u> verstoßen* (22–23) **not** violate the dancing ban'
- *es handele sich schließlich **nicht** <u>um ein</u>*   'after all it's **not** about a music
  <u>*Musikverbot*</u> (31–32) ban'

Note that there are a number of words which follow similar rules to those for *nicht*. Among these are *nie* 'never', *auch* 'also', *kaum* 'hardly' and *schon* 'already'.[102]

---

[99] This also applies to participles used as adjectives.

[100] *Nicht nur* 'not only' acts as one unit here. Similar expressions with *nicht* which follow the same word order are *nicht mehr* 'no more/no longer', *noch nicht* 'not yet', *bestimmt nicht* 'certainly not', *überhaupt nicht* 'not at all/definitely not', *auch nicht* 'not ... either.'

[101] This is only if there is not an adjective/adverb or a stressed pronoun in the same sentence that needs negating, in which case *nicht* would precede the adjective/adverb or pronoun. Furthermore, if the prepositional phrase is fronted for emphasis, as in lines 35–37 of our text, *nicht* tends not to precede it but follows the general rule of going to the end of the clause: *<u>Auf die eigene Meinung</u> ... kommt es **nicht** an.*

[102] *Nichts* 'nothing' acts like an ordinary direct object: e.g. *Ich weiß **nichts*** 'I don't know anything', *Ich habe ihm **nichts** gesagt* 'I didn't tell him anything'.

22.1b *Nicht ... , sondern*

In sentences of the type '**Not** X **but** Y', 'but' is rendered not by the usual word *aber* but by *sondern*: e.g. *Denn es handele sich schließlich **nicht** um ein Musikverbot, **sondern** um ein Verbot, öffentlich Tanzbewegungen zu vollziehen* 'Because after all it's not about a music ban **but** a ban on performing dance movements in public' (31–33).

22.2 *KEIN* 'NOT A', 'NO'

Kein is used, instead of *nicht*, to negate an **indefinite noun** (i.e. a noun which appears with an indefinite article or with no article at all) and takes the place of the indefinite article. Thus, a sentence such as 'That's not a good reason' would not be **Das ist nicht ein guter Grund* but *Das ist* **kein** *guter Grund*. Similarly, *Ich habe* **keine** *Milch* 'I have no milk' (not **Ich habe Milch nicht*) and, in the plural, *Ich mag* **keine** *Oliven* 'I don't like olives' (contrast: *Ich mag <u>die</u> Oliven nicht* 'I don't like <u>those</u> olives').

Kein takes the same endings as the indefinite article (see **Table 3.2**) but also has a plural form:

Table 22.1 Forms of *kein*

	Masc.	**Fem.**	**Neut.**	**Plural**
N	*kein Mann*	*keine Frau*	*kein Kind*	*keine Kinder*
A	*keinen Mann*	*keine Frau*	*kein Kind*	*keine Kinder*
D	*keinem Mann*	*keiner Frau*	*keinem Kind*	*keinen Kindern*
G	*keines Mannes*	*keiner Frau*	*keines Kindes*	*keiner Kinder*

Examples from the text are: **Kein** *Tanz an Karfreitag* (nom. masc. sg.) 'No dance on Good Friday' (1), *Simon hat auch* **kein** *Verständnis* (acc. neut. sg.) 'Simon also does not understand' (literally: 'Simon has no understanding') (12–13).

Consider the examples in **Table 22.2**, which demonstrate how *kein* is used with indefinite nouns and *nicht* with definite nouns:

Table 22.2 Use of *kein* with indefinite nouns

Definite	**Indefinite**
*Der Student hat die Prüfung **nicht** bestanden*	***Kein** Student hat die Prüfung bestanden*
*Ich habe meinen Wein **nicht** ausgetrunken*	*Ich trinke **keinen** Wein*
*Er hat es seinem Freund **nicht** gesagt*	*Er hat **keinem** Menschen etwas gesagt*
*Ich mag diese Blumen **nicht***	*Ich kaufe **keine** Blumen. Sie sind zu teuer.*

Other points to note in the text

- Subjunctive in reported speech: *dass ... die Kirche sich ins eigene Fleisch* **schneide***, wenn sie den jungen Leuten das Tanzen* **verbiete** *(13–15), Man* **sei** *bei einer Freundin zum Geburtstag eingeladen, gut möglich, dass dort auch getanzt* **werde** *(20–21), Denn es* **handele** *sich schließlich nicht um ein Musikverbot (31–32), ob er eine solche Regelung noch für zeitgemäß* **halte** *(34)* (see **Ch. 17**).

- Conditional sentences: *Selbst wenn er religiös* **wäre***,* **wollte** *er sich den Spaß hieran* **nicht** *nehmen lassen* 'Even if he **were** religious, he **wouldn't** want to let the fun of this be taken away from him' (7–9), *Soweit es sich im privaten Rahmen bewegen* **sollte***,* **würden** *die Gastgeberin und ihre Freunde nicht gegen das Tanzverbot verstoßen* 'As long as it **was** held in private, the hostess and her friends **would** not violate the dancing ban' (22–23) (see **16.2**).

- Adjectives with strong endings: *höchster protestantischer ... wichtigster katholischer Feiertag* (2–3), *mit kurzen braunen Haaren* (7), *zwei junge Frauen* (16), *öffentliche Veranstaltungen* (24, 28) (see **5.1–5.2**)
- Relative pronouns: in *einem Land, in dem viele Religionen zusammenleben* (10–11), *die Kirche, die junge Menschen braucht* (13), *nicht nur solche, auf denen getanzt wird* (25) (see **Ch 9**).

Discover more about negation

22.3 *NICHT*

22.3a With indefinite nouns

In some contexts, *nicht* can appear with an indefinite noun, instead of *kein*:

- When a **preposition** precedes the article and noun: e.g. *Ich will <u>mit</u> einem Computer **nicht** arbeiten* 'I don't want to work with a computer'.
- When *nicht* is negating a **verb** rather than a noun: e.g. *Hier darf man **nicht** Rad <u>fahren</u>* 'You can't cycle here' (where *Rad* is seen as part of the verb *Rad fahren*).
- When **emphasis** is required: e.g. *Das ist **nicht** eine Maus, sondern eine Ratte!* 'That's **not** a mouse but a rat!'
- When *ein* means 'one': e.g. *Nicht ein Mensch ist gekommen* 'Not one person came'.

22.3b Placing of *nicht* for emphasis

If the speaker wishes to emphasise the negation of a particular element in the sentence, *nicht* is placed in front of that element, even though under normal circumstances it would usually follow it. Some examples are:

Er ist gestern nicht gekommen.	*Er ist **nicht** gestern gekommen, sondern vorgestern.*
Ich habe den Prof. nicht gesehen.	*Ich habe **nicht** den Prof. gesehen sondern seinen Assistenten.*

22.4 *KEIN* AS A PRONOUN

When the noun is omitted but understood, *kein-* can stand in for the noun, in which case it takes the same endings as it would have done if the noun had been present, e.g. *Wo sind die Brötchen? – Ich habe keine gekauft* 'Where are the bread rolls? – I didn't buy **any**' (= *keine Brötchen*), except in the **masc. nom. sg.** and the **neut. nom./acc. sg.**, which take *-er* and *-(e)s* respectively (compare *einer*, **3.2b(ii)**):

Kein Student hat die Prüfung bestanden	*Keiner hat die Prüfung bestanden*
Ich habe kein Buch mitgenommen	*Ich habe keines/keins mitgenommen*

EXERCISES

Vocabulary topic: *Freizeit und Hobbys*

1 Make the following sentences negative by inserting *nicht* into the correct place:

1 Wolfgang tanzt.
2 Er geht in die Disco.
3 Jutta hat das neueste Buch von Bernhard Schlink gelesen.
4 Mein Vater liest oft Zeitung, weil er viel Freizeit hat.
5 Sie interessieren sich für klassische Musik.
6 Meine Eltern sehen fern.
7 Meine Mutter will mir den selbstgebackenen Marmorkuchen geben.
8 Mit dieser alten Nähmaschine kannst du nähen.
9 Ich will, dass du in einer Band spielst.
10 Er ist der beste Sänger im Chor.

2 Make the following sentences negative by using *nicht* or *kein* (+ necessary endings) where appropriate:

1 Er treibt Sport.
2 Hast du die Briefmarkensammlung mit?
3 Er hat die zwei Modellschiffe selber gebaut.
4 Es kommt eine neue Folge von „Tatort" im Fernsehen.
5 Natürlich habe ich den neuen Film von Heiner Lauterbach gesehen.
6 Ich bin gestern ins Kino gegangen.
7 Wir sammeln Schmetterlinge.

3 EMPHASIS/CONTRAST: Answer the following questions negatively using *nicht ... sondern* (or *kein ... sondern*) + the words underlined. Where present, place *nicht* in front of the element to be emphasised:

Example: Hast du meinen Mann auf der Fete gesehen? – Nein, <u>seinen Freund</u>.
Answer: Nein, ich habe nicht deinen Mann auf der Fete gesehen, sondern seinen Freund.

1 Hast du meinen Mann im Fitnesszentrum gesehen? – Nein, <u>in der Kneipe</u>.
2 Hast du mit Bernhard Tennis gespielt? – Nein, <u>mit Fredi</u>.
3 Warst du mit Klaus im Theater? – Nein, <u>in der Oper</u>.
4 Hast du einen CD-Spieler gekauft? Nein, <u>einen DVD-Spieler</u>.
5 Zeichnest du die Landschaft? Nein, <u>die Pferde in dem Feld da</u>.
6 Möchte er Bücher zum Geburtstag? Nein, <u>Computerspiele</u>.

4 Answer the following questions negatively using the appropriate form of the PRONOUN *kein* in place of the words underlined:

Example: Hast du <u>Schlittschuhe</u>?
Answer: Nein, ich habe keine.

1 Hast du <u>ein Skateboard</u>?

2 Hat er <u>einen Trainingsanzug</u>?

3 Sind sie mit <u>zwei</u> von ihren Freunden joggen gegangen?

4 <u>Welcher Squaschschläger</u> gefällt dir?

5 Brauchst du <u>Federbälle</u>?

23 | Questions

Rheinwiderhall

Wie heißt der Bürgermeister von Wesel? – Esel!
Wer sind seine Räte und Schreiber? – Räuber!

Die Herrn sind alle weltbekannt,
5 An allen Orten viel genannt
Im Land, im Land.
Das Echo hat sich Maul verbrannt,
Das Echo hat sich Maul verbrannt.

Was tun sie in Zünften und Zechen? – Zechen!
10 **Was** werden sie niemals vergessen? – Essen!
Die Herrn sind alle …

Was sind die gelehrten Doktoren? – Toren!
Ist ihnen die Weisheit beschwerlich? – Schwerlich!
Die Herrn sind alle …

15 **Was** haben die Väter geschaffen? – Affen!
Wie werden die jungen Geschlechter? – Schlechter!
Die Herrn sind alle …

Man munkelt von ihren Talenten? – Enten!
Doch die sich durch Tugend empfehlen? – Fehlen!
20 Sie sind ja alle weltbekannt,
An allen Orten laut genannt …

Deutsches Volkslied von W. von Zuccalmaglio (1803–1869)

der Widerhall – echo	*gelehrt* – learned, erudite
der Bürgermeister – mayor	*der Tor* – fool
der Esel – donkey	*beschwerlich* – arduous, difficult
die Räte – council	*schwerlich* – hardly
der Räuber – robber	*der Affe* – monkey
nennen – to name, mention	*jungen Geschlechter* – young families
sich das Maul verbrennen –	*man munkelt* – there are rumours
to say too much	*die Ente* – duck
die Zunft – guild	*sich empfehlen* – to be recommended
die Zeche – mine, pit	*die Tugend* – virtue
zechen – to booze	*fehlen* – to be missing

⌕ Questions in the text

There are three ways of forming a question in German, all of which are present in the above text.

23.1 SUBJECT-VERB INVERSION

Simple 'yes/no' questions (i.e. those that can be answered with a 'yes' or 'no', e.g. 'Are you going out tonight?') are formed by inverting the order of the subject and the verb: *Ist Ihnen die Weisheit beschwerlich?* 'Is wisdom difficult for them?' (13).

23.2 INTONATION OR QUESTION MARK

Alternatively, but less commonly, the sentence can be left as it is and, in the written language, a question mark is added: *Man munkelt von ihren Talenten?* 'It is rumoured that they have talent?' (18), *Doch die sich durch Tugend empfehlen?* 'But those who are recommended by their virtue?' (19). In the spoken language, a rising intonation is used.

23.3 INTERROGATIVES

In addition, specific interrogatives can be used, such as 'who?', 'what?', 'where?', 'why?' etc., which are immediately followed by the verb: *wie* (2, 16), *wer* (3), *was* (9, 10, 12, 15). A list of commonly used interrogatives in German is given in **Table 23.1**.

Table 23.1 Interrogatives

wann	*Wann fängt die Vorlesung an?*	**When** does the lecture begin?
warum?*	*Warum kann er nicht kommen?*	**Why** can't he come?
was? [*wo-* (*wor-* before vowel) with preposition]	*Was hast du gesagt?* *Womit kann ich Ihnen helfen?*	**What** did you say? **What** can I help you **with**?
was für? + noun [*für* does not require the accusative here]	*Was für <u>ein</u> Hund ist das?* *In was für ein<u>em</u> Haus* *wohnt er?*	**What sort of** dog is it? **What sort of** house does he live in?
welcher? [with same endings as *dieser*, see **8.1**]	*<u>Welches</u> Brot/<u>welchen</u> Wein* *möchten Sie?*	**Which** bread/**which** wine would you like?
wer? [acc. *wen*, dat. *wem*] [gen. *wessen* 'whose?']	*Wer bist du?* *Wen kennst du?* *Wessen Mantel ist das?* †	**Who** are you? **Who**(m) do you know? **Whose** coat is that?
wie? [*wie lange* *wie oft* *wieviel* *wie viele*]	*Wie fährt man nach Rom?* *Wie lange bleibst du noch?* *Wie oft kommst du?* *Wieviel Brot?* *Wie viele Eier?*	**How** do you get to Rome? **How long** are you staying? **How often** do you come? **How much** bread? **How many** eggs?
wo? [*woher* *wohin*]	*Wo wohnst du?* *Woher kommst du?* *Wohin gehst du?*	**Where** do you live? **Where** do you come from? **Where** are you going to?

* Other words for 'why' are *wieso* (colloquial), *weshalb* (formal) and *wozu* (= 'what for').

† A more commonly used alternative to *wessen* is *von wem*: e.g. *Von wem sind diese Schuhe?* 'Whose shoes are these?'

Other points to note in the text

- Noun plurals: **-"e**: *Räte* (3); **-(e)n**: *Zechen* (9), *Doktoren* (12), *Toren* (12), *Affen* (15), *Enten* (18), *Herrn* (4, 11, 17) [more usually: *Herren*]; **-er**: *Geschlechter* (16), **-**: *Schreiber* (3), *Räuber* (3); **-"**: *Väter* (15). **Dative** plurals in *-n*: *Orte-n* (5), *Zünfte-n* (9), *Talente-n* (18) (see **Ch. 2**).
- Possessives: *seine* (3), *ihren* (18) (see **7.3**).
- *Sein*-passive: [*sind*] *an allen Orten ... genannt* '[are] mentioned in all places' (5, 21). *Sind* is omitted but understood (see **18.5**).
- Demonstrative pronoun omitted: *Doch die sich ...* (instead of *Doch **die**, die sich*) 'But those who....' (19). This was permissible in older stages of German but is now considered ungrammatical.

Discover more about interrogatives

23.4 INTERROGATIVES USED WITH PREPOSITIONS

When used with **prepositions**, the interrogatives immediately follow, which means that there is no splitting of interrogative and preposition, unlike in English:

*Bis **wann** muss ich es machen?*	**When** do I have to do it <u>by</u>?
*Seit **wann** arbeiten Sie hier?*	**How long** have you worked here (<u>for</u>)?
*Auf **wen** wartest du?*	**Who** are you waiting <u>for</u>?

Note that if *was* appears with a preposition it becomes *wo-* (*wor-* before vowels), e.g. *Wor<u>auf</u> wartest du?* '**What** are you waiting <u>for</u>?'

23.5 INTERROGATIVES IN INDIRECT QUESTIONS

As is the case in English, interrogatives in German can be used in indirect questions of the type 'He asked me **what** I was doing and **who**(m) I was doing it with'. In this case, the interrogative is similar to a subordinating conjunction in that, in German, it sends the finite verb to the end of the clause (and is preceded by a comma in writing): e.g. *Er fragte mich,* **was** *ich <u>machte</u> und mit* **wem** *ich es <u>machte</u>*. Other examples are:

Ich weiß nicht, **wann** *er kommt*[103]	I don't know **when** he's coming
Ich verstehe nicht, **warum** *du das tust*	I don't understand **why** you do that
Ich fragte ihn, in **welchem** *Haus er wohnt*	I asked him **which** house he lived in

---

[103] Not to be confused with the conjunction *wenn* 'if/when': e.g. *Sag es mir,* **wenn** *du fertig bist* 'Tell me **when** you're ready/finished'.

✎ EXERCISES

Vocabulary topic: *Nach dem Weg fragen*

1 Write questions to the following answers using interrogatives for the words and phrases underlined:

Example: Man muss <u>beim Verkehrsampel</u> links abbiegen.
Answer: Wo muss man links abbiegen?

1 Das Krankenhaus liegt <u>gegenüber dem Park</u>.
2 <u>Das</u> ist der kürzeste Weg zum Postamt.
3 Man muss <u>mit dem Bus</u> fahren.
4 Zu Fuß dauert es <u>ungefähr eine halbe Stunde</u>.
5 Zum Bahnhof muss man <u>ziemlich weit</u> gehen.
6 Man muss <u>um vier Uhr</u> losfahren um am Flughafen rechtzeitig anzukommen.

2 Fill in the gaps with an appropriate interrogative:

1 Entschuldigen Sie, bitte. __ komme ich am besten zum Markt?
2 „__ darf man hier nicht rechts abbiegen?" – „Weil das eine Einbahnstraße ist."
3 __ Richtung muss ich jetzt nehmen?
4 In __ Straße hat er sein Geschäft?
5 __ kann mir am besten den Weg zum Fußballstadion erklären?
6 Von __ hast du den Straßenplan bekommen? Von Peter?

3 Make yes/no questions out of the following statements:

Example: Das ist eine Einbahnstraße.
Answer: Ist das eine Einbahnstraße?

1 Man muss geradeaus fahren um in die Stadtmitte zu kommen.
2 Ich kann einfach auf der Straße bis zum großen Kreisverkehr bleiben.
3 Der Taxifahrer ist in die dritte Straße rechts abgebogen.
4 Du nimmst die zweite Straße links nach den Zebrastreifen.
5 Nur beim Fußgängerübergang darf man über die Straße gehen.
6 Wir sind auf dem falschen Weg. Wir müssen umdrehen.

4 Take your answers to questions 1 and 2 above and make them into indirect questions by preceding them with ***Ich weiß nicht***:

Example: Wo muss man links abbiegen?
Answer: Ich weiß nicht , wo man links abbiegen <u>muss</u>.

For question 2(1) omit 'Entschuldigen Sie, bitte'.

24 | Prepositions

Text

Studieren in England

„Die Lehre ist hier studentengerechter", glaubt Kathrin Brost, 27, die gerade einen Master-Kurs **in** Umweltmanagement **an** der Uni Durham **in** Englands Nordosten abschließt. Ein deutscher Dozent **an** einer britischen
5 Elite-Uni sagt es noch deutlicher: „Die Unis gehören **zu** den wenigen Dingen, die dieses Land vernünftig hingekriegt hat. Im Vergleich **zu** hier sind die deutschen Hochschulen verkommen."

Der Bachelor-Abschluss **nach** drei bis vier Jahren sowie Master-Kurse **von** einem oder zwei Jahren sind zwar mittlerweile auch **an** deutschen Unis
10 zu haben. Doch das zusätzliche Plus, **in** der Weltsprache Englisch zu studieren, lockt immer mehr Lernwillige **auf** die Insel. Viele kommen schon **nach** dem Abitur. Daran hat auch die Einführung **von** Studiengebühren **für** Bachelor-Studenten [...] nichts geändert. **Auf** „fast 5000" schätzt Sebastian Fohrbeck, **bis vor** kurzem Leiter des Londoner Büros des Deutschen
15 Akademischen Austauschdienstes (DAAD), die Zahl jener, die ihr ganzes Studium **auf** der Insel absolvieren.

Curt Schmitt, 25, ist so einer. **Nach** dem Abitur kam der Westfale [...] **zum** Geschichtsstudium **an** die London School of Economics (LSE) und erlebte dort, wo**von** seine Kommilitonen **in** Deutschland meist nur träumen:
20 „**Mit** meinem Tutor hatte ich intensive Gespräche. Aber auch die anderen Professoren waren **für** jeden Anfänger ansprechbar." [...].

Die oft gelobte Verschulung und die strukturierten Kurse haben aber auch Nachteile. „Ich habe einen sehr guten Überblick **über** alle Strömungen **in** meinem Fachgebiet bekommen", berichtet Sabine Grenz, 32, die **nach**
25 Studienabschluss **in** Köln und vier Berufsjahren gerade **an** der LSE einen Master **in** Gender Studies absolviert hat. „**Am** Tiefgang hat es aber gelegentlich gefehlt."

Auch diesen Satz hören die DAAD-Betreuer immer wieder. Wor**an** das liegt? „**Von** den Bachelor-Studenten wird ohnehin weniger
30 Wissenschaftlichkeit erwartet als **in** Deutschland", glaubt Grieshop. [...]. Besonders **in** den ersten beiden Studienjahren müssen die angelsächsischen Studenten viel Grundwissen aufholen. Die deutschen Studenten glänzen **in** der Regel **durch** eine breitere Allgemeinbildung als viele Studenten **aus** Übersee, zumal **aus** den USA, hat Christopher Coker
35 beobachtet, der **an** der LSE Internationale Beziehungen lehrt. „Die Deutschen wollen immer gründlich sein."

Aus einem Artikel von Sebastian Borger, *Uni-Spiegel (Online)*. 32/10/00.

die Lehre – teaching	*die Verschulung* – organisation like a school
studentengerecht – fair to students	*die Strömung* – current thinking, trend
der Dozent – lecturer	*das Fachgebiet* – subject area
hinkriegen – to get right	*der Studienabschluss* – degree
verkommen – bad, neglected	*absolvieren* – to graduate
das Abitur – A-Levels	*der Betreuer* – advisor, guide
die Studiengebühr – tuition fee	*die Wissenschaftlichkeit* – scientific rigour
der Westfale – the Westphalian	*aufholen* – to catch up
der Kommilitone – classmate	*glänzen* – to shine
gelobt – praised	*Studenten aus Übersee* – overseas students

Prepositions in the text

24.1 USE OF CASE WITH PREPOSITIONS

A major difficulty for English learners of German is the fact that prepositions always require the following noun or pronoun to be in the accusative, genitive or dative, which is evident when an article, pronoun and/or adjective is used. This is indicated in our text with underlining: e.g. *mit* + dative: *Er kam **mit** dem Hund/**mit** seiner Frau/**mit** guten Freunden.*

24.1a Prepositions taking one case

Accusative: *durch* (33), *für* (21).

Dative: *aus* (34), *mit* (20), *nach* (8, 12, 17), *von* (9, 12, 29), *zu* (5, 18).[104]

Genitive :   Less common, hence no examples in text (see **Table 24.1** for examples).

[104] *Zum* (18), and later *am* (26), are contracted forms of the preposition + *dem* (see **24.1d**).

24.1b Prepositions taking two alternative cases

Some prepositions may take the **accusative or dative** depending on the construction that they are in. Examples from the text are *an, auf, in, über, unter, vor*. Generally speaking, if the meaning of the preposition implies **movement towards** the following noun, the **accusative** is used, otherwise the dative is the norm.[105] Contrast the following:

*Ich fahre nicht gern **in** die Stadt*	I don't like driving into town.
*Ich fahre nicht gern **in** der Stadt*	I don't like driving in town.

Even though both sentences express movement, only the first one implies movement *towards* the following noun, which is suggested by the use of '-to' in English. Examples from the text are: *an* + **dat.** (3, 4, 9, 25, 35) 'at the University etc.' vs. *an* + **acc.** (18) 'to the London School of Economics'; *auf* + **dat.** (16) 'on the island' vs. *auf* + **acc.** (11) 'onto the island'. Other examples have the dative: *in* + **dat.** (10, 24, 33), *vor* + **dat.** (14). *Über* 'above' follows the same rule, yet when it means 'about' it takes the accusative (see line 23).

[105] Unless the preposition is linked with a particular verb (see **24.6**).

24.1c Scope of preposition + case

Case is not simply assigned to the element which immediately follows the preposition but to the **whole noun phrase**, i.e. to the noun and any articles, pronouns and adjectives preceding it: e.g. *in den ersten beiden Studienjahren* (31). Even if another element, e.g. a numeral or a proper name, appears between preposition and noun phrase, case is still assigned: e.g. *nach drei bis vier Jahren* (8). Similarly, if the preposition refers to two or more noun phrases, they all have to be in the appropriate case. Consider the following examples (not from the text):

- *Er kam **mit** seiner Frau, seinem Bruder und seinen Kindern.*   He came with his wife, his brother and his children.
- *Er arbeitet **bei** der VOEST, einer sehr großen Stahlfabrik in Linz.*   He works at the VOEST, a very big steelworks in Linz.

24.1d Contracted forms: preposition + article

These are commonly used in speech and writing when the articles do not need to be stressed: e.g. *an, bei, in, von* and *zu* + *dem* = **am, beim, im, vom, zum**; *an, in* + *das* = **ans, ins**; *zu* + *der* = **zur**: e.g. **zum** *Geschichtsstudium* (18), **am** *Tiefgang* (26).[106]

Other contractions such as **aufs** (*auf* + *das*), **fürs** (*für* + *das*), **ums** (*um* + *das*) are common in speech but only used in less formal styles of writing, or in some set phrases, e.g. **ums** *Leben kommen* 'to lose one's life'.

> [106] If they appear with a full article, e.g. *an dem, in dem*, it usually means that the article is a demonstrative or relative pronoun: e.g. *an **dem** Tag* 'on **that** day'; *der Tag, an **dem** wir uns treffen* 'the day on **which** we are meeting'.

24.2 DIFFERENT MEANINGS OF PREPOSITIONS

A further difficulty for English learners of German lies in the fact that many German prepositions do not correspond directly to English ones, i.e. they may have different meanings depending on the context in which they are used. For instance, the preposition *an* usually means 'on', yet it has a number of different meanings in the text: *an der Uni* (3) 'at the University', *kam … an die LSE* (18) 'came … to the LSE', and when linked with particular verbs: *am Tiefgang hat es … gefehlt* (26–27) 'it was … lacking in depth', *Woran das liegt?* (28–29) 'What's the reason for this? etc. The different meanings of the most common prepositions in German are discussed in **24.5**.

The meanings of other prepositions in the text are:

auf = 'on' (16), 'onto' (11), 'at' (13) with *schätzen* 'to estimate at'
aus = 'from' (34)
bis = 'up to/until' (14)
durch = 'through' (33)
für = 'for' (12, 21)
in = 'in' (1, 3, 10, 19, 24, 25, 26, 30, 31), 'as' (33) in set phrase 'as a rule'
mit = 'with' (20)
nach = 'after' (8, 12, 17, 24)

über = 'about' (23), yet here corresponds to English 'of' in 'I have a good overview <u>of</u> ...'

vor = 'ago', when used with expressions of time. Here *vor kurzem* (14) = 'recently'

von = 'of' (9, 12, 19, 29)

zu = 'to' (5, 6, 18)

24.3 *DA-* AND *WO-* PLUS PREPOSITION

If a preposition occurs with pronouns meaning 'it', 'them', 'that' and 'those' referring not to persons but to **things**, *da-* (or *dar-* before a vowel) is used and the preposition is added on the end: ***Daran*** *hat die Einführung von Studiengebühren ... nichts geändert* (12–13), literally: 'the introduction of student fees hasn't changed anything <u>about that</u>'. If it occurs in a question with *was?* or with a relative pronoun referring to things, not people, then *wo-* (*wor-* before a vowel) + preposition is used: ***Woran*** *das liegt?* (28–29) [not **an was*] '<u>what</u>'s the reason <u>for</u> this?', ***wovon*** *seine Kommilitonen ... nur träumen* (19) [not **von was*] '<u>about which</u> his fellow students...only dream'.[107]

> [107] For further details and examples see **7.5** for preposition + 'it', **8.6** for preposition + 'this/that', **9.4** for preposition + 'which/that' and **23.4** for preposition + interrogatives.

Other points to note in the text

- Comparative constructions: *studentengerechter* (2), *deutlicher* (5), *weniger ... als* (29–30), *breiter- ... als* (33) (see **6.1, 6.6**).
- Demonstratives: *dieses Land* (6), *diesen Satz* (28); as pronoun: *die Zahl jener* (15); with preposition: *daran* (12) (see **8.1, 8.6**).
- Relative pronouns: *die ... abschließt* (2–4), *die ... hingekriegt hat* (6), *die ... absolvieren* (15–16), *die ... absolviert hat* (24–26), *der ... lehrt* (35); and with preposition: *wovon ... träumen* (19), *woran* (28) (see **Ch. 9**).
- Elements (other than subject) placed at beginning of clause, causing the verb to follow immediately: *Im Vergleich zu hier* **sind** (6–7), *Daran* **hat** (12), *Auf „fast 5000"* **schätzt** (13), *Nach dem Abitur* **kam** (17), *Mit meinem Tutor* **hatte** (20), *Am Tiefgang* **hat** (26), *Auch diesen Satz* **hören** (28), *Von den Bachelorstudenten* **wird** (29), *Besonders in den ersten beiden Studienjahren* **müssen** (31). Contrast *Aber auch ...* followed by normal word order (20–21) (see **26.1a(ii)**).

Discover more about prepositions

24.4 CASE

Tables **24.1** and **24.2** set out the most common prepositions in German and the cases they take. Students are advised to learn the prepositions together with an article and noun (in **Table 24.1**) and in whole sentences (in **Table 24.2**), since this makes it easier to remember which case is needed:

Table 24.1 Prepositions taking one case

Accusative only		Genitive only		Dative only	
durch den Wald	'through'	**außerhalb** des Dorfes	'outside'	**ab** dem 1. Mai	'from'
für den Chef	'for'	**innerhalb** eines Monats/Bezirks	'inside/within'	**aus** dem Fenster	'from, out of'
gegen den Baum	'against'	**statt** des Essens	'instead of'	**außer** dem Kind	'except for'
ohne den Vater	'without'	**trotz** des Regens	'in spite of'	**bei** (de)m Bäcker	'at'
um den Park	'round'			**mit** dem Auto	'with/by'
		während des Tages	'during'	**gegenüber** dem Haus	'opposite'
		wegen des Verkehrs*	'because of'	**nach** dem Krieg	'after'
				seit dem Tag	'since'
				von (de)m Chef	'from, of'
				zu (de)m Geschäft	'to'

* *Wegen* is often used with the dative in spoken German, e.g. *wegen* **dem** *Verkehr*.

Table 24.2 Prepositions taking accusative or dative

Dative	Accusative
Der Spiegel hängt **an** <u>der</u> Wand 'The mirror is hanging **on** the wall'	Er hängt den Spiegel **an** <u>die</u> Wand 'He hangs the mirror **on** the wall'
Er sitzt **auf** <u>dem</u> Stuhl 'He is sitting **on** the chair'	Er setzt sich **auf** <u>den</u> Stuhl 'He sits down **on** the chair'
Büsche wachsen **entlang** <u>der</u> Straße 'Bushes are growing **along** the road'	Er fährt <u>die</u> Straße **entlang** 'He drives **along** the road'
Er steht **hinter** <u>dem</u> Baum 'He is standing **behind** the tree'	Er geht **hinter** <u>das</u> Haus 'He goes **behind** the house'
Er arbeitet **in** <u>der</u> Stadt 'He works **in** town'	Er fährt **in** <u>die</u> Stadt 'He drives **into** town'
Er wohnt **neben** <u>dem</u> Krankenhaus 'He lives **next to** the hospital'	Er stellt das Glas **neben** <u>die</u> Flasche 'He puts the glass **next to** the bottle'
Das Bild hängt **über** <u>dem</u> Kamin 'The picture is hanging **above** the fireplace'	Er hängt das Bild **über** <u>den</u> Kamin 'He hangs the picture **above** the fireplace'
Er sucht seine Schuhe **unter** <u>dem</u> Bett 'He looks for his shoes **under** the bed'	Die Maus läuft **unter** <u>das</u> Bett 'The mouse runs **under** the bed'
Er wartet **vor** <u>dem</u> Haus 'He is waiting **in front of** the house'	Er stellt sein Fahrrad **vor** <u>das</u> Haus 'He puts his bike **in front of** the house'
Er sitzt **zwischen** <u>der</u> Chefin und <u>der</u> Sekretärin 'He is sitting **between** the boss and the secretary'	Er setzt sich **zwischen** <u>die</u> Chefin und <u>die</u> Sekretärin 'He sits down **between** the boss and the secretary'

As outlined in **24.1(b)**, the accusative is usually used to indicate movement towards a noun/ pronoun, as the examples in the above table illustrate. Thus, taking the last sentence as an example: *Er sitzt zwischen **der** Chefin und **der** Sekretärin* denotes position (i.e. he is already sitting down between them), while *Er setzt sich zwischen **die** Chefin und **die** Sekretärin* denotes movement (i.e. he is in the process of sitting down between them).[108]

[108] Note that *entlang* usually precedes a noun in the dative but follows a noun in the accusative (see **Table 24.2**).

24.5 ALTERNATIVE MEANINGS

Below is a list of common prepositions with more than one meaning. Only the frequently used meanings are given as a rough guide:

Accusative

• *bis*	until, up to:	*Ich warte **bis** vier Uhr.*
	by (with time):	*Können Sie es **bis** nächsten Dienstag liefern?*
• *durch*	through:	*Ich ging **durch** die Tür.*
	by (in passive):	*Es wurde **durch** fleißige Arbeit geschafft.*[109]
• *gegen*	against:	*Der Besen lehnt **gegen** den Zaun; Ich bin **gegen** die Todesstrafe.*
	around (time):	*Sie kommt **gegen** halb drei.*
• *um*	round:	*Sie saßen **um** das Feuer; Er fuhr zu schnell **um** die Kurve.*
	at (time):	*Sie kommt **um** halb fünf.*
	around (with ages)/ approximately:	*Sie ist **um** die dreißig* (note use of article).

[109] See **18.4** for the use of *von* versus *durch* in the passive.

Dative

• *aus*	out of:	*Er kam **aus** dem Büro.*
	from (place):	*Sie kommt **aus** Hamburg/**aus** der Türkei.*
• *bei*	at (house, business):	*Er wohnt noch **bei** den Eltern; Ich kaufe **bei** Aldi ein.*
	near (place):	*Sie wohnt **bei** München/**bei** der Brücke.*
	in (weather):	***Bei** schlechtem Wetter ist die Straße gesperrt.*
• *gegenüber*	opposite:	*Er saß **gegenüber** seiner Frau.*
	towards:	*Seiner Frau **gegenüber** ist er sehr zärtlich.*[110]
• *mit*	with:	*Ich war **mit** meinem Freund zu Hause.*
	by (transport):	*Ich fahre lieber **mit** dem Auto als mit **dem** Bus.*
	at (age, speed):	***Mit** 16 darf man heiraten; Er fuhr **mit** 120 km/h.*
• *nach*	to (places):	*Er fährt **nach** Amsterdam/**nach** Frankreich* (with proper nouns).
	after:	*Wir sehen uns **nach** der Arbeit.*
• *seit*	since:	***Seit** letztem Juli arbeite ich an diesem Projekt.*
	for (= 'since'):	*Ich wohne **seit** einem Jahr in England.*

- *von*   from: *Ich warte auf einen Anruf **von** meinem Chef.*

           by (in passive):   *Er wurde **von** dem neuen Chef entlassen.*

           of: *Er ist ein Freund **von** Klaus; Das ist sehr nett **von** dir.*

- *zu*   to: *Ich fahre **zum** Supermarkt/**zu** meiner Freundin.*

                               *Sie ist immer sehr nett **zu** mir* (used when expressing an attitude).

           at/on: *Er kommt **zu** Weihnachten/**zu** Ostern/**zu** meinem Geburtstag* (used for festive occasions).

> [110] *Gegenüber*, when meaning 'opposite', may precede or follow the noun, depending on the type of noun used. It always follows pronouns, e.g. *Er wohnt **mir** gegenüber* 'He lives opposite **me**', and tends to follow nouns when it means 'towards' a person, e.g. ***Seiner Frau** gegenüber ist er sehr zärtlich* 'He is very affectionate towards **his wife**'. Otherwise it usually precedes the noun.

Accusative or dative

- *an*   on (the side of):   *Das bild hängt **an** der Wand; Ich hänge es **an** die Wand.*

  (dat.)   on (days & dates):   *Wir kommen **am** Montag/**am** vierten Mai.*

  (dat.)   at (the side of):   *Wir saßen **am** Tisch; Er klopft **an** der Tür.*

  (acc.)   to (the side of):   *Alle gingen **an** den Tisch/**ans** Fenster; Ich gehe **an** die Tür.*

- *auf*   on (top of):   *Er saß **auf** dem Bett; Er setzte sich **auf** das Bett.*

  (dat.)   at (some events):   *Ich war **auf** dem Markt/**auf** einem Konzert/**auf** einer Fete.*

  (acc.)   to (some events):   *Ich ging **auf** den Markt/**auf** ein Konzert/**auf** eine Fete.*

  (acc.)   in (languages):   *Hat er es **auf** Deutsch oder **auf** Englisch gesagt?*

- *in*   in: *Er sitzt **im** Haus; Er geht **ins** Haus; Ich gehe **in** drei Tagen.*

  (dat.)   at (with buildings):   *Sie ist **im** Geschäft/**in** der Schule/**in** der Stadt.*

  (acc.)   to (with buildings):   *Sie geht **ins** Geschäft/**in** die Schule/**in** die Stadt.*

  (dat.)   on (TV, radio etc.):   *Es kommt ein guter Film **im** Fernsehen/**im** Kino.*

- *über*   above/over: *Das Bild hängt **über** dem Kamin; Ich hänge es **über** das Kamin.*

           (with ages):   *Er ist **über** sechzig.*

  (acc.)   about: *Er redet immer **über** seine Arbeit; Ein Film **über** den Tod.*

- *unter*   under/below: *Der Hund liegt **unter** dem Tisch/läuft **unter** den Tisch.*

           (with ages):   *Er ist **unter** zwanzig.*

  (dat.)   among(st):   *Sie ist die klugste **unter** den Schülern.*

- *vor*   in front of: *Er steht **vor** dem Haus; Er stellt sein Fahrrad **vor** das Haus.*

  (dat.)   before: *Kannst du **vor** Montag dem zwanzigsten kommen?*

  (dat.)   ago: *Ich habe ihn **vor** langer Zeit gesehen: **vor** zwei Jahren.*

Notes:

- *für*, when denoting time, is often omitted, e.g. 'I'm going to Italy for two weeks' = *Ich fahre für zwei Wochen nach Italien* or *Ich fahre zwei Wochen nach Italien*, 'I was in the office for four hours' = *Ich war für vier Stunden im Büro* or *Ich war vier Stunden im Büro* or *ich war vier Stunden lang im Büro* (*lang* is often used when referring to the past).
- *in* is omitted before **dates**: e.g. *Ich bin 1935 geboren* (OR: *Ich bin **im Jahre** 1935 geboren*).

- *ohne* is usually used without the indefinite article *ein(-e, -en)*: e.g. *Ich bin* **ohne** *Regenschirm ausgegangen* 'I went out without an umbrella'. **Ohne zu** + **infinitive** renders 'without -ing': e.g. *Er kam herein* **ohne zu** *klopfen* 'he came in without knocking'.

- Use of **two** prepositions: Some prepositions require a second preposition in some circumstances, e.g. *vorbei* 'past' occurs with *an* (+ dat.): e.g. *Ich fuhr* **an** *dem Haus* **vorbei** 'I drove past the house'; *bis* 'until', 'up to' requires *zu* (+ dat.) or *an* (+ acc.) before an article: e.g. *bis Frankfurt* vs. **bis** *zum Schloss* 'up to the castle', **bis** *ans Meer* 'up to the sea'. *Bis auf* means 'except': e.g. *Alle kamen* **bis auf** *den Chef* 'everyone came, except the boss'.

- Common phrases with unpredictable prepositions are: **nach** *Hause* 'home' (e.g. *Ich fahre jetzt nach Hause*), **zu** *Hause* 'at home' (e.g. *Ich will heute zu Hause bleiben*), **im** *Urlaub* 'on holiday' (e.g. *Er ist im Urlaub/Er fährt in Urlaub*), or, colloquially, **auf** *Urlaub*, **in** *dem Alter* 'at that age', **auf** *dem Niveau* 'at that level'.

24.6 COMMON VERBS AND ADJECTIVES TAKING A PREPOSITION

24.6a Choice of preposition and case

A number of verbs and adjectives co-occur with a set preposition, the most problematic being those whose prepositions differ from the English equivalents: e.g. 'to wait for' = *warten* **auf** (not *für). In these constructions, prepositions which can take an accusative **or** dative usually take an **accusative** (particularly if the verb is simple: i.e. is not prefixed or part of a compound): e.g. *Ich warte auf den Mann.*[111] **Tables 24.3** and **24.4** list common verbs and adjectives taking a set preposition which is often different from the English equivalent. Students are advised to learn these in phrases which make the case of the preposition explicit:

[111] This is a tendency rather than a hard and fast rule: e.g. *fehlen an* 'to lack' takes the dative, as can be seen in our text (26–27).

Table 24.3 Verbs + preposition

ACCUSATIVE		
an	Ich **denke** <u>an</u> dich.	think of
	Er **erinnert** mich <u>an</u> meinen Vater.	remind of
	Ich **erinnere mich** <u>an</u> die Geschichte.	remember
auf	Ich **freue mich** <u>auf</u> das Wochenende.	look forward to
	Ich **konzentriere mich** <u>auf</u> die Arbeit.	concentrate on
	Ich **passe** <u>auf</u> das Baby **auf**.	look after
	Ich **verlasse mich** <u>auf</u> dich.	rely on
	Ich **warte** <u>auf</u> dich.	wait for
für	Ich **danke** dir <u>für</u> das Geschenk.	thank for
	Ich **interessiere mich** <u>für</u> die Literatur.	be interested in
in	Ich **verliebte mich** <u>in</u> meinen Chef.	fall in love with
über	Ich **denke** <u>über</u> die Situation **nach**.	think about/consider
	Ich **möchte** <u>über</u> meine Probleme **sprechen**.	talk about
	Ich **freue/ärgere mich** <u>über</u> seine Entscheidung.	be happy/angry about
um	Ich **bitte** dich <u>um</u> Entschuldigung.	ask for
	Es **handelt sich** <u>um</u> viel Geld.	be about
	Ich **mache mir Sorgen** <u>um</u> dich	worry about

DATIVE

an	Ich **arbeite** <u>an</u> einem Projekt.	work on
	Er **leidet** <u>an</u> einer Ohrenentzündung.	suffer from
	Er **starb** <u>an</u> einem Herzinfarkt.	die of
	Ich **nehme** <u>an</u> einem Wettbewerb **teil**.	take part in
mit	Ich **fange** <u>mit</u> meiner neuen Arbeit **an**.	begin
	Kannst du da<u>mit</u> aufhören?*	stop
	Kann ich <u>mit</u> dir **sprechen**?	speak/talk to
nach	Ich **fragte** <u>nach</u> einem Kaffee.	ask for
	Es **schmeckt/riecht** <u>nach</u> Knoblauch.	taste/smell of
von	Er **erzählt** mir <u>von</u> seiner Jugend.	tell/talk about
	Es **hängt** <u>von</u> der Situation **ab**.	depend on
	Ich **träume** jede Nacht <u>von</u> dir.	dream of
vor	Ich **habe Angst/fürchte mich** <u>vor</u> Mäusen.	be afraid of
	Ich will es <u>vor</u> ihm **verbergen**.	hide from
zu	Er **gratuliert** mich <u>zu</u> meinem Geburtstag.	congratulate on

---

* For the use of *da* + preposition see **24.3**.

Table 24.4 Adjectives + preposition

ACCUSATIVE

an	Ich bin <u>an</u> dieses Wetter **gewöhnt**.	accustomed/used to
auf	Ich bin **böse/wütend** <u>auf</u> dich.	angry/furious with
	Sie ist **eifersüchtig/neidisch** <u>auf</u> ihre Schwester.	jealous/envious of
	Ich bin sehr **neugierig** <u>auf</u> deinen neuen Freund.	curious about
	Ich bin **gespannt** <u>auf</u> den Urlaub.	excited about
	Sie ist sehr **stolz** <u>auf</u> ihren Sohn.	proud of
um	Er ist **besorgt** <u>um</u> seine Tochter.	worried about

DATIVE

an	Ich bin <u>an</u> der Geschichte **interessiert**.	interested in
	Ich bin **schuld** <u>an</u> dem Unfall.	to blame for
mit	Sie ist <u>mit</u> einem Arzt **verheiratet**.	married to

---

Often adjectives take the same preposition as their related verbs: e.g. *abhängig **von*** 'dependent on' (< *abhängen von*), *besorgt **um*** 'worried about' (< *sich Sorgen machen um*), *dankbar **für*** 'thankful for' (< *jemandem danken für*), *verliebt **in*** 'in love with' (< *sich verlieben in*). Similarly, **nouns** usually (but not always!) take the same prepositions as their related adjectives and/or verbs: e.g. *der Gedanke **an**, die Erinnerung **an**, die Bitte **um**, das Interesse **an**, die Wut **auf**, der Eifersucht **auf**, die Schuld **an**.*

24.6b *Da*- plus preposition before whole clause

When the verb, adjective etc. + preposition is not followed by a noun/pronoun object but by a whole clause, *da-* (*dar-* before vowels) + preposition is used. Contrast the following pairs:

<u>Object</u>	<u>Clause</u>
*Ich denke **an** <u>dich</u>.*	*Ich denke **daran**, <u>was ich machen würde</u>.*
*Ich warte **auf** <u>dich</u>.*	*Ich warte **darauf**, <u>dass du einen Fehler machst</u>.*

*Ich dachte **über** <u>das Problem</u> nach.*   *Ich dachte **darüber** nach, <u>was passiert war</u>.*

*Ich bin **auf** <u>den Urlaub</u> gespannt.*   *Ich bin **darauf** gespannt, <u>was passieren wird</u>.*

These forms with *da(r)-* are often omitted in the spoken language and in some less formal styles of writing, e.g. *Ich bin gespannt, was passieren wird* 'I'm eager to see what'll happen'. They tend to be omitted with adjectives and nouns rather than with verbs, yet there are some verbs which also allow omission, e.g. *Sie fragte ihn (**danach**), was er jetzt machen würde* 'She asked him what he would do now'.

✎ EXERCISES

Vocabulary topic: *Studium*

1 Put the bracketed words into the correct case which is determined by the preposition in bold print:

  1 Ich studiere an [eine deutsche] Universität .

  2 Welche Kurse zählen für [der] Abschluss?

  3 Nach [das erste] Semester muss ich einen Deutschkurs ablegen.

  4 Über [die] Sprachwissenschaft weiß ich sehr wenig.

  5 Er ist während [die] Vorlesung eingeschlafen.

  6 Die Assistentin kam in [der] Seminarraum und schrieb etwas Unverständliches an [die] Tafel.

  7 Er war vor [sein] Vortrag sehr nervös.

  8 Über zweihundert Studenten saßen in [der] Hörsaal.

2 Fill in the gaps by choosing an appropriate preposition for the context and put the bracketed words into the correct case. Some contexts may permit two or more possible prepositions:

  1 Der heutige Student kann sehr leicht __ [Computer] umgehen.

  2 Das ist der Lehrer, __ [der] ich Spanisch gelernt habe.

  3 Er macht sich __ [die mündliche] Prüfung sorgen.

  4 Ich wartete __ [die] Universitätsbibliothek __ [mein Kommilitone].

  5 Die nächste Vorlesung konzentriert sich__ [das] Ende der Weimarer Republik.

  6 Ich freue mich überhaupt nicht __ [die] kommenden Klausuren.

  7 Ich muss __ [die] nächsten vier Wochen lernen.

  8 Der neue Doktorand arbeitet sehr eifrig __ [seine] Doktorarbeit.

  9 Ich habe __ [die] Studenten gehört, dass der Leistungsdruck dieses Jahr sehr hoch ist.

  10 Sie war __ [ihre] ausgezeichneten Noten sehr zufrieden.

  11 „Fahren wir __ [der] Bus oder __ [das] Auto __ [die] Uni?" „__ [der] Bus. __ [der] Uniparkplatz ist es immer voll."

  12 Ich muss __ vier [Hauptseminare] und zwei [Proseminare] teilnehmen.

✎ FURTHER EXERCISES

3 Insert the correct prepositions and put the capitalised articles and pronouns into the correct case. Use the contracted forms of the articles where appropriate:

Example: Er war gestern __ DAS Theater. (at)

Answer: Er war gestern im Theater.

1 Ich möchte kurz schauen, was heute __ DAS Fernsehen ist. (on)
2 Er geht morgen __ SEINE Freundin __ EIN Rockkonzert. (with, to)
3 Ich gehe lieber __ DAS Kino. (to)
4 Heute gibt es ein Sommerfest __ DAS großen Zelt und vorne __ DER Rasen ist die Kinderunterhaltung. (in, on)
5 Der Chef hat uns __ EINE Fete __ ER zu Hause eingeladen. (to, at)
6 Er sprach __ SEINE Lieblingsfernsehserie. (about)
7 Wir wollen heute abend __ DER Garten grillen. Hast du Lust, __ WIR zu kommen? (in, to)
8 Wollen wir heute __ DIE Disco gehen? Wir können __ DAS Taxi fahren. (to, by)
9 Wann warst du das letzte Mal __ DIE Oper? Ach, __ VIELE Jahren. (at, ago)
10 Was machen wir __ UNSER Hochzeitstag? Gehen wir __ DAS Restaurant. (on, to)

4 Complete the following story by filling in the gaps with any prepositions you feel are appropriate. Remember to make any necessary changes to articles (using contractions where possible), pronouns, adjectives etc.:

Norbert hat wieder Liebeskummer

Ich bin gestern abend __ der Bus __ die Stadt gefahren. Ein hübsches Mädchen saß alleine __ der Bus. Sie erinnerte mich __ meine Ex-Freundin und ich verliebte mich sofort __ sie. Ich setzte mich __ sie und fing an, __ sie __ eine halbe Stunde __ Fußball zu reden. (Ich komme nämlich __ Dortmund und bin ein Fan __ Borussia). Sie interessierte sich aber nicht __ Fußball. Sie wusste nichts __ Fußball und nahm __ unser Gespräch wenig teil. __ eine Weile merkte ich, dass sie sich langweilte und ich wechselte das Thema __ das Eishockey. Ich informierte sie __ die verschiedenen Positionen __ Spiel, nannte ein paar Mannschaften, __ die ich mich erinnern konnte, aber sie gähnte nur. „Ich bin __ Sport, gar nicht interessiert", sagte sie, und ich merkte Ärger __ ihre Stimme. Ok, dachte ich, ich werde mich __ etwas Neutrales konzentrieren. Ich dachte __ ein neues Thema: Fernsehen. „Hast du gestern das Snooker __ Fernsehen gesehen?", fragte ich und gab ihr Informationen __ die verschiedenen Kreidesorten, die man __ der Billardstock tun kann . Warum rollte sie die Augen? Ich wollte nur freundlich sein __ sie. Schließlich fragte ich sie, „Willst du __ ich __ das Bett gehen"? Sie verpasste mir einen Schlag __ der Kopf __ ihr Regenschirm. Frauen: ich verstehe sie einfach nicht!

5 Insert the correct prepositions, preceded by *da(r)*- where appropriate, and put the bracketed articles, pronouns and adjectives into the correct form. Use contracted articles where appropriate:

Example: Er sprach oft __, wie er das Leben __ [die ehermalige DDR] sehr schwierig gefunden hat.

Answer: Er sprach oft darüber, wie er das Leben in der ehemaligen DDR sehr schwierig gefunden hat.

1 „Ich freue mich sehr __ [dein] Besuch." „Ja, ich freue mich auch __, dich wiederzusehen."

2 „Kommst du heute Abend __ [das] Essen?" „Es hängt __ ab, ob ich länger arbeiten muss oder nicht."

3 Er ist sehr stolz __, dass seine Frau einen Bestseller geschrieben hat.

4 Du bist selber __ schuld, dass du dich __ [deine] Freunden gestritten hast.

5 Ich bin __ gewöhnt, meinen eigenen Weg zu gehen, aber jetzt muss ich mich __ [andere] Leute verlassen.

6 Kannst du mich __ erinnern, die Telefonrechnung zu bezahlen, bevor wir __ Urlaub fahren?

7 „Was ist das Problem?" „Es handelt sich __, dass zwei Jugendliche __ [eine alte] Frau eingebrochen sind und achthundert Euro __ [ihre] Ersparnissen gestohlen haben, die __ [ihre] Matratze versteckt waren."

8 Der Gedanke __, dass er __ [ein] Jahr seine Frau betrügt, gefällt mir überhaupt nicht.

6 Translate the following sentences into German:

1 Are you driving into town? Wait for me! (*Use* du).

2 I've been talking to your friend about his new book. He likes talking about it.

3 He sat down on the bench and worried about his wife. (*Use past*)

4 The bottle is standing on the table with a glass next to it.

5 He's still sitting at the desk. What's he working on?

For further exercises on prepositions see Revision Text 2, Ex. 1.

25 | Conjunctions

Text

Bärbel: Was ist los mit deinem Mann?

Marion: Er ist ein Dreckschwein. Nein, er ... ich weiß nicht ... ich kann mich mit ihm nirgendwo sehen lassen, **weil** er ist mir oft auch peinlich. Erstens: er putzt sich zweimal im Jahr die Zähne.

5 Teddy: Reicht das doch nicht aus?

Marion: Ja, für dich würde das reichen, genau.

Bärbel: Küsst du ihn noch?

Marion: **Wenn** es unbedingt sein muss, aber nur so ganz kurz [...].

Teddy: Liebst du deinen Mann? Du sagst, dein Mann ist ein Dreckschwein

10 ... er ... ich meine, es kommt mir nicht so vor, **als ob** du ihn überhaupt liebst.

Alex: Und, ich meine, deine Zähne kommen mir nicht gerade gepflegt vor, muss ich ganz ehrlich sagen.

Marion: Moment, ich putz' sie mir aber! **Und** ich weiß, wie man sich wäscht,

15 ich weiß, was ein Stück Seife ist, was ein Waschlappen ist, was ein Handtuch ist.

Bärbel: Also, er putzt sich nicht die Zähne. Duscht er?

Marion: Jetzt, **seitdem** er eine Arbeit hat, ja [...].

Bärbel: In welchem Abstand hat er dann vorher geduscht? [...].

20 Marion: **Je nachdem** wie sehr ich gedrängelt hab'.

Bärbel: Wechselt er die Klamotten?

Marion: **Wenn** ich super danach guck', dann ja. **Aber** heute hab' ich's ihn alleine machen lassen und ..., guck ihn dir an! [...].

Bärbel: **Aber** du hast ihn ja trotzdem ..., ich meine, ihr kennt euch schon

25 relativ lange. Du hast ihn vor einem Jahr geheiratet.

Marion: Ich hab' nicht gesagt, **dass** ich ihn nicht liebe.

Alex: Du erzählst, du liebst ihn **und** erzählst gleichzeitig, der Mann ist ein Schwein. **Entweder** ich liebe auch einen **oder** ich behaupte, er ist ein Schwein.

30 Marion: Moment, **als** wir uns kennengelernt haben, war ja auch alles in Ordnung [...].

Bärbel: OK, ich würde sagen, wir holen deinen Mann mal 'rein. Er heißt Karl **und** wir werden sehen, **ob** er stellvertretend für viele Männer in Deutschland ist, **oder ob** er eine Ausnahme ist. Herzlich willkommen, Karl!

Aus: *Barbel Schäfer* Talkshow, RTL, 10/11/00.

das Dreckschwein – dirty pig	*je nachdem* – it depends
sich sehen lassen – to be seen	*drängeln* – to push
peinlich – embarrassing	*die Klamotten* – clothes, clobber
ausreichen – to be enough	*behaupten* – to claim, assert
gepflegt – well looked after	*hereinholen* – to bring in
der Waschlappen – flannel	*stellvertretend* – representative
der Abstand – interval	*die Ausnahme* – exception

Conjunctions in the text

25.1 WORD ORDER AFTER CONJUNCTIONS

A conjunction is a word used to link two clauses together and appears either between the clauses, e.g. 'I saw him **as** I got off the bus', or at the beginning of the whole sentence, e.g. '**As** I got off the bus I saw him'. This is also the case in German, yet here there is an added complication. In German there are two main categories of conjuction with regard to their influence on the position of the **following finite verb**: co-ordinating conjunctions, which do not affect word order; and subordinating conjunctions, which send the following finite verb to the end of the clause (see the underlined verbs in the text for their position after the conjunction). The latter group is much larger than the former and, because of the change in word order involved, needs particular attention. A list of the most commonly used conjunctions is given in **Tables 25.1** and **25.2**.

Table 25.1 Common co-ordinating conjunctions

aber	but	**oder**	or
(after negative: **sondern**, see 22.1b)		(or **beziehungsweise**, often abbreviated to **bzw.** in writing)	
denn	as/because	**und**	and
entweder ... oder	either ... or	**weder ... noch**	neither ... nor

Examples of co-ordinating conjunctions in the text are *und* (14, 27, 32), *aber* (22, 24), *oder* (34), *entweder ... oder* (28).[112]

---

[112] As in English, the subject of the sentence can be omitted after the conjunction if it has already appeared beforehand: e.g. *Du liebst ihn und* (*du* omitted) *erzählst* ... 'You love him and say ...' (27)

Table 25.2 Common subordinating conjunctions

als	when (*in past*)	*obwohl*	although
als ob	as if/as though	*ohne dass*	without (+ clause)
angenommen, dass	assuming that	*seit(dem)*	since (re: time)
bevor/ehe	before	*sobald*	as soon as
bis	until/by the time	*so dass*	so (that)
da	as/since (= because)	*solange*	as long as
damit	so (that)	*soweit*	as far as
dass	that	*vorausgesetzt, dass*	provided that
es sei denn, dass	unless	*während*	while
je nachdem	depending on	*weil*	because
nachdem	after	*wenn*	if/when/whenever
ob	whether/if	*wie*	as/like

Examples of subordinating conjunctions in the text are *wenn* (8, 22), *als ob* (10), *seitdem* (18), *je nachdem* (20), *dass* (26)[113], *als*, meaning 'when', (30), *ob* (33, 34). As *weil* is also a subordinating conjunction; it usually sends the verb to the end, although in colloquial spoken German it may be followed by normal word order, which is the case in this text (3). This may be due to confusion between *weil* and the co-ordinating conjunction *denn* which also means 'because' but is much less commonly used.

[113] As in English, *dass* can optionally be omitted after *sagen, erzählen* and *meinen* (see lines 27–28, where *dass* is omitted before *du liebst ihn* and *der Mann ist ein Schwein*).

25.2 INTERROGATIVES BEHAVING LIKE CONJUNCTIONS

In addition to the 'proper' conjunctions listed in **25.1**, some other elements may behave like conjunctions in that they send the finite verb to the end of the clause when linking two clauses together. This is very often the case with interrogatives such as *was* 'what', *wer* 'who', and *wie* 'how' when used in indirect questions (see **23.5**). Examples from the text are: *wie man sich wäscht* 'how one washes' (14), *was ein Stück Seife ist, was ein Waschlappen ist, was ein Handtuch ist* 'what a piece of soap is, what a flannel is, what a towel is' (15–16).

These interrogatives can also be used with *auch* (following the subject) to render the meanings 'what**ever**', 'who**ever**', 'how**ever**' etc. In this case, they often appear at the beginning of the sentence: e.g. (not in text): *Was du auch denkst, ich finde ihn in Ordnung* '**Whatever** you (may) think, I find him alright'; *Wie fleißig er auch arbeitet, wird er nie richtig geschätzt* '**However** hard he works he's never really appreciated'.

Other points to note in the text

- Features of spoken German: **i)** pauses (2, 10, 23, 24); **ii)** filler words and phrases: *ich meine* (10, 12, 24), *auch* (3, 28, 30), *ja* (30), *OK* (32); **iii)** dropping of -e in the first person singular present: *putz'* (14), *hab'* (20, 22, 26), *guck'* (22); **iv)** abbreviated forms: *es* → *'s* (22), *herein* → *'rein* (32); **v)** use of indicative instead of subjunctive in reported speech: *Du sagst, dein Mann* **ist** (9), *dass ich ihn nicht* **liebe** (26), *Du erzählst, du* **liebst** ... *der Mann* **ist** (27).
- Reflexive pronouns: accusative: *mich* (2), *sich* (14); dative: *sich* (4, 17), *mir* (10, 12, 14), *dir* (23). Reciprocal 'each other': *euch* (24), *uns* (30) (see **Ch. 20**).
- Questions: *Was ... ?* (1), *Reicht ... ?* (5), *Küsst ... ?* (7), *Liebst ... ?* (9), *Duscht ... ?* (17), *In welchem ... ?* (19), *Wechselt ... ?* (21) (see **Ch. 23**).
- Relative order of objects: **i)** <u>pronouns</u> – acc. + dat.: *ich putz'* **sie mir** (14), *guck* **ihn dir** *an* (23), *ich kann* **mich** *mit* **ihm** (2); 2 accusatives: *hab' ich's ihn* (22); **ii)** <u>pronoun + noun</u>: *er putzt sich ... die Zähne* (4, 17) (see **26.8b**).

Discover more about conjunctions

25.3 NOTES ON INDIVIDUAL CONJUNCTIONS

25.3a Differences in meaning

Some of the conjunctions listed in **25.1** can be problematic in that they may have different meanings depending on the context in which they are used. Some common difficulties are discussed below:

- *Als/wenn* both mean 'when', yet *als* is used when referring to the **past** (past tense, perfect, pluperfect) and *wenn* refers to the present and future: e.g. *Als wir uns <u>kennengelernt haben</u>* (line 30 of text) '**When** we met each other' vs. *Wenn wir uns am Wochenende <u>sehen</u>* '**When** (or **whenever**) we see each other at the weekend'. If *wenn* is used to refer to the past it means 'whenever': e.g. *Wenn wir uns <u>gesehen haben</u>* '**Whenever** we saw each other'.
- *Wenn* means both 'if' and 'when'. It is sometimes evident from the context which meaning is required (e.g. if used with a subjunctive or conditional it means 'if'), but this is often not the case: e.g. *Wenn es unbedingt sein muss* (line 8 of text) could mean '**If** it's really necessary' or '**When**(ever) it's really necessary'. When a speaker wants to make it absolutely clear that s/he means 'if' and not 'when', s/he can use *falls*: e.g. *Falls ich bis 8 Uhr nicht fertig bin* '**If** (it's the case that) I'm not ready by 8 o'clock'. When 'if' also means 'whether', *ob* is used: e.g. *Ich weiß nicht, ob er heute kommt* 'I don't know if/whether he's coming today'.
- *Damit/so dass* both mean 'so (that)', but *damit* expresses purpose (i.e. 'in order that/in order to'[114]) while *so dass* expresses result (i.e. 'with the result that'): e.g. *Der Chef gab mir einen Laptop, damit ich zu Hause arbeiten konnte* 'The boss gave me a laptop **so that** (= in order that) I could work at home' vs. *Der Laptop war kaputt, so dass ich zu Hause nicht arbeiten konnte* 'The laptop didn't work, **so (that)** I couldn't work at home'.
- When *als ob* 'as if' is used with a verb in a tense other than the present, the conditional or conditional perfect tends to be used, as this introduces an idea which does not correspond to reality (see **Ch. 16**): e.g. *Er tat, als ob er mich nicht gesehen <u>hätte</u>* 'He acted **as if** he hadn't seen me'.

114 When the subject of both clauses is the same, *um ... zu* + infinitive usually renders 'in order to': e.g. *Ich stand heute früher auf*, **um** *den Bus nicht* **zu verpassen** 'I got up earlier **in order** not **to miss** the bus' (rather than: *damit ich den Buss nicht verpassen würde*). This is also the case with *ohne ... dass*/*ohne ... zu*: e.g. *Er ging*, **ohne dass** <u>ich</u> *ihm etwas sagen konnte* 'He went away without me being able to say anything to him' vs. *Er ging* **ohne** *etwas* **zu sagen** 'He went away without saying anything'.

25.3b Commas

Most conjunctions (except *und* and, in some contexts, *oder*, see **28.3(ii)**) are preceded by a **comma**. In addition, some (but not all, see **Table 25.2**) conjunctions with *dass* require a comma before *dass*: e.g. *Ich komme um fünf Uhr nach Hause*, **es sei denn, dass** *ich länger arbeiten muss* 'I'm coming home at five o'clock, unless I have to work longer'. Commas tend to be used before *dass* when the preceding element contains a verb (or part of a verb such as a past participle, e.g. *an**genommen**, dass* 'assuming that'; *voraus**gesetzt**, dass* 'provided that').

25.4 THE SCOPE OF CONJUNCTIONS

Sometimes a conjunction can refer to a whole sentence rather than just one clause. In this case, if the sentence consists of two or more clauses and the conjunction is a subordinating one, **every verb in the sentence** must go to the end of its respective clause: e.g. ***Als*** *er mit seinem Essen fertig* <u>war</u>, *es aber noch nicht weggeräumt* <u>hatte</u> ... 'When he had finished his meal but had not yet cleared away ...'; *Ich wusste*, ***dass*** *ich ihn schon gesehen* <u>hatte</u>, *mit ihm gesprochen* <u>hatte</u> *und ihm sogar meine Telefonnummer gegeben* <u>hatte</u> 'I knew that I had already seen him, had spoken to him and had even given him my telephone number'. (Alternatively, to avoid repetition, the first two instances of *hatte* can be omitted: *Ich wusste*, ***dass*** *ich ihn schon gesehen, mit ihm gesprochen und ihm sogar meine Telefonnummer gegeben* <u>hatte</u>.)

25.5 USE OF ENGLISH '-ING'

It is often the case in English that constructions with '-ing' are used instead of conjunctions: e.g. 'Walk**ing** down the street I noticed ...', 'He left the house **saying** that he would be late back'. These constructions must be translated into German using an appropriate conjunction and an ordinary finite verb. Some examples are:

- *Als ich in die Stadt* <u>fuhr</u>, *bemerkte ich ...*   Driv**ing** into town I noticed ...
- *Er saß im Garten* **und** <u>beobachtete</u> *die Vögel*   He sat in the garden watch**ing** the birds.
- ***Da*** *ich ihn nicht beleidigen* <u>wollte</u>, *nahm*   Not want**ing** to offend him, I accepted
  ich seine Einladung an   his invitation.

Similarly '**by** + -ing' is often translated using ***indem***, which acts like a subordinating conjunction in that it sends the finite verb to the end of the clause:

- *Man bekommt gute Noten*, ***indem*** *man*   You get good marks **by** work**ing** hard.
  fleißig <u>arbeitet</u>

- *Ich habe ihn beleidigt, **indem** ich ihm keinen Kaffee angeboten <u>habe</u>.*

I insulted him **by** not offer**ing** him any coffee.

✎ EXERCISES

Vocabulary topic: *Umweltschutz und Wiederverwertung*

1 Join the following clauses using the conjunctions given in brackets and change the word order where necessary:

Example: Ich weiß nicht. Die Mülltrennung ist noch sinnvoll. [ob]
Answer: Ich weiß nicht, ob die Mülltrennung noch sinnvoll <u>ist</u>.

  1 In Deutschland wurde zu Beginn der 90er Jahre mit der Verpackungsverordnung ein Farbleitsystem für den Hausmüll eingeführt. Jeder wurde verpflichtet seinen Müll zu trennen. [und]
  2 Man trennt den Müll zu Hause. Man kann zu einer nahe gelegenen Recyclinganlage gehen. [entweder … , oder]
  3 Wir sollten abgelaufene Medikamente zurück zur Apotheke bringen. Sie können sehr schädlich sein. [weil]
  4 Händler sind verpflichtet, alte und defekte Elektrogeräte ordnungsgemäß zu entsorgen. Sie haben die neuen Geräte geliefert. [nachdem]
  5 Manche Leute bringen Sperrmüll (größere Gegenstände wie alte Sofas, Bücherregale usw.) zum Wertstoffhof. Andere lassen diese Sachen auf dem Bürgersteig. Jemand möchte etwas für sich nehmen. [aber; falls].
  6 Lärmbelästigung ist weitgehend vermeidbar. Altglas wird nur zwischen 8 und 22 Uhr in die Behälter eingeworfen. [wenn]
  7 Papier gehört in die blaue Tonne, Verpackungen in die gelbe Tonne und Kompost in die braune. Der Rest landet in der grauen Restmülltonne. [während]
  8 Die Supermärkte haben auch eine wichtige Rolle gespielt. Sie haben die Verwendung der Plastiktüten drastisch reduziert und Sammelbehälter für z.B. Batterien zur Verfügung gestellt. [indem]
  9 Jeder kann mit dem Sammelverhalten dazu beitragen. Abfälle können durch Sammelsysteme wiederverwendet, stofflich verwertet und somit umweltkonform behandelt werden. [dass]
  10 Gegner der Mülltrennung behaupten, unser mühsam getrennter Müll werde nicht getrennt wiederverwertet. Er werde letztendlich wieder zusammen gekippt. [sondern].

2 Subordinate clauses (i.e. those beginning with a subordinating conjunction) may often BEGIN a sentence. Take your answers to question 1 (3, 4 and 8) above and place the subordinate clause at the beginning:

Example: Ich weiß nicht, ob die Mülltrennung noch sinnvoll ist.
Answer: Ob die Mülltrennung noch sinnvoll ist, weiß ich nicht.

3 Translate the bracketed conjunctions into German and join the clauses together, changing word order where necessary:

Example: [*After*] ich hatte über Klimawandel gelesen. Ich machte mir Sorgen.
Answer: Nachdem ich über Klimawandel gelesen <u>hatte</u>, <u>machte</u> ich mir Sorgen.

1 Die große Mehrheit der Klimaforscher ist der Ansicht. [*That*] die globale Erwärmung wird überwiegend vom Menschen verursacht.

2 [*Although*] die Temperaturen global ansteigen. Es kann kurzzeitig und regional auch weiterhin zu Kältewellen kommen.

3 [*When*] der Treibhauseffekt wird durch das Verbrennen fossiler Brenstoffe und die Emission des Gases Kohlendioxid verursacht. Es heißt anthropogene (menschengemachte) globale Erwärmung.

4 [*When*] in den späten 1950er Jahren wurde erstmals nachgewiesen, dass der Kohlendioxidgehalt der Atmosphäre ansteigt. Wissenschaftler starteten regelmäßige Messungen des CO_2-Gehalts der Atmosphäre.

5 Politische Vorgaben zum Klimaschutz müssen durch entsprechende Maßnahmen umgesetzt werden. [*so that*] Treibhausgasemissionen können vermindert werden.

6 Man kann die Energieeffizienz verbessern. [*If*] man bietet eine Dienstleistung oder ein Produkt mit weniger Energieverbrauch als zuvor an. Das heißt beispielsweise. [*That*] in einer Wohnung muss weniger geheizt werden, ein Kühlschrank benötigt weniger Strom oder ein Auto hat einen geringeren Benzinverbrauch.

7 Im Gegensatz zu fossilen Energieträgern wird bei der Nutzung der meisten erneuerbaren Energien kein Kohlendioxid ausgestoßen. [*As/since*] sie sind weitgehend CO_2-neutral.

8 Manchmal begründen wir unsere Mangel an Aktivität gegen die globale Erwärmung. [*By*] wir sagen. [*That*] man kann selbst nicht viel tun. [*As long as*] die Wirtschaft ist so mächtig.

9 Was Klimaschutz betrifft sagen wir [*that*] die Handlungen eines Einzelnen bewirken nicht viel. [*Unless*] andere bzw. andere Länder tun auch etwas dagegen.

4 Translate the following sentences into German using an appropriate conjunction for the context, and using the past tense rather than the perfect for questions 2–4:

1 He's on TV discussing the most recent developments in climate change. [zum Thema Klimawandel]

2 Wanting to do something for the environment, I bought some energy-saving lightbulbs. [energiesparende Glühbirnen]

3 My neighbour saved a lot of energy in the long run by installing solar panels. [langfristig, Sonnenkollektoren]

4 The Environment Minister was photographed making a speech at the G8 summit last month. [der G8-Gipfel]

For further exercises on conjunctions see Revision Text 2, Ex. 2 and for exercises on interrogatives functioning as subordinating conjunctions see Ch. 23, Ex. 4.

26 | Word order

Die Deutschen und ihre Autos

Lasst uns ehrlich sein, der deutsche Mann liebt Maschinen. Man muss nur den Männern in der Kneipe zuhören, wie sie darüber diskutieren, wohin sie ihr Auto zur Reparatur bringen; ein Motorschaden, ein abgebrochener
5 Scheibenwischer wird mit ebenso tiefer Besorgnis geschildert wie der gebrochene Knöchel einer Tochter [...]. Wenn ein deutscher Mann die Wahl hätte, würde er sich mit seinem Audi beerdigen lassen, seinem treuen Gefährten. [...]
Es gibt ein zentrales Paradox in Deutschland. Auf den ersten Blick
10 scheint es ein Land zu sein, das besessen von der Autobahn ist; nicht nur die fehlenden Tempolimits – obwohl es mich immer verwundern wird, dass Touristen aus China nur deshalb nach Deutschland reisen, um mit ihrem Porsche mit Höchstgeschwindigkeit von einer Stadt zur nächsten fahren zu können. Nein, auch die Hochgeschwindigkeitszüge, der ICE, der
15 Transrapid. Die gesamte Maschinenbau-Industrie ist eher um das Prinzip der Geschwindigkeits-Maximierung aufgebaut als daran interessiert, Energie zu sparen. Und doch, und doch gibt es keine unbeweglichere Gesellschaft in Europa als die Deutschlands. Die Leute sind lieber arbeitslos und bleiben in ihrem Dorf als für einen neuen Job 100 Kilometer
20 weit weg zu ziehen. Das soziale System fördert Stillstand. Das Mietrecht macht es unprofitabel, umzuziehen. Die unterschiedlichen Schulsysteme machen es beinahe unmöglich, ein Kind von einer Schule in Berlin auf eine bayerische Schule umzuschulen. [...]
Heute ist die Propaganda zum Klimaschutz so stark, dass britische
25 Politiker mit dem Fahrrad zur Arbeit fahren (auch wenn sie zugegebener- maßen von einem chauffierten Auto begleitet werden, in dem sich ihre Dokumente und Aktentaschen befinden). Schon bald, vielleicht in einer Generation, werden Kinder im Kindergarten verspottet werden, deren Vater ein großes Auto fährt. [...]
30 Und so ist die Ära der großen, fetten Limousinen bald vorbei, selbst für den deutschen Mann. Wie wird er nun seine Männlichkeit messen? Anhand der Größe seiner Fahrradluftpumpe? [...]

Von Roger Boyes, zuerst erschienen auf www.goethe.de, März 2007.

der Motorschaden – engine failure	*unbeweglich* – immobile
der Scheibenwischer – windscreen wiper	*die Gesellschaft* – society
die Besorgnis – concern, anxiety	*fördern* – to promote
der Knöchel – ankle	*das Mietrecht* – tenancy laws
beerdigen – to bury	*zugegebenermaßen* – admittedly
der treue Gefährte – faithful companion	*verspotten* – to mock, ridicule
besessen von – obsessed with	*anhand* (+ gen.) – by
die Geschwindigkeit – speed	*die Fahrradluftpumpe* – bicycle pump

Word order in the text

26.1 ORDER OF VERBS

In order to get to grips with the order of verbs in German, it is important to understand what a **clause** is. A clause is the part of a sentence which contains the **finite verb**. The finite verb is the part of the verb that shows person, number and tense (e.g. *ich **mache*** shows first person singular present). Thus examples a) show sentences containing one clause, and examples b) show sentences containing two clauses:

a)   *Ich **fahre** gern nach Deutschland*
   *Sie **haben** ihre Eltern besucht*

b)   *Ich **spreche** Deutsch und mein Freund **spricht** Englisch*
   *Er **ist** ins Kino gegangen, aber der Film **hat** ihm nicht gefallen*

26.1a In main clauses

i)   In an ordinary German main clause, the finite verb is always the **second** 'idea', while infinitives, past participles and separable prefixes appear at the **end**. This is known as the **verbal bracket**. The following examples show the finite verbs in bold print and the infinitives and participles underlined:[115]

• *Man **muss** nur den Männern in der Kneipe <u>zuhören</u>* (2–3)	One simply **has to** <u>listen</u> to the men in the pub
• *Wie **wird** er nun seine Männlichkeit <u>messen</u>?* (31)	How **will** he <u>measure</u> his masculinity now?
• *Die ... Maschinenbau-Industrie **ist** eher um das Prinzip der Geschwindigkeits-Maximierung <u>aufgebaut</u>* (15–16)	The mechanical engineering industry **is** <u>based</u> on the principle of maximising speed

[115] Note that expressions preceded by *als* 'than' and *wie* 'as' can appear outside the clause: *ein abgebrochener Scheibenwischer wird mit ebenso tiefer Besorgnis geschildert <u>wie der gebrochene Knöchel einer Tochter</u>* 'a broken windscreen wiper is described with as much concern <u>as a daughter's broken ankle</u>' (4–6).

ii) If an expression of time or some other element appears at the beginning of the clause, the finite verb must still be in second position, which means that the subject (underlined here) has to **follow** the verb. As you can see from our text, this is extremely common:

- *Auf den ersten Blick **scheint** es (9–10)*   At first sight <u>it</u> **seems**
- *Doch **gibt** <u>es</u> keine unbeweglichere*   Yet <u>there</u> **is** no more immobile
  Gesellschaft (17–18)   a society
- *Heute **ist** <u>die Propaganda</u> … so stark (24)*   Today <u>the propaganda</u> **is** so strong
- *Schon bald, vielleicht in einer Generation,*   Soon, perhaps in a generation,
  ***werden** <u>Kinder</u> … verspottet werden (27–28)*   <u>children</u> **will** be ridiculed…
- *So **ist** <u>die Ära</u> … bald vorbei (30)*   Thus <u>the era</u> **is** soon to be over

This 'verb second' rule also applies if the subject and verb are directly preceded by a co-ordinating conjunction such as *und, aber, oder, denn* etc. (see **Table 25.1**), or after words which are 'cut off' from the clause by a comma:

- <u>*Und doch*</u>, <u>*und*</u> *doch **gibt** es … (17)*   And still, and still there **is** ….
- *Die Leute **sind** lieber arbeitslos <u>und</u>*   The people **prefer** to be jobless
  ***bleiben** in ihrem Dorf (18–19)*   and **stay** in their village

This last example shows that the subject can be omitted if referring to the same person or thing more than once (i.e. instead of *Die Leute sind lieber arbeitslos und <u>sie</u> **bleiben** …*).

iii) The finite verb appears at the **beginning** of the clause if it is in the imperative: ***Lasst** uns ehrlich sein* 'Let's be honest' (2) and in yes/no questions, e.g. ***Komst** du jetzt?* '**Are** you coming now?' (not in text).

26.1b In subordinate clauses

i) The finite verb appears at the **end** of subordinate clauses: i.e. those clauses preceded by a **subordinating conjunction** such as *dass, wenn, weil, da, obwohl* etc. (see **Table 25.2**), a **relative pronoun** such as *der Mann, **der** neben mir wohnt* (see **Ch. 9**) and **interrogatives used indirectly** such as *ich weiß, **wer** du wirklich bist* (see **23.5**). The first set of examples shows subordinating conjunctions sending the finite verb to the end of the clause, the second set shows relative pronouns and the third set shows interrogatives used indirectly.

- <u>*Wenn*</u> *ein deutscher Mann die Wahl **hätte** (6–7)*   <u>if</u> a German man **had** the choice
- <u>*obwohl*</u> *es mich immer verwundern **wird** (11)*   <u>although</u> it'll always surprise me
- <u>*dass*</u> *Touristen aus China nach Deutschland*   <u>that</u> tourists from China **travel**
  ***reisen** (11–12)*   to Germany

- *ein Land, <u>das</u> besessen von der Autobahn*   a country <u>that</u> **is obsessed** with
  ***ist** (10)*   the motorway
- *Auto, in <u>dem</u> sich ihre Dokumente … **befinden***   car in <u>which</u> their documents …
  (26–27)   **can** be found

- *Kinder, <u>deren</u> Vater ein großes Auto **fährt*** (28–29)

  children <u>whose</u> father **drives** a big car

- *<u>wie</u> sie darüber **diskutieren*** (2)
- *<u>wohin</u> sie ihr Auto zur Reparatur* **bringen** (3–4)

  <u>how</u> they **discuss**

  <u>where</u> they **are** taking their car for repair

ii) If, within a sentence, a main clause follows a subordinate clause, the finite verb of the main clause must come **first**: e.g. (subordinate clause underlined):

- *<u>Wenn ein deutscher Mann die Wahl hätte</u>,* **würde** *er sich ... beerdigen lassen* (6–7)

  <u>If a German man had the choice</u> he **would** have himself buried …

26.1c (*Um*) ... *zu* + infinitive

Constructions with *zu* + infinitive (with or without *um*, see **Ch. 21**) are usually treated as a **separate clause**, which means that they **follow** the clause that introduces them. The infinitive itself always appears at the end of its clause (with *zu*):

- *Auf den ersten Blick scheint es ein Land **zu sein*** (9–10)
  'At first sight it appears **to be** a country'

- *Die unterschiedlichen Schulsysteme machen es beinahe unmöglich, ein Kind von einer Schule in Berlin auf eine bayerische Schule **umzuschulen*** (21–23)
  'The different school systems make it almost impossible **to move** a child from a school in Berlin to a Bavarian school'

- *... dass Touristen aus China nach Deutschland reisen **um** mit ihrem Porsche ... fahren **zu können*** (11–14)
  '... that tourists from China travel to Germany in order to drive their Porsche ...'

The last example shows how the finite verb *reisen* is sent to the end of its own clause, before the *um ... zu* clause, and not to the end of the whole sentence (not **dass Touristen aus China nach Deutschland um mit ihrem Porsche fahren zu können **reisen***).

26.2 ORDER OF SUBJECTS AND OBJECTS

In German, the order of subjects and objects is much more flexible than in English. For instance, if the speaker wishes to emphasise or shift the focus onto a particular subject or object, this is often done by a change in word order. Therefore it is unwise to give hard and fast rules for the position of subjects and objects within a German sentence, so only general tendencies can be given which reflect the most common usage.

26.2a Subjects

Subjects usually begin a clause and precede the finite verb: *der deutsche **Mann** liebt Maschinen* '**the German man** loves machines' (2, and see **26.1a(i)** for more examples), unless another element begins the clause, in which case the subject is placed after the verb: *Heute ist **die Propaganda** ... so stark* 'Today, **the propaganda** ... is so strong' (24) (see **26.1a(ii)**). Being in a subordinate clause does not affect the order of subjects and objects: ***der deutsche Mann** liebt Maschinen* → *weil **der deutsche Mann** Maschinen liebt.*

26.2b Objects

Accusative objects[116] usually come later in the clause: after the subject and verb, and also after many expressions of time and some expressions of manner. On the other hand, they tend to precede *nicht* (see **Ch. 22**), and phrases beginning with a preposition that are not expressions of time or manner:

• *Das soziale System fördert **Stillstand*** (20)	The social system promotes **immobility**
• *Wie wird er <u>nun</u> **seine Männlichkeit** messen?* (31)	How will he measure **his masculinity** <u>now</u>?
• *Es gibt **ein zentrales Paradox** <u>in Deutschland</u>* (9)	There's a **central paradox** <u>in Germany</u>

---

[116] For the relative order of accusative and dative objects, see **26.8**.

26.2c Pronouns preceding nouns

There is a general tendency in German word order for pronouns (particularly the small unstressed ones such as personal and reflexive pronouns) to precede nouns, irrespective of whether they are the subject or object, e.g. *Auto ..., in dem **sich** <u>ihre Dokumente und Aktentaschen</u> befinden* 'car ... in which their documents and briefcases can be found' (26–27). Here, the subject (underlined) follows the accusative reflexive pronoun *sich*, as the subject is a noun phrase (see **26.8** for further discussion).

26.3 EXPRESSIONS OF TIME, MANNER AND PLACE

Again, the order of expressions of time, manner and place is quite flexible in German, depending on the focus that the speaker is using. Probably the most frequently used order is Time-Manner-Place: e.g. *Ich fahre* [*jeden Tag*]$_{\text{Time (when?)}}$ [*mit dem Bus*]$_{\text{Manner (how?)}}$ [*in die Uni*]$_{\text{Place (where?)}}$ Examples from the text are:

• *um* [*mit ihrem Porsche mit Höchstgeschwindigkeit*$_M$] [*von einer Stadt zur nächsten*$_P$] *fahren zu können* (12–14)
  'in order to drive at top speed from one town to the next with their Porsche'

• *dass britische Politiker* [*mit dem Fahrrad*$_M$] [*zur Arbeit*$_P$] *fahren* (24–25)
  'that British politicians travel to work by bike'

26.4 ELEMENTS PLACED AT THE BEGINNING OF THE CLAUSE

It is often the case that some words and phrases are placed at the beginning of the clause, before the subject and verb. These can be objects, expressions of time, manner or place, or adverbs. In some contexts this can be a way of emphasising the elements in question, while in others it is simply done without any special emphasis being intended (e.g. it is especially common with expressions of time). Examples from the text are: *Auf den ersten Blick* (9–10), *Auch* (14), *Und doch* (17), *Heute* (24), *Schon bald, vielleicht in einer Generation* (27–28), *Und so* (30).

26.5 ELEMENTS PLACED AT THE END OF THE CLAUSE

It is also possible to place elements **after the final verb** in the clause (i.e. outside the verbal bracket). This is often done in the spoken language where these elements are added as an afterthought or by way of explanation or emphasis. This occurs much less in the written language and, where it does occur, it usually indicates emphasis: *Wenn ein deutscher Mann die Wahl hätte, würde er sich mit seinem Audi beerdigen lassen,* **seinem treuen Gefährten** 'If a German man had the choice he would have himself buried with his Audi, **his faithful companion**' (6–8).

Other points to note in the text

- Relative pronouns: *das* (10), *dem* (26), *deren* (28) (see **Ch. 9**).
- Conditional in 'if' clause: *Wenn ein deutscher Mann die Wahl* **hätte, würde** *er sich mit seinem Audi beerdigen* **lassen** (6–7) (see **16.4**).
- Imperative in the *ihr*-form: **lasst** *uns* (2) (see **11.4**).
- Passives: *ein abgebrochener Scheibenwischer* **wird ... geschildert** (4–5), *wenn sie ...* **begleitet werden** (25–26), *werden Kinder ...* **verspottet werden** (28); *sein*-passive: *Die gesamte Maschinenbau-Industrie* **ist ... aufgebaut** (15–16) (see **Ch. 18**).

Discover more about word order

26.6 MULTIPLE SUBORDINATE CLAUSES

It is sometimes the case that an element that sends the following finite verb to the end, e.g. a subordinating conjunction or relative pronoun, has scope over more than one clause and therefore over more than one finite verb. This means that it is not sufficient simply to send the closest following verb to the end of the clause and leave the others. In this case, the finite verbs all go to **the end of their respective clauses**. Note that they do not 'pile up' at the end of the sentence:

Sie ist traurig, <u>weil</u> sie kein Geld **hat**, *ihre Miete nicht bezahlen* **kann** *und ihre Eltern ihr nicht helfen* **wollen**
'She is sad because she hasn't any money, can't pay her rent and her parents don't want to help her'.

26.7 DOUBLE INFINITIVE CONSTRUCTIONS IN SUBORDINATE CLAUSES

When a finite verb is sent to the end of a subordinate clause containing a double infinitive construction, i.e. when a modal verb is used with another verb in the perfect, pluperfect, conditional perfect or future (see **21.4b**), the finite verb does not go to the very end of the clause but to the position immediately preceding the two infinitives, e.g. *Ich* **habe** *es nicht machen können* → *weil ich es nicht* **habe** <u>*machen können*</u> 'because I haven't been able to do it'.

26.8 RELATIVE ORDER OF SUBJECT, ACCUSATIVE OBJECT AND DATIVE OBJECT

As with most aspects of word order in German, the relative position of subjects and objects is much more flexible than in English, depending on the focus which the speaker wants to give to these elements and on the wider context. Below are some basic guidelines for commonly used word order patterns in constructions where the subject and objects all **follow the finite verb**, as this is often problematic for English learners of German.

26.8a Nouns

The usual order for subjects and objects when they are all nouns following the verb is: **subject-dative object-accusative object**:

- *Nachher erzählte der Vater$_S$ seinem Sohn$_D$*   Afterwards the father told his son
  eine Geschichte$_A$.   a story
- *Gestern gab der Student$_S$ dem Lehrer$_D$*   Yesterday the student gave the
  seinen Aufsatz$_A$.[117]   teacher his essay
- *Wie will dein Freund$_S$ seiner Mutter$_D$*   How will your friend tell his
  diese Nachricht$_A$ beibringen?   mother this news?

This does not apply when the objects are **personal pronouns**, however, as pronouns usually precede nouns which follow the finite verb, irrespective of case (see **26.8b**).

> [117] And with the expression of time **not** at the beginning: *Der Student gab dem Lehrer **gestern** seinen Aufsatz.*

26.8b Personal pronouns

Personal pronouns following a finite verb usually come **immediately after the verb** (or, in subordinate clauses, the conjunction), which means that **personal pronouns tend to precede all nouns** in this position:

- *Trotzdem hat **ihr** der Chef eine*   Despite this her boss gave her
  Gehaltserhöhung gegeben.[118]   a salary increase
- *Morgen muss **dich** dein Freund abholen.*   Tomorrow your friend must pick
  Mein Auto ist kaputt.   you up. My car is broken.
- *Er weiß, dass **mir** der Kollege geholfen hat.*   He knows that the colleague helped me

> [118] Reflexive pronouns occupy the same position as the personal pronouns: e.g. *Gestern hat **sich** der Chef geärgert.* By contrast, demonstrative pronouns and other types of pronoun tend to come after the noun: e.g. *Siehst du die Äpfel? – Gestern habe ich dem Chef **einen** gegeben; Gestern hat sie dem Chef **das** gesagt* (OR *Gestern hat sie **das** dem Chef gesagt* for a different emphasis).

When the subject and both objects are all personal pronouns the usual order is: **subject-accusative-dative**:

- *Außerdem hat **er es ihr** nicht erzählt.*   Besides, he didn't tell it to her
- *Brauchst du heute deine Schlittschuhe?*   Do you need your skates today?
  *Kannst **du sie mir** leihen?*   Can you lend me them?

26.9 PHRASES BEGINNING WITH PREPOSITIONS

Following the general tendency in German for short, unstressed words to come early after the finite verb and longer items to follow (e.g. pronouns coming before nouns), prepositional phrases, which consist of a preposition and noun phrase, are large items and therefore tend to come even **later in the clause**, e.g. *Ich habe gestern meiner Mutter einen Ring **zum Geburtstag** geschenkt* 'I gave my mother a ring **for her birthday**', in which the prepositional phrase follows the expression of time and two objects (dative and accusative).

If, however, a phrase beginning with a preposition is itself an expression of time, manner or place (e.g. *zum ersten Mal*), then it will usually follow the rules set out in **26.3**.

26.10 POSITION OF ADJECTIVES

Most predicative adjectives (i.e. those which do not precede a noun) occur at the **end** of the clause, e.g. *Ich war dort bei dem schönen Wetter richtig **glücklich*** 'I was really **happy** there with that lovely weather'.

In clauses where the verb has been sent to the end or there is a past participle or infinitive present, the adjective precedes these verbs: e.g. *weil ich dort bei dem schönen Wetter richtig glücklich <u>war</u>*.

26.11 SOME COMMON GERMAN SENTENCE PATTERNS

Tables 26.1 and **26.2** illustrate some commonly used German sentence patterns. Students are advised to pay particular attention to the word order.

Table 26.1 Verbs and expressions of time, manner and place

Conj.	1st pos.	2nd pos.	Time	Manner	Place	Participle/ Infinitive	Verb sent to end
	Uta	fährt	heute	mit dem Zug	nach Berlin		
	Heute	fährt Uta		mit dem Zug	nach Berlin		
und	Uta	ist	heute	mit dem Zug	nach Berlin	gefahren	
weil	Uta		heute	mit dem Zug	nach Berlin	gefahren	ist

Table 26.2 Subjects, objects and prepositional phrases

1st pos.	2nd pos.	Pro-nouns	Inverted noun subj.	Dat. noun	Time	Acc. noun	Prepositional phrase
Uta	gab			ihrem Mann	heute	ein Buch	zum Geburtstag
Heute	gab		Uta	ihrem Mann		ein Buch	zum Geburtstag
Heute	gab	ihm	Uta			ein Buch	zum Geburtstag
Heute	gab	sie ihm				ein Buch	zum Geburtstag
Heute	gab	sie es ihm					

✎ **EXERCISES**

Vocabulary topic: *Zeit, Tage und Termine*

1 Insert the bracketed finite verbs into the correct place in the sentence:

1 Joachim am Samstag um acht Uhr eine Fete. [macht]

2 Diese Woche die Kinder zu ihren Großeltern. [fahren]

3 Leider es nicht möglich, vor dem vierundzwanzigsten Mai den Flug zu buchen. [ist]

4 Am 2. März ich bis sieben Uhr abends, aber den nächsten Tag ich frei. [arbeite, habe]

5 Karl, ich am Montag nicht kommen. [kann]

6 Stell dir vor, sie am 12. Februar hundert Jahre alt! [wird]

7 Wo du gestern Morgen um halb neun? [warst]

8 Ich glaube, er am 16. April Geburtstag. [hat]

9 Schade, dass ich dich am ersten Januar nicht. [sah]

10 Der siebzehnte Juni der Tag, an dem wir uns. [war, kennenlernten]

11 Weißt du, ob deine englischen Freunde in Deutschland am 24. oder 25. Dezember Weihnachten und was sie an dem Tag? [feiern, essen]

12 Seine Mutter besorgt, weil er gestern Abend nicht nach Hause und sie auch nicht. [war, kam, anrief]

13 Ich froh, dass ich es jeden Tag, vor halb sechs mit meiner Arbeit fertig zu sein. [bin, schaffe]

14 Bevor ich dieses Jahr in Urlaub, ich einen neuen Koffer. [fahre, brauche]

15 Da wir am 4. Juli unseren Hochzeitstag, wir abends in ein schönes Restaurant. [haben, gehen]

2 Return to Question 1 above and put the bracketed verbs into the PERFECT tense, paying particular attention to where you place the auxiliary and past participle in the sentence.

3 Rearrange the following words and phrases to make proper sentences, paying particular attention to the order of the expressions of time, manner and place:

1 Jens, zur Arbeit, mit dem Auto, immer, fährt.

2 Mein Vater, am Bahnhof, morgen um halb acht, kommt, an.

3 Die Kinder, auf der Wiese, heute, fröhlich, spielen.

4 Wir, für vier Tage, nach Wien, dieses Wochenende, mit dem Schnellzug, fahren.

5 Meine Freundin, mit ihrem neuen Ehemann, auf Besuch, morgen Abend, kommt.

6 Ich, werde, warten, auf dich, auf dem Hauptplatz, um viertel vor drei.

✎ **FURTHER EXERCISES**

4 Put the bracketed subjects and objects into the correct order in the sentence:

1 Wollte schenken [er, Blumen, seiner Lehrerin].

2 Hat erklärt [sie, die Ursache des Problems, ihrem Chef].

3 Gestern habe gekauft [von H&M, ich, einen neuen Pulli, meinem Mann].

4 Ich hoffe, dass schon gegeben hast [du, die Nachricht, deinem Freund].

5 Hast schon gesagt [du, es, deiner Mutter]?

6 „Kannst leihen [du, einen Stift, mir]?" „Sicher. Ich kann geben [einen, dir]. Ich habe genug davon".

7 Ich glaube, dass schämt [wegen seines schlechten Benehmens, er, sich].

8 Ich weiß, dass zu sagen hast [du, etwas, mir]. Sag [es, mir]!

9 Dein Freund hat wegen seines Fahrrads angerufen. Kannst zurückgeben [du, es, ihm]?

10 „Was hält deine Mutter von unseren Urlaubsfotos?" „Habe noch nicht gezeigt [ich, sie, ihr]."

5 Make proper sentences out of the following dialogue by changing the order of the words and phrases where necessary:

Birgit: Du, meine Ohrringe, hast gesehen? Ich, sie, an, gehabt, gestern, habe, aber, ich, heute, sie, kann, finden, nicht mehr.

Kerstin: Ja, mir, du, sie, hast geliehen, gestern Abend. Du, sie, zurückhaben, willst?

Birgit: Nein, kein Problem, ist, das. Ich, vergessen, hatte, bloß,[119] dass, ich, hatte, geliehen, dir, sie.

Kerstin: Und, hast, geliehen, auch[119], deine Goldkette, du, mir.

Birgit: Ja, das, ich, weiß.

Kerstin: Du, in die Disco, gehst, heute Abend?

Birgit: Nein, ich, ins Bett, gehe, früher, heute Abend, weil, ich, fahre, nach Frankfurt, mit meiner Schwester, morgen, und, muss, aufstehen, sehr früh.

Kerstin: OK, ich, versuchen, ruhig zu sein, werde, wenn, von der Disco, später, ich, zurückkomme, damit, ich, nicht, aufwecke, dich.

Birgit: Gut. Viel Spaß!

---

[119] The rules for the position of *bloß* and *auch* are similar to those for *nicht* (see **22.1A**).

Other word-order related exercises are: word order after conjunctions (Ch. 25, Exs 1–3); word order after relative pronouns (Ch. 9, Exs 2–3); word order with modals (Ch. 21, Ex. 3); position of nicht (Ch. 22, Exs 1–3); position of separable prefixes (Ch. 19, Exs 1–3) and position of reflexive pronouns (Ch. 20, Exs 2–3).

For further exercises on word order see Revision Text 1, Ex. 4 and Revision Text 4, Ex. 4 (position of verbs), Revision Text 2, Ex. 2 (conjunctions) and Revision Text 3, Ex. 4 (relative clauses).

27| Word formation

Andere Länder, andere Tischsitten

Die Ellbogen dürfen nicht auf den Tisch, Schmatzer werden verpönt und es wird ordentlich mit Messer und Gabel gegessen [...]. Doch was passiert, wenn der gut erzogene Deutsche seine Heimat verlässt? Häufig wird
5 vergessen, dass Tischsitten [...] von Land zu Land unterschiedlich sind [...].
[I]n den USA wird für gewöhnlich nur mit einer Hand gegessen, während die zweite seelenruhig im Schoß liegt. Dies soll einer Legende nach ein Vermächtnis aus dem Wilden Westen sein. Weil man dort zu jeder Zeit auf der Hut vor Feinden sein musste, behielt man stets – und so auch beim
10 Essen – eine Hand an der Waffe. Und so kam es, dass viele Amerikaner heutzutage zunächst ihr Essen zerschneiden, um es anschließend einhändig mit der Gabel zu sich zu nehmen.
Kaum zu glauben, aber in Japan gilt es als Kompliment an den Chefkoch wenn gerülpst und geschlürft wird. Das zeugt davon, dass das Essen
15 mundet und der Tischgast sich wohl fühlt [...]. Wer in Japan mit Stäbchen isst, sollte keineswegs zu wild mit selbigen hantieren. Die Esswerkzeuge dürfen vor allen Dingen nicht gekreuzt werden oder in den Reis gesteckt werden [...]. Außerdem sollten die Stäbchen weder aneinander gerieben noch abgeleckt werden. Wie bei uns der nackte Zeigefinger, so gilt es in
20 Japan als Beleidigung, mit einem Stäbchen auf eine andere Person zu zeigen [...].
Hat man in Russland genug gegessen, so lässt man einen Rest seines Essens auf dem Teller liegen. Doch nicht etwa, weil man diesen nicht mehr schafft, sondern aus reiner Höflichkeit. Durch diese Geste weiß nämlich der
25 Koch, dass er seinen Job gut gemacht und nicht etwa zu wenig Essen zubereitet hat. (Während es in Deutschland als unhöflich gilt, nicht aufzuessen.) [...]
Dass immer noch in vielen Ländern, darunter auch Indien, mit der Hand gegessen wird, dürfte bekannt sein. Doch vergessen Europäer bei einem
30 Besuch Indiens oft etwas Entscheidendes: Die linke, die 'unreine' Hand darf gar nicht eingesetzt werden. Warum? In Indien benutzt man zum Beispiel nur die linke Hand zum Reinigen nach dem Toilettengang. Somit versteht sich diese Tischregel von selbst [...].

© web.de, 2011 [http://web.de/magazine/essen-geniessen/essen/]

die Tischsitte – table etiquette	*rülpsen* – to burp
der Schmatzer – noisy eater	*schlürfen* – to slurp
verpönt – frowned upon	*munden* – to taste good
gut erzogen – well brought up	*das Stäbchen* – chopstick
der Schoß – lap	*hantieren* – to handle
das Vermächtnis – legacy	*das Esswerkzeug* – implement for eating
auf der Hut sein – to be on guard	*unrein* – unclean
einhändig – with one hand	*einsetzen* – to put to use

♀ Word formation in the text

This chapter deals with the way in which words are derived from other words in German. This is a highly complex issue, as there are usually different ways of deriving words of a similar meaning and there often is no apparent 'reason' for the choice of derivation (e.g. if we say *schlafen* → *der Schlaf* why are *Essen* → **der Ess* or *trinken* → **der Trink* incorrect, the correct forms being *das Essen* and *das Getränk*?). Moreover, it is hardly ever the case that a German derivation corresponds to a single English equivalent. For these reasons, this chapter does not set out hard-and-fast rules for word formation in German but simply lists the most common forms of derivation which the student is encouraged to recognise.

27.1 THE FORMATION OF NOUNS

In German, nouns can be formed from other words (nouns, adjectives, verbs) usually by adding a suffix. The noun formation processes used in our text are listed below. Note that they usually have a particular gender associated with them:

27.1a *-er* (less commonly *-ler*) added to verb stems and many nouns (gender: masculine)

These are most commonly **agent nouns** (nouns that denote a person who carries out the action of a verb): e.g. *schmatzen* 'to eat noisily' → verb stem *schmatz-* → agent noun *der Schmatzer* 'the noisy eater' (2).[120]

-er can also be added to place names to denote someone's origin: *Europa* → *der Europäer* 'the European' (29). This example shows that *-er* sometimes triggers umlaut (compare e.g. *backen – der Bäcker* 'baker'). Note that nouns derived from place names can sometimes have irregularities, as they are often derived from adjective bases: *Amerika* → *der Amerika<u>n</u>er* (10) (c.f. *amerikan- isch*), hence the insertion of 'n'. Noun formation with *-er* is a highly productive process.[121]

---

[120] *-er* can also be used to denote the **instrument** that carries out a particular action: e.g. *schälen* 'to peel' → *der Kartoffelschäl**er** 'the potato peeler'.

[121] This means that the rule is still in operation today, rather than being a relic from the past. Thus if new words enter the language, the rule can apply to them: e.g. *programmieren* → *der Programmier**er*.

27.1b *-heit* (with some words *-keit*[122]) added to adjectives (gender: feminine)

These are added to **adjectives** to form nouns denoting a particular quality, often corresponding to English '-ness' or '-ity'. There is only one example in the text: *die Höflichkeit* 'politeness' (24) (< *höflich*). Other examples are: *gesund* → *die Gesundheit* 'health', *schön* → *die Schönheit* 'beauty', *einsam* → *die Einsamkeit* 'loneliness'.

> [122] Usually in words ending with *-bar, -ig, -lich, -sam* and sometimes *-el, -er*.

27.1c *-ung* added to verb stems (gender: feminine)

This is a very frequently used productive suffix which derives nouns from verbs. It sometimes renders English '-ing' or '-ion', referring to the action described by the verb: *beleidigen* 'to insult' → *die Beleidigung* 'the insult' (20). Other examples not from the text are: *vorlesen* → *die Vorlesung* 'lecture', *sich entschuldigen* → *die Entschuldigung* 'apology'.

27.1d Verb stems used as nouns (gender: masculine)

These also denote an action and tend to be used with prefixed verbs (i.e. verbs with separable or inseparable prefixes): *besuchen* → *der Besuch* 'the visit' (30). Other examples are: *anfangen* → *der Anfang, beginnen* → *der Beginn* 'beginning'. This process is less productive than the addition of *-ung*.

27.1e Infinitival nouns (gender: neuter)

The use of an infinitive form as a noun is an extremely frequent and productive way of deriving nouns which refer to the action described by the verb. It very frequently corresponds to an English present participle in '-ing'. Examples from the text are *das Essen*, which can either mean 'eating', referring to the action (10), or 'food' (14, 23, 25); *das Reinigen* 'cleaning' (32). The last example shows that this rule can apply to verbs which already have a derived noun (e.g. *die Reinigung*) to make it clear that it is an **action** that is being referred to (e.g. *die Reinigung* could also mean the place where something is cleaned, such as a dry cleaner's shop).

27.1f Adjectival nouns (gender: masculine or feminine for people, neuter for things)

These are nouns which describe a person or thing and look like an adjective (with the appropriate ending). Examples from the text are: *Deutsche* 'Germans' (4), which is plural and not preceded by an article. Other forms of this word are: *der Deutsche* 'the German man', *die Deutschen* 'the Germans', *ein Deutscher* 'a German man', *eine Deutsche* 'a German woman' etc. (see **5.5**).

When referring to things, a neuter form is used: *etwas Entscheidendes* 'something crucial' (30). Other forms of this would be: *das Entscheidende* 'the crucial thing'.

27.1g Diminutive nouns (gender: neuter)

These nouns are used to mean 'little', either in the literal sense of 'small' or when used as a term of endearment (or sometimes condescension). The most frequently used suffix is *-chen*, and the preceding stressed vowel is umlauted: *der Stab* 'stick' → *das Stäbchen* 'little stick', which in this text means 'chopstick' (15, 18). The less common suffix *-lein* is added after nouns ending in *ch* and *g*, for ease of pronunciation (e.g. *Buch* → *Büchlein* 'little book'), and is often found in more poetic language instead of *-chen*.

See **27.5** for more noun-forming processes.

27.2 THE FORMATION OF ADJECTIVES

In German, adjectives can be formed from nouns, verbs and other adjectives in the following ways, as illustrated in the text. Note that all of these are common and productive.

27.2a *-lich* added to nouns (where possible, umlaut is usually added)

This sometimes, but not always, corresponds to English *-ly*: *Name* → *nämlich* 'namely' (24), *Hof* → *höflich* 'courteous, polite' (26), *Unterschied* → *unterschiedlich* 'different' (5).

Less commonly, *-lich* can be added to **adjectives** and **verb** stems: *gewöhnen* → *gewöhnlich* 'usually', which is used as an adverb here (6).

27.2b *-ig* added to nouns (where possible, umlaut is usually added)

This usually denotes possession of a particular characteristic associated with the noun: *eine Hand* → *einhändig* 'one-handed' (12), *Ruhe* → *ruhig* 'peaceful, calm' (7), *Haufen* → *häufig* 'frequent' (4).[123]

> [123] Unstressed *-e* and *-en* is dropped before adding the suffix. Note that the last example shows a weaker semantic link with its associated noun: *der Haufen* 'heap, pile'.

27.2c *un-* prefixed to adjectives

As in English, this is used to denote the **negative** of the meaning of the adjective: *rein* → *unrein* 'unclean' (30), *höflich* → **un**höflich 'impolite' (26).

27.2d Past and present participles

These can be used unchanged as adjectives (or adverbs). Examples from the text are: past participles *erzogen* 'brought up' (4), *bekannt* 'well-known' (28); present participles *entscheidend* 'crucial', used as a noun here *Entscheidendes* (30), *anschließend* 'following', used here as an adverb meaning 'afterwards' (11).

See **27.6** for more adjective-forming processes.

27.3 THE FORMATION OF VERBS

The infinitive forms of German verbs are formed from nouns and adjectives by the addition of *-(e)n*. Examples from the text are: *Mund* 'mouth' → *munden* 'to taste good' (15), *Zeuge* 'witness' → *zeugen* 'to testify' (14).[124]

Verbs can also be derived from other verbs by the addition of a **prefix**, which can either be separable or inseparable. The most commonly used separable prefixes have already been discussed in **Ch. 19**. This chapter will deal primarily with inseparable prefixes.

> [124] *-n* occurs after *-e*, *-el*, *-er*, and *-en* occurs elsewhere. Some words umlaut the preceding stressed vowel: e.g. *Hammer* → *hämmern* 'to hammer', and words of Latin origin add *-ieren*: e.g. *Telefon* → *telefonieren*.

27.3a Inseparable prefixes[125]

i) *be-* added to verbs, nouns and adjectives. This is commonly used to form **transitive** verbs: e.g. *steigen* 'climb' → *den Berg besteigen* 'to climb the mountain'. The meaning of the derived verb sometimes differs from that of the original one, as we can see in our text: *nutzen* 'to be of use' → *benutzen* 'to use' (31), *halten* 'to hold' → *behalten* 'to keep' (9).

ii) *er-* added to verbs, nouns and adjectives. This often expresses **achievement** or **conclusion** of an action: e.g. *schießen* 'to shoot' → *erschießen* 'to shoot dead'. There is one example in the text: *ziehen* 'to raise' → *erziehen* 'to raise' in the sense of 'to bring up', 'to educate', appearing here in its past participle form *erzogen* (4).

iii) *ent-* added to verbs, nouns and adjectives. This often denotes **escaping**: e.g. *entlaufen* 'run away', or **removing** something: e.g. *entdecken* 'to uncover, discover'.

iv) *ver-* added to verbs, nouns and adjectives. This often expresses the meaning of **dying away**, e.g. *vergehen* 'die away, fade' or, when reflexive, doing something wrongly, e.g. *sich verplanen* 'plan badly'. The examples in our text do not have these meanings, however, and are semantically far removed from their original verb: *vergessen* 'to forget' (5) (< *essen*, with the addition of 'g'), *verstehen* 'understand' (32).

v) *zer-* added to verbs. This usually conveys the meaning of **in pieces**: *schneiden* 'cut' → *zerschneiden* 'cut into pieces' (11).

vi) *ge-* added to verbs. This is no longer productive and occurs with relatively few verbs, hence its absence from our text. It is not associated with a particular meaning: e.g. *stehen* 'to stand' → *gestehen* 'to admit'.

[125] Some other prefixes which are commonly used inseparably are *hinter-* 'behind' (e.g. *hintergehen* 'to go behind someone's back', *miss-* '-mis' (e.g. *missverstehen* 'to misunderstand'), *wider-* 'against' (e.g. *widersprechen* 'to contradict').

27.3b Separable prefixes

Separable prefixes (see **19.2–19.3**) in the text are: *ablecken* 'to lick' (19), *zubereiten* 'to prepare' (26), *aufessen* 'to eat up' (27), *einsetzen* 'to put to use' (31).

27.4 COMPOUNDING

27.4a Types of compound

A compound is a word made up of two or more words that can also be used independently, e.g. *das Haus + die Frau = die Hausfrau* 'housewife', the gender and plural form being determined by the last word in the compound. Compounds can consist of nouns, adjectives and verbs,[126] in different combinations, e.g. *die Hausfrau, die Putzfrau* (< *putzen*) 'cleaning lady', *blaugrün* 'bluey-green' or 'blue and green', *tierliebend* 'animal loving'. The most common type of compound in German is the noun compound, which consists of two or more nouns. In fact, German is famous for its noun compounds, some of which can be very long. Examples of compounds from the text are:

[126] And less commonly, prepositions and numerals.

noun + noun	die **Tischsitte** 'table etiquette' (1, 5), der **Chefkoch** 'head chef' (13), der **Tischgast** 'guest at the table' (15), **die Tischregel** 'table rule' (33)
verb + noun	das **Esswerkzeug** 'eating implement' (16), whose noun element consists of two nouns Werk + Zeug
preposition + noun	das **Beispiel** 'example' (31)
numeral + adjective	**einhändig** 'one-handed' (12)

Many compounds in German are written together as one word,[127] whereas their English equivalents might have two separate words or even be a whole phrase.

> [127] If a compound word is a relatively new coinage and part of a particular specialist terminology, it is likely to be written with a hyphen: e.g. der Erasmus-Student, das Buddy-Programm.

27.4b Linking elements

Compounding in German is further complicated by the fact that many compounds have a particular element linking the two halves of the compound, the use of which is not always predictable. For instance, the first word in the compound may have a suffix which **looks like a noun plural** ending (and have umlaut if the plural form has umlaut): e.g. 'bookshelf' is not *Buchregal but Bücherregal. Examples of this type in the text are: seelenruhig 'calmly' (literally 'soul calmly') (7), der Toilettengang 'going to the toilet' (32). Indeed, these examples show that nouns ending in -e prefer to add n when another element follows.

Alternatively, a linking 's' (or 'es' after words of one syllable) may appear, e.g. Freundeskreis 'circle of friends' (not in text). This is particularly common after the suffixes -(k)eit, -ion, -ung, -ling and -tät: e.g. Gesundheitsfanatiker 'fitness freak'.

When the first element of the compound is a verb stem of one syllable, the linking element 'e' is sometimes used. There is one example of this in our text: der Zeigefinger 'index finger' (19).

Other points to note in the text

- Passive: werden verpönt (2), wird ... gegessen (3,6), wird vergessen (4–5), wenn gerülpst und geschlürft wird (14), gekreuzt werden (17), gesteckt werden (17–18), abgeleckt werden (19), eingesetzt werden (31); and a verb being used reflexively with a passive meaning: somit **versteht sich** diese Tischregel 'so this table rule is easily understood' (32–33) (see **Ch. 18**).
- Modal verbs: dürfen (2); and with another infinitive: **soll ... sein** (7–8), **sein musste** (9), **sollte ... hantieren** (16), **dürfen ... gekreuzt werden** (17), **sollten ... abgeleckt werden** (18–19), **dürfte bekannt sein** (29), **darf ... eingesetzt werden** (30–31); and lassen plus bare infinitive: **lässt ... liegen** (22–23) (see **21.3–21.4**).
- Um ... zu plus infinitive: **um** es... zu sich **zu nehmen** 'in order to eat it' (11–12) (see **21.2**).
- Zu plus infinitive: zu glauben (13), zu zeigen (20–21), aufzuessen (27) (see **21.1**).
- Da- plus preposition before a clause: Das zeugt **davon**, dass... 'that testifies to the fact that ...' (14) (see **24.6b**).

Discover more about word formation

27.5 NOUNS

Other ways of forming nouns which do not appear in our text are:

27.5a Nouns referring to people

In addition to the highly frequent *-er* (see **27.1a**), there are three further noun deriving suffixes that usually refer to people:

i) *-ist* added to words of Latin origin (gender: masculine)

This suffix is often added to the stems of *-ieren* verbs, e.g. *spezialisieren* 'to specialise' → *der Spezialist* 'specialist', and is also added to nouns: for example, to the names of musical instruments that are of Latin origin, e.g. *Gitarre* → *der Gitarrist* 'guitarist'.[128]

ii) *-ling* added to adjectives (gender: masculine)

This productively denotes a person associated with a particular characteristic: e.g. *feige* 'cowardly' → *der Feigling* 'coward'.

iii) *-in* added to nouns to denote the female equivalent (gender: feminine)

This suffix is productively added to nouns referring to people, e.g. *der Freund* 'friend' → *die Freundin* 'female friend/girlfriend', and can also be used with some animal names: *der Fuchs* 'fox' → *die Füchsin* 'vixen'. Where possible, it occurs with umlaut.

---

[128] Note that the final vowel drops before adding the suffix, to avoid two vowels coming together.

27.5b -e added to verb stems and adjectives (gender: feminine)

When added to verb stems, this can denote an action, e.g. *lieben* 'to love' → *die Liebe* 'the love', or refer to the instrument of an action, e.g. *bürsten* 'to brush' → *die Bürste* 'the brush'. Only the process referring to the instrument is productive.

When added to an adjective it denotes a quality, often corresponding to English 'th', e.g. *lang* 'long' → *die Länge* 'length', *stark* 'strong' → *die Stärke* 'strength', and the preceding vowel takes an umlaut. This is no longer productive.

27.5c -ei added to nouns (gender: feminine)

This denotes the **place** where someone works: e.g. *der Bäcker* 'baker' → *die Bäckerei* 'bakery', *der Abt* 'abbot' → *die Abtei* 'abbey'.

27.5d -erei added to verb stems (gender: feminine)

This denotes a repeated (often irritating) action, corresponding to English '-ing' used in a pejorative way: e.g. *herumfahren* 'to drive around' → *die Herumfahrerei* 'the driving around'.

27.5e Other less frequent suffixes

i) *-nis* (fem. or neut.) which derives abstract nouns from verbs and adjectives but is no longer productive: e.g. *sich ereignen* 'to happen' → *das Ereignis* 'event'

ii) *-schaft* (fem.) which is productively added to nouns (and to adjectives, but not productively) to denote a collective, e.g. *Mann* → *die Mannschaft* 'team', or state, corresponding to English '-hood': e.g. *Mutter* → *die Mutterschaft* 'motherhood'

iii) *-tum* (neut.) which is productively added to nouns (and to adjectives, but not productively) referring to persons and expresses a characteristic or collective: e.g. *der Heide* 'heathen' → *das Heidentum* means both 'heathenism' and 'heathens'.

27.5f *Ge ... (e)* added to nouns (gender: neuter)

This denotes **collective nouns**. It is used with umlaut where possible (and 'e' becomes 'i'): e.g. *Berg* 'mountain' → *das Gebirge* 'mountain range', *Tier* 'animal' → *das Getier* 'creatures', *Stein* 'stone' → *das Gestein* '(layer of) stones'. Often the final *-e* is absent.

When used with a **verb** stem (and without umlaut), this has the same meaning as *-erei* (see **27.5d**): e.g. *schreien* 'to shout/scream' → *das Geschrei* 'shouting/screaming'.

27.5g Prefixes

Some frequent prefixes used to derive nouns from other nouns are: ***mit-***, corresponding to English 'co-', 'fellow-' (e.g. *der **Mit**bewohner* 'fellow occupant/flatmate'), ***nicht-***, corresponding to English 'non-' (e.g. *der **Nicht**raucher* 'non-smoker'), ***scheiß-***, literally 'shit', which is often used in colloquial German to express displeasure (e.g. *die **Scheiß**arbeit* 'shitty job').

27.6 ADJECTIVES

Adjective formations not dealt with in the text are:

27.6a *-isch* added to nouns (umlaut is sometimes added)

This is often used with geographical names, e.g. *amerikan**isch**, engl**isch*** and words of Latin origin, *e.g. Praktik* 'practice' → *prakt**isch*** 'practical'. When used with nouns of German origin it denotes a particular characteristic associated with that noun, and is often pejorative, e.g. *Kind* → *kind**isch*** 'childish'.

27.6b *-bar* added to verb stems (no umlaut)

This is extremely productive and usually corresponds to English '-able'/'-ible', e.g. *machen* 'to do' → *mach**bar*** 'doable', *lesen* 'to read' → *les**bar*** 'legible', or to a passive in English, e.g. *erreichen* 'to reach' → *Er ist nicht erreich**bar*** 'He cannot be reached'.

27.6c *-mäßig* added to nouns (no umlaut)

This is also very productive and has a variety of meanings, the most common being 'relating to/according to', e.g. *Gesetz* 'law' → *gesetz**mäßig*** 'according to the law/legal', and '-like': e.g. *Schüler* 'school pupil' → *schüler**mäßig*** 'like a school pupil'.

27.6d *-voll* and *-los* added to nouns (no umlaut)

-voll corresponds to English '-ful', e.g. *das Wunder* 'wonder' → *wunder**voll*** 'wonderful'; *-los* corresponds to English '-less', e.g. *die Mühe* 'effort' → *mühe**los*** 'effortless'. Both suffixes are productive.

27.6e Less productive suffixes

There are a small number of less productive adjective-forming suffixes: *-en* (with some words *-ern* + umlaut) added to nouns denoting a material, e.g. *Gold* → *gold**en*** 'golden', *Holz* → *hölz**ern*** 'wooden'; *-haft* added to nouns to describe a quality associated with the noun, e.g. *Märchen* 'fairy-tale' → *märchen**haft*** 'like a fairy-tale'; *-sam* added to verb stems or nouns to express a tendency, e.g. *schweigen* 'to be quiet' → *schweig**sam*** 'taciturn/quiet'.

✎ EXERCISES

Vocabulary topic: *Berufe*

1 Form words for professions based on the verbs and nouns below. Give first the masculine and then the feminine form:

1 lehren	**5** Garten	**9** malen	**13** Piano
2 arbeiten	**6** Physik	**10** Wissenschaft	**14** Gitarre
3 backen	**7** Sport	**11** komponieren	**15** Trommel
4 tanzen	**8** übersetzen	**12** Politik	**16** Tisch

2 Rewrite the following sentences using a compound noun to denote the appropriate profession, remembering that some of these compounds might need linking elements. Note that there is no article directly before the profession:

Example: Er pflegt Kranke.
Answer: Er ist Krankenpfleger.

1 Er spielt Fußball.
2 Er arbeitet in einem Büro.
3 Sie führt eine Gruppe.
4 Er ist Professor an der Universität.
5 Er ist ein Arzt, der sich auf Kinder spezialisiert.
6 Er ist ein Beamter, der für Sicherheit verantwortlich ist.
7 Er fährt einen Bus.
8 Er verkauft Autos.
9 Sie lehrt Schwimmen.
10 Sie leitet eine Abteilung.

3 Translate the following sentences into German (if marked *, use the past tense):

1 She is my boss.
2 She is the new doctor.
3 She's a very good cook.
4 My sister is a farmer.
5 She wants to become a singer.
6 The lecturer waited for her students*.

7 The professor lost her glasses*.
8 The cleaner wanted her money*.
9 The waitress was unfriendly*.
10 My girlfriend is a psychologist.
11 My neighbour, Lena, is a lawyer.
12 She's a bad writer. Her books are boring.

✎ FURTHER EXERCISES

4 a Translate the following groups of words into English:

1 Haus, Häuschen, häuslich, Häuslichkeit.
2 Mann, männlich, Männlichkeit, mannhaft, Mannschaft, bemannen.
3 lesen, Leser, Lesung, lesbar, Lesbarkeit, Leserschaft, sich verlesen.
4 Freund, Freundin, unfreundlich, Freundlichkeit, befreunden.

5 Macht, machtlos, mächtig, Mächtigkeit, entmachten.

6 reden, Rede, Reden, Gerede, Rederei, Redner, rednerisch.

7 fühlen, fühlbar, Fühler, Gefühl, gefühlvoll, gefühllos.

8 brechen, unbrechbar, zerbrechen, zerbrechlich, Zerbrechlichkeit.

9 schlagen, Schlag, Schläger, Schlägerei, unschlagbar, erschlagen, zerschlagen.

10 sprechen, Sprecher, Sprache, sprachlos, Sprachlosigkeit, besprechen, Besprechung, entsprechen, versprechen, sich versprechen, widersprechen.

4 b Take the nouns from 4a and show their gender by adding the appropriate definite article.

5 Make compounds out of the following pairs of words, adding linking elements where required. Give the gender of the compound noun and translate your answers into English:

1 Haus, Tür	**6** Kleid, Schrank	**11** Buch, Regal
2 wohnen, Zimmer	**7** bügeln, Brett	**12** Sicherheit, Schloss
3 baden, Zimmer	**8** Gast, Zimmer	**13** alt, Papier
4 Straße, Lampe	**9** Bett, Decke	**14** Wohnung, Suche
5 Küche, Fenster	**10** Hund, Haus	**15** gefrieren, Truhe

For further exercises on deriving nouns see Revision Text 4, Ex. 5.

28| Punctuation and spelling

Text

Halloween „beglückt" uns bald wieder

Bald ist es wieder so weit. Halloween „beglückt" uns wieder. Über den Sinn
und Unsinn von Halloween könnte man ja ganze Bücher schreiben. Woher
kommt der Name Halloween eigentlich? "All Hallows Evening". Zu Deutsch,
5 der Abend vor Allerheiligen. Ursprünglich ist Halloween ein keltischer Brauch.
In der Nacht vom 31. Oktober auf den 1. November verabschiedeten die
Druiden den Sommer. Die kalte, lange Winterzeit brach an. Die Druiden
glaubten, dass in dieser Nacht die Toten auf die Erde zurückkehrten.
   Einwanderer aus England und Irland brachten diesen Brauch in die USA,
10 als sie zwischen 1830 und 1850 zu Hunderttausenden auswanderten. Dort
wurde er von anderen Volksgruppen übernommen.
   In unserer doch eher kleineren Gemeinde werden wir auch jedes Jahr
wieder „beglückt" mit diesem amerikanischen „Import-Brauch". Aber hier
findet doch noch ein gewisser Gegenpol in Form eines von der Schule
15 organisierten Räbeliechtli-Umzugs statt. Das finde ich gut so. Und meine
Feststellung in Sachen Halloween-Aktivitäten ist: Tendenz eher abnehmend.
Was meinen Sie zu Halloween?

Aus dem Blog von Willi Müller, 28/10/08 [www.reiseerfahrung.info].

beglücken – to make happy	*der Einwanderer* – immigrant
der Sinn – sense	*auswandern* – to emigrate
der Unsinn – nonsense	*die Gemeinde* – community
Allerheiligen – All Saints	*der Gegenpol* – counterpart
ursprünglich – originally	*der Räbeliechtli-Umzug* – procession
der Brauch – custom, tradition	with lanterns (in Switzerland)
verabschieden – to see off	*die Feststellung* – observation
der Druide – Druid	*abnehmend* – waning, decreasing

℘ Punctuation and spelling in the text

28.1 PUNCTUATION

On the whole, German punctuation is fairly similar to that of English: e.g. using a capital letter at
the beginning of a sentence and a full stop at the end. There are, however, a couple of areas of

divergence which may cause problems for English learners of German: i) the use of capitals for nouns; ii) the use of commas:

28.1a Use of capitals for nouns

In English, capital letters are used for proper nouns (i.e. names of people, places, titles etc., e.g. 'Mary', 'England', 'Prime Minister') while in German they are used for **all nouns** (including nouns derived from other parts of speech, such as adjectives and verbs). Some examples from the text are: *Sinn* (2), *Unsinn* (3), *Bücher* (3), *Name* (4), *Deutsch* (4), *Abend* (5), *Brauch* (5), *Nacht* (6); also numerals used as nouns: *Hunderttausenden* (10).[129]

By contrast, with certain exceptions (see **28.4**), *adjectives* are usually not capitalised, even when they are derived from the names of countries: *mit diesem **amerikanischen** Import-Brauch* (13). Such adjectives would always have a capital letter in English: e.g. 'this imported American custom'. This can also be seen in line 5: *ein **keltischer** Brauch* 'a Celtic tradition'.

If a compound word is written with a hyphen, then both nouns are capitalised: *Import-Brauch* (13), *Räbeliechtli-Umzug* (15), *Halloween-Aktivitäten* (16).

The personal pronoun *Sie*, meaning 'you' in the polite form is always capitalised: *Was meinen Sie?* 'What do you think?' (17).

> [129] Note that adjectives are capitalised when used as nouns: e.g. *der Große* 'the big one', *das Wichtigste* 'the most important thing'. Other elements that are capitalised when used as nouns are fractions: e.g. *zwei Drittel* 'two thirds', and points of the compass: e.g. *im Norden* 'in the north'.

28.1b Commas

i) In general, commas are used in German to **separate one clause with a finite verb from another**. Examples from the text are (with the finite verbs underlined):

- *Die Druiden <u>glaubten,</u> dass in dieser Nacht die Toten ... <u>zurückkehrten</u>* (7–8)
  'The Druids believed that the dead returned ... on this night'
- *Einwanderer aus England und Irland <u>brachten</u> diesen Brauch in die USA, als sie zwischen 1830 und 1850 ... <u>auswanderten</u>* (9–10)
  'Immigrants from England and Ireland brought this tradition to the USA when they emigrated between 1830 and 1850'

In English, commas may be used after introductory parts of the sentence not containing a finite verb: e.g. 'After a long discussion(,) they decided to go'. In German, where these introductory words are followed by a finite verb appearing in second position (see **26.1aii**), commas are not possible: *In unserer doch eher kleineren Gemeinde <u>werden</u> wir auch jedes Jahr wieder „beglückt"* 'In our rather smaller community, we are also "made happy" every year' (12–13). A comma between *Gemeinde* and the following finite verb would not be correct. Also, in line 6 it is not possible to place a comma between *November* and the following verb *verabschiedeten*, although it would be possible in English.

Similarly, adverbial phrases such as 'however', 'naturally' etc. are often followed by a comma in English when they appear at the beginning of the sentence. This is not possible in German if a finite verb follows: *Ursprünglich <u>ist</u> Halloween ein keltischer Brauch* 'Originally(,) Halloween is a Celtic tradition' (5).

If, however, there is no finite verb to follow, a comma can be used: *Zu Deutsch, der Abend vor Allerheiligen* 'In German, the evening of All Saints' (4–5), where it is being used instead of a colon.

ii) Commas are used to separate words in a **list**. It is particularly common to separate adjectives from each other, as in the text: *die kalte, lange Winterzeit* 'the cold, long winter time' (7).

28.1c Further notes on punctuation

- **Quotation marks** in German traditionally take the form „ ", e.g. *„beglückt"* (1, 2, 13) *„Import-Brauch"* (13). In some texts, particularly in more recent journalistic texts and texts published online, " " is used, as in English. It is interesting that the writer of this blog uses both: *"All Hallows Evening"* (4). Perhaps this is because he is quoting an English expression. However, in most texts, authors just stick to one form.

- **Ordinal numbers**, e.g. '1st', '2nd', '3rd', '4th', are indicated by placing a full stop after the number: *In der Nacht vom 31. Oktober auf den 1. November* (6).

- **Question marks and exclamation marks** are used similarly in German and English. *Woher kommt der Name ... eigentlich?* 'Where does the name actually come from?' (3–4) *Was meinen Sie zu Halloween?* 'What do you think of Halloween?' (17).

- **Colons** are used similarly in German and English, e.g. before an explanation: *Meine Feststellung ... ist: Tendenz eher abnehmend* 'my observation is: the tendency is somewhat decreasing' (15–16).[130] It is particularly common before direct quotations. **Semi-colons** are much less frequent in German (note the lack of examples in the text).

- **Hyphens** are used with some compound words, particularly new coinages: *Import-Brauch* (13), *Räbeliechtli-Umzug* (15), *Halloween-Aktivitäten* (16). They are also used to indicate that the second part of a compound word (whether originally hyphenated or not) has been omitted to avoid repetition: e.g. *Sommer- und Winterzeit* 'summer (time) and winter time' (not in text).

[130] Some writers use a capital after colons, as if starting a new sentence, although this is not compulsory and practice varies.

28.2 SPELLING

The main difficulty for foreign learners of German is knowing when to use the letter *ß*, sometimes referred to as the *scharfes s* or the *eszet*, and when to use *ss*. The rule of distribution for these alternatives is that *ß* **should only be used after long vowels and diphthongs**: e.g. *groß* 'big', *Maß* 'measurement', *heißen* 'to be called'; contrast the short vowels in e.g. *Ross* 'horse', *Hass* 'hate' and *wissen* 'to know'. In our text there are no examples of *ß* because the words containing a double *s* have short vowels rather than long ones: *dass* (8), *gewisser* (14). In older texts you will find some uses of *ß* after short vowels, e.g. *daß*. This is no longer permissible.

Other points to note in the text

- 'Verb 2nd' rule causing subject-verb inversion: *Bald **ist** es* (2), *Über den Sinn und Unsinn von Halloween **könnte** man* (2–3), *Ursprünglich **ist** Halloween* (5), *In der Nacht vom 31. Oktober auf den 1. November **verabschiedeten** die Druiden* (6–7), *Dort **wurde** er* (10–11), *In unserer doch* *eher kleineren Gemeinde **werden** wir* (12), *hier **findet** doch ein gewisser Gegenpol* (13–14), *Das finde ich* (15) (see **26.1aii**).

- Subordinating conjunctions sending finite verb to end of clause: ***dass** in dieser Nacht die Toten auf die Erde <u>zurückkehrten</u>* (8), ***als** sie zwischen 1830 und 1850 zu Hunderttausenden <u>auswanderten</u>* (10) (see **25.1**).

- Use of simple past tense when narrating a sequence of past events: *verabschiedeten* (6), *brach ... an* (7), *glaubten* (8*), zurückkehrten* (8), *brachten* (9), *auswanderten* (10), *wurde* (11) (see **12.1**).

- Passive: *Dort **wurde** er ... **übernommen*** 'There it was taken over' (10–11), ***werden** wir ... „**beglückt** "* 'We are "made happy"' (12–13) (see **Ch. 18**).

Discover more about punctuation and spelling

28.3 FURTHER NOTES ON COMMAS

In addition to the main comma rule given in **28.1**, which states that commas are used to separate clauses with a finite verb, the following must also be heeded:

i) Commas are always used before **subordinate clauses**, even if the preceding clause does not have a finite verb. This applies to clauses beginning with a subordinating conjunction (a), a relative pronoun (b) or a question word used indirectly (c):

    a) *Ich gehe ins Bett, <u>weil</u> ich müde bin*   I'm going to bed because I'm tired
    b) *Der Mann, <u>der</u> im Garten sitzt*   The man who is sitting in the garden
    c) *Egal, <u>wer</u> kommt*   No matter who's coming

ii) Before a **main clause**, commas are usually used, except before ***und***: e.g. *Er öffnete den Wein und sie holte die Gläser* 'He opened the wine and she fetched the glasses'. The other exception is ***oder***, which omits a preceding comma if the subjects of both clauses are the same: e.g. *Ich spiele Tennis oder gehe ins Schwimmbad* 'I play tennis or go swimming'. If the subjects are different, some writers prefer to insert a comma: e.g. *Wir könnten Tennis spielen(,) oder willst du lieber schwimmen gehen?* 'We could play tennis, or would you prefer to go swimming?'

iii) Clauses with **infinitives** and **participles**. In older texts, these were often separated off by commas: e.g. *Ich habe versucht, mit dir <u>zu sprechen</u>* 'I tried to talk to you'. Nowadays, however, commas are **no longer obligatory** before or after these types of clause: e.g. *Ich habe versucht(,) dich mit meinem neuen Handy <u>anzurufen</u>* 'I tried to ring you with my new mobile', provided that their omission does not impede the reader's understanding of the sentence.

iv) Commas are used in German to show a **decimal point**, while English uses a full stop: e.g. *17,5 Prozent der Befragten* '17.5 per cent of those asked'. Conversely, where English would use a comma to indicate thousands, German uses a full stop: e.g. *23.000 Einwohner* '23,000 inhabitants'.

28.4 PLACE NAMES CAPITALIZED, ALSO AS ADJECTIVES

As stated in **28.1a** adjectives are not capitalised, which means that adjectives derived from the names of **countries** have a small letter in German and a capital in English: e.g. *meine deutsche Freundin* vs. 'my **German** friend'.[131] Adjectives in *-er* derived from **town names** do begin with a capital letter, however: e.g *meine Londoner Kollegin* vs. *meine englische Kollegin*.

[131] If, however, the adjective appears in a title or name, then it is capitalised, as titles and names are always capitalised in German: e.g. *das Deutsche Reich* 'the German Empire'.

28.5 PUNCTUATION IN LETTER WRITING

German letters, both formal and informal, have certain features of punctuation which English speakers must be aware of:

i) Formal headings of address may be followed by an **exclamation mark**: e.g. *Lieber Karl!* 'Dear Karl', although this is becoming slightly old-fashioned and is now usually replaced by a comma, as in English.

ii) If a comma is used after a form of address, the first sentence of the letter does **not begin with a capital letter**: e.g.

Lieber Karl,
es tut mir Leid, dass ich seit langem nicht geschrieben habe.

iii) One often finds the pronoun *du* (and related *dich, dein* etc.) capitalised in older letters. This practice is no longer common.

✎ EXERCISES

Vocabulary topic: *deutsche Geschichte*

1 Add the necessary punctuation: capital letters, full stops, commas, quotation marks, and change *ss* to *ß* where appropriate:

1914 In europa beginnt der erste weltkrieg.

1917 Nach der abdankung des zaren im frühjahr übernehmen in der oktoberrevolution die bolschewiki unter lenin die macht in russland.

1918 Deutschland wird republik.

1933 Hitler wird reichskanzler. Der aufbau des terroristischen führerstaates beginnt.

1939 Deutschland überfällt polen. Der zweite weltkrieg bricht aus.

1942 Auf der wannseekonferenz beschliessen die nazis die juden ganz europas systematisch zu ermorden.

1945 Hitler begeht selbstmord. Der zweite weltkrieg endet mit deutschlands bedingungsloser kapitulation.

1948 Mahatma (grosse seele) ghandhi dessen methode des passiven widerstandes indien den weg in die unabhängigkeit geebnet hat wird opfer eines attentats.

1949 Das grundgesetz für die bundesrepublik deutschland wird verabschiedet. In ost-berlin nimmt der volkskongress die verfassung der deutschen demokratischen republik an.

1953 Im märz stirbt der sowjetische diktator josef stalin. Im juni wird ein arbeiteraufstand in der ddr von russischen truppen brutal niedergeschlagen.

1961 Die führung der ddr lässt die berliner mauer errichten.

1962 Die kuba-krise bringt die welt an den rand des atomkriegs.

1965 Die usa schicken verstärkt soldaten nach vietnam. Der krieg eskaliert.

1968 Schwere studentenunruhen in der bundesrepublik richten sich gegen notstandsgesetzgebung vietnamkrieg und spiesserrepublik.

1977 Der terror der RAF erreicht in einer beispiellosen serie von attentaten seinen höhepunkt.

1985 Michail gorbatschow generalsekretär des ZK der KPdSU verkündet das reformprogramm der perestrojka.

1989 Das sozialistische regime der ddr bricht nach 40 jahren herrschaft zusammen.

1990 Die wiedererrichteten länder der ddr treten am 3 oktober der brd bei.

1991 In jugoslawien bricht der bürgerkrieg aus.

1993 Mit dem inkrafttreten des vertrags von maastricht entsteht die europäische union deren ziel ein wirtschaftlich und sozial geeintes europa ist.

Aus: *Der Stern – History* (*Online*), 31.1.01.

2 Insert commas where necessary:

Doch der Vormarsch der Alliierten ging an allen Fronten wenn auch von Stockungen begleitet etappenweise voran. Im Februar und März 1945 eroberten sie die linksrheinischen Gebiete Deutschlands. Nachdem amerikanische Truppen am 7. März bei Remagen und britische Einheiten am 24. März bei Wesel den Rhein überschritten hatten rückten die Amerikaner (zusammen mit der 1. französischen Armee) nach Süddeutschland vor. Sie besetzten auch Vorarlberg Tirol das Salzkammergut Oberösterreich und den Westen Böhmens bis zur Linie Karlsbad-Budweis-Linz. Im Norden erreichten die Engländer am 19. April 1945 die Elbe bei Lauenburg während amerikanische Verbände ins Zentrum des Reiches vorstießen und am 25. April 1945 mit den Sowjets bei Torgau zusammentrafen. Weiterzumarschieren lehnte der alliierte Oberbefehlshaber General Eisenhower jedoch aus politischen und militärischen Gründen ab da er sich mit der Masse seiner Streitkräfte der Eroberung des deutschen „Alpen-Reduit" zuwenden wollte. Der Osten des Reiches wurde im Zeitraum vom Januar bis zum Mai 1945 von der sowjetischen Armee erobert vor der Millionen von Deutschen unter unsagbaren Leiden nach Westen zu fliehen versuchten.

Aus: Klaus Hildebrand: *Das Dritte Reich*. © R. Oldenbourg Verlag GmbH, 1987.

For further exercises on punctuation and spelling see Revision Text 2, Ex 4.

Appendix 1: Common strong and irregular verbs[132]

[132] Verbs beginning with a prefix are usually derived from basic verbs and, consequently, often have the same irregularities as the basic verbs: e.g. *verstehen* is like *stehen* (*ich verstand, ich habe verstanden*), *ankommen* is like *kommen* (*ich kam an, ich bin angekommen*). For this reason, it is not necessary to include all prefixed verbs in the following list.

Infinitive[133]	Past Stem[134]	Past Participle[135]	
backen	backte[136]	gebacken	*bake*
befehlen (du befiehlst, er befiehlt)	befahl	befohlen	*command*
beginnen	begann	begonnen	*begin*
beißen	biss (bisse)	gebissen	*bite*
bersten (es birst or berstet)	barst	geborsten	*burst*
betrügen	betrog	betrogen	*deceive*
biegen	bog	(ist)_{Int.} gebogen	*bend*
bieten	bot	geboten	*offer*
binden	band (bände)	gebunden	*bind*
bitten	bat (bäte)	gebeten	*ask for/request*
blasen (du bläst, er bläst)	blies	geblasen	*blow*
bleiben	blieb (bliebe)	ist geblieben	*stay*
braten (du brätst, er brät)	briet	gebraten	*roast/fry*
brechen (du brichst, er bricht)	brach (bräche)	(ist)_{Int.} gebrochen	*break*
brennen	brannte	gebrannt	*burn*
bringen	brachte (brächte)	gebracht	*bring/take*
denken	dachte (dächte)	gedacht	*think*
dringen	drang	(ist)_{Int.} gedrungen	*penetrate*
dürfen (ich/er darf, du darfst)	durfte (dürfte)	gedurft	*be allowed*

[133] Irregularities in the present tense are given in brackets after the infinitive. Note that the forms with *er* 'he' also occur with *sie* 'she' and *es* 'it'. The *es*-form is given instead of *du* and *er* where it is most appropriate to the context.

[134] This is used in the *ich*- and *er/sie/es*-forms. The other persons need additional endings: e.g. *du befahlst, wir/sie/Sie befahlen, ihr befahlt*. The same applies to the *Konjunktiv II* stems given in brackets after the past stems. Only *Konjunktiv II* stems which are still in use are included, although note that many of these sound stilted if used in spoken German (see **16.2b** for usage). Archaic forms are omitted.

[135] If a verb takes *sein* in the (plu)perfect, this is indicated by *ist*, otherwise it takes *haben*. Verbs which take *haben* when used transitively but *sein* when used intransitively (see **13.3b** for details) are marked (*ist*)_{Int.}

[136] Older form *buk*.

Infinitive[133]	Past Stem[134]	Past Participle[135]	
erschrecken (du erschrickst, er erschrickt)	erschrak	ist erschrocken	*be frightened*[137]
essen (du/er isst)	aß (äße)	gegessen	*eat*
fahren (du fährst, er fährt)	fuhr (führe)	(ist)$_{Int.}$ gefahren	*go/drive*
fallen (du fällst, er fällt)	fiel (fiele)	ist gefallen	*fall*
fangen (du fängst, er fängt)	fing (finge)	gefangen	*catch*
finden	fand (fände)	gefunden	*find*
fliegen	flog (flöge)	(ist)$_{Int.}$ geflogen	*fly*
fliehen	floh	ist geflohen	*flee*
fließen	floss	ist geflossen	*flow*
fressen (du/er frisst)	fraß	gefressen	*eat (of animals)*
frieren	fror	(ist)$_{Int.}$ gefroren	*freeze*
gebären	gebar	geboren	*give birth*
geben (du gibst, er gibt)	gab (gäbe)	gegeben	*give*
gedeihen	gedieh	ist gediehen	*thrive*
gehen	ging (ginge)	ist gegangen	*go*
gelingen	gelang (gelänge)	ist gelungen	*succeed*
gelten (es gilt)	galt	gegolten	*be valid*
genießen	genoss	genossen	*enjoy*
geschehen (es geschieht)	geschah (geschähe)	ist geschehen	*happen*
gewinnen	gewann	gewonnen	*win*
gießen	goss	gegossen	*pour*
gleichen	glich (gliche)	geglichen	*resemble*
gleiten	glitt	ist geglitten	*slide/glide*
graben (du gräbst, er gräbt)	grub	gegraben	*dig*
greifen	griff (griffe)	gegriffen	*grasp/seize*
haben (du hast, er hat)	hatte (hätte)	gehabt	*have*
halten (du hältst, er hält)	hielt (hielte)	gehalten	*hold*
hängen[138] (du hängst, er hängt)	hing (hinge)	gehangen	*hang*
heben	hob	gehoben	*lift*
heißen	hieß (hieße)	geheißen	*be called*
helfen (du hilftst, er hilft)	half	geholfen	*help*
kennen	kannte	gekannt	*know*
klingen	klang (klänge)	geklungen	*sound*
kommen	kam (käme)	ist gekommen	*come*
können (ich/er kann, du kannst)	konnte (könnte)	gekonnt	*be able*
kriechen	kroch	ist gekrochen	*creep/crawl*
laden (du lädst, er lädt)	lud	geladen	*load*
lassen (du/er lässt)	ließ (ließe)	gelassen	*let*
laufen (du läufst, er läuft)	lief (liefe)	(ist)$_{Int.}$ gelaufen	*run*
leiden	litt (litte)	gelitten	*suffer*
leihen	lieh (liehe)	geliehen	*lend/borrow*
lesen (du/er liest)	las	gelesen	*read*
liegen	lag	gelegen	*lie*
lügen	log	gelogen	*tell lies*

[137] The transitive verb (*jemanden*) *erschrecken* 'to frighten (s.o.)' is regular: *erschreckte, erschreckt*.
[138] The transitive verb (*etwas*) *hängen* 'to hang (sth.)' is regular: *hängte, gehängt*.

Infinitive[133]	Past Stem[134]	Past Participle[135]	
mahlen	mahlte	gemahlen	*grind*
meiden	mied (miede)	gemieden	*avoid*
messen (du/er misst)	maß	gemessen	*measure*
mögen (ich/er mag, du magst)	mochte (möchte)	gemocht	*like*
müssen (ich/er muss, du musst)	musste (müsste)	gemusst	*have to/must*
nehmen (du nimmst, er nimmt)	nahm (nähme)	genommen	*take*
nennen	nannte	genannt	*call/name*
pfeifen	pfiff (pfiffe)	gepfiffen	*whistle*
preisen	pries (priese)	gepriesen	*praise*
raten (du rätst, er rät)	riet (riete)	geraten	*advise*
reiben	rieb (riebe)	gerieben	*rub*
reißen	riss (risse)	(ist)_{Int.} gerissen	*tear/rip*
reiten	ritt (ritte)	(ist)_{Int.} geritten	*ride (a horse)*
rennen	rannte	(ist)_{Int.} gerannt	*run/race*
riechen	roch	gerochen	*smell*
rufen	rief (riefe)	gerufen	*shout/call*
salzen	salzte	gesalzen	*salt*
saufen	soff	gesoffen	*drink (of animals) /booze*
saugen	saugte/sog	gesaugt/gesogen	*suck*
schaffen	schuf	geschaffen	*create*[139]
scheiden	schied (schiede)	(ist)_{Int.} geschieden	*separate/depart*
scheinen	schien (schiene)	geschienen	*shine/seem*
scheißen	schiss (schisse)	geschissen	*shit*
schelten (du schiltst, er schilt)	schalt	gescholten	*scold*
scheren	schor	geschoren	*shear/clip*
schieben	schob	geschoben	*shove/push*
schießen	schoss	(ist)_{Int.} geschossen	*shoot*
schlafen (du schläfst, er schläft)	schlief (schliefe)	geschlafen	*sleep*
schlagen (du schlägst, er schlägt)	schlug (schlüge)	geschlagen	*hit/strike/beat*
schleichen	schlich (schliche)	ist geschlichen	*creep*
schließen	schloss (schlösse)	geschlossen	*shut*
schmeißen	schmiss (schmisse)	geschmissen	*chuck*
schmelzen (es schmilzt)	schmolz	(ist)_{Int.} geschmolzen	*melt*
schneiden	schnitt (schnitte)	geschnitten	*cut*
schreiben	schrieb (schriebe)	geschrieben	*write*
schreien	schrie	geschrie(e)n	*shout/scream*
schreiten	schritt (schritte)	ist geschritten	*stride*
schweigen	schwieg (schwiege)	geschwiegen	*be silent*
schwellen (es schwillt)	schwoll	ist geschwollen	*swell*
schwimmen	schwamm	(ist)_{Int.} geschwommen	*swim*
schwingen	schwang	geschwungen	*swing*
schwören	schwor	geschworen	*swear (an oath)*
sehen (du siehst, er sieht)	sah (sähe)	gesehen	*see*
sein (ich bin, du bist, er ist wir sind, ihr seid, sie sind)	war (wäre)	ist gewesen	*be*

[139] *Schaffen* meaning 'to manage to do something' is regular: *schaffte, geschafft.*

Infinitive[133]	Past Stem[134]	Past Participle[135]	
singen	sang (sänge)	gesungen	*sing*
sinken	sank	ist gesunken	*sink*
sitzen	saß (säße)	gesessen	*sit*
sollen (ich/er soll, du sollst)	sollte (sollte)	gesollt	*should*
spinnen	spann	gesponnen	*spin/be stupid*
sprechen (du sprichst, er spricht)	sprach (spräche)	gesprochen	*speak*
springen	sprang (spränge)	ist gesprungen	*jump*
stechen (du stichst, er sticht)	stach	gestochen	*stab/prick/sting*
stehen	stand (stünde)	gestanden	*stand*
stehlen (du stiehlst, er stiehlt)	stahl	gestohlen	*steal*
steigen	stieg (stiege)	ist gestiegen	*rise/climb*
sterben (du stirbst, er stirbt)	starb (stürbe)	ist gestorben	*die*
stinken	stank	gestunken	*stink*
stoßen (du/er stößt)	stieß (stieße)	(ist)_{Int.} gestoßen	*bump/push*
streichen	strich (striche)	(ist)_{Int.} gestrichen	*stroke*
streiten	stritt (stritte)	gestritten	*quarrel*
tragen (du trägst, er trägt)	trug (trüge)	getragen	*carry/wear*
treffen (du triffst, er trifft)	traf (träfe)	getroffen	*meet/hit*
treiben	trieb (triebe)	(ist)_{Int.} getrieben	*drive/propel/drift*
treten (du trittst, er tritt)	trat (träte)	(ist)_{Int.} getreten	*step/tread*
trinken	trank (tränke)	getrunken	*drink*
tun	tat (täte)	getan	*do*
verbergen (du verbirgst, er verbirgt)	verbarg	verborgen	*hide*
verderben (du verdirbst, er verdirbt)	verdarb	(ist)_{Int.} verdorben	*spoil*
vergessen (du/er vergisst)	vergaß (vergäße)	vergessen	*forget*
verlieren	verlor	verloren	*lose*
verschwinden	verschwand (verschwände)	ist verschwunden	*disappear*
verzeihen	verzieh (verziehe)	verziehen	*forgive*
wachsen (du/er wächst)	wuchs (wüchse)	ist gewachsen	*grow*
waschen (du wäschst, er wäscht)	wusch	gewaschen	*wash*
weichen	wich (wiche)	gewichen	*yield/give way*
weisen	wies (wiese)	gewiesen	*point*
werben (du wirbst, er wirbt)	warb	geworben	*recruit/advertise*
werden (du wirst, er wird)	wurde	ist geworden	*become*
werfen (du wirfst, er wirft)	warf	geworfen	*throw*
wiegen	wog	gewogen	*weigh*
wissen (ich/er weiß, du weißt)	wusste (wüsste)	gewusst	*know*
wollen (ich/er will, du willst)	wollte (wollte)	gewollt	*want*
ziehen	zog (zöge)	(ist)_{Int.} gezogen	*pull/move*
zwingen	zwang	gezwungen	*force*

Appendix 2: Article and adjective endings

Some students may find it easier to learn article and adjective endings together within the context of a whole sentence rather than as isolated words or endings. The following tables provide a list of simple sentences that should be learned by heart. This will enable students to generalise the different case and number ending patterns to other words, provided that the gender of the noun is known.

Adjectives without articles (strong endings)

MASC.	*Nom.*	Stark**ER** Kaffee schmeckt mir
	Acc.	Ich mag stark**EN** Kaffee
	Dat.	Brot mit stark**EM** Kaffee
	Gen.	Der Geschmack stark**EN** Kaffee**S**
FEM.	*Nom.*	Warm**E** Milch schmeckt mir
	Acc.	Ich mag warm**E** Milch
	Dat.	Brot mit warm**ER** Milch
	Gen.	Der Geschmack warm**ER** Milch
NEUT.	*Nom.*	Frisch**ES** Brot schmeckt mir
	Acc.	Ich mag frisch**ES** Brot
	Dat.	Käse mit frisch**EM** Brot
	Gen.	Der Geschmack frisch**EN** Brot**ES**
PLURAL	*Nom.*	Selbstgebacken**E** Kekse schmecken mir
	Acc.	Ich mag selbstgebacken**E** Kekse
	Dat.	Kaffee mit selbstgebacken**EN** Kekse**N**
	Gen.	Der Geschmack selbstgebacken**ER** Kekse

Definite article + adjective (weak endings)

MASC.	*Nom.*	**DER** stark**E** Kaffee schmeckt mir
	Acc.	Ich mag **DEN** stark**EN** Kaffee
	Dat.	Brot mit **DEM** stark**EN** Kaffee
	Gen.	Der Geschmack **DES** stark**EN** Kaffee**S**
FEM.	*Nom.*	**DIE** warm**E** Milch schmeckt mir
	Acc.	Ich mag **DIE** warm**E** Milch
	Dat.	Brot mit **DER** warm**EN** Milch
	Gen.	Der Geschmack **DER** warm**EN** Milch
NEUT.	*Nom.*	**DAS** frisch**E** Brot schmeckt mir
	Acc.	Ich mag **DAS** frisch**E** Brot
	Dat.	Käse mit **DEM** frisch**EN** Brot
	Gen.	Der Geschmack **DES** frisch**EN** Brot**ES**
PLURAL	*Nom.*	**DIE** selbstgebacken**EN** Kekse schmecken mir
	Acc.	Ich mag **DIE** selbstgebacken**EN** Kekse
	Dat.	Kaffee mit **DEN** sebstgebacken**EN** Kekse**N**
	Gen.	Der Geschmack **DER** selbstgebacken**EN** Kekse

Indefinite article + adjective (strong and weak endings)

MASC.	*Nom.*	Das ist **EIN** stark**ER** Kaffee
	Acc.	Ich möchte **EINEN** stark**EN** Kaffee
	Dat.	Brot mit **EINEM** stark**EN** Kaffee
	Gen.	Der Geschmack **EINES** stark**EN** Kaffee**S**
FEM.	*Nom.*	Das ist **EINE** warm**E** Milch
	Acc.	Ich möchte **EINE** warm**E** Milch
	Dat.	Brot mit **EINER** warm**EN** Milch
	Gen.	Der Geschmack **EINER** warm**EN** Milch
NEUT.	*Nom.*	Das ist **EIN** frisch**ES** Brot
	Acc.	Ich möchte **EIN** frisch**ES** Brot
	Dat.	Käse mit **EINEM** frisch**EN** Brot
	Gen.	Der Geschmack **EINES** frisch**EN** Brot**ES**

Appendix 3: Revision texts

Gemeinsamer Urlaub führt oft zum Scheidungsrichter

DÜSSELDORF – Nach Angaben der nordrhein-westfälischen Verbraucher-Zentrale wird etwa jede dritte Scheidung in Deutschland nach einem gemeinsam verbrachten Urlaub beantragt. Zwei Psychologen haben
5 deshalb die häufigsten Gründe für Krisen und Ratschläge zur Krisenvermeidung in einem Artikel des neu erschienenen Ratgebers „Chance Psychotherapie" veröffentlicht. Der gemeinsame Urlaub bedeute für viele Paare mehr Stress als Erholung. „Der Urlaub ist dann ein Risikofaktor, wenn die Beziehung ohnehin schon gefährdet ist", sagte
10 Psychologe und Autor Ralf Dohrenbusch. Viele Paare könnten nicht damit umgehen, dass sie im Urlaub plötzlich so viel Zeit miteinander verbringen „müssten". „Im Alltag gibt es verschiedene Strategien, wie man sich aus dem Weg gehen kann, zum Beispiel Treffen mit Freunden", so der Psychologe. Diese Möglichkeiten habe man im Urlaub naturgemäß
15 nicht.

Viele Paare stellten insgesamt zu hohe Erwartungen an die gemeinsame Urlaubszeit. „Wenn die dann nicht erfüllt werden, wird die Enttäuschung auf den Partner projiziert", so der Psychologe. Schwierige und unbefriedigende Situationen wie etwa ein schlechtes Hotel oder
20 ungewohnte klimatische Bedingungen verstärkten das Stressgefühl zusätzlich. „Auch ein stabiles Beziehungssystem kann dadurch akut gefährdet werden, und wenn im Urlaub plötzlich andere Regeln aufgestellt werden, sind meist beide überfordert" […].

Aus: *Der Spiegel (Online)*, 27/8/00.

der Scheidungsrichter – divorce court judge	*ohnehin* – anyway
die Angabe – detail, statement	*die Beziehung* – relationship
die Verbraucherzentrale – consumer centre	*gefährdet* – in danger
beantragen – to apply for	*umgehen mit* – to deal, cope with
der Ratschlag – advice	*die Enttäuschung* – disappointment
veröffentlichen – to publish	*die Bedingung* – condition
die Erholung – relaxation	*überfordert* – overtaxed, overstressed

🔎 ANALYSIS[140]

1 Identify the *werden*-passives in the text. There are five in total. See **Ch. 18**.

2 Find the two *sein*-passives in the text and translate them literally into English, showing how their meaning differs from that of their corresponding *werden*-passives. See **Ch. 18**.

3 Explain the use of the *Konjunktiv I* in lines 7 and 14 as opposed to the ordinary indicative in lines 8–9. See **Ch. 17**.

4 Identify the forms *könnten* and *müssten* in lines 10 and 12 respectively and explain their use. See **Ch. 17**.

5 Identify the forms *stellten* and *verstärkten* in lines 16 and 20 respectively and explain their use. How do these forms compare to *könnten* and *müssten* mentioned in Question 4 above? See **Ch. 17**.

6 Explain the lack of ending on *gemeinsam* (line 4, contrast *gemeinsame* in line 17), *neu* (6) and *akut* (21). See **Ch. 5**.

7 What sort of adjective is *häufigsten* in line 5? What does it mean? See **Ch. 6**.

8 Identify the pronoun *sich* in line 13 and translate it into English. Why is it directly preceded by *man* in this text? See **Ch. 20**.

9 What sort of pronoun is *die* in line 17? Explain its use. See **Ch. 8**.

10 Explain the use of *damit* and *dadurch* in lines 11 and 21 respectively. How would you translate each one into English? See **Chs 24** and **8**.

11 Why is *durch* used instead of *von* to refer to the agent of the passive clause in line 21? See **Ch. 18**.

12 In line 1, why is the article absent before *Gemeinsamer Urlaub* but present in *zum Scheidungsrichter*? See **Ch. 4**.

[140] Answers to the analysis questions can be found in the key to the revision texts at the back of the book.

🖎 EXERCISES

All exercises are based on Revision Text 1. Complete each of these without looking at the text or at the other exercises in this section:

1 Put the capitalised nouns into the plural (see **Ch. 2**), or into the dative plural if the context requires it (see **Ch. 3**):

Nach ANGABE; Zwei PSYCHOLOGE; die häufigsten GRUND für KRISE und RATSCHLAG; viele PAAR; verschiedene STRATEGIE; Treffen mit FREUND; Diese MÖGLICHKEIT; hohe ERWARTUNG; Schwierige SITUATION; klimatische BEDINGUNG; andere REGEL.

2 Put the italicised articles, pronouns and nouns into the correct case. Use the contracted forms of articles where appropriate (see **Chs 3** and **24**):

Gemeinsamer Urlaub führt oft zu *der* Scheidungsrichter. Nach Angaben *die* nordrhein-westfälischen Verbraucher-Zentrale wird etwa *jede* dritte Scheidung in Deutschland nach *ein* gemeinsam verbrachten Urlaub beantragt. Zwei Psychologen haben deshalb *die* häufigsten Gründe für Krisen und Ratschläge zu *die* Krisenvermeidung in *ein* Artikel *der* neu erschienenen *Ratgeber* „Chance Psychotherapie" veröffentlicht. Viele Paare könnten nicht damit umgehen, dass sie in *der* Urlaub plötzlich so viel Zeit miteinander verbringen müssten. „In *der* Alltag gibt es verschiedene Strategien, wie man sich aus *der* Weg gehen kann, zum Beispiel Treffen mit *Freunde*", so *der* Psychologe. Viele Paare stellten insgesamt zu hohe Erwartungen an *die* gemeinsame Urlaubszeit. „Wenn *die* dann nicht erfüllt werden, wird *die* Enttäuschung auf *der* Partner projiziert".

3 Insert the correct adjective endings where appropriate (see **Ch. 5** and **Appendix 2**):

Gemeinsam_ Urlaub führt oft zum Scheidungsrichter. Nach Angaben der nordrhein_-westfälisch_ Verbraucher-Zentrale wird etwa jede dritt_ Scheidung in Deutschland nach einem gemeinsam_ verbracht_ Urlaub beantragt. Zwei Psychologen haben deshalb die häufigst_ Gründe für Krisenvermeidung in einem Artikel des neu erschienen_ Ratgebers … veröffentlicht. Der gemeinsam_ Urlaub bedeute für viele Paare mehr Stress als Erholung[…]. Schwierig_ und unbefriedigend_ Situationen wie etwa ein schlecht_ Hotel oder ungewohnt_ klimatisch_ Bedingungen verstärkten das Stressgefühl zusätzlich.

4 Insert the bracketed verb forms into the correct position in the following sentences (see **Ch. 26**):

1 Nach Angaben der nordrhein-westfälischen Verbraucher-Zentrale etwa jede dritte Scheidung in Deutschland nach einem gemeinsam verbrachten Urlaub. (wird beantragt)

2 Zwei Psychologen deshalb die häufigsten Gründe für Krisen und Ratschläge zur Krisenvermeidung in einem Artikel des neu erschienenen Ratgebers „Chance Psychotherapie." (haben veröffentlicht)

3 Der Urlaub ist dann ein Risikofaktor, wenn die Beziehung ohnehin schon. (ist gefährdet)

4 Viele Paare könnten nicht damit umgehen, dass sie im Urlaub plötzlich so viel Zeit miteinander. (müssten verbringen)

5 Im Alltag es verschiedene Strategien (gibt), wie man sich aus dem Weg, zum Beispiel Treffen mit Freunden. (gehen kann)

6 „Wenn die dann nicht (werden erfüllt), die Enttäuschung auf den Partner." (wird projiziert)

7 Auch ein stabiles Beziehungssystem dadurch akut. (kann gefährdet werden)

8 Und wenn im Urlaub plötzlich andere Regeln (werden aufgestellt), meist beide. (sind überfordert)

5 Insert the bracketed words into the correct position in the following clauses. Note that *oft* and *schon* often follow the same word order rules as *nicht* (see **Ch. 22**):

1 Gemeinsamer Urlaub führt zum Scheidungsrichter. (oft)

2 … , wenn die Beziehung ohnehin gefährdet ist. (schon)

3 Viele Paare könnten damit umgehen, … (nicht)

4 Diese Möglichkeiten habe man im Urlaub naturgemäß. (nicht)

5 Wenn die dann erfüllt werden, … (nicht)

☞ Now go back to the text to check your answers.

Karneval: Eine Übersicht

Karneval bezeichnet die vielen verschiedenen Festivitäten, die vor der österlichen Fastenzeit stattfinden. Im Karneval wird dem grauen Alltag Farbe verliehen: Kinder wie Erwachsene verkleiden sich, gehen zu
5 Karnevalsumzügen oder Kostümfesten und denken so wenig wie möglich an Schule, Arbeit und andere unangenehme Dinge.

Karneval wird in ganz Deutschland gefeiert, aber die größten Veranstaltungen finden in den vorherrschend katholischen Gebieten wie dem Rheinland und Süddeutschland statt. Wie bei so vielen deutschen
10 Traditionen heben sich die Gebräuche in den einzelnen Regionen deutlich voneinander ab. In manchen Gebieten, wie zum Beispiel Köln, gehört Karneval zur Geschichte der Stadt und ist das vielleicht wichtigste Fest des Jahres. In Städten wie München gehört Karneval ebenfalls zur lokalen Tradition, wird aber eher privat als öffentlich gefeiert. In Städten
15 protestantischer Prägung wie Berlin wird Karneval zwar inzwischen auch gefeiert, hat aber keine echte Tradition [...].

Die wichtigsten Tage in der Karnevalszeit sind Weiberfastnacht und Rosenmontag. Die Daten, an denen sie gefeiert werden, sind von Jahr zu Jahr unterschiedlich, da ihre Festlegung von Ostern abhängig ist, einem
20 beweglichen Fest. Weiberfastnacht feiert man am Donnerstag und Rosenmontag am Montag vorm Faschingsdienstag [...]. Weiberfastnacht ist der Tag, an dem die meisten Deutschen in irgendeiner Form Karneval feiern: sei es auf der Arbeit, in der Schule, in Vereinen und Verbänden oder zuhause mit Freunden. Das Wichtigste an allen Aktivitäten im
25 Karneval ist, dass der normale Alltag auf den Kopf gestellt wird: Jeder kann sich verkleiden wie er möchte, darf die üblichen Konventionen und Regeln außer acht lassen und sich nach Herzenslust amüsieren [...].

Rosenmontag ist der Tag, an dem die großen Karnevalsumzüge veranstaltet werden. Die größten und bekanntesten Umzüge finden in
30 Köln, Düsseldorf und Mainz statt. Die Umzüge bestehen aus großen bunten dekorierten Karnevalswagen, riesigen Puppen (meist Karikaturen bekannter Politiker), Gruppen von Clowns, Bands, Kapellen, tanzenden Funkenmariechen und kostümierten Corps. Wenn die Prozession an den (ebenfalls verkleideten) Zuschauern vorbeifährt, werfen die Leute auf den
35 Wagen Bonbons und Schokolade in die Menge. Die dekorierten Karnevalswagen tragen oft ein bestimmtes Motto. Da Karneval traditionsgemäß eine unkonventionelle Zeit ist, werden besonders Politiker und ihre Politik häufig Zielscheibe satirischer Kritik.

Am Aschermittwoch ist der Karneval offiziell zu Ende [...].

österlich – Easter (adjective)	*der Verein* – club
die Fastenzeit – time of fasting	*der Verband* – association
sich verkleiden – to wear fancy dress	*auf den Kopf stellen* – turn upside down
der Umzug – procession	*die Kapelle* – (traditional music) band
die Veranstaltung – event	*das Funkenmariechen* – majorette
vorherrschend – predominantly	*das Corps* – corps, troops
der Gebrauch – custom, tradition	*ebenfalls* – equally, also
sich abheben – to stand out	*Aschermittwoch* – Ash Wednesday
die Prägung – character	*die Menge* – crowd
Faschingsdienstag – Shrove Tuesday	*die Zielscheibe* – target

⚲ ANALYSIS¹⁴¹

1   Identify the case forms of the following words and explain why they are being used: *dem* (3), *der* (12), *des* (13), *einem* (19), *der* (25), *ein* (36), *satirischer* (38). See **Ch. 3**.

2   What sort of pronoun is *sich* in line 10? Why is it appearing before the subject? See **Ch. 20**.

3   Why is the bare infinitive (i.e. without *um* or *zu*) used in lines 26 and 27? See **Ch. 21**.

4   Find examples of relative pronouns in the text and explain their form in terms of gender, number and case. There are 4 occurrences in total. See **Ch. 9**.

5   Why is the subjunctive (*Konjunktiv I*) used in line 23? See **Ch. 18**.

6   Why does the superlative *bekanntesten* in line 29 add *e* before the superlative ending? See **Ch. 6**.

7   Identify the form of *möchte* in line 26 and give its meaning. See **Ch. 17**.

8   Explain the presence of *sich* in line 27. See **Ch. 20**.

9   Explain the presence of umlaut in *vorbeifährt* (34). See **Ch. 10**.

10   Explain why *der* is used in line 23 and, by contrast, *die* is used in line 35. See **Ch. 24**.

11   What does *an* mean in line 28, and what is its meaning in line 6? Why are these meanings different? See **Ch. 24**.

12   Why is the contracted form *am* used in lines 20 and 21 but the full forms *an dem* in lines 22 and 28? See **Ch. 24**.

¹⁴¹ Answers to the analysis questions can be found in the key to the revision texts at the back of the book.

✎ EXERCISES

All exercises are based on Revision Text 2. Complete each of these without looking at the text or at the other exercises in this section:

1   Put the capitalised nouns, pronouns, articles and adjectives into the case required by the underlined prepositions (see **Ch. 24**):

   1   Festivitäten, die <u>vor</u> DIE ÖSTERLICHE FASTENZEIT stattfinden.

2 Sie denken so wenig wie möglich <u>an</u> Schule, Arbeit und ANDERE UNANGENEHME DINGE.

3 Die größten Veranstaltungen finden <u>in</u> DIE VORHERRSCHEND KATHOLISCHEN GEBIETE statt.

4 Wie <u>bei</u> so VIELE DEUTSCHE TRADITIONEN heben sich die Gebräuche <u>in</u> DIE EINZELNEN REGIONEN deutlich voneinander ab.

5 Die wichtigsten Tage <u>in</u> DIE KARNEVALSZEIT.

6 Weiberfastnacht ist der Tag, an dem die meisten Deutschen <u>in</u> IRGENDEINE FORM Karneval feiern: sei es <u>auf</u> DIE ARBEIT, <u>in</u> DIE SCHULE, <u>in</u> VEREINE und VERBÄNDE oder zuhause <u>mit</u> FREUNDE.

7 Das Wichtigste <u>an</u> ALLE AKTIVITÄTEN.

8 Dass der normale Alltag <u>auf</u> DER KOPF gestellt wird.

9 Die Umzüge bestehen <u>aus</u> GROSSE BUNTE DEKORIERTE KARNEVALSWAGEN.

10 Wenn die Prozession <u>an</u> DIE ZUSCHAUER <u>vorbei</u>fährt, werfen die Leute <u>auf</u> DER WAGEN Bonbons und Schokolade.

2 Translate the capitalised conjunctions into German and make the necessary word order changes where appropriate (see **Ch. 25**):

1 Karneval wird in ganz Deutschland gefeiert, BUT die größten Veranstaltungen finden in den vorherrschend katholischen Gebieten wie dem Rheinland und Süddeutschland statt.

2 Die Daten, an denen sie gefeiert werden, sind von Jahr zu Jahr unterschiedlich, AS/SINCE ihre Festlegung ist von Ostern abhängig.

3 Das Wichtigste an allen Aktivitäten im Karneval ist, THAT der normale Alltag wird auf den Kopf gestellt.

4 WHENEVER die Prozession fährt an den Zuschauern vorbei, die Leute werfen auf den Wagen Bonbons und Schokolade.

5 AS/SINCE Karneval ist traditionsgemäß eine unkonventionelle Zeit, besonders Politiker und ihre Politik werden häufig Zielscheibe satirischer Kritik.

3 Put the following sentences with *man* into the passive, taking care not to change the tense. Do not mention an agent. (see **Ch. 18**):

Example: Man fängt den Hund.
Answer: Der Hund wird gefangen.

1 Man feiert Karneval in ganz Deutschland.

2 Die Daten, an denen man sie feiert. [sie *refers to* die wichtigsten Tage]

3 Dass man den normalen Alltag auf den Kopf stellt.

4 Der Tag, an dem man die großen Karnevalsumzüge veranstaltet.

5 Im Karneval verleiht man dem grauen Alltag Farbe.

4 Add commas and capital letters to the following sentences. Where SS appears, decide whether to use *ss* or *ß*. (see **Ch. 28**):

1 Karneval bezeichnet die vielen verschiedenen festivitäten die vor der österlichen fastenzeit stattfinden.

2 Karneval wird in ganz deutschland gefeiert aber die gröSSten veranstaltungen finden in den vorherrschend katholischen gebieten wie dem rheinland und süddeutschland statt.

3 Wie bei so vielen deutschen traditionen heben sich die gebräuche in den einzelnen regionen deutlich voneinander ab.

4 Die daten an denen sie gefeiert werden sind von jahr zu jahr unterschiedlich da ihre festlegung von ostern abhängig ist.

5 Das wichtigste an allen aktivitäten im karneval ist daSS der normale alltag auf den kopf gestellt wird.

6 Da karneval traditionsgemäSS eine unkonventionelle zeit ist werden besonders politiker und ihre politik häufig zielscheibe satirischer kritik.

☞ Now go back to the text to check your answers.

Die eifrigsten Bratmaxe in ganz Europa

Deutsche Grillpartys sind einzigartig – soviel steht fest. Das Wort "Barbecue" ist wohl vom mexikanisch-spanischen "barbocoa" abgeleitet, was "heilige Feuerstätte" bedeutet. Die Amerikaner übernahmen die
5 Grillsitte zuerst und machten sie zum Teil der Kleinstadtidylle: ein Haus, ein Auto, eine Frau, zwei rotbäckige Kinder und einen Grill im Garten. Indem man Steaks im Freien grillte, ließ man seine Nachbarn wissen, dass man es zu etwas gebracht hatte. In Deutschland wurde zwar erst später draußen gegrillt, jedoch geriet es in den 1950ern bald zum
10 Volkssport. Heute gelten die Deutschen als eifrigste Bratmaxe in ganz Europa. Natürlich genießen auch andere Völker hin und wieder ein über Kohle gebrutzeltes Stück Fleisch. Aber sie folgen keinem derart ausgeklügelten Ritual wie die Deutschen, für die der Grill eine wahrhaft "heilige Feuerstätte" ist.
15   Der deutsche Grillabend ist zu einem der wichtigsten Gemeinschaftserlebnisse der Vororte geworden. Vor allem ist es der Moment, in dem der deutsche Büroangestellte, der sich normalerweise tagsüber von seinem Revier fernhält, die Herrschaft über seinen Grund und Boden ausübt. Will man sich ins Gedächtnis rufen, dass Grillen eine
20 Erfindung der Steinzeit ist, muss man nur einmal an einem Sommerabend bei einem Fußballspiel der Deutschen eine Straße entlangschlendern. Das Tier zu jagen – also Würstchen, Steaks und Hackfleisch im Supermarkt zu kaufen – ein Feuer zu entfachen und es zu beaufsichtigen, ist absolute Männersache. [...].
25   Deutsche Männer können stundenlang über die richtige Wahl des Fleisches (Hühnerfleisch gilt als zu weibisch für den männlichen Grillgeschmack, weil es a) zu wenig Fett hat und b) schwer zuzubereiten ist, ohne Lebensmittelvergiftungen zu verursachen), über die richtige Rindfleischmarinade, den richtigen Moment zur Beigabe von Kräutern,
30 den Einfluss von Rauch, die richtige Ausrüstung (das deutsche Alpha-Männchen lehnt den runden, transportierbaren Kugelgrill ab), den richtigen Anzünder, den Umgang mit Aluminiumfolie und die Schmorzeit vor dem Wenden des Grillspießes dozieren. [...].
   Das Landgericht München hat soeben verfügt, dass Nachbarn, die sich
35 durch den über den Zaun ziehenden Qualm, den Geruch von Fleisch, das Gebrutzel und Gezische gestört fühlten, akzeptieren müssten, dass das Grillen zum deutschen Sommer gehöre. Solange der Grillabend in einem "angemessenen" Rahmen abläuft, kann der wütende Nachbar nicht dagegen klagen. Aber was heißt denn "angemessen"? Das Münchner
40 Gericht legte fest, dass 26 Grillabende in einem Zeitraum von vier Monaten angemessen seien. Das Stuttgarter Landgericht war hier strenger – nur drei Grillabende pro Jahr seien akzeptabel, und diese dürften nicht länger als zwei Stunden dauern. [...]. Seltsam? Eigentlich nicht, nur typisch deutsch.

Von Roger Boyes, © Goethe-Institut, 2008 [www.goethe.de].

eifrig – keen	*die Lebensmittelvergiftung* – food poisoning
der Bratmax – barbecue freak	*das Hühnerfleisch/Rindfleisch* – chicken/beef
einzigartig – unique	*die Kräuter* – herbs
die Feuerstätte – fireplace	*die Ausrüstung* – equipment
die Grillsitte – barbecue habit	*der Kugelgrill* – kettle grill
rotbäckig – rosy-cheeked	*der Anzünder* – lighter
zu etwas bringen – to accomplish	*die Schmorzeit* – roasting time
ausgeklügelt – elaborate	*der Spieß* – skewer
das Gemeinschaftserlebnis – community experience	*dozieren über* – to pontificate about
der Vorort – suburb	*das Landgericht* – district court
der Büroangestellte – office worker	*verfügen* – to decree
das Revier – patch, hunting ground	*der Qualm* – smoke
ausüben – to carry out, practise	*brutzeln* – to sizzle
das Hackfleisch – mince	*zischen* – to hiss
entfachen – to kindle	*angemessen* – appropriate
beaufsichtigen – to oversee	*der Rahmen* – scale, setting
	festlegen – lay down, stipulate

⚲ ANALYSIS[142]

1 What type of word is *indem* in line 7 and what is the equivalent English construction? See **Ch. 25**.

2 Identify the tense form of *gebracht hatte* in line 8 and explain why it is being used here. See **Ch. 14**.

3 Why is there no adjective ending on *wahrhaft* in line 13, despite its appearance before a noun? See **Ch. 5**.

4 Why does *Stuttgarter* have the adjective ending *-er* in line 41, instead of the usual weak ending for singular nouns *-e*? See **Ch. 5**.

5 What is the name of the constructions in lines 11–12: *ein **über Kohle gebrutzeltes** Stück Fleisch* and line 35: *den **über den Zaun ziehenden** Qualm*. Translate them into English. See **Ch. 5**.

6 Account for the word order of *hat* in line 27 and *ist* in line 28. See **Ch. 26**.

7 Why is the infinitive *dozieren* in line 33 not preceded by *zu*? See **Ch. 21**.

8 Identify the word *sich* in line 34 and explain why it is needed here. See **Ch. 20**.

9 Why does *müssten* appear **after** the infinitive *akzeptieren* in line 36? See **Ch. 26**.

10 Why is the subjunctive being used in lines 36, 37, 41, 42 and 43? See **Ch. 17**.

11 Why is *deutschen* written with a small letter in line 37 but with a capital in line 10? And why is *Stuttgarter* written with a capital letter in line 41? See **Ch. 28**.

12 What sort of word is *Männchen* in line 31? See **Ch. 27**.

[142] Answers to the analysis questions can be found in the key to the revision texts at the back of the book.

🖉 EXERCISES

All exercises are based on Revision Text 3. Complete each of these without looking at the text or at the other exercises in this section:

1 Put the capitalised verbs into the present tense (see **Ch. 10**):

1 Das Wort "Barbecue" SEIN wohl vom mexikanisch-spanischen "barbocoa" abgeleitet, was "heilige Feuerstätte" BEDEUTEN.

2 Der Moment, in dem der deutsche Büroangestellte, der sich normalerweise tagsüber von seinem Revier FERNHALTEN, die Herrschaft über seinen Grund und Boden AUSÜBEN.

3 WOLLEN man sich ins Gedächtnis rufen, dass Grillen eine Erfindung der Steinzeit SEIN, MÜSSEN man nur einmal an einem Sommerabend bei einem Fußballspiel der Deutschen eine Straße entlangschlendern.

4 Hühnerfleisch GELTEN als zu weibisch für den männlichen Grillgeschmack, weil es zu wenig Fett HABEN.

5 Solange der Grillabend in einem "angemessenen" Rahmen ABLAUFEN, KÖNNEN der wütende Nachbar nicht dagegen klagen.

2 Put the capitalised verbs into the past tense (see **Ch. 12**):

1 Die Amerikaner ÜBERNEHMEN die Grillsitte zuerst und MACHEN sie zum Teil der Kleinstadtidylle.

2 Indem man Steaks im Freien GRILLEN, LASSEN man seine Nachbarn wissen, dass man es zu etwas gebracht HABEN.

3 In Deutschland WERDEN zwar erst später draußen gegrillt, jedoch GERATEN es in den 1950ern bald zum Volkssport.

4 Das Münchner Gericht FESTLEGEN, dass 26 Grillabende in einem Zeitraum von vier Monaten angemessen seien. [NB *festlegen* is a separable verb].

5 Das Stuttgarter Landgericht SEIN hier strenger.

3 Put the capitalised verbs into the correct form of the subjunctive to indicate reported speech. Decide for each verb whether to use the *Konjunktiv I* or the *Konjunktiv II* (see **Ch. 17**):

1 Das Landgericht München hat soeben verfügt, dass Nachbarn, die sich durch den über den Zaun ziehenden Qualm [...] gestört FÜHLEN, akzeptieren MÜSSEN, dass das Grillen zum deutschen Sommer GEHÖREN.

2 Das Münchner Gericht legte fest, dass 26 Grillabende in einem Zeitraum von vier Monaten angemessen SEIN.

3 Das Stuttgarter Landgericht war hier strenger – nur drei Grillabende pro Jahr SIND akzeptabel, und diese DÜRFEN nicht länger als zwei Stunden dauern.

4 Translate the capitalised relative pronouns into German (see **Ch. 9**) and move the underlined verbs to the necessary position:

1 Die Deutschen, für WHOM der Grill <u>ist</u> eine wahrhaft "heilige Feuerstätte."

2 Der Moment, in WHICH der deutsche Büroangestellte <u>übt</u> die Herrschaft über seinen Grund und Boden <u>aus</u>.

3 Der deutsche Büroangestellte, WHO <u>hält</u> sich normalerweise tagsüber von seinem Revier <u>fern</u>.

4 Nachbarn, WHO <u>fühlten</u> sich durch den über den Zaun ziehenden Qualm [...] gestört.

5 Put the capitalised articles (and nouns, where appropriate) into the genitive to give the meaning 'of' (see **Ch. 3**):

1 Zum Teil DIE Kleinstadtidylle

2 Bei einem Fußballspiel DIE DEUTSCH_ [*plural*]

3 Die richtige Wahl DAS FLEISCH_

4 Eine Erfindung DIE Steinzeit

5 Vor dem Wenden DER GRILLSPIEß_

☞ Now go back to the text to check your answers.

Die Sehnsucht der Deutschen nach der freien Natur

[...]. Aktiv sein ist wieder in. Tatsache ist jedoch, dass die meisten jungen Deutschen in Städten leben und größtenteils den Bezug zur Natur verloren haben. Sie mögen eine romantische Vorstellung von stillen Seen
5 und läutenden Kuhglocken auf Berghängen hegen. Doch der deutsche Städter verbringt seine Wochenenden gewöhnlich in der Stadt und seine Ferien überwiegend in fernen, exotischen Ländern.

Dabei kleidet sich der urbane Deutsche so, als ob er gerade die Zugspitze erklimmen wollte. In jeder Fußgängerzone sieht man heute
10 robuste Outdoorbekleidung, und es gilt als modisch durchaus vertretbar, beim Zeitungskauf oder dem Genuss eines Caffè Latte wärmeisolierte Jacken und feste Wanderschuhe zu tragen. Niemand findet es lächerlich, in einer leichten Polarjacke mit einem Allradwagen zum Bäcker zu fahren, um Croissants zu besorgen. [...].
15 Männer wollen heute so ausschauen, als seien sie eins mit der Natur. Auf einer Party in Berlin liegt man momentan mit einem rotkarierten Holzfällerhemd nie daneben. Demzufolge sind Norwegerpullis, Napapijri-Kleidung (das heißt „nördlicher Polarkreis" auf Finnisch) und Ontariojacken äußerst gefragt. Es ist bekannt, dass deutsche Männer gut
20 Windeln wechseln und über ihre Gefühle reden können; nun müssen sie beweisen, dass sie auch einen Grizzlybären mit bloßen Händen erwürgen und es mit einem Rudel Huskys aufnehmen können. Und das, während sie mit ihrer Freundin Gesichtscreme kaufen.

Aber in Deutschland ist eine viel tiefgreifendere Wandlung im Gange:
25 Man sehnt sich nach dem Leben in der Natur als einem Ausgleich zum hektischen Stadtalltag. Die deutschen Männer und Frauen scheinen zu Wurzeln zurückkehren zu wollen, die sie nie hatten. Infolgedessen kaufen sich einige von ihnen Wochenendhäuser auf dem Land, damit sie – so glauben sie – ihren Sprösslingen wenigstens ein Gefühl einer
30 nichtstädtischen Kindheit vermitteln können, wie im See zu angeln oder Brot zu backen.

Von Roger Boyes, © Goethe-Institut, 2010 [www.goethe.de].

die Sehnsucht – longing	*daneben* – wrong
der Bezug – connection	*demzufolge* – consequently
die Kuhglocke – cowbell	*gefragt* – in demand
der Berghang – mountainside	*die Windel* – nappy
hegen – to harbour	*erwürgen* – strangle to death
überwiegend – predominantly	*das Rudel* – pack
die Zugspitze – 'Zugspitze' mountain	*es aufnehmen* – to rival
vertretbar – reasonable	*die Wandlung* – transformation
lächerlich – ridiculous	*der Ausgleich* – compensation
der Allradwagen – four-wheel drive	*die Wurzel* – root
rotkariert – red-chequered	*der Sprössling* – offspring
der Holzfäller – lumberjack	*vermitteln* (+ dat.) – to convey, provide

⚲ ANALYSIS[143]

1 Identify the case forms of the following words and explain why these cases are being used in each context: *der* (1), *den* (3), *der* (8), *dem* (11), *nördlicher* (18), *einem* (25), *ihren* (29). See **Ch. 3**.

2 Why does the noun *Grizzlybär* end in *-en* in line 21? See **Ch. 3**.

3 Why does *Caffè Latte* in line 11 not have a genitive ending? See **Ch. 3**.

4 Find the *-s* plurals in the text (there are 3 in total) and explain why *-s* is used to mark plural on these words. See **Ch. 2**.

5 Why is *sich* used in line 8 and why does it precede the subject? See **Ch. 20**.

6 Identify the form *seien* in line 15 and explain its meaning. See **Ch. 17**.

7 What type of word is *während* in line 22? What does it mean and what effect does it have on the following finite verb? See **Ch. 25**.

8 What is the meaning of *damit* in line 28? See **Ch. 25**.

9 Identify the form *die* in line 27 and account for its number and case. See **Ch. 9**.

10 Explain the relative word order of *gewöhnlich in der Stadt* in line 6 and of *mit einem Allradwagen zum Bäcker* in line 13. See **Ch. 26**.

11 Explain the relative word order of *ihren Sprösslingen … ein Gefühl* in line 29. See **Ch. 26**.

12 Explain the meaning of *nie* in lines 17 and 27 and account for its position in the sentence. See **Ch. 22**.

[143] Answers to the analysis questions can be found in the key to the revision texts at the back of the book.

✎ EXERCISES

All exercises are based on Revision Text 4. Complete each of these without looking at the text or at the other exercises in this section:

1 Put the capitalised articles and adjectives into the correct form, where appropriate (see Chs 1 for gender, 3 for case and 5 for adjectives):

1 Tatsache ist jedoch, dass die MEIST__ JUNG__ Deutschen in Städten leben und größtenteils D__ Bezug zur Natur verloren haben.

2 Doch D__ DEUTSCH__ Städter verbringt seine Wochenenden gewöhnlich in D__ Stadt.

3 Sie mögen EIN__ ROMANTISCH__ Vorstellung von STILL__ Seen und LÄUTEND__ Kuhglocken auf Berghängen hegen.

4 Beim Zeitungskauf oder dem Genuss EIN__ Caffè Latte.

5 Dabei kleidet sich D__ URBAN__ Deutsche so, als ob er gerade die Zugspitze erklimmen wollte.

6 Das heißt „NÖRDLICH__ Polarkreis" auf Finnisch.

7 Es ist bekannt, dass DEUTSCH__ Männer gut Windeln wechseln.

8 D__ DEUTSCH__ Männer und Frauen scheinen zu Wurzeln zurückkehren zu wollen.

9 Aber in Deutschland ist EIN__ viel TIEFGREIFENDER__ Wandlung im Gange.

10 Damit sie ihren Sprösslingen wenigstens EIN__ Gefühl EIN__ NICHTSTÄDTISCH__ Kindheit vermitteln können.

2 Fill in the gaps with the appropriate personal pronoun or possessive, taking care to use the correct case form (see **Ch. 7**):

1 Dabei kleidet sich der urbane Deutsche so, als ob __ gerade die Zugspitze erklimmen wollte. (*he*)

2 Männer wollen heute so ausschauen, als seien __ eins mit der Natur. (*they*)

3 Infolgedessen kaufen sich einige von __ Wochenendhäuser auf dem Land. (*them*)

4 In jeder Fußgängerzone sieht __ heute robuste Outdoorbekleidung. (*one*)

5 Doch der deutsche Städter verbringt __ Wochenenden gewöhnlich in der Stadt. (*his*)

6 Es ist bekannt, dass deutsche Männer gut Windeln wechseln und über __ Gefühle reden können. (*their*)

7 Damit sie __ Sprösslingen wenigstens ein Gefühl einer nichtstädtischen Kindheit vermitteln können. (*their*)

8 Und das, während sie mit __ Freundin Gesichtscreme kaufen. (*their*)

3 Decide whether to use *zu*, *um ... zu* or a bare infinitive in the following sentences, filling in the gaps where appropriate (see **Ch. 21**):

1 Es gilt als modisch durchaus vertretbar, __ beim Zeitungskauf oder dem Genuss eines Caffè Latte wärmeisolierte Jacken und feste Wanderschuhe __ tragen.

2 Nun müssen sie __ __ beweisen.

3 Niemand findet es lächerlich, __ in einer leichten Polarjacke mit einem Allradwagen zum Bäcker __ fahren, __ Croissants __ besorgen.

4 Sie mögen __ eine romantische Vorstellung von stillen Seen und läutenden Kuhglocken auf Berghängen __ hegen.

5 Die deutschen Männer und Frauen scheinen __ zu Wurzeln zurückkehren __ wollen.

6 Damit sie ihren Sprösslingen wenigstens ein Gefühl einer nichtstädtischen Kindheit vermitteln __ können, wie __ im See __ angeln oder __ Brot __ backen.

4 Move the underlined verbs to the correct position in the sentence where necessary (see **Ch. 26**):

1 Tatsache ist jedoch, dass die meisten jungen Deutschen <u>leben</u> in Städten und <u>haben</u> größtenteils den Bezug zur Natur verloren.

2 Dabei der urbane Deutsche <u>kleidet sich</u> so, als ob er gerade die Zugspitze <u>wollte</u> erklimmen.

3 In jeder Fußgängerzone man <u>sieht</u> heute robuste Outdoorbekleidung.

4 Niemand findet es lächerlich, <u>zu fahren</u> in einer leichten Polarjacke mit einem Allradwagen zum Bäcker.

5 Auf einer Party in Berlin man <u>liegt</u> momentan mit einem rotkarierten Holzfällerhemd nie daneben.

6 Es ist bekannt, dass deutsche Männer <u>können</u> gut Windeln wechseln und über ihre Gefühle reden.

7 Die deutschen Männer und Frauen scheinen <u>zu wollen</u> zu Wurzeln zurückkehren, die sie <u>hatten</u> nie.

8 Infolgedessen einige von ihnen <u>kaufen sich</u> Wochenendhäuser auf dem Land, damit sie <u>können</u> <u>vermitteln</u> ihren Sprösslingen wenigstens ein Gefühl einer nichtstädtischen Kindheit.

5 Derive nouns from the following nouns, adjectives and verbs, and add the definite article to each one to show its gender (see **Ch. 27**):

1	*deutsch*	'the German' (masc.)	**7**	*kaufen*	'the purchase'
2	*deutsch*	'the Germans' (pl.)	**8**	*genießen*	'the enjoyment'
3	*Kind*	'the childhood'	**9**	*backen*	'the baker'
4	*Stadt*	'the townie'	**10**	*fühlen*	'the feeling'
5	*vorstellen*	'the picture, image'	**11**	*wandeln*	'the change'
6	*bekleiden*	'the clothing'	**12**	*ausgleichen*	'the balance, compensation'

☞ Now go back to the text to check your answers.

Appendix 4: Key to exercises

1 GENDER

1 1. das, ein, ein, ein. 2. der, eine. 3. die, die. 4. das, ein, eine. 5. das, die. 6. das, eine, das. 7. das, die, ein, die. 8. die, die, die. 9. das (*this is an exception to the rule that nouns ending in* –us *are masc.*), ein, eine, ein, das, das, das. 10. der, eine, ein, die, der, der, der, der.

2 **Column 1:** der Bruder, der Schnee, der Liebling, der Frühling, der Whisky, der Lehrer, der Tourismus, der Polizist, der Osten, der Motor. **Column 2:** die Blume, die Regierung, die Politik, die Gesundheit, die Universität, die Natur, die Höhe, die Erde, die Freundin, die Bäckerei. **Column 3:** das Foto, das Ereignis, das Kind, das Französisch, das Viertel, das Lesen, das Grün, das Geräusch, das Fräulein, das Klima.

2 NOUN PLURALS

1 Tomaten, Äpfel, 12 Eier, Vollwertnudeln, Zwiebeln, Weintrauben, 6 Brötchen, 2 Dosen Thunfisch, Kartoffeln, Erdbeeren, Joghurts (or Joghurt), Kaffeefilter, Champignons, Pfirsiche, Pizzas, 2 Kisten Bier, Kräuter, Datteln, Bonbons, 4 Flaschen Wein, Gewürze, Erdnüsse, Muesliriegel, verschiedene Fruchtsäfte.

2 Rosinen, Esslöffel, Klümpchen, Rosinen, Zutaten, Minuten, Stückchen, Lauchzwiebeln, Paprikaschoten, Zucchini, Lauchzwiebeln, Stücke, Schoten, Streifen, Zucchini, Stifte, Kichererbsen, Rosinen, Mandeln, Häufchen, Portionen, Kalorien, Joule, Ballaststoffe, Stunden.

3 1. Ossis. 2. Schuhe. 3. Zeitungen. 4. Kekse. 5. Scheiben. 6. Schlüssel (Schluessel). 7. Hüte (Huete).

3 CASE

1 1. den Mann meiner Schwester. 2. der Junge. 3. den Chef. 4. mein Vater. 5. den Freund des Nachbarmädchens. 6. den Kindern einen Kuss. 7. einer von den Nachbarn. 8. der Assistentin … der Chef. 9. der Junge seinen Vater. 10. des Lehrers.

2 1. Er hat Angst vor den Lehrern. 2. Sie schrie die Hunde wütend an. 3. Ich sagte den Müttern, dass die Kinder böse waren. 4. Verärgert erklärte ich den Arbeitern die Ursache der Probleme. 5. Warum müssen die Frauen immer über ihre Gefühle reden? 6. Er macht seinen Freunden Sorgen.

3 1. Ich sagte den Kollegen, dass ich krank war. 2. Ich fragte den netten Arzt, ob er mir etwas geben könnte. 3. Der schüchterne Schüler wollte dem strengen Lehrer nicht antworten. 4. Er hat seinem Vater einen roten Pullover zu Weihnachten geschenkt. 5. Ich habe versucht meiner neuen Nachbarin zu helfen. 6. Es würde meine Frau sehr freuen, wenn Sie sie besuchen würden. 7. Mmm! Hast du frische Plätzchen gekauft? Ja, aber ich habe nur eines/ eins übrig. 8. Er folgte einer der hübschen Studentinnen nach Hause. 9. Schmeckt den Kindern der neue Saft? 10. Du musst den Eltern gehorchen! 11. Wir suchen einen von den Gästen. Er heißt Benno Andlinger. 12. Er gratulierte seinem alten Onkel zum Geburtstag. 13. Ich bin einer guten Freundin in der Stadt begegnet. 14. Wir haben einen Ausflug nach Wien gemacht. Es hat den Schülern dort sehr gefallen. 15. Wer hat dem Kind diesen blöden Witz erzählt?

4 1. Das ist das Auto eines Freundes. 2. Das ist Peters Frau. 3. Es war die Idee der Chefin. 4. Hast du Annas Bücher gesehen? 5. Was ist die Hauptstadt Brasiliens? 6. Ich bin mit dem Fortschritt der Kinder sehr zufrieden. 6. Der Film handelt von der Untergang der „Titanic".

5 1. Nachbarn. 2. Kunden. 3. Taxifahrer. 4. Herrn … Journalisten. 5. Löwen, Tiger, Elephanten, Bären, Hund. 6. Kommissar … Kollegen. 7. Studenten. 8. des Professors. In colloquial German the weak -(e)n can be omitted.

6 des Elternhauses, der, der, des Studentenwerks, einem, einer, ein, das, den, die, den, das, des Studiums, den, die, Der, den, den.

4 USE OF ARTICLES

1 1. no article. 2. ein, der. 3. no article, der. 4. die, den. 5. eine. 6. ein, der. 7. no article, einen (der Kredit *means 'loan' here*), die. 8. der. 9. einen. 10. einen, der. 11. no article, no article. 12. no article, einer (or no article), den, eine.

2 1. zum. 2. im, no article, no article. 3. im, die. 4. no article. 5. den, die, zum, die. 6. den, am. 7. der. 8. das, das. 9. no article, no article (*because idiom: 'age before beauty'*). 10. no article, no article, no article. 11. der, no article. 12. no article, der. 13. der (*genitive*). 14. no article, dem. 15. am, no article, no article.

5 ADJECTIVES

1 deutsches Bier, der englische Tee, diese schwedischen Fleischklöße, holländischer Käse, ein schottischer Lachs, welcher österreichische Wein?, spanische Oliven, keine belgischen Pralinen, das frische französische Brot, mein griechischer Schafskäse.

2 1. guten. 2. schönes, großen, heutigen. 3. europaweiten, riesigen. 4. weltberühmte, hoher. 5. schicken italienischen. 6. kleine, teueren französischen, vierzigsten.

3 europäischen, wichtigste, junger, deutsche, neuer technischer, deutsch-amerikanischen, befragten, wichtiges, englische, weltweiten, amerikanischen, britischen, englische, andere, verschiedenen, feinen, kulturellen,[144] eigenen, universellen, sprachliche, meistverbreitete, meistgesprochene, sechziger, siebziger, lange, lokale, deutschsprachigen, intensiven, persönlichen.

[144] fein *and* kulturell *are linked syntactically to the previous plural article* die; *therefore they have a weak ending, even though they do not directly follow the article.*

4   unruhigen, ungeheueren, panzerartig, harten, gewölbten, braunen, bogenförmigen, geteilten, gänzlichen, vielen, sonstigen, kläglich, dünnen, richtiges, kleines, wohlbekannten, auseinandergepackte, illustrierten, hübschen, vergoldeten, schweren, ganzer, trübe.

5   Meine schönen alten Häuser haben zwei besonders große Schlafzimmer. 2. Die schwarzen Hemden mit den weißen Streifen hingen im Kleiderschrank. 3. Gute Weine sind selten billig. Nimm diese zwei französischen, zum Beispiel. 4. Diese frischgepflückten Blumen sind für meine neuen Freundinnen. 5. Sie ist trotz der verspäteten Züge relativ früh nach Hause gekommen.

6   a   1. panzerartig harten, 2. von bogenförmigen Versteifungen geteilten, 3. im Vergleich zu seinem sonstigen Umfang kläglich dünnen, 4. nur etwas zu kleines.

    b   1. Seine vor zwei Tagen achtzig gewordene Mutter. 2. Ein von mehreren Akademikern viel gelobter Schriftsteller. 3. Ein von den Deutschen eingeführtes Gesetz. 4. Sie bieten vier von der Gemeinde finanzierte Arbeitsplätze an. 5. Sie haben keinen für die Stelle geeigneten Kandidaten gefunden.

7   1. Hier kommt die Unfreundliche. 2. Sie spielte mit dem Kleinen. 3. Der Chef feuerte den Angestellten. 4. Sie war die Freundin des Gestorbenen. 5. Wir müssen für die Armen mehr spenden. 6. Ich habe etwas Interessantes gelesen. 7. Ich muss dir leider etwas Trauriges mitteilen.

8   1. Er hat eine ungewöhnlich große Nase. 2. Was für ein unglaublich schmutziges Zimmer! 3. Sie hat eine geschmackvoll eingerichtete Wohnung. 4. Es war ein unangenehm heißer Tag.

6 COMPARATIVES AND SUPERLATIVES

1   1. Ein Teich ist tiefer als eine Pfütze. 2. Der Fernsehturm in Berlin ist höher als das Rathaus. 3. Eine Autobahn ist breiter als eine Gasse. 4. Ein Supermodel ist schlanker als die durchschnittliche Frau. 5. Ein Sumo-Ringer is dicker als ein Rennreiter. 6. Ein Einzelbett ist schmaler/schmäler als ein Doppelbett. 7. Die Preise bei Aldi sind niedriger als die Preise bei anderen Supermärkten.

2   1. Der Teich ist der tiefste. 2. Der Fernsehturm ist der höchste. 3. Die Autobahn ist die breiteste. 4. Das Supermodel ist das schankste. 5. Der Sumo-Ringer ist der dickste. 6. Das Einzelbett ist das schmalste/schmälste. 7. Die Preise bei Aldi sind die niedrigsten.

3   1. längeren, längsten. 2. kürzere, kürzeste. 3. kleinere, kleinste. 4. größeren, größten. 5. dünnere, dünnste.

4   1. jünger. 2. älteste. 3. älter, langsamer. 4. beste. 5. reicher, arroganter. 6. wärmer, kälter. 7. klügsten. 8. höchste. 9. billigeren or billigsten. 10. stärker.

5   1. Das teuerste/am teuersten. 2. am besten. 3. am liebsten. 4. am lautesten. 5. nasseste/nässeste.

7 PERSONAL PRONOUNS AND POSSESSIVES

1   1. du, mir, sie. 2. wir, uns. 3. Sie, Sie, Ihnen. 4. ihr, euch, man. 5. er, mich, mir. 6. er, du, ihn, dir.

2   1. ihnen, ihre. 2. seine, ihn, mich, ihm. 3. meine, ihre, sie. 4. deinen, er. 5. unsere, sie, ihr. 6. Sie, Ihre. 7. ihr, euer, sie, euch. 8. mein, deinen, deiner. 9. ihrer, ihrem (= Marions Mann) *or* deren (= der Mann ihrer Freundin). 10. unser, wir, uns, unseres, sie.

3   1. Das ist mein Lippenstift – Das ist meiner. 2. Das ist dein Zimmer – Das ist dein(e)s. 3. Das sind seine Schuhe – Das sind seine. 4. Das ist unser Wagen – Das ist unserer. 5. Das sind eure Bücher – Das sind eure. 6. Das sind ihre Ohrringe – Das sind ihre. 7. Das ist ihr Baby – Das ist ihr(e)s. 8. Das ist Ihr Kaffee – Das ist Ihrer.

4   1. sie. 2. sie. 3. er. 4. ihn. 5. es *or* er. 6. es *or* er. 7. dafür. 8. darauf *or* auf sie. 9. davon. 10. ihn.

5   1. You can't/aren't allowed to smoke here. 2. A new bridge has just been built *or* They've just built a new bridge. 3. That can really get on your nerves. 4. The Germans are considered to be very hardworking/industrious. 5. The weather here can really depress you.

8 DEMONSTRATIVES

1   1. den, diesen. 2. der, dieser. 3. der, dieser. 4. den, diesen. 5. des, dieses. 6. den, diesen.

2   1. die da, diese da. 2. der da, dieser da. 3. denen da, diesen da. 4. den da, diesen da. 5. der da, dieser da. 6. denen da, diesen da. 7. der da, dieser da. 8. die da, diese da.

3   1. den. 2. das. 3. das. 4. derjenige. 5. demjenigen. 6. von dem *or better* davon. 7. an das *or better* daran.

4   1. Ich weiß es nicht. Den habe ich seit langem nicht gesehen. 2. Der ist im Urlaub. 3. Ja, von denen habe ich diese Uhr gekriegt. 4. Der habe ich eine CD gegeben. 5. Dem schmecken Fisch und Meeresfrüchte überhaupt nicht.

9 RELATIVE PRONOUNS

1   1. die. 2. der, die. 3. den. 4. das. 5. denen. 6. was. 7. der (or welcher *if you want to avoid* der der). 8. den. 9. was. 10. dem.

2   1. Sein Chef, von dem er Selbstbehauptungstraining bekommen hat. 2. Ihre Anti-Depressiva, auf die sie sich zu sehr verlässt. 3. Die Neurose seiner Frau, von der er mehr als genug hat. 4. Der Persönlichkeitstest, mit dem ich nichts anfangen kann. 5. Der Psychiater, dessen Papiere auf dem Tisch liegen. 6. Meine Beraterin, deren Vorschläge mir sehr geholfen haben. 7. Die Vergangenheitsbewältigung, mit der der Autor sich viel beschäftigt (*or* mit welcher). 8. Der Eheberater, auf den sie lange gewartet haben. 9. Die Psychotherapie, worüber ich nicht viel weiß. 10. Schwere Depressionen, woran er seit langem leidet.

3   1. Meine Tochter ist sehr ängstlich, was echt ein Problem ist. 2. Mein Patient hat einen Minderwertigkeitskomplex, woran wir arbeiten müssen. 3. Er hat irgendeine Psychose aber lässt sich nicht helfen, womit die Ärzte nicht umgehen können. 4. Mein Kollege is asozial, was meine Arbeit sehr schwierig macht. 5. Mein Mann ist von Natur aus Optimist, wofür ich sehr dankbar bin.

4 Du hast schöne Augen, / Die aufleuchten, wenn du sprichst. / Augen, mit denen du mir ins Herz schauen kannst / Und etwas sehen, was ich geheimhalten will. / Und dein Mund, der immer lächelt, / Den ich immer küssen will (*or* möchte), / Zu dem ich immer zurückkomme / In meinen Gedanken. / Aber dein großes Herz, das alle Schulden verzeiht, / In dem ich mich zu Hause fühle, / Das ist das[145], woran ich am meisten denke. / Das Beste an dir.

[145] *A pronoun or noun is needed before a relative: literally 'that which', although it can be omitted in colloquial speech.*

10 PRESENT TENSE

1 **a** 1. kannst. 2. findet, gefällt. 3. Wie spricht man „Chrysantheme" aus? 4. liest. 5. denke, sind, ist.

1 **b** ist, macht, fühlt sich, bin, glaubt, anführt, wird, denkt, wappnet sich für den Moment auf (or auf für den Moment, *as in the original text the prepositional object is placed outside the verbal bracket, see* **26.5** *on word order*), hat, heißt, vertraut, setzen wir ... Kultur ein.

2 1. fischt. 2. hängen hundert Hemden raus. 3. entwächst. 4. magst. 5. bremst, brennt. 6. tut, tut er seine Tute wieder in den Tutkasten rein. 7. ist, besitzt. 8. schwitzt, schweißt.

3 1. geht, bringt es auch zwei Flaschen Apfelsaft mit, fragt, wollen, antwortet, trinken. 2. sitzt, meint, weißt, glaubst, soll. 3. fragt, sprechen, spreche, schlafen, bin. 4. müssen, befiehlt, singen. 5. sagt, steht, ist, sind, herumstehen, haben. 6. fragt, bist, geht, bist, habe. 7. läuft, kommt, bin.

4 1. *remains perfect*. 2. wohnt. 3. *remains perfect*. 4. sind. 5. habe.

5 Down: 1. fängt [faengt]. 2. betrachte. 3. spricht. 4. rettet.
Across: 3. steuerst. 5. regnet. 6. hängt [haengt].

11 IMPERATIVE

1 1. Komme/komm heute Abend mit! 2. Gib mir einen Kuss! 3. Bleibt brav zu Hause! 4. Sagen Sie mir Bescheid! 5. Räumt euer Zimmer auf! 6. Entschuldigen Sie mich, bitte! 7. Iss dein Gemüse! 8. Sage/sag das noch einmal! 9. Nimm deinen Regenschirm mit! 10. Wasche/wasch Hände! 11. Ruhe/ruh dich aus! 12. Stelle/stell dir die Situation vor! 13. Gehen wir ins Kino! 14. Setzen wir uns! 15. Den Rasen nicht betreten [*general imperative*].

12 PAST TENSE

1 1. buchten. 2. reservierten. 3. übernachtete. 4. wolltest. 5. amüsiertet. 6. kaufte. 7. spielten. 8. dauerte. 9. wanderten. 10. frühstückten.

2 1. hatte. 2. schwammen. 3. flogen. 4. kamen um halb elf am Flughafen an. 5. aßen. 6. kostete. 7. nahm alles mit der Videokamera auf. 8. waren. 9. reiste um 16 Uhr ab. 10. sahen uns die schönsten Städte an.

3 Down: 1. redete. 2. fanden. 3. starrte. 4. tranken.
Across: 4. tadelten. 5. antwortete. 6. endeten.

4 kamen, traten, sagte, gebar, waren, war, waren, starb, stand mitten in der Nacht auf, nahm mir mein Kind weg, schlief, legte, legte, aufstand, war, ansah, war, rief, entgegnete, stritten, begann, fuhr fort, brachte, entschied, bat, regte, rief, befahl, hörte, schauten mit Ehrfurcht zu ihm auf, erkannten, war, sprach.

13 PERFECT TENSE

1 1. Wir haben auf den Bus gewartet. 2. Der Zug hat Verspätung gehabt. 3. Ich habe eine Rückfahrkarte gebraucht. 4. Habt ihr ein neues Auto gekauft? 5. Wir haben unser altes Motorrad verkauft. 6. Sie haben sich am Bahnhof getroffen. 7. Wir haben im Nichtrauchercoupé gesessen. 8. Hast du die Straßenbahn gesehen?

2 1. sind. 2. bin. 3. hat. 4. ist. 5. habe. 6. hast. 7. habe. 8. ist. 9. hat. 10. sind. 11. hat. 12. bist, bin.

3 1. Der Junge ist nach Hause gelaufen. 2. Die Teekanne ist zum Boden gefallen und ist gebrochen. 3. Du hast das Weinglas gebrochen. 4. Die Kinder sind in ihrem Zimmer geblieben und haben gespielt. 5. Wir sind mit KLM nach Amsterdam geflogen. 6. Er hat heute zum ersten Mal sein Modellflugzeug geflogen, aber leider ist es abgestürzt. 7. Der Schüler hat einen Mitschüler ins Gesicht geschlagen. 8. Der Lehrer ist ins Zimmer hereingekommen. 9. Ich habe mich aufs Bett hingelegt. 10. Der Dieb ist in das Haus eingebrochen.

4 stattgefunden hat, gegeben hat, musste, habe Näheres darüber einmal auf Urlaub von einem aus jener Klasse erfahren, haben einen hübschen Burschen unter sich gehabt, waren, haben damals die Sache zu weit getrieben, verstand, handelte, fühlte, wusste, zuckte, ist dir nicht aufgefallen, geworden ist, hat er kaum mehr etwas sagen lassen (lassen *behaves like a modal verb here, hence the double infinitive in the perfect*), hieß[146], hat er sich wahrscheinlich gedacht, versprochen haben (*this is a future perfect,* see **15.4**), geirrt haben, bist du darauf gekommen, bin ihnen einmal nachgegangen.

[146] Past is used in original but perfect is also possible: hat … geheißen.

14 PLUPERFECT TENSE

1 1. geregnet hatte. 2. hatte es geschneit. 3. war untergegangen. 4. hatte einen Sturm gegeben, waren umgefallen. 5. war in letzter Zeit am Meer sehr windig gewesen. 6. gehagelt hatte.

2 **Ex. 2** 1. waren. 2. war. 3. hatte. 4. war. 5. hatte. 6. hattest. 7. hatte. 8. war. 9. hatte. 10. waren. 11. hatte. 12. warst, war. **Ex. 3.** 1. Der Junge war nach Hause gelaufen. 2. Die Teekanne war zum Boden gefallen und war gebrochen. 3. Du hattest das Weinglas gebrochen. 4. Die Kinder waren in ihrem Zimmer geblieben und hatten gespielt. 5. Wir waren mit KLM nach Amsterdam geflogen. 6. Er hatte heute zum ersten Mal sein Modellflugzeug geflogen, aber leider war es abgestürzt. 7. Der Schüler hatte einen Mitschüler ins Gesicht geschlagen. 8. Der Lehrer war ins Zimmer hereingekommen. 9. Ich hatte mich aufs Bett hingelegt. 10. Der Dieb war in das Haus eingebrochen.

3 1. Ich war im Nebel nach Hause gefahren. 2. Ich fuhr (gerade) von der Arbeit nach Hause, als das Gewitter anfing. 3. Es war ziemlich warm gewesen und das Eis war geschmolzen. 4. Ich sonnte mich (gerade) im Garten, als das Telefon klingelte. 5. Es war den ganzen Tag bewölkt gewesen.

15 FUTURE

1 1. Welche Partei wird nächstes Jahr an der Macht sein? 2. Es wird wahrscheinlich eine Koalition geben. 3. Welchen Kandidaten wirst du wählen? 4. Die nächste Wahl wird im Juni dieses Jahres stattfinden. 5. Alle Parteien werden das Verhältniswahlrecht unterstützen. 6. In welchem Wahlkreis werdet ihr nächstes Jahr sein? 7. Ich werde dem Innenminister schreiben. 8. Er wird wahrscheinlich Außenminister werden. 9. Der Abgeordnete wird seine Wähler vertreten. 10. Die Politiker, die an die Macht kommen werden, sind die, die dem Publikum zuhören werden.

2 1. Die Regierung wird ihre Ausgaben reduziert haben. 2. Die Linken werden mehr in das Schulwesen investiert haben. 3. Der Bundeskanzler wird zurückgetreten sein. 4. Die Rechten werden sich aufgelöst haben. 5. Er wird Mitglied des Europaparlaments gewesen sein.

3 1. treffen (*future expressed by* um drei Uhr). 2. fahrt (*future expressed by* wann). 3. wird schön sein (ist *would be ambiguous here: 'it is nice/it will be nice'*). 4. wird regnen (*future used for predictions*). 5. kommt um 18 Uhr an (*future expressed by* um 18 Uhr). 6. Morgen wird es schneien (*future used for predictions*). *One could also say Morgen schneit es because Morgen is present, but it is more common for weather predictions to use the future tense.* 7. machst (*future expressed by* morgen Abend). 8. wird er machen (*present would be ambiguous: 'what is he doing/what will he do'*).

4 1. Klaus wird wahrscheinlich noch arbeiten. 2. Er wird wahrscheinlich noch schlafen. 3. Peter wird es wahrscheinlich schon gemacht haben. 4. Die Nachbarn werden wahrscheinlich schon abgereist sein. 5. Er wird es wahrscheinlich seiner Frau erzählt haben.

16 CONDITIONAL

1 1. Ich würde die Blumen gießen. 2. Er würde die neuen Pflanzen eingraben. 3. Wir möchten auf der Terasse frühstücken. 4. Es wäre schön beim Brunnen zu sitzen. 5. Ich würde es schwierig finden, den großen Busch zurückzuschneiden. 6. Wir müssten eigentlich den Rosenstrauch düngen. 7. Der Baum würde im Winter seine Blätter verlieren. 8. Könntest du Unkraut jäten? Ich hätte eine Schaufel. 9. Ich sollte einen richtigen Komposthaufen machen. 10. Wüsstest du zufällig (*or* würdest du zufällig wissen), wo der Rechen sein könnte?

2 1. Der Gärtner hätte es besser gemacht. 2. Ich hätte eine Regentonne gekauft, aber sie war zu groß zu transportieren. 3. Ein guter Spaten wäre zu teuer gewesen. Deshalb habe ich die Schaufel genommen. 4. Ich hätte den Gartenzaun streichen sollen, aber es war zu viel Arbeit. 5. Rhododendren haben eigentlich sehr kleine Wurzeln. Du hättest sie in einen Topf pflanzen können. 6. Eine schöne Elster wäre in den Garten geflogen, aber die Katze hat sie weggescheucht.

3 1. Wenn es nicht regnen würde, wäre die Erde sehr trocken 'If it didn't rain the soil would be very dry'. 2. Wenn sie Geld hätten, würden sie einen Wintergarten kaufen 'If they had money they would buy a conservatory'. 3. Wenn ich ein Glashaus hätte, könnte ich Tomaten ziehen

'If I had a greenhouse I would be able to grow tomatoes' (*or 'I could grow tomatoes'*). 4. Wenn das Wetter besser wäre, würden die Kletterpflanzen höher wachsen 'If the weather was better the climbers would grow higher'. 5. Wenn du mir den Gartenschlauch geben würdest, würde ich den Rasen spritzen 'If you gave me the hose I would water the grass'. 6. Wenn wir jetzt die Zwiebeln pflanzen würden, würden die Krokusse und Narzissen im Frühling kommen (*also possible:* kämen die Krokusse und Narzissen im Frühling) 'If we planted the bulbs now the crocuses and daffodils would come in the spring'. 7. Wenn der Blumenstock verwelken würde, müsste ich ihn umtopfen 'If the pot plant wilted I would have to re-pot it'. 8. Wenn du mir helfen wolltest, könntest du den Gartenschuppen aufbauen 'If you wanted to help me you could put up the garden shed'.

4 1. Wenn es nicht geregnet hätte, wäre die Erde sehr trocken gewesen 'If it hadn't rained the soil would have been very dry'. 2. Wenn sie Geld gehabt hätten, hätten sie einen Wintergarten gekauft 'If they had had money they would have bought a conservatory'. 3. Wenn ich ein Glashaus gehabt hätte, hätte ich Tomaten ziehen können 'If I had had a greenhouse I would have been able to grow tomatoes (or *'could have grown tomatoes')'*. 4. Wenn das Wetter besser gewesen wäre, wären die Kletterpflanzen höher gewachsen 'If the weather had been better the climbers would have grown higher'. 5. Wenn du mir den Gartenschlauch gegeben hättest, hätte ich den Rasen gespritzt 'If you had given me the hose I would have watered the grass'. 6. Wenn wir jetzt die Zwiebeln gepflanzt hätten, wären die Krokusse und Narzissen im Frühling gekommen 'If we had planted the bulbs now the crocuses and daffodils would have come in the spring'. 7. Wenn der Blumenstock verwelkt wäre, hätte ich ihn umtopfen müssen 'If the pot plant had wilted I would have had to re-pot it'. 8. Wenn du mir hättest helfen wollen, hättest du den Gartenschuppen aufbauen können 'If you had wanted to help me you could have put up the garden shed'.

17 SUBJUNCTIVE IN REPORTED SPEECH

1 **a** 1. Das Formel 1 Team teilte mit, der Ferrari-Fahrer könne voraussichtlich aus dem Krankenhaus entlassen werden. Die Ärzte stellten nach eingehenden Untersuchungen fest, kein medizinischer Eingriff sei nötig. 2. Der jüngere der beiden Brüder sagte, er wolle diesen Kampf unbedingt und er hoffe, dass er bald diese Chance bekomme. Er sagte, er warte auf große Kämpfe. Zu 70 Prozent sei er zufrieden, 30 Prozent müsse er sich noch erarbeiten. 3. Wenn der Vertrag unter Dach und Fach sei, ergänzte der Trainer, komme Schmidt bereits in der nächsten Woche mit ins Trainingslager nach Österreich. 4. Es könne nicht sein, betonte der Kapitän, dass es nur als Pflichtübung gelte, in der Nationalmannschaft zu spielen. Jeder müsse es wollen. Es müsse eine Ehre sein. 5. Die dreimalige Olympiasiegerin sagte, sie sei froh, dass sie es versucht habe. Sie werde nichts in Zweifel ziehen, jetzt liege alles hinter ihr. 6. Als sie über die Ziellinie gelaufen sei, seien jahrelang angestaute Gefühle aufgekommen, jubelte die Siegerin. Seit sie neun sei, habe sie davon geträumt, im Olympia-Team zu stehen. Jetzt sei der Traum wahr. 7. Eigentlich habe er gar nicht so recht mit diesem Sieg gerechnet, weil er diese Rallye nicht gekannt habe, erklärte der 32 Jahre alte Finne. Daher freue er sich umsomehr darüber.

1 **b** 1. Der Trainer sagte am Sonntag, sie hätten sich am Wochenende mit Beck und Ajax so weit geeinigt, dass man davon ausgehen könne, er komme zu ihnen. 2. Deichmanns Anwalt Michael Exner kommentierte, Heinz Deichmann solle sich erst einmal in Ruhe auf Sydney vorbereiten, dann würden sie weitersehen. 3. Der Vorsitzender des DLV-Bundesausschusses Leistungssport sagte, natürlich fehlten die großen Reißer. Aber sie hätten eine sehr ausgeglichene Mannschaft, wobei die Frauen gegenüber dem letzten Jahr deutlich im Aufwind seien. Bei den Männern müsse man sehen. Der erste Tag sei nie der Tag der Deutschen gewesen. Die big points würden sicher morgen kommen. 4. Maatz fügte hinzu, nach einer EM oder großen Turnieren habe es immer einen Schnitt gegeben. Einige hörten aus Altersgründen auf, andere würden durch das Sieb fallen. Wenn ein neuer Trainer komme, habe man andere Vorstellungen. 5. Die Australier rechneten zu 90 Prozent damit, dass sie zum Endspiel nach Spanien reisen müssten und nicht gegen die USA im heimischen National Tennis Centre in Melbourne antreten könnten, berichtete die australische Presseagentur APA. 6. Der Coach meinte, die MetroStars würden die Entscheidung treffen. Der Müller habe da nur noch wenig zu sagen […] Er (or, *to make it clear*, Der Coach) glaube, dass er die falsche Einstellung habe. Es drehe sich hier nicht alles um den einen Stürmer, das habe es nie getan. Der Coach erklärte, sie hätten einige Fragen an den Spieler zu seiner Verletzung und seiner Einstellung zur Mannschaft gehabt. Alle hätten ihre Meinung gesagt.

2 1. Paul sagte, er würde lieber Squash als Tennis spielen. 2. Mein Bruder sagte, Matthäus hätte zwei Tore innerhalb fünf Minuten geschossen. 3. Meine Freundin meinte, sie würde sich überhaupt nicht für Autorennen interessieren. 4. Benno sagte, der Schiedsrichter hätte ihm die gelbe Karte gezeigt. 5. Unsere Gegner drohten uns, sie würden uns mit fünf zu null schlagen. 6. Anton sagte, er müsste sich beeilen. Er würde gleich ins Fußballstadion gehen. 7. Sabine sagte, sie wüsste nicht, ob er gewonnen hätte. 8. Mein Schilehrer sagte, man müsste beim Schifahren immer auf der Piste bleiben, sonst könnte ein Unfall passieren. 9. Mein Vater sagte, es würde nichts schöneres als Pferderennen geben! (*less commonly in speech*: es gäbe). 10. Ulrike sagte, sie hätte mit ihm Badminton spielen wollen, aber er hätte keine Zeit gehabt.

3 könne, wisse, sei, einleuchte, sei, hätten, könne, herausstelle, gebe, werde, könne, gestorben sei, grolle, habe, stehe, sei, werde, habe sich aus … für Katharina ergeben, habe mit großer Zuneigung … über sie gesprochen, sei, vorliege, seien, verachte, sei.

4 Was gilt überhaupt als Diät? Jede zweite Frau in Deutschland möchte weniger wiegen. 44 Prozent der Frauen zwischen 20 und 60 Jahren wollten kalorienbewusst essen. Fast die Hälfte der befragten Frauen habe angegeben, schon einmal eine Diät gemacht zu haben, sagte Miglietti. Allerdings würden 88 Prozent so genannte *Formula-Diäten*, also das Ersetzen einer Mahlzeit durch einen Drink, nicht als Diät angesehen. Auch eine Mahlzeit ausfallen zu lassen, werde von 80 Prozent nicht als Abmagerungskur empfunden. Der Griff zur Tüte: Miglietti erklärte, dass jede siebte Frau zur Gruppe der *unkritischen Pflichtesserinnen* gehöre. Diese *Trash-Fress-Frauen* würden häufig zu Fertiggerichten greifen oder beschäftigten sich neben dem Essen noch mit anderen Dingen. Vor allem junge Singles im Alter von 20 bis 30 Jahren gehörten zu dieser Gruppe. 43 Prozent der Frauen würden beim Fernsehen essen, 42 Prozent würden sich vom leckeren Anblick der Speisen verleiten lassen, erklärte die Journalistin. 80 Prozent der Frauen hätten angegeben, gesundheitsbewusst zu kochen. Demgegenüber hätten allerdings 54 Prozent erklärt, sie benutzten auch Halbfertig- oder Fertigprodukte wie Soßenpulver. 62 Prozent müssten immer Salziges oder Süßes zum Knabbern zu Hause haben. Ein entspanntes Verhältnis zum Essen hätten nur 40 Prozent der 20- bis 60-Jährigen. Sie seien auch eher mit ihrem Gewicht zufrieden.

18 PASSIVE

1 1. Musik wird oft als Wahlfach genommen. 2. Die Hausarbeit muss bis Montag abgegeben werden. 3. Fragen können während der Gruppenarbeit gestellt werden. 4. Das Klassenzimmer wird aufgeräumt. 5. Wie viele Fächer werden hier unterrichtet?

2 1. Der Unterricht wurde gestört. 2. Die Prüfungen sind verschoben worden. 3. Dieses Thema war schon drei Mal besprochen worden, aber trotzdem fanden es die Schüler sehr schwierig zu verstehen. 4. Die Übungen sind nicht gemacht worden. 5. Keine Taschenrechner dürfen benutzt werden. 6. Die Schüler werden nächsten Monat in diesem Fach geprüft werden.

3 1. Der Lehrer wurde von den Schülern beleidigt. 2. Das Problem ist von dem (*or* vom) Klassensprecher erwähnt worden. 3. Klaus war von dem/vom Sportlehrer für die Fußballmannschaft der Schule ausgewählt worden. 4. Das Hockeyturnier wurde durch das schlechte Wetter ruiniert. 5. Die Konzentration der Prüfungskandidaten ist durch das Geräusch des Rasenmähers gestört worden. 6. Der Unruhestifter wird von dem/vom Direktor aus der Schule herausgeschmissen werden. 7. Peter wurde wegen seiner schlechten Noten von den Lehrern gezwungen sitzenzubleiben. 8. Sechs Auszeichnungen sind von den Prüfern erteilt worden. 9. Der Schüleraustausch war von den Organisatoren wegen Mangel an Interesse gestrichen worden. (NB: *Placing the agent after* Mangel an Interesse *would make the sentence ambiguous: i.e. 'lack of interest from the organisers'.*) 10. Er kann wegen Schwänzerei der Schule verwiesen werden.

4 Werden-passives: Unbeschadet des staatlichen Aufsichtsrechtes <u>wird</u> der Religionsunterricht in Übereinstimmung mit den Grundsätzen der Religionsgemeinschaften <u>erteilt</u>; Kein Lehrer darf … <u>verpflichtet werden</u>; <u>wird gewährleistet</u>; <u>gefördert wird</u>; <u>errichtet werden</u> soll. Sein-passive: nicht genügend <u>gesichert ist</u>. Zu + infinitive-passives: Die Genehmigung <u>ist zu erteilen</u>; Die Genehmigung <u>ist zu versagen</u>; <u>ist</u> nur <u>zuzulassen</u>.

5 1. Meinem Sohn ist bedroht worden. 2. Mein Mann ist mitten in der Nacht angerufen worden. 3. Auf keinen wird bei uns in der Firma Rücksicht genommen. 4. Über Geld wird oft geredet, aber es gibt wichtigere Dinge im Leben. 5. Meiner Freundin wurde nach Hause gefolgt. 6. Die Nachbarn waren nicht eingeladen worden. 7. Den Angestellten ist nichts gesagt worden. 8. Mit Elektrizität wird nicht herumgespielt! 9. Schau! Mir sind diese leckeren Pralinen geschenkt worden. 10. Der Brief war noch nicht weggeschickt worden.

6 **a** 1. Man störte den Unterricht. 2. Man hat die Prüfungen verschoben. 3. Man hatte dieses Thema schon drei Mal besprochen … 4. Man hat die Übungen nicht gemacht. 5. Man darf keine Taschenrechner benutzen. 6. Man wird die Schüler nächsten Monat in diesem Fach prüfen.

6 **b** 1. Man hat meine Handtasche gestohlen! 2. Was kann man machen/tun? 3. Man hat mir einen Scheck gegeben (or Man gab mir einen Scheck). 4. Man beschreibt ihn oft als arrogant.

7 1. Die Tasse ist gebrochen 'The cup is broken'. 2. Der Nagel ist gebogen 'The nail is bent'. 3. Mein Bruder ist gesehen worden 'My brother has been seen'. 4. Maria ist eben geküsst worden 'Maria has just been kissed'. 5. Das Kind ist angezogen 'The child is dressed'. 6. Die Zeitung ist gelesen worden 'The newspaper has been read'.

8 1. Der Dieselmotor wurde von Rudolf Diesel erfunden. 2. Das Flugzeug wurde von Orville und Wilbur Wright erfunden. 3. Die Atombombe wurde von Robert Oppenheimer erfunden. 4. Das Dynamo wurde von Michael Faraday erfunden. 5. Der Personenaufzug ist von Elisha A. Otis erfunden worden. 6. Die Glühbirne ist von E.A. Edison und J. Swan erfunden worden. 7. Das Automobil ist von Carl Benz erfunden worden. 8. Das Thermometer ist von Daniel Gabriel Fahrenheit erfunden worden. 9. Die Buchdruckerkunst war von Johannes Gutenberg erfunden worden. 10. Die Fotografie war von Louis-Jacques Daguerre erfunden worden. 11. Der Rundfunk war von Guglielmo Marconi erfunden worden. 12. Der Sportschuh wurde von Adolf (Adi) Dassler erfunden (*Hence the brand name Adidas*). 13. Die Batterie wurde von Alessandro Volta erfunden. 14. Der Computer wurde von Konrad Zuse erfunden. 15. Das Gummi ist von Charles Goodyear erfunden worden. 16. Der Blitzableiter ist von Benjamin Franklin erfunden worden.

19 SEPARABLE VERBS

1 1. Wir ziehen am Samstag in unser neues Haus ein. 2. Ich ziehe heute um. 3. Wann ziehst du aus? 4. Die Männer streichen gerade das Wohnzimmer an. 5. Die Gäste setzen sich am Tisch hin. 6. Ich versuche aus dem Küchenfenster hinauszuschauen, aber es ist zu schmutzig. 7. Wir haben vor die neuen Gardinen aufzuhängen. 8. Drehst du den Wasserhahn auf?

2 1. Wir sind am Samstag in unser neues Haus eingezogen. 2. Ich bin heute umgezogen. 3. Wann bist du ausgezogen? 4. Die Männer haben gerade das Wohnzimmer angestrichen. 5. Die Gäste haben sich am Tisch hingesetzt. 6. Ich habe versucht aus dem Küchenfenster hinauszuschauen, aber es ist zu schmutzig gewesen. 7. Wir haben vorgehabt die neuen Gardinen aufzuhängen. 8. Hast du den Wasserhahn aufgedreht?

3 1. Er war müde und legte sich aufs Sofa hin. 2. Als er ins Badezimmer hereinkam, saß sie schon im Bad. 3. Ich ersetze diesen alten Teppich. 4. Wir richten eine neue Küche ein. 5. Hast du die alte Tapete weggerissen? 6. Die Katze hat meine neue Bettdecke zerrissen. 7. Wenn du das Fenster aufmachst … 8. Der Maurer versucht die Wand zu verputzen. 9. Ich habe keine Zeit dieses Geschirr abzutrocknen. 10. Man hat das Zimmer noch nicht hergerichtet. 11. Schalt(e) den Fernseher aus! 12. Er überzieht den Esstisch mit einer bunten Tischdecke.

20 REFLEXIVE VERBS

1 1. Er bemüht sich sehr das Rauchen aufzugeben. 2. Du hast dich erkältet. 3. Wir haben uns mit dem Whiskeytrinken krank gemacht. 4. Als ich schwanger war, habe ich mich jeden

Morgen übergeben. 5. Die Kinder hatten vor zwei Wochen eine Grippe, aber jetzt haben sie sich erholt. 6. Ihr müsst euch warm anziehen, sonst bekommt ihr einen Schnupfen.

2   1. Habt ihr euch die Zähne geputzt? 2. Ich werde mich duschen und mir die Haare waschen. 3. Du hast einen Unfall gehabt? Hast du dir wehgetan? 4. Du bist ganz schmutzig. Hast du dich heute nicht gewaschen? 5. Ich habe mir das Bein gebrochen. 6. Ich muss mich beeilen. Ich habe einen Arzttermin. 7. Sie müssen sich ärztlich untersuchen lassen. 8. Er hat aufgehört sich zu rasieren. Der Stoppelbart passt ihm sehr gut. 9. Wir schämen uns beide wegen unseres Gewichts. 10. Hast du dir das Handgelenk verstaucht?

3   1. Interessierst du dich für Fußball? 2. Er arbeitet für eine andere Firma. 3. Ich freue mich sehr auf die Sommerferien. 4. Erinnert ihr euch an letzten Silvester? 5. Ich habe vergessen, wieviel ich für das Auto bezahlt habe. 6. Nein, das stimmt nicht. Sie müssen sich geirrt haben. 7. Er langweilt sich zu Hause. 8. Kannst du dir vorstellen, wie ich mich gefühlt habe? 9. Er hat erzählt, dass ihn seine Frau verlassen habe. 10. Wir wollten uns irgendwo hinsetzen, aber es gab keinen Platz.

21 INFINITIVES AND MODAL VERBS

1   1. Nach offiziellen Angaben sei es zu spät gewesen (um) den Opfern des Flugzeugabsturzes zu helfen. 2. Sicherheitsbeamte haben es geschafft einen Banküberfall zu verhindern. 3. Aufständische sind sofort auf Konfrontationskurs gegangen um ihren Plan durchzuführen. 4. Der Finanzminister will die Benzinpreise erhöhen um mehr Geld in den Straßenbau investieren zu können. 5. Der Soldat hat versucht sich mit der deutschen Botschaft in Kontakt zu setzen um Näheres über seine Kamaraden zu erfahren. 6. Der Außenminister will mit den anderen EU-Ländern zusammenarbeiten. Er will, dass sie alle bald zu einer Vereinbarung kommen. 7. Auf Anordnung des Verteidigungsministers musste der Kampf gegen den Terrorismus fortgeführt werden, obwohl keine Spur der vermuteten Massenvernichtungswaffen zu finden war. 8. Laut Berichten aus dem betroffenen Gebiet ist es noch zu früh (um) festzulegen, genau wie viele Menschen beim Erdbeben und der darauffolgenden Flutwelle ums Leben kamen, aber es ist zu befürchten, dass mehr als zwanzigtausend Menschen umgekommen sind. 9. Während des Hochwassers hatten viele Pendler Schwierigkeiten zur Arbeit zu fahren. Sie wollten die Überschwemmungsgebiete vermeiden und benutzten deshalb die Nebenstraßen, aber die meisten konnten nicht durchkommen und lange Staus haben sich gebildet. 10. Die Polizei hat eine Rufnummer veröffentlicht um mögliche Zeugen des Autounfalls zu erreichen. 11. Der Polizeichef behauptet, er brauche mehr Hinweise aus der Bevölkerung um diesen Mordfall zu lösen. Er und seine Kollegen brauchten auch mehr Zeit um Spuren nachzugehen und Beweise zu sammeln (*avoid repetition of* um). 12. Der Attentäter hatte die Absicht das Landesgericht in die Luft zu sprengen, aber um seinen Plan auszuführen musste er den Sprengstoff hineinschmuggeln, und er konnte das nicht machen ohne erwischt zu werden. 13. Die Bundeskanzlerin hatte keine Zeit an der Pressekonferenz teilzunehmen. Sie musste sofort nach Brüssel reisen. 14. Manche Leute wollen, dass wir in Deutschland die Todesstrafe einführen um Kriminelle von größeren Straftaten wie Vergewältigung und Mord abzuschrecken. 15. Die Gewerkschaft ruft ihre Mitglieder auf zu streiken, um bessere Arbeitsverhältnisse zu fordern, aber die Mehrheit will das Risiko nicht eingehen, ihre Arbeit zu verlieren. 16. Der Angeklagte wurde des Mordes schuldig gesprochen und wurde zu einer lebenslänglichen Gefängnisstrafe verurteilt. Die Frau des Ermordeten sagte, der Mörder habe es verdient seine Freiheit zu verlieren und von der Gesellschaft ausgeschlossen zu werden. 17. Die Regierung will, dass wir eine höhere Einkommenssteuer zahlen um unsere Renten zu sichern. Gleichzeitig steigt das Rentenalter, so dass wir länger arbeiten müssen. Es ist nicht zu fassen!

2 1. Die Direktoren des großen Konzerns wollten vierhundert Arbeitsplätze abbauen. 2. Die Pressefreiheit musste gewährleistet werden. 3. Der Rockstar könnte die Reporter gegen Verleumdung klagen. 4. Die Einwanderungsbehörde muss die Zahl der Einwanderer einschränken. 5. Laut dem Bildungsminister dürfen die Studiengebühren nicht erhöht werden. 6. Die Regierung sollte ein neues Gesetz gegen das Rauchen in der Öffentlichkeit einführen. 7. Der Täter soll brutal vorgegangen sein. 8. Beim Banküberfall ließen die Räuber den Tresor öffnen (*i.e. got someone else to do it*).

3 1. Die Direktoren des großen Konzerns haben vierhundert Arbeitsplätze abbauen wollen. 2. Die Pressefreiheit hat gewährleistet werden müssen. 3. Der Rockstar hat die Reporter gegen Verleumdung klagen können. 4. Die Einwanderungsbehörde hat die Zahl der Einwanderer einschränken müssen. 5. Laut dem Bildungsminister haben die Studiengebühren nicht erhöht werden dürfen. 6. Die Regierung hat ein neues Gesetz gegen das Rauchen in der Öffentlichkeit einführen sollen. 8. Beim Banküberfall haben die Räuber den Tresor öffnen lassen.

4 1. Ich möchte vier Brötchen. 2. Darf ich hier rauchen? 3. Musst du heute arbeiten? 4. Du darfst deine Schlüssel nicht vergessen. 5. Du musst nicht auf mich warten. 6. Er soll ziemlich reich sein. 7. Ich sollte ihn anrufen, aber ich habe es vergessen. 8. Wo ist Peter? Er könnte bei seiner Freundin sein. 9. Er müsste um halb sechs kommen. 10. Ich wollte eben (*or* gerade) einen Tee machen. 11. Du hättest mich gestern anrufen sollen. 12. Er hätte länger bleiben können, aber er wollte nicht. 13. Wer hat mein Bier getrunken? Es könnte Peter gewesen sein. 14. Ich hätte nicht gehen können. 15. Sie hätten sowieso nicht kommen wollen. 16. Normalerweise hätte ich an einem Samstag nicht arbeiten müssen, aber mein Kollege war krank.

22 NEGATION

1 1. Wolfgang tanzt nicht. 2. Er geht nicht in die Disco. 3. Jutta hat das neueste Buch von Bernhard Schlink nicht gelesen. 4. Mein Vater liest nicht oft Zeitung, weil er nicht viel Freizeit hat. 5. Sie interessieren sich nicht für klassische Musik. 6. Meine Eltern sehen nicht fern. 7. Meine Mutter will mir den selbstgebackenen Marmorkuchen nicht geben. 8. Mit dieser alten Nähmaschine kannst du nicht nähen. 9. Ich will nicht, dass du in einer Band spielst. 10. Er ist nicht der beste Sänger im Chor.

2 1. Er treibt keinen Sport. 2. Hast du die Briefmarkensammlung nicht mit? 3. Er hat die zwei Modellschiffe nicht selber gebaut. 4. Es kommt keine neue Folge von „Tatort" im Fernsehen. 5. Natürlich habe ich den neuen Film von Heiner Lauterbach nicht gesehen. 6. Ich bin gestern nicht ins Kino gegangen. 7. Wir sammeln keine Schmetterlinge.

3   1. Nein, ich habe deinen Mann nicht im Fitnesszentrum gesehen, sondern in der Kneipe.
2. Nein, ich habe nicht mit Bernhard Tennis gespielt, sondern mit Fredi. 3. Nein, ich war mit
Klaus nicht im Theater, sondern in der Oper. 4. Nein, ich habe keinen CD-Spieler gekauft,
sondern einen DVD-Spieler. 5. Nein, ich zeichne nicht die Landschaft, sondern die Pferde in
dem Feld da. 6. Nein, er möchte keine Bücher zum Geburtstag, sondern Computerspiele.

4   1. Nein, ich habe keines (or keins). 2. Nein, er hat keinen. 3. Nein, sie sind mit keinen von
ihren Freunden joggen gegangen. 4. Keiner gefällt mir. 5. Nein, ich brauche keine.

23 QUESTIONS

1   1. Wo liegt das Krankenhaus? 2. Was ist der kürzeste Weg zum Postamt? 3. Wie muss man
fahren? (or Womit muss man fahren? *to indicate means of transport*). 4. Wie lange dauert es
zu Fuß? 5. Wie weit muss man zum Bahnhof gehen? 6. Wann (*or* Um wieviel Uhr) muss man
losfahren um am Flughafen rechtzeitig anzukommen?

2   1. wie. 2. warum. 3. welche. 4. welcher. 5. wer. 6. wem.

3   1. Muss man geradeaus fahren um in die Stadtmitte zu kommen? 2. Kann ich einfach auf der
Straße bis zum großen Kreisverkehr bleiben? 3. Ist der Taxifahrer in die dritte Straße rechts
abgebogen? 4. Nimmst du die zweite Straße links nach den Zebrastreifen? 5. Darf man nur
beim Fußgängerübergang über die Straße gehen? 6. Sind wir auf dem falschen Weg? Müssen
wir umdrehen?

4   **Ex. 1.** 1. Ich weiß, wo das Krankenhaus liegt. 2. Ich weiß, was der kürzeste Weg zum Postamt
ist. 3. Ich weiß, wie (*or* womit) man fahren muss. 4. Ich weiß, wie lange es zu Fuß dauert.
5. Ich weiß, wie weit man zum Bahnhof gehen muss. 6. Ich weiß, wann (*or* um wieviel Uhr)
man losfahren muss um am Flughafen rechtzeitig anzukommen. **Ex. 2.** 1. Ich weiß, wie ich
am besten zum Markt komme. 2. Ich weiß, warum man hier nicht rechts abbiegen darf. Weil
das eine Einbahnstraße ist. 3. Ich weiß, welche Richtung ich nehmen muss. 4. Ich weiß, in
welcher Straße er sein Geschäft hat. 5. Ich weiß, wer mir am besten den Weg zum
Fußballstadion erklären kann. 6. Ich weiß, von wem du den Straßenplan bekommen hast.
Von Peter.

24 PREPOSITIONS

1   1. einer deutschen. 2. den. 3. dem ersten. 4. die. 5. der. 6. den, die. 7. seinem. 8. dem (*or the
contracted form* im).

2   1. mit Computern. 2. bei dem (*or* von dem). 3. um die mündliche. 4. in der (*or* vor der, hinter
der, neben der, bei der), auf meinen Kommilitonen ('weak' noun, see **3.3b**) (*or* mit meinem
Kommilitonen 'with') 5. auf das. 6. auf die. 7. in den (*or* während der – *colloquial* während
den -, für die). 8. an seiner. 9. von den. 10. mit ihren. 11. mit dem, mit dem, in die, mit dem,
auf dem. 12. an vier Hauptseminaren und zwei Proseminaren.

3   1. im. 2. mit seiner, auf ein. 3. ins. 4. im, auf dem. 5. auf eine, bei ihm. 6. über seine. 7. im, zu
uns. 8. in die, mit dem. 9. in der, vor vielen. 10. an unserem (*or* zu unserem), ins.

4   mit dem Bus in die Stadt, im Bus, an meine Ex-Freundin, in sie, neben sie (*or* zu ihr), mit ihr
(*either* für *or no preposition before* eine halbe Stunde), über Fußball, aus Dortmund, von

Borussia, für Fußball, über Fußball (*or* von Fußball), an unserem Gespräch, nach einer Weile, zum Eishockey, über die verschiedenen Positionen im Spiel, an die, an Sport, in ihrer Stimme, auf etwas Neutrales, an ein neues Thema, im Fernsehen, über die verschiedenen Kreidesorten, auf den Billardstock, zu ihr (*or* mit ihr), mit mir ins Bett, auf den Kopf mit ihrem Regenschirm.

5 1. „Ich freue mich sehr auf deinen Besuch." „Ja, ich freue mich auch darauf, dich wiederzusehen." 2. „Kommst du heute Abend zum Essen?" „Es hängt davon ab, ob ich länger arbeiten muss oder nicht." 3. Er ist sehr stolz darauf, dass seine Frau einen Bestseller geschrieben hat (*Here,* darauf *can be omitted in spoken German*). 4. Du bist selber daran schuld, dass du dich mit deinen Freunden gestritten hast (*Here,* daran *can be omitted in spoken German*). 5. Ich bin daran (*or* daran *can be omitted in speech*) gewöhnt, meinen eigenen Weg zu gehen, aber jetzt muss ich mich auf andere Leute verlassen. 6. Kannst du mich daran erinnern, die Telefonrechnung zu bezahlen, bevor wir in Urlaub (*colloquial* auf Urlaub) fahren? 7. „Was ist das Problem?" „Es handelt sich darum, dass zwei Jugendliche bei einer alten Frau eingebrochen sind und achthundert Euro von ihren Ersparnissen gestohlen haben, die unter ihrer Matratze versteckt waren." 8. Der Gedanke daran, dass er seit einem Jahr seine Frau betrügt, gefällt mir überhaupt nicht (*Here,* daran *can be omitted in spoken German*).

6 1. Fährst du in die Stadt? Warte auf mich! 2. Ich habe mit deinem Freund über sein neues Buch geredet/gesprochen. Er redet/spricht gern darüber. 3. Er setzte sich auf die Bank und machte sich Sorgen um seine Frau. 4. Die Flasche steht auf dem Tisch mit einem Glas daneben. 5. Er sitzt (immer) noch am Schreibtisch. Woran arbeitet er?

25 CONJUNCTIONS

1 1. In Deutschland wurde zu Beginn der 90er Jahre mit der Verpackungsverordnung ein Farbleitsystem für den Hausmüll eingeführt und jeder wurde verpflichtet seinen Müll zu trennen. 2. Entweder man trennt den Müll zu Hause, oder man kann zu einer nahe gelegenen Recyclinganlage gehen. 3. Wir sollten abgelaufene Medikamente zurück zur Apotheke bringen, weil sie sehr schädlich sein können. 4. Händler sind verpflichtet, alte und defekte Elektrogeräte ordnungsgemäß zu entsorgen, nachdem sie die neuen Geräte geliefert haben. 5. Manche Leute bringen Sperrmüll (größere Gegenstände wie alte Sofas, Bücherregale usw.) zum Wertstoffhof, aber andere lassen diese Sachen auf dem Bürgersteig, falls jemand etwas für sich nehmen möchte. 6. Lärmbelästigung ist weitgehend vermeidbar, wenn Altglas nur zwischen 8 und 22 Uhr in die Behälter eingeworfen wird. 7. Papier gehört in die blaue Tonne, Verpackungen in die gelbe Tonne und Kompost in die braune, während der Rest in der grauen Restmülltonne landet. 8. Die Supermärkte haben auch eine wichtige Rolle gespielt, indem sie die Verwendung der Plastiktüten drastisch reduziert und Sammelbehälter für z.B. Batterien zur Verfügung gestellt haben. 9. Jeder kann mit dem Sammelverhalten dazu beitragen, dass Abfälle durch Sammelsysteme wiederverwendet, stofflich verwertet und somit umweltkonform behandelt werden können. 10. Gegner der Mülltrennung behaupten, unser mühsam getrennter Müll werde nicht getrennt wiederverwertet, sondern er werde letztendlich wieder zusammen gekippt.

2 3. Weil sie sehr schädlich sein können, sollten wir abgelaufene Medikamente zurück zur Apotheke bringen. 4. Nachdem sie die neuen Geräte geliefert haben, sind Händler verpflichtet, alte und defekte Elektrogeräte ordnungsgemäß zu entsorgen. 8. Indem sie die Verwendung der Plastiktüten drastisch reduziert und Sammelbehälter für z.B. Batterien zur Verfügung gestellt haben, haben die Supermärkte auch eine wichtige Rolle gespielt.

3 1. Die große Mehrheit der Klimaforscher ist der Ansicht, dass die globale Erwärmung überwiegend vom Menschen verursacht wird. 2. Obwohl die Temperaturen global ansteigen, kann es kurzzeitig und regional auch weiterhin zu Kältewellen kommen. 3. Wenn der Treibhauseffekt durch das Verbrennen fossiler Brenstoffe und die Emission des Gases Kohlendioxid verursacht wird, heißt es anthropogene (menschengemachte) globale Erwärmung. 4. Als in den späten 1950er Jahren erstmals nachgewiesen wurde, dass der Kohlendioxidgehalt der Atmosphäre ansteigt, starteten Wissenschaftler regelmäßige Messungen des CO_2-Gehalts der Atmosphäre. 5. Politische Vorgaben zum Klimaschutz müssen durch entsprechende Maßnahmen umgesetzt werden, damit Treibhausgasemissionen vermindert werden können. 6. Man kann die Energieeffizienz verbessern, wenn man eine Dienstleistung oder ein Produkt mit weniger Energieverbrauch als zuvor anbietet. Das heißt beispielsweise, dass in einer Wohnung weniger geheizt werden muss, ein Kühlschrank weniger Strom benötigt oder ein Auto einen geringeren Benzinverbrauch hat. 7. Im Gegensatz zu fossilen Energieträgern wird bei der Nutzung der meisten erneuerbaren Energien kein Kohlendioxid ausgestoßen, da sie weitgehend CO_2-neutral sind. 8. Manchmal begründen wir unsere Mangel an Aktivität gegen die globale Erwärmung, indem wir sagen, dass man selbst nicht viel tun kann, solange die Wirtschaft so mächtig ist. 9. Was Klimaschutz betrifft sagen wir, dass die Handlungen eines Einzelnen nicht viel bewirken, es sei denn, dass andere bzw. andere Länder auch etwas dagegen tun.

4 1. Er ist im Fernsehen und diskutiert über die neuesten Entwicklungen zum Thema Klimawandel (*or* bespricht die …). 2. Da ich etwas für die Umwelt machen wollte, kaufte ich (einige) energiesparende Glühbirnen. (*or* Da ich für die Umwelt etwas machen wollte …). 3. Mein Nachbar sparte langfristig viel Energie, indem er Sonnenkollektoren installierte. 4. Der Umweltminister wurde fotografiert, während (*or* als) er letzten Monat auf dem G8-Gipfel eine Rede hielt.

26 WORD ORDER

1 1. Joachim macht am Samstag um acht Uhr eine Fete. 2. Diese Woche fahren die Kinder zu ihren Großeltern. 3. Leider ist es nicht möglich, vor dem vierundzwanzigsten Mai den Flug zu buchen. 4. Am 2. März arbeite ich bis sieben Uhr abends, aber den nächsten Tag habe ich frei. 5. Karl, ich kann am Montag nicht kommen. (*If a word is separated from the clause by a comma, it does not count as belonging to the clause.*) 6. Stell dir vor, sie wird am 12. Februar hundert Jahre alt! 7. Wo warst du gestern Morgen um halb neun? 8. Ich glaube, er hat am 16. April Geburtstag. 9. Schade, dass ich dich am ersten Januar nicht sah. 10. Der siebzehnte Juni war der Tag, an dem wir uns kennenlernten. 11. Weißt du, ob deine englischen Freunde in Deutschland am 24. oder 25. Dezember Weihnachten feiern und was sie an dem Tag essen? 12. Seine Mutter war besorgt, weil er gestern Abend nicht nach Hause kam und sie auch nicht anrief. 13. Ich bin froh, dass ich es jeden Tag schaffe, vor halb sechs mit meiner Arbeit fertig zu sein. 14. Bevor ich dieses Jahr in Urlaub fahre, brauche ich einen neuen Koffer. 15. Da wir am 4. Juli unseren Hochzeitstag haben, gehen wir abends in ein schönes Restaurant.

2 1. Joachim hat am Samstag um acht Uhr eine Fete gemacht. 2. Diese Woche sind die Kinder zu ihren Großeltern gefahren. 3. Leider ist es nicht möglich gewesen, vor dem vierundzwanzigsten Mai den Flug zu buchen. 4. Am 2. März habe ich bis sieben Uhr abends gearbeitet, aber den nächsten Tag habe ich frei gehabt. 5. Karl, ich habe am Montag nicht kommen können. 6. Stell dir vor, sie ist am 12. Februar hundert Jahre alt geworden! 7. Wo bist du gestern Morgen um halb neun gewesen? 8. Ich glaube, er hat am 16. April Geburtstag gehabt. 9. Schade, dass ich dich am ersten Januar nicht gesehen habe. 10. Der siebzehnte Juni ist der Tag gewesen, an dem wir uns kennengelernt haben. 11. Weißt du, ob deine englischen Freunde in Deutschland am 24. oder 25. Dezember Weihnachten gefeiert haben und was sie an dem Tag gegessen haben? 12. Seine Mutter ist besorgt gewesen, weil er gestern Abend nicht nach Hause gekommen ist und sie auch nicht angerufen hat. 13. Ich bin froh gewesen, dass ich es jeden Tag geschafft habe, vor halb sechs mit meiner Arbeit fertig zu sein. 14. Bevor ich dieses Jahr in Urlaub gefahren bin, habe ich einen neuen Koffer gebraucht. 15. Da wir am 4. Juli unseren Hochzeitstag gehabt haben, sind wir abends in ein schönes Restaurant gegangen.

3 1. Jens fährt immer mit dem Auto zur Arbeit. 2. Mein Vater kommt morgen um halb acht am Bahnhof an (*or* Morgen kommt mein Vater um halb acht am Bahnhof an). 3. Die Kinder spielen heute fröhlich auf der Wiese (*or* Heute spielen die Kinder fröhlich auf der Wiese). 4. Wir fahren dieses Wochenende für vier Tage mit dem Schnellzug nach Wien (*or* Dieses Wochenende fahren wir für vier Tage mit dem Schnellzug nach Wien). 5. Meine Freundin kommt morgen Abend mit ihrem neuen Ehemann auf Besuch (*or* Morgen Abend kommt meine Freundin mit ihrem neuen Ehemann auf Besuch). 6. Ich werde um viertel vor drei auf dem Hauptplatz auf dich[147] warten (*or* Um viertel vor drei werde ich auf dem Hauptplatz auf dich warten).

4 1. Er wollte seiner Lehrerin Blumen schenken. 2. Sie hat ihrem Chef die Ursache des Problems erklärt. 3. Gestern habe ich meinem Mann einen neuen Pulli von H&M gekauft (*or* Gestern habe ich meinem Mann von H&M einen neuen Pulli gekauft). 4. Ich hoffe, dass du deinem Freund die Nachricht schon gegeben hast. 5. Hast du es deiner Mutter schon gesagt? 6. „Kannst du mir einen Stift leihen?" „Sicher. Ich kann dir einen geben. Ich habe genug davon." 7. Ich glaube, dass er sich wegen seines schlechten Benehmens schämt. 8. Ich weiß, dass du mir etwas zu sagen hast. Sag es mir! 9. Dein Freund hat wegen seines Fahrrads angerufen. Kannst du es ihm zurückgeben? 10. „Was hält deine Mutter von unseren Urlaubsfotos?" „Ich habe sie ihr noch nicht gezeigt."

5 1. B: Hast du meine Ohrringe gesehen? Ich habe sie gestern an gehabt, aber ich kann sie heute nicht mehr finden (*or* Gestern habe ich sie an gehabt, aber heute kann ich sie nicht mehr finden). K: Ja, du hast sie mir gestern Abend geliehen (*or* Ja, gestern Abend hast du sie mir geliehen). Willst du sie zurückhaben? B: Nein, das ist kein Problem. Ich hatte bloß vergessen, dass ich sie dir geliehen hatte. K: Und du hast mir deine Goldkette auch geliehen. (*To place emphasis on* Goldkette *we could say:* Und du hast mir auch deine Goldkette geliehen *or* Und deine Goldkette hast du mir auch geliehen.) B: Ja, das weiß ich. K: Gehst du heute Abend in die Disco? B: Nein, ich gehe heute Abend früher ins Bett, weil ich morgen mit meiner

Schwester nach Frankfurt fahre und sehr früh aufstehen muss. K: OK. Ich werde versuchen ruhig zu sein, wenn ich später von der Disco zurückkomme, damit ich dich nicht aufwecke. B: Gut. Viel Spaß!

[147] *Phrases beginning with prepositions that are not expressions of time, manner or place but 'belong' to the verb usually come late in the sentence – see **26.9**.*

27 WORD FORMATION

1   1. Lehrer, Lehrerin. 2. Arbeiter, Arbeiterin. 3. Bäcker, Bäckerin. 4. Tänzer, Tänzerin. 5. Gärtner, Gärtnerin. 6. Physiker, Physikerin. 7. Sportler, Sportlerin. 8. Übersetzer, Übersetzerin. 9. Maler, Malerin. 10. Wissenschaftler, Wissenschaftlerin. 11. Komponist, Komponistin. 12. Politiker, Politikerin. 13. Pianist, Pianistin. 14. Gitarist, Gitaristin. 15. Trommler, Trommlerin. 16. Tischler, Tischlerin.

2   1. Er ist Fußballspieler. 2. Er ist Büroarbeiter. 3. Sie ist Gruppenführerin. 4. Er ist Universitätsprofessor. 5. Er ist Kinderarzt. 6. Er ist Sicherheitsbeamter. 7. Er ist Busfahrer. 8. Er ist Autoverkäufer. 9. Sie ist Schwimmlehrerin. 10. Sie ist Abteilungsleiterin.

3   1. Sie ist meine Chefin. 2. Sie ist die neue Ärztin. 3. Sie ist eine sehr gute Köchin. 4. Meine Schwester ist Bäuerin. 5. Sie will Sängerin werden. 6. Die Dozentin wartete auf ihre Studenten. 7. Die Professorin verlor ihre Brille. 8. Die Putzfrau wollte ihr Geld. 9. Die Kellnerin war unfreundlich. 10. Meine Freundin ist Psychologin. 11. Meine Nachbarin, Lena, ist Anwältin. 12. Sie ist eine schlechte Schriftstellerin. Ihre Bücher sind langweilig.

4   **a**   1. house, little house (cottage), domestic, domesticity. 2. man, manly (*or* masculine), manliness (or masculinity), manful/valiant, team, to man (or staff, or crew, e.g. a ship). 3. to read, reader, a reading, legible, legibility, readership, to misread. 4. friend, girlfriend, unfriendly, friendliness, to befriend. 5. power, powerless, powerful/mighty, powerfulness/mightiness, to remove power. 6. to speak/talk/give a speech, speech, speaking (the act of), talk (pejorative), chatter (pejorative), speaker/orator, oratorical. 7. to feel, perceptible, feeler (of insect), feeling, sensitive, insensitive/without feeling. 8. to break, unbreakable, to break into pieces/shatter, fragile/breakable, fragility. 9. to hit/strike a blow/beat, blow, hitter (or racquet in sports), fight, unbeatable, to beat to death, to smash to pieces. 10. to speak, speaker, speech/language, speechless, speechlessness, to discuss, discussion, to correspond, to promise, to say wrongly/make a slip of the tongue, to contradict.

4   **b**   1. das Haus, das Häuschen, die Häuslichkeit. 2. der Mann, die Männlichkeit, die Mannschaft. 3. der Leser, die Lesung, die Lesbarbeit, die Leserschaft. 4. der Freund, die Freundin, die Freundlichkeit. 5. die Macht, die Mächtigkeit. 6. die Rede, das Reden, das Gerede, die Rederei, der Redner. 7. der Fühler, das Gefühl. 8. die Zerbrechlichkeit. 9. der Schlag, der Schläger, die Schlägerei. 10. der Sprecher, die Sprache, die Sprachlosigkeit, die Besprechung.

5   1. die Haustür 'front door'. 2. das Wohnzimmer 'living room'. 3. das Badezimmer 'bathroom'. 4. die Straßenlampe 'street lamp'. 5. das Küchenfenster 'kitchen window'. 6. der Kleiderschrank 'wardrobe'. 7. das Bügelbrett 'ironing board'. 8. das Gästezimmer 'guest room'. 9. die Bettdecke 'blanket/bedcover'. 10. das Hundehaus 'kennel'. 11. das Bücherregal 'bookshelf'. 12. das Sicherheitsschloss 'safety lock'. 13. das Altpapier 'paper for recycling'. 14. die Wohnungssuche 'flat hunting'. 15. die Gefriertruhe 'freezer/deep freeze'.

28 PUNCTUATION AND SPELLING

1 **1914** In Europa beginnt der Erste Weltkrieg. **1917** Nach der Abdankung des Zaren im Frühjahr übernehmen in der Oktoberrevolution die Bolschewiki unter Lenin die Macht in Russland. **1918** Deutschland wird Republik. **1933** Hitler wird Reichskanzler. Der Aufbau des terroristischen Führerstaates beginnt. **1939** Deutschland überfällt Polen. Der Zweite Weltkrieg bricht aus. **1942** Auf der Wannseekonferenz beschließen die Nazis die Juden ganz Europas systematisch zu ermorden. **1945** Hitler begeht Selbstmord. Der Zweite Weltkrieg endet mit Deutschlands bedingungsloser Kapitulation. **1948** Mahatma („Große Seele") Ghandhi, dessen Methode des passiven Widerstandes Indien den Weg in die Unabhängigkeit geebnet hat, wird Opfer eines Attentats. **1949** Das Grundgesetz für die Bundesrepublik Deutschland wird verabschiedet. In Ost-Berlin nimmt der Volkskongress die Verfassung der Deutschen Demokratischen Republik an. **1953** Im März stirbt der sowjetische Diktator Josef Stalin. Im Juni wird ein Arbeiteraufstand in der DDR von russischen Truppen brutal niedergeschlagen. **1961** Die Führung der DDR lässt die Berliner Mauer errichten. **1962** Die Kuba-Krise bringt die Welt an den Rand des Atomkriegs. **1965** Die USA schicken verstärkt Soldaten nach Vietnam. Der Krieg eskaliert. **1968** Schwere Studentenunruhen in der Bundesrepublik richten sich gegen Notstandsgesetzgebung, Vietnamkrieg und Spießerrepublik. **1977** Der Terror der RAF erreicht in einer beispiellosen Serie von Attentaten seinen Höhepunkt. **1985** Michail Gorbatschow, Generalsekretär des ZK der KPdSU, verkündet das Reformprogramm der Perestrojka. **1989** Das sozialistische Regime der DDR bricht nach 40 Jahren Herrschaft zusammen. **1990** Die wiedererrichteten Länder der DDR treten am 3. Oktober der BRD bei. **1991** In Jugoslawien bricht der Bürgerkrieg aus. **1993** Mit dem Inkrafttreten des Vertrags von Maastricht entsteht die Europäische Union, deren Ziel ein wirtschaftlich und sozial geeintes Europa ist.

2 Doch der Vormarsch der Alliierten ging an allen Fronten, wenn auch von Stockungen begleitet, etappenweise voran. Im Februar und März 1945 eroberten sie die linksrheinischen Gebiete Deutschlands. Nachdem amerikanische Truppen am 7. März bei Remagen und britische Einheiten am 24. März bei Wesel den Rhein überschritten hatten, rückten die Amerikaner (zusammen mit der 1. französischen Armee) nach Süddeutschland vor. Sie besetzten auch Vorarlberg, Tirol, das Salzkammergut, Oberösterreich und den Westen Böhmens bis zur Linie Karlsbad-Budweis-Linz. Im Norden erreichten die Engländer am 19. April 1945 die Elbe bei Lauenburg, während amerikanische Verbände ins Zentrum des Reiches vorstießen und am 25. April 1945 mit den Sowjets bei Torgau zusammentrafen. Weiterzumarschieren lehnte der alliierte Oberbefehlshaber General Eisenhower jedoch aus politischen und militärischen Gründen ab, da er sich mit der Masse seiner Streitkräfte der Eroberung des deutschen „Alpen-Reduit" zuwenden wollte. Der Osten des Reiches wurde im Zeitraum vom Januar bis zum Mai 1945 von der sowjetischen Armee erobert, vor der Millionen von Deutschen unter unsagbaren Leiden nach Westen zu fliehen versuchten.

Appendix 5: Key to revision texts: analysis questions

REVISION TEXT 1

1 wird ... beantragt, erfüllt werden, wird ... projiziert, kann ... gefährdet werden, aufgestellt werden.

2 gefährdet ist (8) literally: 'is endangered' (or more naturally: 'at risk'), sind ... überfordert (22) 'are overstretched'. These both express a **state**. If *sein* was replaced by *werden* then an **action** would be expressed: i.e. 'is being endangered' (*or* 'put at risk'), 'are being overstretched' (see line 21 for an example of *gefährdet* with *werden*).

3 The *Konjunktiv I* is used, primarily in written German, to express reported (otherwise known as 'indirect') speech: i.e. here it conveys what was said by the psychologists in their article. By contrast, where the speech is direct (i.e. a direct quotation indicated by inverted commas) the ordinary indicative is used.

4 These are *Konjunktiv II* forms and are used to indicate reported speech in contexts where the *Konjunktiv I* form would be identical to the indicative. For instance, the *KI* form of *können* in the plural is *können*, which looks like an indicative. *Könnten* is used to make it clear that this is a subjunctive which is used to report what the psychologist is saying.

5 These are also *Konjunktiv II* forms, but as they are regular verbs these forms appear identical to the ordinary past tense forms. We know that these are *Konjunktiv II* forms because they appear in reported speech where some sort of subjunctive is needed (and the *Konjunktiv I* would not be possible as it is identical to the indicative in the plural, see Answer 4 above). They cannot be ordinary past tense forms because the article is written largely in the present, as it expresses a general present-day trend. In spoken German, the *Konjunktiv II* forms of regular verbs are usually replaced with *würde* + infinitive: e.g. *Viele Paare würden zu hohe Erwartungen ... stellen.*

6 There is no grammatical ending on these forms because they are used as adverbs.

7 This is the superlative form of the adjective *häufig*, meaning 'most frequent'.

8 This is a reflexive pronoun in the third person singular form. As the expression *jemandem aus dem Weg gehen* takes the dative (e.g. *Er ging mir aus dem Weg*) we know that *sich* must be in the dative, although this third person form is identical to the accusative. In this context it has a reciprocal rather than a reflexive meaning: i.e. it means 'each other' rather than 'oneself' if translated into English: 'there are different strategies for avoiding each other'. With regard to word order, the reflexive pronoun occupies the same position as the direct object: i.e. it follows the subject (and verb but in this sentence the verb has been sent to the end of the clause because of *wie*).

9   It is a demonstrative pronoun, meaning literally 'those' (= 'those expectations'). It occurs instead of the personal pronoun *sie* 'they' for extra emphasis.

10   Because the verb *umgehen* takes the preposition *mit* 'to deal with', it is necessary to have *damit* before a following clause (see **24.7b**). Literally this means 'Many couples cannot deal **with it** that on holiday they have to spend so much time with each other'. A more natural translation would be 'deal with the fact that …'. *Dadurch* is slightly different in that it is not linked to a particular verb but *da* refers specifically to what has been said before (= 'this' or 'that'): 'Difficult and unsatisfactory situations such as a bad hotel or unaccustomed weather conditions further increase stress levels. Even a strong relationship can be acutely jeopardised **by this**'.

11   *Durch* refers back to an idea (i.e. 'difficult situations') rather than to a person who is the direct agent of the verb.

12   The definite article tends to be used more when it appears in its contracted form after a preposition, even in contexts which allow it to be dropped (in this case, in a news headline).

REVISION TEXT 2

1   *Dem* is the dative form of *der*. The dative is used because the verb *verleihen* takes the dative; *der* is the genitive form of *die*, meaning '<u>of</u> the'; *des* is the genitive form of *das*, meaning 'of the'; *einem* is the dative form of *ein*. The dative is used because the article is dependent on the preceding preposition *von*; *der* is in the nominative, marking the subject of the sentence; *ein* is the accusative form of the neuter indefinite article, marking the direct object. The form is identical to the nominative; *satirischer* appears in the genitive (-*er* marks the genitive singular of feminine nouns), meaning '<u>of</u> satirical'.

2   *Sich* is a reflexive pronoun. It appears before the subject here because the subject and verb have been inverted. Instead of coming directly after the verb, the subject follows *sich* because *sich* is a pronoun and the subject is a full noun phrase. (There is a general tendency in German word order for small unstressed pronouns, such as personal pronouns and reflexives, to come before nouns when they appear in this middle position in the sentence.)

3   The bare infinitives are used because they follow modal verbs (*kann, darf*). Modal verbs always occur with a bare infinitive and never with *zu* or *um … zu*.

4   *Die* (2) is a plural relative pronoun, referring to the noun *Festivitäten*. It is in the nominative case because it is the subject of the relative clause; *denen* (18) is a plural relative pronoun, referring to the noun *Daten*. It is in the dative case because it follows the preposition *an*; *dem* (22 and again in 28) is a masculine singular relative pronoun, referring to the noun *Tag*. It is in the dative case because it follows the preposition *an*.

5   The subjunctive is used in *sei es* because this is a set phrase. Its English equivalent is also a subjunctive: 'be it'.

6   *Bekanntesten* adds *e* because the adjective *bekannt* ends in -*t*. Adjectives ending in -*t*, -*d*, -*s*, -*ß*, -*sch* and -*z* insert *e* for ease of pronunciation.

7   *Möchte* is the *Konjunktiv II* form of *mögen*. Here, the *Konjunktiv II* is used to express conditional meaning: 'would like'.

8   *Sich* is present here because it belongs to the reflexive verb *sich amüsieren* 'to enjoy oneself'.

9   *Vorbeifährt* umlauts the *a* because its base verb *fahren* has umlaut in the third person singular present form: *er fährt*.

10   *Der* is the dative form of the feminine singular *die* and appears in line 23 after the prepositions *auf* and *in*. These prepositions are taking the dative because they are referring to position: 'at work', 'at school'. By contrast *die* appears in the accusative after *in* in line 35 because movement towards the noun is being expressed: 'throw sweets and chocolate in**to** the crowd'.

11   In line 28 *an* means 'on', which is its usual meaning. However, in line 6 it means 'about', because it is a part of the verb *denken* (*denken an etwas* = 'to think about something').

12   *Am* is used when the preposition *an* comes together with the definite article *dem*. The reason why *an dem* is used in lines 22 and 28 is that *dem* here is not a definite article but a relative pronoun, meaning 'which'.

REVISION TEXT 3

1   *Indem* is a subordinating conjunction, which sends the verb to the end of the clause. The English equivalent is 'by' followed by an '-ing' construction: 'By barbecuing steaks outside'.

2   *Gebracht hatte* is a pluperfect form ('had brought') and is used to refer to an action further back in the past than the time of the narrative: i.e. what they **had done** before starting to barbecue.

3   The fact that there is no adjective ending indicates that this word is not an adjective but an adverb, meaning 'truly'.

4   *Stuttgarter*: Adjectives derived from place names always take the ending *-er*, irrespective of the case, gender and number of the following noun.

5   These are known as extended attributes (or expanded attributes) and mean 'a piece of meat grilled (literally: sizzled) over coal' and 'the smoke wafting over the fence' respectively.

6   *Hat* and *ist* have been sent to the end of their respective clauses by the subordinating conjunction *weil* in line 27.

7   This is a bare infinitive because it is occurring together with the modal verb *können* in line 25 (despite its considerable distance from the verb here). Modal verbs always take a bare infinitive.

8   *Sich* is a reflexive pronoun and is needed here because it goes with the verb *fühlen*. *Sich fühlen* 'to feel' is a reflexive verb.

9   The finite verb *müssten* is sent to the end of its clause by the subordinating conjunction *dass* in line 34, despite the fact that a relative clause intervenes.

10   The subjunctive is being used to indicate reported speech: i.e. telling us what the district courts have decreed.

11   Adjectives are written with small letters, even the names of nationalities, whereas nouns are written with capitals: *zum deutschen Sommer* shows *deutsch* as an adjective and *die Deutschen* is an adjectival noun ('the Germans/the German people'). As *Stuttgarter* is an adjective, one would expect a small letter; however names of places form an exception to the rule and are always capitalised.

12 This is the diminutive form of the noun *Mann*, which is formed by adding *-chen* and umlauting the stressed vowel. Usually diminutive forms indicate smallness, but in this word it means 'male'.

REVISION TEXT 4

1 *Der* is the genitive form of the plural definite article and is used to mean 'of the'; *den* is the accusative form (masc. sg.) and is used because *Bezug* is the direct object of the verb *verlieren*; *der* is the nominative form (masc. sg.) and is used because the noun *Deutsche* is the subject of the verb *sich kleiden*; *dem* is the dative form (masc. sg.) and is used because it is dependent on the preceding preposition *bei*, which takes the dative; *nördlicher* is an adjective with a nominative ending (masc. sg.) and is used because the following noun *Polarkreis* is the subject of the verb *heißen*; *einem* is a dative form (masc. sg.) and is used because it is dependent on the preceding preposition *nach*, which takes the dative; *ihren* is in the dative form (plural) because it is the indirect object of the verb *verleihen* and expresses the meaning '<u>to</u> their' in English ('to their offspring').

2 *Bär* is a weak masculine noun, which means that it adds *-en* in all forms except the nominative singular. Here it is in the accusative singular form.

3 Proper names and foreign words often appear without an ending in the genitive. They form exceptions to the rule that adds *-(e)s* to masculine and neuter singular nouns.

4 *Croissants* (14), *Norwegerpullis* (17), *Huskys* (22). Words ending in a vowel other than *-e* take an *-s* plural, which accounts for the latter two examples, as do some words of foreign origin, which accounts for the first example.

5 It is used because the verb *kleiden* is reflexive here, and *sich* is the appropriate reflexive pronoun (third person form). It precedes the subject because it is a small unstressed pronoun and the subject is a full noun phrase.

6 *Seien* is the *Konjunktiv I* form of the verb *sein* (third person plural). It is used here to express something that is unreal: 'as if they were at one with nature' refers to a pretence rather than a reality. Subjunctive forms are often used after *als* when it means *als ob* 'as if'.

7 Here, *während* is a subordinating conjunction, meaning 'while', and it sends the following finite verb to the end of the clause. (It is not to be confused with *während* + noun, which is a preposition meaning 'during': e.g. *während des Krieges*.)

8 *Damit* means 'so that' and expresses intention (i.e. 'in order that').

9 *Die* is a relative pronoun meaning 'which' or 'that'. It is a plural form because it refers back to the plural noun *Wurzeln* 'roots' and it is in the accusative form because it is the direct object of the verb *hatten* in the relative clause (the subject is *sie*).

10 Expressions of time usually precede those of place, hence *gewöhnlich in der Stadt*. Expressions of manner also tend to precede expressions of place, hence *mit einem Allradwagen zum Bäcker*.

11 When accusative and dative objects appear in the middle part of clauses (i.e. in their normal order without having been fronted), the usual order is dative first and then accusative when both objects are nouns. *Ihren Sprösslingen* is the dative object and *ein Gefühl* the accusative.

12 *Nie* means 'never' and its word order is the same as that of *nicht*. The word order rules for *nicht* state that it usually appears at the end of the clause (or if a verb has been sent to the end and is occupying that position, then *nicht* appears immediately before it). This accounts for the position of *nie* in line 27. If, however, the clause contains an adjective or adverb that is being negated, *nicht* and *nie* appear immediately before it. This explains *nie daneben* 'never wrong' in line 17.

Recommended reading

For further details on aspects of German grammar covered in this book and information on more specific grammatical topics not dealt with here I recommend the following:

Dodd, William *et al.* (2003) *Modern German Grammar: A Practical Guide.* 2nd edition. London and New York. Routledge.

DUDEN (2000) *Die deutsche Rechtschreibung.* 25th edition. Mannheim, Bibliographisches Institut: Dudenverlag.

DUDEN (2009) *Grammatik der deutschen Gegenwartssprache.* 8th edition. Mannheim, Bibliographisches Institut: Dudenverlag.

Durrell, Martin (1992) *Using German.* Cambridge: Cambridge University Press.

Durrell, Martin (2011) *Hammer's German Grammar and Usage.* Fifth edition. London: Hodder.

Eisenberg, Peter (2006) *Grundriss der deutschen Grammatik.* Vols 1 and 2. 3rd edition. Stuttgart, Weimar: Metzler.

Fleischer, Wolfgang and Irmhild Barz (2007) *Wortbildung der deuschen Gegenwartssprache.* 3rd edition. Tübingen: Max Niemeyer.

Fox, Anthony (2005) *The Structure of German.* 2nd edition. Oxford: OUP.

Helbig, Gerhard and Joachim Buscha (2007) *Deutsche Grammatik. Ein Handbuch für den Ausländerunterricht.* 15th edition. Berlin and Munich: Langenscheidt.

Lockwood, W. B. (1987) *German Today: The Advanced Learner's Guide.* Oxford: Clarendon Press.

Weinrich, Harald (2007) *Textgrammatik der deutschen Sprache.* 4th edition. Hildesheim and New York: Olms.

West, Jonathan (1992) *Progressive Grammar of German 2: Sentences and Their Realisation.* Dublin: Authentik.

Zifonun, Gisela *et al.* (1997) *Grammatik der deutschen Sprache.* Berlin and New York: de Gruyter.

Useful websites with free online grammar exercises

www.deutsch-lernen.com/
www.grammatiktraining.de/
www.schubert-verlag.de/aufgaben/index.htm
www.duden.de/grammatiktest
http://german.about.com

Index

Bold is used to highlight the pages which deal with the topic in more detail.